Dreamweaver CS6

TOM NEGRINO • DORI SMITH

 Peachpit Press

Visual QuickStart Guide
Dreamweaver CS6
Tom Negrino and Dori Smith

Peachpit Press
1249 Eighth Street
Berkeley, CA 94710
510/524-2178
510/524-2221 (fax)

Find us on the Web at www.peachpit.com
To report errors, please send a note to errata@peachpit.com
Peachpit Press is a division of Pearson Education

Editor: Nancy Peterson
Production Editor: Katerina Malone
Copyeditor: Scout Festa
Compositor: Danielle Foster
Indexer: Emily Glossbrenner
Cover Design: RHDG / Riezebos Holzbaur Design Group, Peachpit Press
Interior Design: Peachpit Press
Logo Design: MINE™ www.minesf.com

ISBN 13: 978-0-321-82252-9
ISBN 10:   0-321-82252-8

9 8 7 6 5 4 3 2 1

Printed and bound in the United States of America

Dedication

To our son, Sean Smith, with love from Mom and Dad

Special Thanks to:

Our patient and cheerful editor, Nancy Peterson, who made this book better, and encouraged us when we were weary. Thanks for pushing us over the finish line.

Virginia DeBolt, who contributed several chapters to previous editions, which we have built upon in this revision. Her work was terrific, and we are grateful for her help.

Katerina Malone, for her excellent production work.

The book's compositor, Danielle Foster, and to Emily Glossbrenner for the index.

Peachpit's Nancy Ruenzel and Nancy Davis, for their many years of friendship and support.

Of course, our gratitude to the members of the Adobe Dreamweaver CS6 team for creating a terrific product.

In Tom's office, the soundtrack for this book included music from my Pandora and Rhapsody subscriptions, and lots of embarrassingly bouncy pop music that shall go unnamed.

Contents at a Glance

Table of Contents

Introduction

Welcome to *Dreamweaver CS6: Visual QuickStart Guide*! Adobe Dreamweaver has long (initially under its previous name, Macromedia Dreamweaver) been the premier visual tool for Web site developers, allowing you to build great-looking Web pages and smoothly running Web sites. Dreamweaver's ease-of-use takes much of the pain out of creating Web sites, without sacrificing flexibility. It's possible to use Dreamweaver to create terrific Web sites without knowing much about HTML, CSS, and JavaScript.

Dreamweaver is a rich, powerful, and deep program, and at first glance, it can be a bit intimidating. We've written this book as a painless introduction to Dreamweaver and its features, and with our help, you will use Dreamweaver to build an excellent Web site.

Using this Book

We've organized the different elements of building Web sites with Dreamweaver CS6 into chapters, and within each chapter are numbered, step-by-step directions that tell you exactly how to accomplish various tasks. You don't have to work through the entire book in order, but it is structured so the more complex material builds on the earlier tasks.

We start with an overview of Dreamweaver, move on to setting up your Web site and creating your first Web page, then discuss how to add content, structure, and interactivity to your pages. Finally, we show you how to work with HTML code and manage your Web site.

When we first decided to write this book, we wanted to take a fresh look at Dreamweaver—at how people use it, and how people *should* use it. Throughout the book, we've tried to show you how to use Dreamweaver using its most modern features, rather than using some of the features that are still in the program but that are "old school." Specifically, we'll show you how to apply styles and lay out your page elements using Cascading Style Sheets, rather than older, obsolete methods. If you don't know what that means, don't worry; it's all explained in Chapters 7 through 9.

For keyboard commands, we've included Mac keyboard shortcuts in parentheses immediately after the Windows shortcut, like this:

To open the Find & Replace dialog, press Ctrl-F (Cmd-F).

While writing this book, we've made the assumption that you're familiar with the basics of using Windows or OS X. You don't need to be a computer expert by any means, but you shouldn't be stumped by concepts like selecting text, using menus, clicking and dragging, and using files and folders. Naturally, you should be familiar with Web surfing and how to use a Web browser to view a Web site.

Tips

TIP Throughout the book we've included many tips that will help you get things done faster, better, or both.

TIP Be sure to read the figure captions, too; sometimes you'll find extra nuggets of information there.

TIP When we're showing HTML, CSS, or JavaScript code, we've used this code font. We also use the code font for Web addresses.

TIP You'll also find sidebars (with gray backgrounds) that delve deeper into subjects.

Getting the most from Dreamweaver

Dreamweaver is a professional-class tool, and it provides professional results. Dreamweaver allows you to build Web sites visually, without needing to know the details of HTML, CSS, and JavaScript. But to best use Dreamweaver, you will still need some fundamental knowledge of what these languages are, and how they work together to make up a Web site. Similarly, you will find it helpful to know basic things such as what a Web page is and what a Web server does.

Where necessary, throughout this book we explain what you'll need to know about HTML, CSS, and JavaScript to work with Dreamweaver. But there is much more to say about these subjects, and there are thousands of books devoted to that job. In fact, we wrote one of the most popular books on JavaScript. You'll find information about that book, as well as some of our favorite Web design and development books written by other authors, in Appendix A.

A note for our Mac-using friends

If you've flipped through this book already, you probably noticed that the vast majority of the screenshots were taken on machines running Windows. That doesn't mean that the book (or its authors) doesn't welcome Dreamweaver users on the Mac. Far from it; in fact, both of us are primarily Mac users, and we are frequent contributors to *Macworld* magazine and other Mac-oriented publications.

However, our crack research department tells us that most Dreamweaver users are running the program on Windows machines, so we have included screenshots that will reflect the experience of the majority of our readers. Happily, Dreamweaver works almost identically on both platforms. In the few cases where there are differences, we've included separate procedures for Windows and for Mac users.

There is one other thing that we *haven't* done in this book that we have done in our previous Mac books. We are no longer telling Mac users to Control-click to bring up a context menu (also known as a shortcut or contextual menu). Instead, we've adopted right-click, because Apple now ships its multiple-button mouse with all of its computers that come with a mouse. If you are using a Mac with a trackpad, just mentally substitute Control-click wherever you see right-click in the book. Better yet, we suggest that you get any USB or wireless mouse with multiple buttons and a scroll wheel. It will really increase your productivity.

There's more online

We've prepared a companion Web site for this book, which you'll find at:

www.dreamweaverbook.com

On this site, you'll find news about the book and links to other online resources that will help you use Dreamweaver CS6 more productively. If we discover any mistakes in the book that somehow got through the editing process, we'll list the updates on the site, too.

Because of space limitations in the paper edition, we're taking some sections that were in previous editions of the book and posting them on the Web site. These bonus chapters have been updated for Dreamweaver CS6. By moving them to the Web, we can also easily keep them up to date between paper editions of the book. If you bought the paper edition, you can download the bonus chapters from our site. If you bought the ebook edition, there's no need to download the bonus chapters; the ebook edition includes all the bonus chapters.

If you have any questions about the book's contents, please first check the FAQ (Frequently Asked Questions) page on the companion Web site. It's clearly marked. If you've read the FAQ and your question isn't answered there, you can contact us via email at **dwcs6@dreamweaverbook.com**. We regret that because of the large volume of email that we get, we cannot, and will not, answer email about the book sent to our personal email addresses or via the contact forms on our personal sites. We can promise that messages sent only to the **dwcs6@dreamweaverbook.com** email address will be read and answered, as time allows. Unfortunately, due to the danger of computer viruses being spread with email attachments, we cannot accept any messages with attachments. We also must limit ourselves to responding to questions about the book; time doesn't permit us to answer general questions about Web design and development.

Let's get started

Every journey begins with a first step, and if you've read this far, your journey with Dreamweaver has already begun. Thanks for joining us, and let's get started building your great Web site.

—Tom Negrino and Dori Smith, June 2012

Introducing Dreamweaver

Welcome to the world of Dreamweaver! The premier Web design and development tool from Adobe may appear a little daunting at first, so this chapter shows you what's what and what's where. Once you understand what all the parts of its interface do, you'll soon find that Dreamweaver is an invaluable application for creating and maintaining Web sites.

In this chapter, you'll learn about the Dreamweaver Welcome screen and document window. Then you'll see the plethora of toolbars and panels included with the software: the menu bar, the Document toolbar, the Browser Navigation toolbar, and the Standard toolbar. The Status bar, the Property inspector, the Insert panel, and other panels are next, and then you'll learn about the included workspace layouts and how to set up your own custom workspace. Finally, there's a summary of the new features in Dreamweaver CS6.

A Quick Tour of Dreamweaver

In this section, you'll learn about the different windows, panels, pages, views, toolbars, and inspectors that make up the Dreamweaver experience. Whether you're a novice to Web design, an experienced pro who's new to Dreamweaver, or someone who primarily wants to know what's new in Dreamweaver CS6, this will bring you up to speed.

The Welcome screen

The first time you launch Dreamweaver, you'll see the Welcome screen, as shown in **A**. This page (which changes based on what you've recently done in Dreamweaver) is your starting point for creating and modifying pages and sites. If you close all your open Dreamweaver windows, the Welcome screen reappears.

New blank pages of each of the below types

A list of recently opened items

Video clips explaining top features

Displays an online interactive tutorial

Shows the New Features documentation in your default browser

Takes your default browser to online training resources

Shows the Dreamweaver Exchange site in your default browser

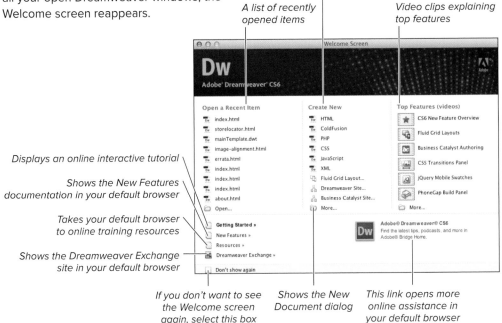

If you don't want to see the Welcome screen again, select this box

Shows the New Document dialog

This link opens more online assistance in your default browser

A Dreamweaver's Welcome screen will soon become familiar—but if you don't want to see it, you can make it go away.

The Welcome screen consists of several sections:

- **Open a Recent Item:** This section contains a list of the nine most recently opened items in Dreamweaver. If you've opened fewer than nine, it shows just that number; if you've never used Dreamweaver, it appears with just a button showing an Open folder; clicking the button displays the Open dialog, just as if you had chosen File > Open.

- **Create New:** If you want to create a new page or site, this is the column for you. Choosing one of these options creates a new HTML, ColdFusion, PHP, CSS, JavaScript, XML, or fluid grid layout file. You can also create a new Dreamweaver or Business Catalyst site. In addition, you can choose More, which will display the New Document dialog **B**, about which you'll learn more later.

continues on next page

B The New Document dialog offers a multitude of choices.

- **Top Features (videos):** If you're the type of person who likes video training, these clips open in your default browser and give you an overview of some of the new features in Dreamweaver CS6. This section may change from time to time as Adobe updates the video selection.

- **Getting Started:** Choosing this option gives you a quick tour of Dreamweaver's functionality. You'll see a short online tutorial on Adobe's Web site.

- **New Features:** This opens the online New Features documentation using your default browser.

- **Resources:** If, despite having this book, you still want further training, you can follow this link to find additional resources on Adobe's site.

- **More Help:** This link, at the lower-right corner of the window, takes you to Adobe's Web site for more help resources.

- **Dreamweaver Exchange:** Dreamweaver is built with an extensible architecture—that is, it's easy to add functionality to Dreamweaver that wasn't included when it shipped. That's done through a technology called *extensions*, which are bits of software that extend Dreamweaver's capabilities.

  You can get additional extensions through the Adobe Dreamweaver Exchange at **www.adobe.com/exchange/** by clicking the Dreamweaver category. Some of them have an additional charge, and some are free, but it's worth checking out what's available when Dreamweaver alone doesn't scratch your itch. See Appendix B "Customizing and Extending Dreamweaver" for more information.

A Windows users will see the Default Editor dialog the first time they launch Dreamweaver.

- **Don't show again:** Adobe knows that although some people love the Welcome screen, other people aren't so fond of it. Throughout this book, you'll see many examples of how you can personalize your copy of Dreamweaver so that it works just the way you want it to. Here, you can choose to never see the Welcome screen again.

If you reconsider, though, it's easy to bring back the Welcome screen: in Dreamweaver, choose Edit (Windows) / Dreamweaver (Mac) > Preferences > General > Document Options, and select the Show Welcome Screen check box.

Editor setup (Windows only)

If you've just launched Dreamweaver for the first time and you're using Windows, you'll see a dialog before the Welcome screen A. The Default Editor dialog lets you choose which file types you want to tell Windows to assign to Dreamweaver as the primary editor. In other words, when you double-click a file with one of the listed extensions, Dreamweaver will launch to edit the file.

Many of these file types are types that are used with the kinds of Web sites that we won't be covering in this book, but unless you have a preference for a different editing program, there's no harm in clicking the Select All button in the dialog. You should make sure that at least the JavaScript, Cascading Style Sheets, and Extensible Markup Language choices are selected. The Default Editor dialog appears only the first time you run Dreamweaver.

The menu bar

The Dreamweaver menu bar looks about like what you'd expect to see on your platform. There is one big difference between the Windows menu bar **A** and the Mac menu bar **B**: the latter also contains a Dreamweaver menu. On it are the About Dreamweaver, Keyboard Shortcuts, and Preferences menu options. On Windows, the first can be found under Help, and the latter two under Edit. And of course, the Windows menu bar is part of the Dreamweaver window, whereas on the Mac the menu bar is always at the top of the screen.

The other big difference is that on Windows, the Layout, Extend Dreamweaver, Site, and Workspace menus and the Search online help field, which together are called the Application bar, usually (if the window is maximized or wide enough) appear as part of the menu bar. On Mac, these appear in a separate toolbar below the menu bar.

TIP On both platforms, you can turn the Application bar off (and on Mac, recover some valuable vertical screen real estate) by choosing Window > Application Bar. Since the Application bar contains items that you probably won't use every day (and are also available via the regular menu bar), hiding it is usually a good idea.

A The Dreamweaver menu bar on Windows.

B The Dreamweaver menu bar on a Mac, which includes an additional Dreamweaver menu and the Application bar below.

The document window

Now that you've opened a file, you see the document window and all its surrounding panels, inspectors, and so on **A**. It may look busy and cluttered at first, but you'll soon learn your way around.

The document window shown here is a blank white Web page, ready for you to add your design and content. If you want, you can just click inside the window and start typing away! The details of creating a Web page are covered in Chapter 3.

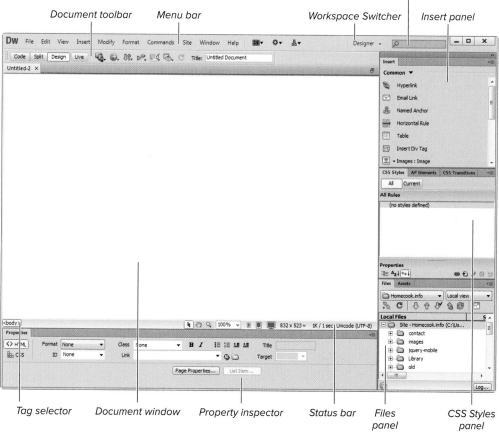

Search online help field

Document toolbar   Menu bar   Workspace Switcher   Insert panel

Tag selector   Document window   Property inspector   Status bar   Files panel   CSS Styles panel

A This shows your basic vanilla Dreamweaver document window, but you can modify it to fit your work habits.

New to Dreamweaver CS6 on the Mac is the *Application frame*, which gathers all of Dreamweaver's panels and windows—including the document window—in a single window, allowing you to move the program's interface as a group. Or to put it another way, Dreamweaver on the Mac can now be made to work like it does on the Windows version, with the exception that the menu bar still stays at the top of the Mac screen instead of being part of the application window, as it is on Windows. If you don't want to use the Application frame on Mac, you can turn it off by clearing the check mark next to Window > Application Frame. Dreamweaver will then display free-floating panels, which can be placed as you wish. Even though we're hard-core Mac users, we preferred using the Application frame, as it requires less mouse travel to get from one panel to another.

If you have multiple files open at once (a fairly common occurrence), you'll see a row of tabs across the top of the document window **B**. To go from one file to another, just click the name of the file you want to edit.

Don't like tabs? Dreamweaver lets you get rid of them:

- **Windows:** When you open a document in Dreamweaver, click the Restore Down button **C** in the upper-right corner of the document window (*not* the one in the Dreamweaver window). Once one document has been moved into its own window, all the others automatically move, too. To go back to the original view, click the Maximize button (which has replaced the Restore Down button) in the upper-right corner of any of the open document windows.

- **Mac:** Tabs are the normal interface in Windows, so Windows users have to manually lose the tabs any time they

index.html ✕	storelocator.html ✕	fishinspector.html ✕
Source Code	showDate.js	homecook.css

B Switch from document to document by clicking the tab with the document name.

C On Windows, the Restore Down button changes Dreamweaver from a tabbed view to a multiple document view.

want to do without them. Dreamweaver allows Mac users to choose whether or not to use tabs (they are active by default). This can be set by choosing Dreamweaver > Preferences > General > Document Options and selecting (or not) "Open documents in tabs."

The Document toolbar

Below any document tabs you have open, you'll find the Document toolbar . The Document toolbar consists of three parts:

- **View mode buttons:** These let you choose between Design, Code, and Split views of your document. This area also includes the Live button, which turns on Live view—a rendered view of your page right in the document window. When you turn on Live view, two more buttons appear: Live Code and Inspect ⓑ. See "Using document views" for more on what each of these does and when you'd want to choose each. Live Code view is discussed in Chapter 17, "Editing Code."

- **The page title:** Every page needs a descriptive title, and here's where you'll change yours. The page title, and how it differs from the name of a page, will be covered in Chapter 3, "Building Your First Page."

- **Miscellaneous buttons:** These contain everything from a "preview in browser" button, to a button to validate content, to a button to show additional visual aids inside Dreamweaver.

| Code | Split | Design | Live | Title: | Untitled Document |

Ⓐ The Document toolbar on Windows.

| Code | Split | Design | Live | Live Code | Inspect |

Ⓑ When you turn on Live view, the Live Code and Inspect buttons are added to the toolbar.

Using document views

The six document views allow you to choose which version of the document you want to see:

- **Design:**  shows a Web page in Design view. This mode, known as WYSIWYG (What You See Is What You Get), allows you to get an idea of how your page will appear when viewed in a browser. For the most part, almost everything you want to do in Dreamweaver can be done in Design view, and this book will be largely about what you can do here (except for Chapter 15, "Working with Content Management Systems," and Chapter 17, "Editing Code").

A A Web page displayed in Design view.

- **Code:**  shows the exact same page in Code view. Here's what the underlying markup and tags look like. Although Chapter 17 will cover the ins and outs of tags, many people work quite well with Dreamweaver without ever using Code view. Note that in Code view, you get a new toolbar (also covered in Chapter 17) down the left side of the document window, with specialized tools to work with code.

B The same Web page displayed in Code view.

Split bar

- **Split:** shows the same page, again, in Split view. If you can't decide whether you want to look at code or design, Split lets you have the best of both, with code in one pane and Design view in another. It's a great way to start to learn about markup, and it's also handy for control freaks (you know who you are) who want to tweak their tags to be just so and simultaneously see how their design looks. You can

C And the same Web page displayed in Split view.

Beatles Discography

Album	Year	Label
Please Please Me	1963	Parlophone
With The Beatles	1963	Parlophone
A Hard Day's Night	1964	Parlophone
Beatles for Sale	1964	Parlophone
Help!	1965	Parlophone
Rubber Soul	1965	Parlophone
Revolver	1966	Parlophone
Sgt. Pepper's Lonely Hearts Club Band	1967	Parlophone
Magical Mystery Tour	1967	Capitol
The Beatles	1968	Apple
Yellow Submarine	1969	Apple
Abbey Road	1969	Apple
Let It Be	1970	Apple

Beatles Discography

Album	Year	Label
Please Please Me	1963	Parlophone
With The Beatles	1963	Parlophone
A Hard Day's Night	1964	Parlophone
Beatles for Sale	1964	Parlophone
Help!	1965	Parlophone
Rubber Soul	1965	Parlophone
Revolver	1966	Parlophone
Sgt. Pepper's Lonely Hearts Club Band	1967	Parlophone
Magical Mystery Tour	1967	Capitol
The Beatles	1968	Apple
Yellow Submarine	1969	Apple
Abbey Road	1969	Apple
Let It Be	1970	Apple

D Live view allows you to see how a page looks in Dreamweaver's regular editing mode (top) and how it would look rendered in a browser (bottom). Note that in Live view the table shows CSS styling, as well as its JavaScript-driven ability to sort the table by clicking its column headings.

resize the amount of space taken up by each of the two views by dragging the split bar between the two panes. With the View > Split Vertically and View > Design View commands, you can also choose to have the split be vertical or horizontal, and to have Design view in the left or top panes rather than the default right or bottom panes.

- **Live:** This view is perfect for giving you a good idea of what pages powered by JavaScript or other code will look like in a browser. With Live view, a browser engine (the cross-platform WebKit, the engine used by Apple's Safari and Google's Chrome browsers) is built into Dreamweaver, and clicking the Live button displays the page using WebKit in the document window **D**.

- **Live Code:** This button splits the window into Live view in the Design pane and opens the Code pane. If your Web page uses JavaScript or Ajax for visual effects, the scripts will actually be rewriting the HTML under script control as the user interacts with the page. Live Code view allows you to see how the HTML changes as you interact with the page in Design pane. You'll learn more abut Live Code view in Chapter 17.

- **Inspect:** This button also enhances Live view. It allows you to turn on CSS Inspect mode, which outlines and highlights the CSS block styles in the Design pane as you move the cursor over the different blocks. There's more about CSS Inspect mode in Chapter 9.

The Browser Navigation toolbar

The Browser Navigation toolbar , which automatically appears when you enter Live view, allows you to navigate from page to page in a natural way when you are using Live view. It includes an address field and the usual Back, Forward, Refresh, and Home buttons. It also includes a button that allows you to access Live view options.

The Related Files bar

Modern Web pages often have several supporting files that help make up the page. For example, what appears to the user as a single Web page may actually consist of an HTML file, a CSS file, and a JavaScript file. The **Related Files** feature adds a bar with the names of these supporting files under the documents tab . You'll learn more about using the Related Files feature in Chapters 7 and 15.

Other toolbars

If you right-click in a blank part of the Document toolbar, you'll see that there are two other bars that aren't enabled by default:

- **Style Rendering bar:** If you've set up your CSS style sheets so that your pages appear differently in, for example, a screen view versus a page designed for printing, this is what you'll use to switch between the two style renderings **C**. Most of the time, you'll just want the default screen view. The Toggle button works a little differently: It toggles the page between a view that includes the rendered CSS styles and a view with CSS styles turned off.

A The Browser Navigation toolbar allows you to move between pages in your site, much as you would in a stand-alone Web browser.

index.html ×
Source Code showDate.js homecook.css — *Related files*

B The Related Files bar makes it easy to switch to files that are attached to the current document, such as CSS or JavaScript files.

Toggle button

C The Toggle button on the Style Rendering toolbar allows you to view the page with or without any attached CSS styles.

D The little-used Standard toolbar gives you access to functions such as Save, Copy, Paste, and Undo.

- **Standard bar:** While Adobe refers to this bar as "standard," it's actually used to make Dreamweaver feel more like a word processing application **D**. Some examples of what it contains—New, Open, Save, Print, Cut, Copy, Paste— give you an idea of what's here. As with the Style Rendering bar, the chances are that Adobe's default for these toolbars (off) is what you'll want to use.

You can turn off any of the four toolbars (Style Rendering, Document, Standard, or Browser Navigation) if you want the cleanest possible layout (for instance, if you're working on a very small screen). To turn them back on, choose View > Toolbars, and select the ones you want to see again.

The Status bar

The Status bar is the bottommost part of the document window. It's often also referred to as the *tag selector*, although that's really the correct name for just the leftmost part. Click anywhere in a document, and the tag selector shows you the current tags based on the current location of the cursor. You can then click any of the tags in the tag selector Ⓐ to select everything contained within that tag. Clicking the `<body>` tag always selects the entire contents of the page.

The rightmost side of the Status bar contains more controls Ⓑ. The Select, Hand, and Zoom tools let you (respectively) select objects on the page, scroll around the page, and zoom into the page. The next control, a pop-up menu, shows the current zoom percentage of the page. Next are three preset window size buttons, for Mobile, Tablet, and Desktop screen sizes. After that is the window size currently being displayed; click this to get a pop-up menu of available window sizes Ⓒ. If you don't like the default values for these last two controls, you can change either or both by selecting Edit Sizes from the pop-up menu, which opens the Window Sizes pane of the Preferences panel. We'll cover this more extensively in Chapter 12. Next is an estimate of how long it would take a browser to download this page. Finally, the status bar tells you the document text encoding for the page. The encoding tells the browser which character set should be used to display the fonts on the page.

Sgt. Pepper's Lonely Hearts Club Band	1967	Parl
Magical Mystery Tour	1967	Cap
The Beatles	1968	App

`<body> <table#theTable> <tr> <td>`

Ⓐ The tag selector at the bottom of the document window makes it easy to select all the contents of a tag.

Select tool	*Zoom tool*	*Window sizes*	*Download time*

`100%` ⌄ 889 x 415 ⌄ 26K / 1 sec Unicode (UTF-8)

Hand tool   *Zoom percentage*   *Current window size*   *Text encoding*

Ⓑ The controls on the right side of the Status bar.

240 x 320	Feature Phone
✓ 320 x 480	Smart Phone
480 x 800	Smart Phone
592w	
768 x 1024	Tablet
1000 x 620	(1024 x 768, Maximized)
1260 x 875	(1280 x 1024, Maximized)
1420 x 750	(1440 x 900, Maximized)
1580 x 1050	(1600 x 1200, Maximized)
1280 x 800	MacBook screen size
Full Size	
Edit Sizes...	
Orientation Landscape	
✓ Orientation Portrait	
Media Queries...	

Ⓒ Use this pop-up menu to choose the dimensions of your document window.

The Property inspector

At the bottom of the screen is the Property inspector Ⓐ. Based on what is selected in the document window, different options appear in this inspector; that is, if you've selected some text, you'll see text options, but if you've selected an image, image options appear. The Property inspector can be used to view and modify the displayed options. The many uses of the Property inspector will be covered throughout the rest of the book.

In the lower-right corner of the inspector is an expand/collapse triangle. Depending on its current state, this either expands or collapses the inspector. This lets you choose whether you want to display the extra information shown in the bottom half.

The Property inspector has two tabs: HTML and CSS. Depending on which tab you're on, Dreamweaver will apply properties of that type. For example, if you're on the HTML tab, select some text in the document window, click the Italic button, and Dreamweaver will apply the style using the HTML <em> tag. If you're on the CSS tab of the Property inspector Ⓑ, select some text, click the Italic button, and Dreamweaver will walk you through creating a new CSS style rule for the selection.

Ⓐ The HTML tab of the Property inspector.

Ⓑ The CSS tab of the Property inspector.

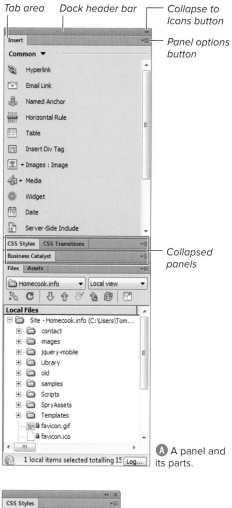

Tab area   Dock header bar   Collapse to Icons button

Panel options button

Collapsed panels

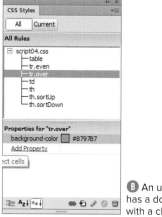

A A panel and its parts.

B An undocked panel has a dock header bar with a close box.

The panels

Along the right side of the Dreamweaver window are *panels*. In the default installation of Dreamweaver **A**, the Adobe BrowserLab, Insert, CSS Styles, AP Elements, Business Catalyst (a Web site hosting service from Adobe), Files, and Assets panels are visible and docked (in the default Designer workspace; more about workspaces later in this chapter). Also available, although not visible until you turn them on, are Databases, Bindings, Server Behaviors, Components, Snippets, CSS Transitions, Tag inspector, Behaviors, History, Frames, Code inspector, and Results. These can all be found under the Window menu.

The different panels appear by default in the *dock area* on the right side of the screen. You can move this area to the left side of the screen by dragging the *dock header bar* at the top of the stack of docked panels.

You can hide, show, move, resize, and rearrange panels to fit the way that you work. There are controls on each panel that help you do these things:

- **Tab area:** At the top of each panel, next to the tab with its name, is a dark gray area. This is the *tab area*. Click and drag this to move the panel to a new location. If you drag the panel out of the dock area, you *undock* the panel **B**, and the dock header bar appears. To dock the panel again, use the tab area to drag the panel back into the dock area.

Double-clicking the tab area will expand and collapse it to show either the whole panel or just the tab area. You can also resize a panel by clicking and dragging its left or bottom edge.

continues on next page

- **Dock header bar:** The bar across the top of an undocked panel is the *dock header bar*. Click and drag the dock header bar to move the panel to a new location. Clicking the close box (Windows) or close button (Mac) closes the panel group; it does not re-dock it. To re-dock, drag the panel back into the dock.

- **Collapse to Icons button:** You can reduce screen clutter by clicking the Collapse to Icons button at the upper-right corner of the dock, which shrinks the panels to icons . To use the iconic panel, click its icon, and the panel appears as a drawer next to the dock .

- **Panel options button:** If you click the panel options button, a menu appears that gives you a variety of options ⓔ based on which panel and tab you're currently on. This example shows the options for the Insert panel. From here, you can hide the labels in the Insert panel, or show its icons in color. The ability to close tabs and move tabs from one panel to another allows you to set up Dreamweaver to work just the way you want it.

TIP Panels have an occasional tendency to go missing. If you have a situation where the Window menu says a panel is open but you can't find it anywhere, choose Window > Arrange Panels to make all currently open panels visible again.

TIP If you want to completely concentrate on working in your document window, you can hide the dock with all of the panels and the Property inspector by pressing F4 or choosing Window > Hide Panels. The panels and inspector shrink down to a thin gray strip on the right and bottom edges of your screen called the reveal strip. Click the reveal strip to briefly show the dock or Property inspector; it will shrink back down after a short delay when you move the cursor away. Press F4 or use the menu choice again to bring the hidden elements back for good.

ⓒ If you need more screen space, you can shrink your panels to icons in the dock area.

ⓓ Clicking a panel icon opens the panel in a drawer next to the dock area.

ⓔ Different panels have different menu options, but these are the most common.

A The Insert panel contains many of the tools you'll use most often to insert objects on your Web pages.

The Insert panel

In the default Designer workspace, the top panel is the Insert panel **A**. As you might have guessed, the Insert panel is used to insert content and objects into your Web page.

The Insert panel has nine categories, which you can switch between with a pop-up menu. You get different tools in each category:

- **Common:** This set of objects contains most commonly used objects, such as links and images.

- **Layout:** This tab includes **div**s and tables: all objects that let you describe how you want to lay out your page.

- **Forms:** The Forms set includes form elements such as text fields, buttons, and check boxes.

- **Data:** If you're someday going to work with external data such as databases, that's when you'll use the Data set.

- **Spry:** Spry is a JavaScript library for designers and developers that allows them to add rich page functionality using Ajax widgets, such as menus, form validation, and tabbed panels. The Spry tab allows you to insert Spry widgets onto your pages, with no coding required.

- **jQuery Mobile:** This section allows you to insert widgets from the jQuery Mobile JavaScript library. It's used when making specialized sites designed for use on mobile devices.

continues on next page

- **InContext Editing:** InContext Editing (ICE) is part of Business Catalyst, a hosted service that Adobe acquired in 2009 and that is now part of the Creative Cloud subscription service. Business Catalyst includes content management, email marketing, e-commerce, and extensive business analytics. ICE allows users to make relatively simple edits to their Web pages from a Web browser, with no other software required. In Dreamweaver, the Insert panel allows you to add certain areas to pages to make them available to ICE end users. Business Catalyst and ICE are outside of the scope of this book.

- **Text:** The Text tab doesn't actually contain objects to insert on the page; instead, it lets you use HTML markup to style text that's already on the page.

- **Favorites:** This starts off empty, but you can modify it to contain just what you'd like it to have. To do this, choose the Favorites set and then right-click. You'll be presented with a dialog that allows you to add your most commonly used objects.

TIP The Insert panel is just a different orientation of the Insert bar, which was a staple of past versions of Dreamweaver. If you're a long-time user and miss the Insert bar, just drag the Insert panel's tab above the document window, and the panel will transform back into the familiar Insert bar **B**. You lose a little vertical space for your document window, but you get back an old friend. Judging by the discussion on Adobe forums, this is the preferred setup for many professional-level users.

TIP If you're ever wondering what an icon on the Insert bar does, just move your cursor over it—a tool tip will appear with the icon's name. If there's a small black triangle to the right of an icon, it means that the object contains related tools and objects. Click the object to view the pop-up menu of choices.

B If you're an old-school Dreamweaver user, you can turn the Insert panel back into the Insert bar.

Setting Up Your Workspace

It's not just a matter of deciding what you *do* want to see—setting up your workspace also means figuring out what you *don't* want to see. Given the toolbars *and* all the possible panels *and* the Property inspector, you can run out of room for the actual Web page you're trying to work on Ⓐ. In Dreamweaver's parlance, a *workspace* is an arrangement of panels, the dock, the document window, and the Property inspector. Here's how to set up a workspace that works for you.

Ⓐ Not all the tools and panels are visible, but this is already an unusable workspace.

The included workspace layouts

Dreamweaver CS6 has preset workspaces that look and work the same on Windows and Mac and are designed for different classes of users:

- App Developer
- App Developer Plus
- Business Catalyst
- Classic
- Coder
- Coder Plus
- Designer (the default workspace)
- Designer Compact
- Dual Screen
- Fluid Layout
- Mobile Applications

These workspaces rearrange the document window, panels, and Property inspector to work more efficiently for each type of user.

The Dual Screen layout isn't associated with a kind of user; rather, it attempts to make the best of your hardware. If you're lucky enough to have two (or more) monitors, the Dual Screen layout attempts to make the most of all of them. For example, the document window is expanded to cover the whole primary monitor, and the panels are moved onto the secondary monitor.

You switch between the different layouts with the Workspace Switcher in the Application bar ⓑ. Just choose from the pop-up menu to switch between workspaces.

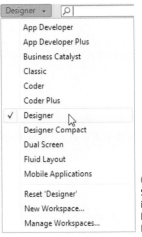

ⓑ The Workspace Switcher makes it easy to change between workspace layouts.

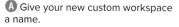

New Workspace

Name: My Workspace

[OK]   [Cancel]

Ⓐ Give your new custom workspace a name.

Manage Workspaces

My Workspace

[OK]

[Rename...]

[Delete]

Ⓑ The Manage Workspaces dialog lets you rename or delete your custom layouts.

Saving custom layouts

Chances are that the workspaces that come with Dreamweaver aren't exactly what you want. No problem! You can save your own workspaces.

To save a custom workspace:

1. Set up your layout just the way you want it. Show or hide panels, and drag them to where you want.

2. From the Workspace Switcher menu, choose New Workspace.

   The New Workspace dialog appears Ⓐ.

3. Enter a name for your custom workspace, and then click OK.

   Your new workspace appears at the top of the Workspace Switcher menu.

TIP If at any point you've added, deleted, and moved around panels and documents to the point where everything's all over the place, you can always go back to the original layout for any workspace by first choosing it from the Workspace Switcher menu, and then choosing Reset [workspace name] from the same menu.

To delete or rename a custom workspace:

1. If you later decide that you don't want a custom workspace any more, or want to give it another name, you can change it. From the Workspace Switcher menu, choose Manage Workspaces.

   The Manage Workspaces dialog appears Ⓑ.

2. Select the workspace you want to change, and then delete or rename your custom layout (but you can't do this to any of the included layouts).

What's New in Dreamweaver CS6

If you've used Dreamweaver before, you'll notice that although some things look similar, some things look very different. A comprehensive description of all the new features in Dreamweaver CS6 would take up an entire chapter, so here are just a few of the highlights:

- **Fluid grid layouts:** This new choice in the New Document dialog **A** lets you design your site based on grids with rows and columns; you use one layout for smart phones, another for tablets, and a third for computer monitors—and which layout is displayed is based on the width of the browser window.

A You begin creating a fluid grid layout in the New Document dialog.

You lay out your **div**s on the grid **B**, and Dreamweaver creates the code to automatically switch between layouts depending on the screen size. See Chapter 12 for more.

- **Improved Multiscreen Preview:** Dreamweaver CS5.5 introduced a new feature, Multiscreen Preview, that works with Live view to show you simultaneous views of three different screen sizes: Mobile, Tablet, and Desktop. Multiscreen Preview makes it much easier to make your Web pages multi-device aware. In CS6, the real-time rendering of the screen sizes is faster and more accurate. We also cover this in Chapter 12.

- **Enhanced Live view:** Dreamweaver has a built-in rendering engine that is based on the latest version of WebKit, the browser engine used in Safari, Chrome, iOS, Android, and other browsers and operating systems. In Dreamweaver CS6, Live view has improved rendering of HTML5 and CSS3 code.

continues on next page

B The grid, in the background, constrains the **div**s with your content areas.

- **CSS transitions:** It's been possible for a long time to change the CSS of a page on the fly when the user interacts with it, in ways such as a hover or a click. Dreamweaver CS6 implements CSS transitions, part of CSS3. With a transition, you can control the timing and other characteristics of the change from one CSS state to another, creating smooth animation effects without JavaScript. Turn to Chapter 14 for more info.

- **W3C validation:** Make sure your pages adhere to Web standards with the new W3C Validator feature. You can validate static or dynamic HTML documents with the W3C validation service from within Dreamweaver. We cover this in Chapter 17.

- **Better code editing:** Dreamweaver has added tools to make it faster and easier to write CSS, JavaScript, browser-specific properties, and jQuery code. With code hinting, Dreamweaver uses pop-up menus to suggest properties and attributes as you type, saving you time.

Starting Your
First Site

Dreamweaver is all about building Web sites. Sure, it has all of the tools you need to create great Web pages. But the basic building block is the site, not the page. You need to define a site in Dreamweaver, which will then be the container for all of the files and folders that will make up your Web site.

When you build sites, you start by creating and testing the site on your local machine. Then, when the site is ready, you will send it over the Internet to your Web server, where it will go live for the world to see. Dreamweaver has all the tools you'll need to create the site, work with its files and folders, and then transfer it to the Web server. That's what we'll be covering in this chapter. So let's get started!

Understanding Local and Remote Sites

Dreamweaver can do a great job of helping you manage all the files and folders that make up your Web site, but for the best results, you'll need to use the program's site management tools to set up and maintain the site. You first need to understand some of the terminology Dreamweaver uses for sites. You'll want to build and test your Web site within a single folder on your hard disk, which Dreamweaver calls the *local root folder*. This folder contains all of the files and folders that make up the site. For example, let's say that you're building a company site that has two sections in it, one for contact information (called **contact**), and the other for information about the company (called **about**). Each of the two sections gets its own folder. These folders are located inside the local root folder (which is usually the site name; in this example, **Homecook.info**). Because each section shares some of the same graphic images, there is also an **images** folder in the local root folder. The site structure would look something like . With one main exception, each of the Web pages that you build for the site will go into either the **about** or **contact** folder or other folders you create for the site (not shown), such as **products** or **reviews**. The exception is the main site page (the one that people see when they load your site in their browsers). That's called the *index page*, and it usually goes in the local root folder (which is also called the *local site*).

A The top folder here is the local root folder, which contains all of the files and folders that make up the Web site.

Static vs. Dynamic Sites

There are two main kinds of Web sites that you can create in Dreamweaver: *static* sites, where you build all of the pages of the site on your local machine, and then upload them to the Web server; and *dynamic* sites, in which all the pages are created from information drawn from a database. The content from a dynamic page is created when the user loads the page. Many e-commerce sites are dynamic sites; for example, when you go to Amazon.com and see pages that greet you by name and offer personalized recommendations, those pages are created and served just for you, based on the programming of Amazon's database.

One big new feature introduced in Dreamweaver CS5 was the ability to work with dynamic sites that are built using content management systems (CMSs). The three supported systems are WordPress, Joomla, and Drupal. These systems create and serve pages dynamically from their internal databases. We'll discuss using Dreamweaver with these systems in Chapter 15, "Working with Content Management Systems." The groups who have created these CMSs have done a lot of programming so that you don't have to, and you can now use Dreamweaver to build on their work.

With the exception of working with the CMS, we're covering how to build static sites with Dreamweaver in this book. Dreamweaver still has plenty of features that allow Web programmers to build database-backed sites from scratch, and those features are so extensive that they would require and deserve a book of their own. When we run into the options that Dreamweaver offers to work with dynamic sites, we'll mention them, but we generally will not cover those options in detail in this book.

After you build the pages for your site, you will use Dreamweaver to copy all of the files and folders (usually over the Internet) to the Web server. Dreamweaver replicates the folder structure from your hard disk on the Web server, so the site's structure and all of the links between the pages are preserved. Dreamweaver refers to the copy of the site on the Web server as the *remote site*. The remote site should always be a mirror image of your local site, and Dreamweaver has tools that can synchronize the two sites (you'll learn more about that later in this chapter and in Chapter 18).

TIP Strictly speaking, you don't have to create all of your site's files within the local root folder. But if you do not, Dreamweaver will often put up dialogs complaining that files aren't in a local site, and you'll lose access to very useful Dreamweaver features, such as the ability to automatically update all links to a file that has been moved to another location in the site. We strongly recommend that you always build your pages in a local site and keep all of the elements that make up those pages in the local root folder.

TIP If you were using Dreamweaver's ability to work with sites built using a database, you could have a third copy of your site on a testing or staging server.

Creating the Local Site

Because the process of setting up your local and remote sites has several steps, Dreamweaver provides a handy Site Setup dialog that contains all the settings. Beginning with Dreamweaver CS5, the process of site definition was considerably streamlined to make it easier and faster.

You'll use the Site Setup dialog to create both the local and remote sites. In this section, however, we'll just create the local site. See "Defining the Remote Server," later in this chapter, for instructions on how to tell Dreamweaver about the remote site.

To create the local site:

1. In the Dreamweaver Welcome screen, click the Dreamweaver Site link **A**.

    or

    Choose Site > New Site.

    The Site Setup dialog appears, set to the Site category **B**.

A Click the Dreamweaver Site link in the Welcome screen to begin creating your site.

B In the Site pane of the Site Setup dialog, enter the name and local site folder of your site.

2. In the Site Name field, enter the name you want for your site.

   The site name is only for your reference; it won't be visible to users of the site.

3. Local Site Folder is the location on your computer where you want to store your files. Click the folder icon to the right of the text field, which brings up the Choose Root Folder dialog, and browse to the folder on your hard disk that contains all of the files for your site. If the folder doesn't already exist, click the New Folder button in the dialog and then name and save the folder. It's usually a good idea to give the folder the same or a similar name to the site name.

   On Windows, select the folder in the dialog, click Open, and then click the Select button.

   or

   On OS X, select the folder in the dialog and click the Choose button.

   The dialog closes and you will return to the Site Setup dialog. The field next to Local Site Folder now shows the path to the folder you just selected.

   That's all you absolutely need to do to define a site and get started with it in Dreamweaver. You can click Save now and start working. As you build your site and Dreamweaver needs additional information, it will prompt you as needed.

   Our recommendation, however, is to go ahead and complete two other items in the Site Setup dialog.

   continues on next page

4. Click the Advanced Settings category in the Site Setup dialog.

The Advanced Settings subcategories appear, with the Local Info category selected **C**.

5. Click the folder icon next to the Default Images Folder field. This brings up the Choose Image Folder dialog inside the local root folder.

6. You need to create the Images folder, so click the New Folder button in the dialog to create the folder. Name it `images`. On Windows, you can create the folder without a naming dialog; on OS X, you'll have to click Create after you enter the name. You will return to the dialog showing the contents of the root site folder, which will now contain the new `images` folder. Click Select (Choose).

You will return to the Local Info category of the Site Setup dialog, with the path to the images folder entered in the Default Images folder field.

C Next, in the Local Info category, you should tell Dreamweaver where the images folder is and the site's Web URL.

Site Setup for Dreamweaver Book	
Default Images folder:	/Users/tom/Documents/Websites/dreamweaverbook	
Site-wide Media Query file:		
Links relative to:	⦿ Document ○ Site Root
Web URL:	http://www.dreamweaverbook.com/

Enter the Web URL if you don't have a remote server defined. If you have a remote server defined, Dreamweaver uses the Web URL specified in the server settings.

Ⓓ When you enter the information about the images folder, Dreamweaver displays the path to the folder.

7. In the Web URL field, enter the Web address of your site, including the leading **http://** **Ⓓ**.

We'll cover the other items in this panel in other places in the book. For now, you can leave them at their default values.

8. Click Save.

In this case, we are only creating the local site. If you want to continue on and define the remote site, go to step 3 in "Defining the Remote Server," later in this chapter.

Getting Organized

Before you dive deeper into Dreamweaver, it's useful to spend some time deciding the structure and design of your site. In fact, this is a great time to push away from the computer and pick up much older design tools: a pencil and pad of paper. While a primer on site design would take up much more space than we have in this sidebar (indeed, entire books are devoted to the subject), before you begin building your site with Dreamweaver, consider the following and then sketch out your designs.

- What do your customers need from your site? Your site's visitors are your customers. Create your sites for them, not for you. Customers can visit your site for a variety of reasons: to purchase something, to get information or entertainment, or to be part of a community. Sites centered on your customer's needs are sites that visitors will return to. Sites driven by company structure or by the designer's ego—not so popular.

- What is the best structure and navigation for your site? Site structure is generally like an upside-down tree or an organizational chart. The index page is the main trunk that branches off to folders with other pages inside (and often other folders with their own pages). On your pad, add the main folders that you'll create from the index page (the home page of your site). Your structure will also determine the site navigation you choose. Again, put yourself in the place of your customers and imagine what they'll need to get around your site. Remember that they may not enter your site at your home page, so make sure the navigation is clear and consistent throughout the site.

Take the time to work out your customer's needs and then the site's structure and navigation on paper before you start creating things in Dreamweaver. You'll end up saving time by avoiding dead ends and wasted effort. To get some suggestions for good Web design books, see the appendix, "Where to Learn More."

Defining the Remote Server

The remote site lives on your Web server, and it is the destination for the files and folders from the local site on your computer's hard disk. Dreamweaver can connect to your Web server in several ways. The most common connection, called *FTP*, is used when your server resides on the Internet or on your company's intranet. Another way to connect is called *SFTP*, for Secure FTP. A third way to connect is via a protocol called *WebDAV* (see the sidebar "What Are FTP, SFTP, FTPS, and WebDAV?").

Before you begin creating a connection to the remote site, you need to ask your network administrator for some information about the Web server you're using. You will need the following:

- The connection type, which will typically be FTP, SFTP, or WebDAV. Dreamweaver CS5.5 added two additional flavors of FTP: FTP over SSL/TLS (implicit encryption) and FTP over SSL/TLS (explicit encryption), both of which, when chosen, add an additional Authentication pop-up menu to the Server Definition dialog; both should be used only at the direction of your site administrator.

- The FTP, SFTP, or WebDAV address for your server.

- The login (sometimes called the username) for the server.

- The password associated with the login.

- The folder's path on the server that contains your Web site.

Once you gather this information, you're ready to define the remote site in Dreamweaver. You'll begin by editing the site definition.

TIP Dreamweaver offers another way to connect to remote sites: RDS, which is used for database-backed sites and will not be discussed in this book.

What Are FTP, SFTP, FTPS, and WebDAV?

If you've never done any Web site maintenance before, you might be baffled by the term *FTP*. It stands for File Transfer Protocol, and it's a common method for transferring files (such as Web pages and images) between two computers connected to the Internet. Web servers often use FTP to send files between the server and the computer of whomever is maintaining the Web site. To do this, the server machine runs an *FTP server* program in addition to the Web server software. Normally you need a program called an *FTP client* on your computer to transfer files to and from an FTP server. Dreamweaver has built-in FTP client functions.

One of the drawbacks to FTP is that it is a protocol with no built-in security; all information is sent "in the clear," including your username, password, and the files themselves. The Secure FTP (SFTP) protocol solves this problem by encrypting all information sent between the SFTP client (in this case, Dreamweaver) and the SFTP server. SFTP uses the Secure Shell protocol to add security to the connection. As a result, it allows encryption but not authentication; the client and the server can't exchange credentials to verify that access is really allowed.

A newer method of adding security to FTP connections is FTPS (though Dreamweaver doesn't use that terminology; it instead uses the more precise FTP over SSL/TLS [implicit encryption] and FTP over SSL/TLS [explicit encryption]). In these methods, Dreamweaver not only encrypts its data transfers with the server, but also exchanges security credentials with the servers. These credentials are in the form of digitally signed server certificates, guaranteed by certificate authorities like Verisign and Thawte. The explicit encryption method allows both secure and insecure clients to use the server, but implements security if the client requests it. The implicit encryption method allows only secure clients to use the server.

The WebDAV protocol provides security and deals with another problem faced by Dreamweaver users: that of ensuring that only one person at a time is modifying a particular Web page. WebDAV locks a file while it is being edited and releases the lock when the page is completed. Dreamweaver has its own system of locking and unlocking files when you use protocols other than WebDAV; in practice, you won't see a difference in the way Dreamweaver works no matter which connection protocol you select.

To define the remote site with FTP or SFTP:

1. Choose Site > Manage Sites.

   The Manage Sites dialog appears **A**.

2. Select the site you want, and then click the Edit Selected Site icon.

   The Site Setup dialog appears.

3. Click the Servers category.

   The Servers pane appears **B** with no servers defined yet.

4. Click the Add New Server button at the bottom of the server list (it looks like a plus sign).

   The Server Definition dialog appears **C**, set to the Basic tab.

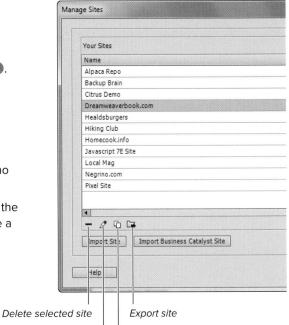

Delete selected site | Export site

Edit selected site | Duplicate site

A Begin adding the remote server to your site definition in the Manage Sites dialog.

Add new server | Server list

B You'll use the Servers category in the Site Setup dialog to enter the remote server information.

C Begin adding the remote server information by giving it a name (we suggest "Remote Server" because that's the name Dreamweaver uses elsewhere in the program).

D You'll need to enter the FTP information in the Server Definition screen. We've blurred some private information here.

5. Enter the name of the server in the Server Name field. Dreamweaver uses the name "Remote Server" elsewhere in the program, and that's what we suggest you do, too.

6. From the pop-up menu labeled "Connect using," choose FTP, SFTP, FTP over SSL/TLS (implicit encryption), or FTP over SSL/TLS (explicit encryption), depending on which kind of connection you are making.

   The dialog changes to show fields you need to fill in for the FTP and SFTP connection types **D**. Depending on your choice, one of the fields will be named FTP Address or SFTP Address.

7. In the FTP or SFTP Address field, enter the hostname or FTP/SFTP address of your Web server.

   The hostname could be a name like `www.peachpit.com` or `ftp.dori.com`. It will usually be the name you would enter into a Web browser without the `http://`. It must begin with `www` or `ftp` and cannot be just the domain name, such as `dori.com`. The name should not contain directories or slashes, such as `www.negrino.com/books/`. You can also enter a numeric IP address in this field, such as `64.28.85.14`.

8. In the Username field, enter the FTP/SFTP login name.

9. Enter the FTP/SFTP password.

   Don't forget that FTP/SFTP logins and passwords are case sensitive on many servers.

10. If you want Dreamweaver to remember the FTP/SFTP login and password (recommended), make sure the Save check box is selected.

continues on next page

11. In the next field, enter the name of the folder on the Web site that contains your site's files and will serve as the root folder for your site.

This folder is also called the *host directory* and is usually a path from the FTP folder to the root folder. Depending on your Web hosting company, this path could be named many different things. Typical host directory names are `htdocs`, `public_html`, and `www/public/docs/`. If you're unsure of the exact name of the host directory, check with your Web hosting company. Sometimes, the FTP host connects to the correct directory automatically, and you can leave the field blank.

12. If you were directed by your site admin to choose FTP over SSL/TLS (implicit encryption) or FTP over SSL/TLS (explicit encryption) in step 6, an Authentication pop-up menu appears in the dialog. For either method, choose either None (encryption only) or Trusted Server from the pop-up menu—again, as directed by the admin.

13. Click the Test button to make sure that Dreamweaver can connect successfully to your Web server.

If Dreamweaver reports an error, check the information you entered.

14. Click Save.

You are returned to the Site Setup dialog. The server you just added now appears in the Server list.

15. Click Save to close the dialog.

To define the remote site with WebDAV:

1. Choose Site > Manage Sites.

The Manage Sites dialog appears.

E If you connect to your Web server via WebDAV, you'll need to enter the connection information.

2. Select the site you want, and then click the Edit Selected Site icon.

The Site Setup dialog appears.

3. Click the Servers category.

The Servers pane appears with no servers defined yet.

4. Click the Add New Server button at the bottom of the server list (it looks like a plus sign).

The Server Definition dialog appears, set to the Basic tab.

5. Enter the name of the server in the Server Name field. Dreamweaver uses the name "Remote Server" elsewhere in the program, and that's what we suggest you do, too.

6. From the pop-up menu labeled "Connect using," choose WebDAV.

The dialog changes to show fields you need to fill in for the WebDAV connection type **E**.

7. Enter the URL of your WebDAV server.

8. In the Username field, enter the WebDAV login name.

9. Enter the WebDAV password.

If you want Dreamweaver to remember the WebDAV login and password (recommended), make sure the Save check box is selected.

10. Click the Test button to make sure that Dreamweaver can connect successfully to your Web server.

If Dreamweaver reports an error, check the information you entered.

11. Click Save.

You are returned to the Site Setup dialog. The server you just added now appears in the Server list.

12. Click Save to close the dialog.

Editing Site Definitions

Once you have created your site definitions, you might need to change them.
For example, you might want to change
the location of the local root folder, or you
may change the path on the remote server.
You'll use the Site Setup dialog.

To change a site definition:

1. Choose Site > Manage Sites.

   The Manage Sites dialog appears.

2. Select the site you want, and then
   click the Edit Selected Site icon.

   The Site Setup dialog appears.

3. Choose the category on the left side of
   the dialog for the kind of change you
   want to make.

   The right side of the dialog changes
   to show the options for the category
   you chose.

4. Make the changes you need to make.

5. Click Save.

Working with the Files Panel

To work with the files and folders that make up your Web sites, you'll use the Files panel. This panel allows you to add and delete files and folders; view and change the local or remote sites; and do other maintenance tasks for your sites.

The Files panel appears at the right side of the Dreamweaver window, docked with other panels. By default, the Files panel is at the bottom of the group of panels. The panel consists of a couple of pop-up menus, a toolbar, and the files area below Ⓐ.

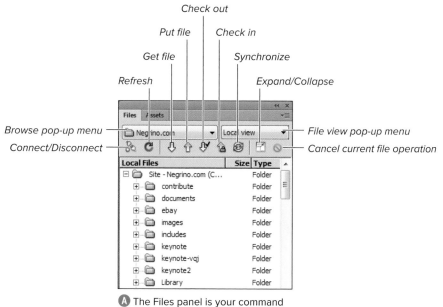

Check out
Put file　Check in
Get file　Synchronize
Refresh　Expand/Collapse
Browse pop-up menu ——
Connect/Disconnect ——
—— File view pop-up menu
—— Cancel current file operation

Ⓐ The Files panel is your command center for working with files in Dreamweaver.

Navigating Disks and Sites

The Browse pop-up menu at the top of the Files panel allows you to browse through your hard disk and easily switch between sites that you have defined. The menu looks a bit different on Windows and OS X, reflecting the differences between the operating systems 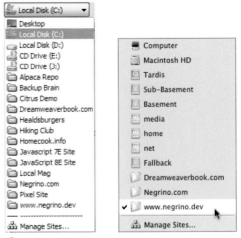. On both platforms, sites you have defined appear in the menu as folders.

To browse your hard disk:

1. In the Files panel, choose the disk you want from the Browse pop-up menu.

   The disk's contents appear in the files area **B**.

2. Navigate to the folder and file that you want.

To switch between defined sites:

In the Files panel, choose the site from the Browse pop-up menu.

A The Browse menu in the Files panel reflects the differences in the Windows (left) and OS X (right) operating systems.

B If you choose your hard disk from the Browse pop-up menu, you can then navigate to any file or folder on the disk.

A To see the files on the remote site, choose Remote server from the File view pop-up menu.

Switching Between Local View and the Remote Server

The File view pop-up menu, next to the Browse pop-up menu, allows you to switch the view in the Files panel between the local and remote sites.

To switch between local and remote views:

1. Choose a site you have defined from the Browse pop-up menu.

    The site's local files appear in the files area, and the File view pop-up menu switches to Local view.

2. From the File view pop-up menu, choose Remote server **A**.

    Dreamweaver connects to the site (you can tell because the Connect/Disconnect button in the Files panel toolbar will highlight), and the remote files appear in the files area.

TIP The File view pop-up menu has two other choices: Testing server and Repository view. We talk about using testing servers in Chapter 15; we won't be discussing Repository view in this book.

Refreshing Views

When you switch to the local or remote views of a site, Dreamweaver scans the contents of your local or remote site folders and displays the current contents. On occasion, the view you're looking at in the Files panel may become out of date. For example, if you happen to upload or delete items on the remote site with a program other than Dreamweaver, those changes won't be shown in the Files panel. Similarly, if you move files into the local root folder by working on the Windows or OS X desktop, you may need to tell Dreamweaver to rescan and refresh its display of the local site.

To refresh the local or remote view:

1. Choose the site you want to refresh from the Browse pop-up menu.

2. Choose the view (Local view or Remote server) you want from the File view pop-up menu.

3. Click the Refresh button in the Files panel toolbar.

    Dreamweaver rescans the site you selected and updates the files area.

Working with Files and Folders

The Files panel is great for organizing all of the files on your site and creating new files and folders. You should do most of your file creation and management in the Files panel, because it can often save you quite a bit of time compared to using another method in Dreamweaver.

For example, you can create a new page by choosing File > New, choosing the kind of page you want from the New Document dialog, and then editing the page. When you save the page, you must navigate to the correct folder in the local site folder, name the page, and then save it. In contrast, to create a new page in a particular folder using the Files panel, you select the folder that you want to contain the page and then choose the New File command, as described next.

TIP Just because the Dreamweaver files area is reminiscent of the Windows Explorer or OS X Finder, don't be fooled into thinking that it is the same and that you could do your local file management on your computer's desktop. Dreamweaver is designed for working with Web pages, and it can do incredibly useful things—like updating the links on a page to work correctly, even if you move the page that contains the links to a different folder on the site.

To create a new file or folder:

1. Use the File view pop-up menu to select the local or remote site. You will usually create files or folders in the local site.

2. Right-click a file or folder in the files area.

   A context menu appears that gives you many options 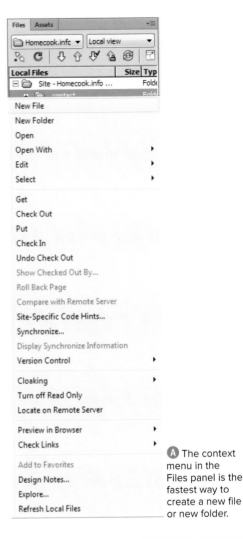.

3. From the context menu, choose New File or New Folder.

   The new file or folder appears in the files area. If you selected a folder in step 2, the new file or folder will be created inside the selected folder.

4. The name of the newly created file or folder ("untitled.html" for a file, or "untitled" for a folder) is selected in the Files panel. Type the name you want.

TIP You could also use the panel options button at the upper-right corner of the Files panel, which gives you a different menu, but it's easier to use the right-click context menu.

To move files or folders:

1. Select a file or folder in the files area. To move multiple items, Ctrl-click (Cmd-click) to select each of the items you want to move.

2. Drag the selected item or items to the new location.

   The Update Files dialog appears **B**.

3. Click Update.

   Dreamweaver updates all of the links in the site that are affected by the move.

A The context menu in the Files panel is the fastest way to create a new file or new folder.

B If you move files that are the target of links, Dreamweaver asks to update the pages that link to the file you moved.

The Edit submenu in the Files panel context menu gives you several options for working with files or folders.

To rename files or folders:

1. Select a file or folder in the files area.

2. Click the name of the file or folder.

   or

   Press F2.

   The name becomes highlighted.

3. Type the new name. Don't forget to add the correct file extension for the file that you're renaming. For example, most Web pages have the file extension `.htm` or (preferably) `.html`.

4. Press Enter (Return).

   The Update Files dialog appears.

5. Click Update.

   Dreamweaver updates all of the files in the site that are affected by the renamed file.

To edit files or folders:

1. Right-click a file or folder in the files area.

2. From the resulting context menu, choose Edit .

3. Choose one of the items in the Edit submenu.

   You can Cut, Copy, Paste, Delete, Duplicate, or Rename the file or folder. If a file operation will affect other files, Dreamweaver may display an "Are you sure?" dialog or the Update Files dialog.

TIP Note the shortcut keys listed next to each of the items in the Edit menu. As you become more comfortable working with files in Dreamweaver, using the shortcut keys can save you time.

Putting and Getting Files

You can copy selected files or folders (or the entire site) between the local and remote sites using the Files panel. Dreamweaver calls moving an item from the local to the remote site *putting* the item; moving the item from the remote to the local site is *getting* the item. If a put or get operation will overwrite a file, Dreamweaver warns you. If you select a folder, Dreamweaver moves the folder and all of the items that it contains. So if you select the local root folder, you can put the entire site up on the remote server in just a couple of clicks. Sometimes, however, you'll want to use Dreamweaver's site synchronization feature rather than putting or getting individual items. See "Synchronizing the Local and Remote Sites," later in this chapter.

Checking Files In and Out

We'll discuss operations with the Check In and Check Out buttons in the Files panel toolbar in Chapter 18, "Managing Your Site."

To put or get a file or folder:

1. In the Files panel, choose Local view or Remote server from the File view pop-up menu.

   The local or remote view is displayed in the files area.

2. Select the file or folder you want to move.

3. Click the Get file or Put file button in the Files panel toolbar.

4. If any of the files that you're transferring are open and have unsaved changes, Dreamweaver asks if you want to save the files before they are sent. Click Yes; if there are multiple files, click Yes to All.

5. Dreamweaver may also display a dialog asking if you want to transfer any dependent files. An example of dependent files would be the graphics on the pages that you are uploading. If the dependent files have already been uploaded to the server, click No; there's no reason to reupload files that haven't changed. If you want to transfer dependent files that have changed, click Yes.

Expanding the Files Panel

Normally, the Files panel will only show either the local site or the remote site. But if you would like to compare the list of files and folders on both sites, you can do that by expanding the Files panel. This feature works slightly differently on Windows and OS X. On Windows, expanding the Files panel causes it to grow to take over the entire screen, replacing the rest of the Dreamweaver interface. On OS X, expanding the Files panel opens the panel in a new window that allows you to see the remote site on the left and the local site on the right Ⓐ.

To expand the Files panel:

Click the Expand/Collapse button in the Files panel toolbar.

TIP To collapse the Files panel, click the Expand/Collapse button again.

Ⓐ On OS X, when you expand the Files panel, it opens in a new window with the remote site on the left and the local site on the right.

A In the Synchronize with Remote Server dialog, you'll need to select the synchronization method you want to use.

Synchronizing the Local and Remote Sites

Having two copies of a Web site—one on your local machine and the other on a Web server—can potentially lead to trouble. It's possible, for example, for you to update several pages on your local site and lose track of just which files you changed. In that case, it might be difficult for you to determine which copy of the site (local or remote) has the latest version of the files. Dreamweaver's Synchronize command compares the local and remote sites and transfers the newer files in either direction.

To synchronize local and remote sites:

1. Click the Synchronize button in the Files panel.

   or

   Choose Site > Synchronize Sitewide.

   The Synchronize with Remote Server dialog appears A.

2. From the Synchronize pop-up menu, choose the files you want to update.

   Your choices are to synchronize all the files in the site, or just files or folders that you selected in the Local view.

continues on next page

3. From the Direction pop-up menu, choose how you would like to copy newer files:

- ▶ **Put newer files to remote** sends newer files from your local site folder to the Web server.

- ▶ **Get newer files from remote** finds newer files on the Web server and copies them to your local site folder. This option also copies completely new files that are on the Web server (ones, for example, that may have been placed there by a coworker) to your local site folder.

- ▶ **Get and Put newer files** synchronizes files both ways. New files on the local site will be transferred to the remote site and vice versa.

4. (Optional) If you want, select the "Delete remote files not on local drive" check box.

This is a good option to choose when you've made substantial deletions in the local site (perhaps because you did a big site cleanup). The wording of this option changes depending on what you chose in step 3. If you chose to transfer newer files from the remote site, the wording changes to "Delete local files not on remote server." If you chose to get and put files, this option becomes inactive.

5. Click Preview.

Dreamweaver connects to the remote site, compares the files you chose to synchronize, and then displays the Synchronize dialog **B**. This allows you to preview the changes that will be made on the site. The Action column in the dialog tells you what Dreamweaver proposes to do to each file.

6. If desired, select one or more files in the Synchronize dialog and choose one of the action buttons at the bottom of the dialog. You have the following choices:

   ▸ **Get** marks the selected files to be retrieved from the remote site.

   ▸ **Put** marks the selected files to be sent to the remote site.

   ▸ **Delete** marks the selected files for deletion.

   ▸ **Ignore** tells Dreamweaver to ignore the selected files for this synchronization.

   ▸ **Compare** opens the local and remote versions of the file so you can compare their differences.

   ▸ **Mark as synchronized** tells Dreamweaver to consider the selected files as already synchronized, so no action will be taken.

7. Click OK.

   Dreamweaver performs the synchronization.

Get | Put | Delete | Ignore | Compare | Mark as synchronized

B You can select actions in the Synchronize dialog that will determine how the files are affected as they are synchronized.

Cloaking Files and Folders

Not every file or folder in your local site needs to be uploaded to the remote site on the Web server. Dreamweaver allows files and folders to be *cloaked*, which means that they will be exempt from synchronization. This can save you a lot of time. Imagine that you're working on a site that contains large movie files. Cloaking the folder that contains the movie files means that while you're working on other parts of the site, Dreamweaver won't take the time to scan through the folders when synchronizing and won't upload any of the files. When you're ready to upload the files, uncloak the movies folder and synchronize the local and remote sites.

To cloak a file or folder:

1. Right-click a file or folder in the Files panel.

2. From the resulting context menu, choose Cloaking, and then from the submenu, choose Cloak .

   In the Files panel, Dreamweaver displays the file or folder with a slash through it, indicating that it is cloaked.

To uncloak a file or folder:

1. Right-click a cloaked file or folder in the Files panel.

2. From the resulting context menu, choose Cloaking > Uncloak or Cloaking > Uncloak All.

A Choosing Cloak from the Files panel context menu keeps a file or a folder and its contents from being affected during synchronization operations.

B The Cloaking category in the Site Setup dialog allows you to set particular kinds of files to always be cloaked.

TIP You can cloak all files of a particular type. Choose Site > Manage Sites, and then select the site you're working on. Click the Advanced Settings category of the Site Setup dialog, and then choose the Cloaking category. Select the "Cloak files ending with" check box, and then enter the file extensions of the kinds of files you want to cloak **B**.

Building Your
First Page

After you've set up your local site, you can begin filling the site with pages. To do that, you'll need to create a page, give it a title, add some content to the page, and save it. To check your work, you should view the page in one or more Web browsers before you upload it to your Web server. Dreamweaver has always made it easy to view your work in different browsers, and the new (as of CS5) integration with Adobe's BrowserLab service makes it even simpler.

If you need a little inspiration, Dreamweaver offers a variety of sample pages that you can use as a jumping-off point for your own creative efforts. You can also choose from a variety of page designs created entirely with CSS.

In this chapter, we'll also briefly discuss how you add text, images, and links to your pages, although we go into those subjects in much greater detail in Chapters 4, 5, and 6, respectively.

In This Chapter

Creating a New Page

The first HTML page that you create in a new site should be the *index* page, which is the page that a Web browser loads automatically when a visitor goes to the site. Depending on how you are naming pages on your site, the index page could have a variety of names, but it is most often named `index.html`. After you create the index page, you will want to create other pages for the site.

As is often the case with Dreamweaver, there is more than one way to do the task at hand. You can create a new page using the Welcome screen, or you can use the New Document dialog.

Using the Welcome screen

The Welcome screen is the fastest way to create a new HTML page. It appears when you have closed all other document windows.

To create a new page from the Welcome screen:

1. Close any open document windows.

   The Welcome screen appears **Ⓐ**. Each of the items in the Welcome screen is a link.

2. In the Create New section, click HTML.

   Dreamweaver creates the new blank HTML page **Ⓑ**.

> **TIP** You can also use the Welcome screen to open pages that you recently worked on. Just click the item's name in the Open a Recent Item section of the Welcome screen.

Using the New Document Dialog

The New Document dialog gives you a bit more flexibility than the Welcome screen when creating new documents. As with the Welcome screen, you can create several different types of new documents, plus it allows you to choose the **doctype** of the new document.

> **TIP** Clicking ColdFusion or PHP in the Create New section of the Welcome screen also creates an HTML page. Clicking CSS creates a new CSS style sheet. Clicking any of the other choices creates documents designed for different Web programming languages that you would normally work with in Code view.

> **TIP** If you don't want to use the Welcome screen at all, you can turn it off in Dreamweaver's Preferences. Choose Edit > Preferences (Dreamweaver > Preferences), and click the General category. Then deselect the check box next to "Show Welcome screen."

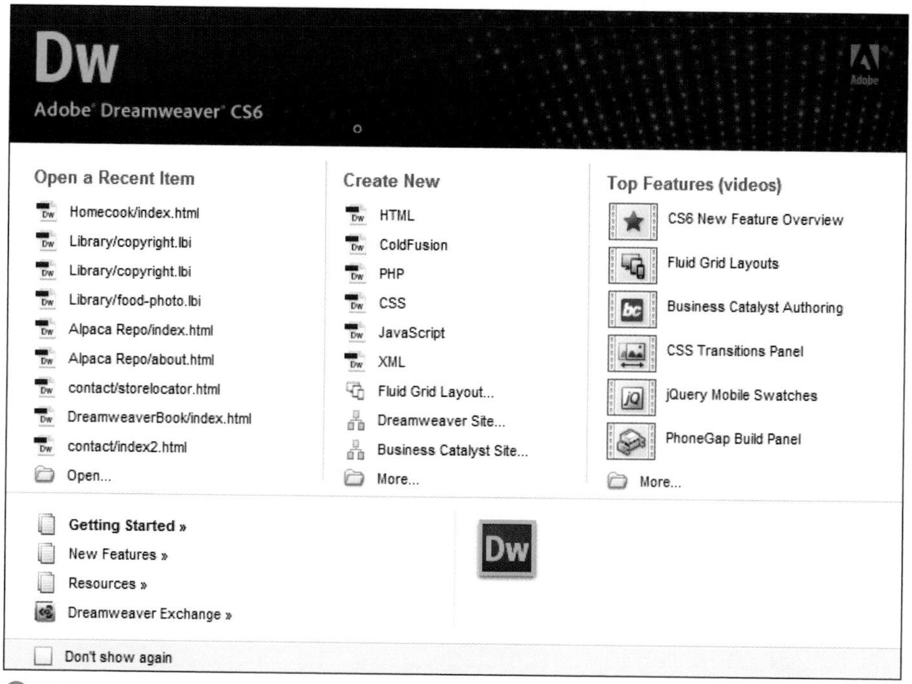

Dw
Adobe Dreamweaver CS6
Open a Recent Item
Homecook/index.html
Library/copyright.lbi
Library/copyright.lbi
Library/food-photo.lbi
Alpaca Repo/index.html
Alpaca Repo/about.html
contact/storelocator.html
DreamweaverBook/index.html
contact/index2.html
Open...
Create New
HTML
ColdFusion
PHP
CSS
JavaScript
XML
Fluid Grid Layout...
Dreamweaver Site...
Business Catalyst Site...
More...
Top Features (videos)
CS6 New Feature Overview
Fluid Grid Layouts
Business Catalyst Authoring
CSS Transitions Panel
jQuery Mobile Swatches
PhoneGap Build Panel
More...
Getting Started »
New Features »
Resources »
Dreamweaver Exchange »
Dw
Don't show again

Ⓐ Click the links in the Welcome screen to open a recent item or create a new item.

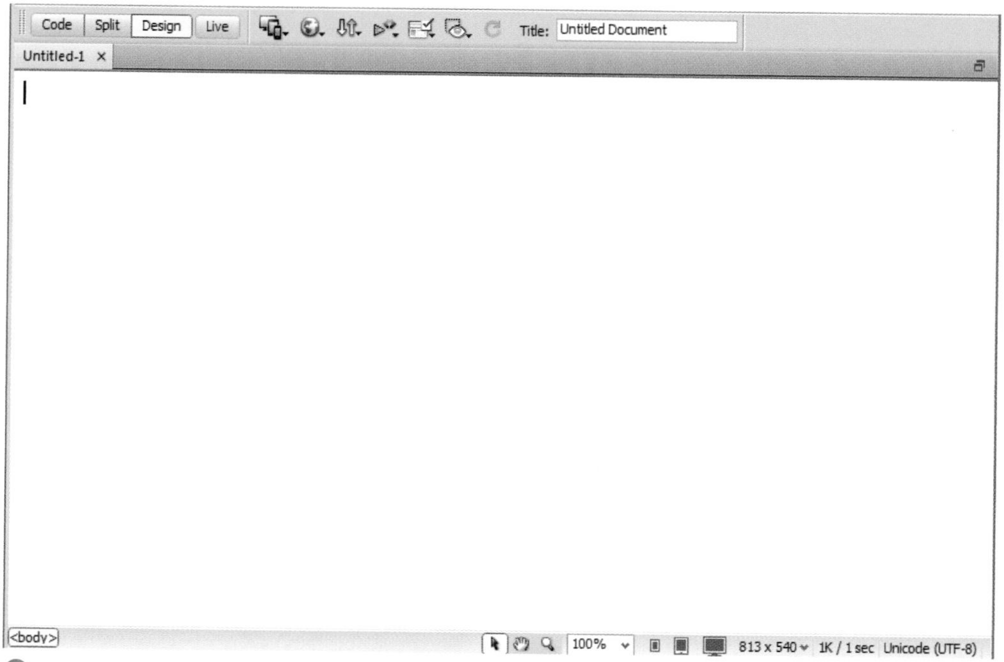

Code
Split
Design
Live
Title:
Untitled Document
Untitled-1 ×
<body>
100%
813 x 540
1K / 1 sec
Unicode (UTF-8)

Ⓑ A brand-new page in Dreamweaver showing the Design view.

To create a new page from the New Document dialog:

1. Choose File > New, or press Ctrl-N (Cmd-N).

   The New Document dialog appears **C** set to the Blank Page tab.

2. Click to choose one of the tabs in the leftmost column.

   The second column changes to show the available items for the tab you selected. The name of this column also changes to match the name of the tab.

   If you chose the Blank Page tab and HTML as the page type, as in **C**, the third column shows a number of CSS starter layouts. These starter layouts are discussed in more detail in Chapter 8.

C You'll probably create most of your new pages from the New Document dialog.

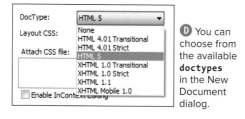

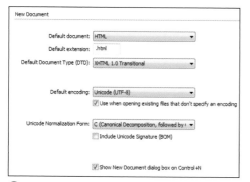

D You can choose from the available **doctypes** in the New Document dialog.

E Change the defaults for new pages in the New Document category of Dreamweaver's Preferences dialog.

Behind the Doctype

If you're not familiar with **doctype**, it's a declaration at the start of an HTML page that specifies the DTD (Document Type Definition) that is in use for the file. Web browsers use the **doctype** declaration to determine how the page should be rendered.

By default, Dreamweaver CS6 inserts the "XHTML 1.0 Transitional" **doctype**, and the code it creates is consistent with that standard. This version also has the option of using the HTML5 **doctype**. HTML5 is an emerging standard that is expected to become the dominant Web standard in the years to come.

3. Click the item you want in the third column.

If Dreamweaver has a preview image of the item you selected available, it appears in the Preview pane (previews are mostly available for sample pages and templates) with its description below the preview area.

4. (Optional) Some of the kinds of documents you can create in this dialog allow you to declare their **doctype**, and for those the DocType pop-up menu will be available. Most of the time the default choice is fine, but if you want, you can change the **doctype** from the pop-up menu **D**.

5. Click Create.

Dreamweaver creates the new document and displays it in a new window.

TIP If you want to change any of the defaults for a new document, click the Preferences button in the New Document dialog. In the resulting dialog **E**, you can change the default document type for the New Document dialog; the extension used for that document; the default document type (DTD); and the default character encoding. You can also choose whether or not you want the New Document dialog to appear when you press Ctrl-N (Cmd-N), or if you just want Dreamweaver to create a new default document.

TIP We'll cover the Blank Template and Page from Template tabs of the New Document dialog in Chapter 15.

Using Sample Pages

Dreamweaver has many sample pages available, which do some of the work of creating new pages for you. The sample pages are often good jumping-off points for your own pages. After you create a document from one of the sample pages, you can customize and modify it as you wish.

The sample pages come in two categories:

- **CSS Style Sheet** chooses external CSS style sheet documents that contain style definitions with a wide variety of looks for your pages. You can click any of the sample style sheets to see a preview and description Ⓐ.

- **Mobile Starters** has three premade jQuery-based pages Ⓑ. Using these pages to create layouts destined for mobile devices is considerably easier than doing it by hand.

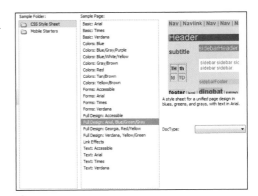

Ⓐ Dreamweaver provides many starter CSS style sheets, which you can preview in the New Document dialog.

Ⓑ You can preview and choose from the predefined jQuery-based mobile starter pages.

To create a page from a sample page:

1. Choose File > New, or press Ctrl-N (Cmd-N).

   The New Document dialog appears.

2. Click the Page from Sample tab in the leftmost column **C**.

   The second column changes to show the available items for the tab you selected. The name of this column also changes to Sample Folder.

3. Click the item you want in the third column.

   The preview image of the item you selected appears in the Preview pane (previews are mostly available for sample pages and templates) with its description below the preview.

4. Click Create.

   Dreamweaver creates the page in a new window.

5. Modify the sample page as you like.

TIP If you're looking for rapid prototyping of sites, one possibility is to download or purchase one of the many free or inexpensive Dreamweaver templates; a quick Google search for "Dreamweaver templates" will turn up a large selection. When you find one that you like, make sure that its layout is CSS based, not table based. It makes no sense to use templates that won't be easy to maintain in the future.

C You can choose from two categories of sample pages.

Titling Your Page

The first thing you should do with your new page is to add a *title*. The title is the text that appears in the title bar of Web browser windows, at the top of the window **A**. You'll enter this text in the Dreamweaver document window.

To add a title to your page:

1. If necessary, open the page you want to title.
2. Click in the Title field at the top of the page's document window.
3. Type in the title **B**.

TIP Don't forget to add the title; it's easy to forget, and when you do forget, it makes it harder for people to find your pages using a search engine. As we write this, a quick Google search for "Untitled Document" in the title of pages brings up more than 117 million hits. Don't be one of them!

A The title of an HTML document appears at the top of a Web browser's window or, for browsers that use tabbed windows (like Firefox does here), as the title of the tab.

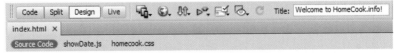

B Enter the title in, well, the Title field.

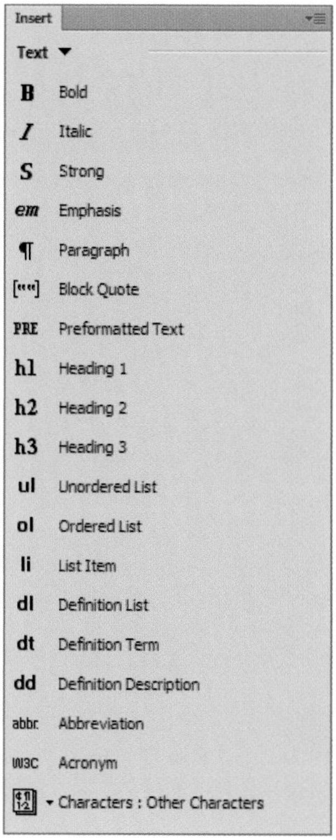
Insert
Text
B Bold
I Italic
S Strong
em Emphasis
¶ Paragraph
Block Quote
PRE Preformatted Text
h1 Heading 1
h2 Heading 2
h3 Heading 3
ul Unordered List
ol Ordered List
li List Item
dl Definition List
dt Definition Term
dd Definition Description
abbr. Abbreviation
W3C Acronym
Characters : Other Characters

A Use the Text category of the Insert panel to format your text using HTML markup.

Adding Text to Your Page

In this section, we'll cover adding a bit of text to your page, just enough to get you started. You'll find a much more detailed discussion of working with text in Dreamweaver in Chapter 4. In short, adding text is a lot like typing text in any word processor.

To add text to a page:

1. On the new page, click to set a blinking insertion point. You can press Enter (Return) to move the insertion point down on the page.
2. Type your text.

   The text appears on the page, aligned to the left.

To format the text:

1. In the Insert panel, choose the Text category from the pop-up menu.

   The Text category of the Insert panel appears **A**.
2. Using the Insert panel and the HTML tab of the Property inspector, apply any formatting you want, as you would with a word processor.

   See Chapter 4 for much more detail about using the Text category of the Insert panel.

TIP This formatting would, of course, add HTML markup to your page. You'll probably want to use CSS formatting for text instead; that's covered in Chapter 7.

Creating Links

To add a hyperlink to a page, you need to select the text you want to turn into a link, and then provide the URL for the link. A URL (Uniform Resource Locator) is the Web address that you would type into the Address bar of a Web browser.

You will find much more information about adding links to your pages in Chapter 6. You'll see how to add links to either text or graphics and lots of other linky goodness.

Ⓐ Begin creating a link by selecting the text that you want to turn into the link.

To add a link to a page:

1. Select the text you want to turn into a link Ⓐ.

   In this example, I want to turn the "HomeCook.info" text at the top of the page into a link to the home page of the site, so I've selected that text.

2. Do one of the following:

   If you are linking to a page in your site, click the Point to File button in the Property inspector Ⓑ and then drag to a file in the Files panel Ⓒ. When you release the mouse button, the filename appears in the Link field.

   or

Point to File button   *Browse for File button*

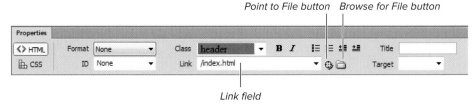

Link field

Ⓑ Click the Point to File button to begin the linking process...

Ⓒ ...then drag to point at the file you want to link to in the Files panel. As you drag, Dreamweaver follows your mouse pointer with an arrow to make it clear which file you're pointing at.

D You can also create a link by clicking the Browse for File button in the Property inspector, which brings up the Select File dialog.

E If the file you are selecting is outside your local root folder, Dreamweaver offers to copy the file to that folder as part of the linking process.

If you are linking to a file on your hard drive (inside or outside of your local site folder), click the Browse for File button in the Property inspector. The Select File dialog appears **D**. Navigate to the file you want to link to, select it, and then click OK (Choose). The filename appears in the Link field. If the file is outside of the local root folder, Dreamweaver lets you know and offers to copy the file into the local root folder **E**.

or

If you are linking to a Web address, click in the Link field in the Property inspector and type the full URL of the link destination. You must include the `http://` portion of the address.

> **TIP** You can also copy a URL from the Address bar of a Web browser (or anywhere else) and paste the URL into the Link field.

> **TIP** You aren't limited to Web links, which begin with `http://`, of course; you can put any valid URL in the Link field, including links for FTP sites, email addresses, and more. Again, see Chapter 6 for more information.

Adding Images

Much of the visual interest in Web pages is provided by images, and Dreamweaver makes it easy to add images to your pages. For much more information about adding images, sound, or movie files to your pages, see Chapter 5.

To add an image to your page:

1. In your document, click where you want the image to appear.

2. In the Common category of the Insert panel, click the Images: Image button 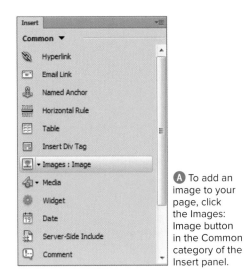.

   The Select Image Source dialog appears **B**.

A To add an image to your page, click the Images: Image button in the Common category of the Insert panel.

B The Select Image Source dialog lets you pick an image and shows you a preview of it as well.

Image Tag Accessibility Attributes

Alternate text: Pixel the cat ▼

Long description: http://

If you don't want to enter this information when inserting objects, change the Accessibility preferences.

OK
Cancel
Help

C Use this dialog to enter the alternate text for an image.

Code | Split | Design | Live

fishinspector.html* ×

Our Fish Inspector

D The image appears on the page at the insertion point.

3. Navigate to the image file you want, and select it.

   Dreamweaver shows you a preview of the image in the Select Image Source dialog.

4. Click OK (Choose).

   If the image is not inside the **/images** directory of your local root folder, Dreamweaver copies the image to that location. Dreamweaver next displays the Image Tag Accessibility Attributes dialog **C**.

5. (Optional, but strongly recommended) Enter a description of the image in the Alternate text field.

   Alternate text is text attached to the image for use by screen readers for the visually impaired or by people who are browsing with images turned off.

6. Click OK.

   The image appears in your document **D**.

TIP The Long description field in the Image Tag Accessibility Attributes dialog links to a file that can contain a full description of the image. This option is not often used.

TIP If you don't want to add alternate text, you can turn off the prompt dialog in the Accessibility category of Dreamweaver's Preferences panel. But you shouldn't; this is a key attribute to add for the benefit of visually impaired visitors to your site.

Naming and Saving Your Page

After you've built your page, you'll want to name it and save it in your local site folder. After you work on the page, you'll need to save your changes. You should get in the habit of saving often; there's nothing more annoying than lost work due to a power failure or because your computer decides to lock up.

It's important to understand the difference between a page's *title* and its *name*. The *title* appears at the top of the page in a Web browser; the *name* is the file's name and will be part of the Web address, or URL, of the page. For example, "Welcome to HomeCook.info!" is the page's title, but `index.html` is the page's name.

To save your page for the first time:

1. Choose File > Save, or press Ctrl-S (Cmd-S).

   The Save As dialog appears 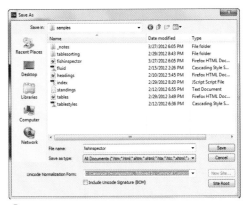.

A Use the Save As dialog to place your new document where you want it inside your local root folder and also to give it a filename.

B The Mac version of the Save As dialog shows you the document's extension and selects the name for you.

What's in a Name?

Your computer may allow you to enter characters in a filename that aren't acceptable in a URL. For example, on the Mac, it's perfectly OK to use the slash (/) in a filename. But you can't use a slash in a URL (Web servers can't handle a slash in a filename), so you *shouldn't* include slashes. Similarly, you can use spaces in filenames on both Windows and Mac, but you cannot have spaces in a URL, so don't use spaces in your filenames. Other characters to avoid include #, $, &, and %. We recommend that for safety's sake, you use only letters, numbers, and the underscore character (to substitute for a space). Remember that some people may want to manually type a URL from your site into a browser, so make things easy for them by using relatively short filenames. Using all lowercase makes it easier for visitors, too.

2. Enter the name for the page.

Dreamweaver gives the page a default name of Untitled-*x*, where *x* is the number of pages you've created since you launched Dreamweaver. On Windows, the dialog shows the name in the "File name" field without showing the extension; on the Mac, the name appears with the extension, but only the name is selected, ready for replacement with whatever you type **B**.

Not all characters are acceptable in a filename; be sure to read the "What's in a Name?" sidebar.

3. You should save the file inside your local site folder. If you want the file to be in a particular folder inside your site, navigate to that folder.

4. Click Save.

To save changes you make in your pages:

Choose File > Save, or press Ctrl-S (Cmd-S).

Opening a Page

Opening a page is straightforward; you'll usually want to use Dreamweaver's Files panel. You can also use the File menu or the Welcome screen if you like.

To open a page:

1. In the Files panel 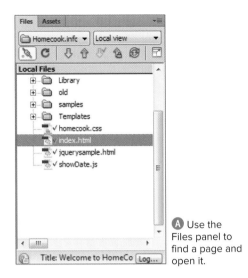, find the page you want to open and double-click it.

   The page opens.

   or

   Choose File > Open, or press Ctrl-O (Cmd-O).

   The Open dialog appears.

2. Navigate to the file, select it, and click Open.

   The file opens in a new window (or in a new tab if you already have open windows).

TIP If you want to open a page that you worked on recently, find the page in the Open a Recent Item category in the Welcome screen, and click it.

TIP Click the Site Root button in the Open or Save As dialog to jump quickly to the site's root folder.

Ⓐ Use the Files panel to find a page and open it.

A Thanks to the widespread acceptance of CSS across all browser makers, pages display similarly in different browsers, provided they are relatively modern, as with this Firefox example. The biggest problem to watch for is old (pre-IE9) versions of Internet Explorer, which had serious CSS rendering issues.

Previewing in a Browser

The page preview you see in Dreamweaver's Design view is useful, but it's no substitute for previewing your pages in real Web browsers. The reason is simple: The Design view shows one rendering of the HTML page, but Web browsers, which may be based on different rendering software (often called "rendering engines"), may show the same page differently. For example, you'll often see pages that look different in Internet Explorer for Windows (especially versions prior to IE9), Mozilla Firefox, Google Chrome, Opera, and Safari on either Mac or Windows. That's because each browser lays out and draws pages in its own way **A**. Even the preview you get in Live view isn't always exactly the same as the most common Windows browsers (Internet Explorer and Firefox). Although Dreamweaver's Live view is much more true to what you'll see in a Web browser—since it uses WebKit, the same rendering engine used by Chrome and Safari—it's still a good idea to preview in more than one real browser, preferably on Mac, Windows, and mobile devices.

By default, Dreamweaver makes your computer's default Web browser the default browser for previewing pages, but you can change that if you prefer.

To preview a page in a Web browser:

1. Save your page.

Dreamweaver requires that the page be saved before it can create a preview. If you forget, a dialog will ask you if you want to save. If you click No in this dialog, the preview that appears will be of the last saved version of the page—not necessarily the latest version—so get used to saving before previewing.

2. Press F12 (Opt-F12).

The page opens in the default preview browser.

or

Choose File > Preview in Browser, and then choose a browser from the submenu **B**.

The page opens in the browser you selected.

or

Click the Preview/Debug in Browser button on the Document toolbar **C**. A pop-up menu appears with the browser choices available on your system.

TIP If you're using the built-in keyboard on a Mac laptop, you may need to press Fn-Opt-F12.

TIP Depending on which Mac and which version of Mac OS X (Mountain Lion, Lion, or Snow Leopard) you're running, F12 could be assigned by the system to Mission Control, Exposé, or Dashboard. On the Mac, Dreamweaver requires that you use Opt-F12 for the primary browser, and Cmd-F12 for the secondary browser. If you have any OS X features that use these keys, you can change them to different keys in the Mission Control, Dashboard & Exposé, Keyboard, or Exposé & Spaces pane of the System Preferences panel.

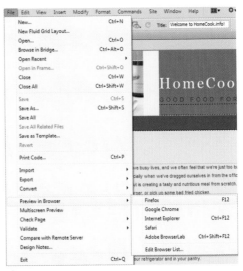

B Choose the browser you want to use for the preview from the Preview in Browser submenu.

C You can also choose your preview browser from the Preview/Debug in Browser button on the Document toolbar.

D You can choose which browsers on your system appear in the Preview in Browser list and also set browsers as your primary and secondary preview browsers.

To set the browsers that appear in the Browser list:

1. Choose File > Preview in Browser, and then choose Edit Browser List from the submenu.

    The Preview in Browser category of the Preferences panel appears **D**.

2. Do one or more of the following:

    ▸ To add a browser to the list, click the + button and then fill out the information in the resulting Add Browser dialog.

    ▸ To remove a browser from the list, select the browser and click the – button.

    ▸ To set a browser as the primary preview browser (this will cause it to open when you press F12 [Opt-F12]), select it and then select the Primary browser check box.

    ▸ To set a browser as the secondary preview browser (this will cause it to open when you press Ctrl-F12 [Cmd-F12]), select it and then click the Secondary browser check box.

3. Click OK to close the Preferences dialog.

TIP Note that there is a choice in **C** that doesn't appear in the list in **D**: Adobe BrowserLab. BrowserLab is an online previewing service that's integrated with Dreamweaver and discussed later in this chapter. You can't remove BrowserLab from the submenu.

Preview Using Preset Screen Sizes

By default, when you view a page in Design or Live view, it takes up the entire document page . Dreamweaver already has a Window Sizes feature, which shrinks the document window to the horizontal and vertical sizes you specify. But the new Resolution Management feature lets you choose from different view settings for your document, regardless of whether you have the Dreamweaver window in a maximized or non-maximized mode.

There is now a Window Size menu that contains a list of common screen sizes, which you can edit to match the window sizes you're targeting with your design.

TIP To make it easier for you to follow along, you can use the demo assets that Adobe has supplied on their Dreamweaver Developer Center site. Download the sample files from www.adobe.com/devnet/dreamweaver/articles/dw_html5_pt3.html. Look for the citrus_pt3_completed.zip sample files. In order to use them, unzip the download, put the sample files on your local hard drive, and then set them up as a site within Dreamweaver by using Site > New Site.

Ⓐ In the Dreamweaver document window, shown here in Live view, you'll see the entire page you're working on.

| Code | Split | Design | Live | Live Code | Inspect |

index.html ×

Source Code citrus_mq.css desktop.css phone.css tablet.css

B Look at your document in Live view in order to properly view different window sizes.

Adobe BrowserLab

Multiscreen Preview

240 x 320	Feature Phone
320 x 480	Smart Phone
480 x 800	Smart Phone
592w	
768 x 1024	Tablet
1000 x 620	(1024 x 768, Maximized)
1260 x 875	(1280 x 1024, Maximized)
1420 x 750	(1440 x 900, Maximized)
1580 x 1050	(1600 x 1200, Maximized)

✓ Full Size

Edit Sizes...

✓ Orientation Landscape

Orientation Portrait

only screen and (max-width:320px)

only screen and (min-width:321px) and (max-width:768px)

Media Queries...

C The drop-down menu, part of the Multiscreen button in the Document toolbar, shows you the preset screen sizes you can display in the document window.

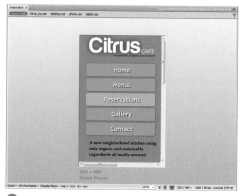

D When this low-resolution screen size is shown in the document window, the linked CSS file springs into action, changing the layout of the page to show the site's logo and menus in a vertical layout.

To display screen sizes:

1. In the Document toolbar, click the Live view button **B**.

   The document renders using the WebKit browser engine.

2. From the Window Size drop-down menu attached to the Multiscreen button in the Document menu, choose one of the preset sizes **C**. For example, 320 x 480 Smart Phone is the nominal size of an iPhone screen.

   The new viewport appears within the document window **D**.

   If you have only one version of the page, the viewport will just be a window into the full-size page, starting from the upper-left corner of the page. But if you've created different CSS layouts for different screen sizes (this is called a *media query*, and there's lots more about those in Chapter 12), the viewport will respect the media query for the selected screen size and will show you the version of the page using the proper CSS layout.

3. (Optional) You can simulate changing the orientation of a mobile device by choosing either Orientation Landscape or Orientation Portrait from the menu.

TIP You can also access the view settings by clicking the Window Size menu in the status toolbar at the bottom of the document window or by choosing View > Window Size.

TIP If you have created media queries for the page, they will also appear in the Window Size menu, below the orientation choices.

TIP One good way to work interactively with your code and design is to use Split view (which shows code in one pane and either Design or Live view in the other) and then choose View > Split Vertically. If you drag the border between the two panes to the right or left—and you have created different CSS layouts for smaller screen sizes—the Live view pane will respect the layout file for the smaller size, and the display will automatically switch the CSS layout and change the view in that pane.

TIP Dreamweaver's resolution management preview does a decent job, but you shouldn't fully rely on it for what your page will really look like when displayed on a mobile device. For example, the Safari browser on an iPhone automatically zooms the page so that you see more of it **E**. As always, there is no true substitute for viewing your pages on as many real-world devices as are important to you.

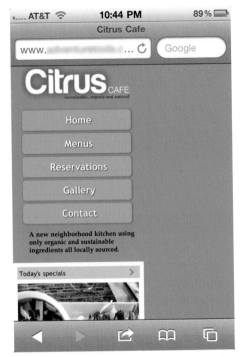

E Whenever possible, preview the page on the actual device you're targeting. As you can see, on a real iPhone, the Safari browser zooms the page to show more of its content.

WebKit Enhancements

Dreamweaver's Live view is powered by WebKit, the browser engine used by Apple's Safari browser (which ships as the default browser on Mac and iOS devices, such as the iPhone and iPad) and by Google Chrome. Other devices in the mobile space, notably Android smart phones and some RIM BlackBerry smartphones, also include the WebKit browser engine.

Dreamweaver CS5.5 updated the built-in WebKit browser engine. Adobe says the new rendering is equivalent to Safari 5.0. Dreamweaver's Live view now renders several CSS properties as described in the W3C specifications for CSS3. CSS rules that include **font-face**, **svg**, and **box-shadow** now render properly.

Its support of the **font-face** property is especially interesting, as it allows you to use non-Web-safe fonts by defining the location of a font resource in the CSS rule. The font resource can be either local to your site or an external reference. See Chapter 7 for more about implementing Web fonts and **font-face** in your documents.

Dreamweaver also supports code hinting for **font-face** and **box-shadow**. You'll see more about code hints in Chapter 17.

To customize screen sizes:

1. From the Window Size menu, choose Edit Sizes.

   Dreamweaver's Preferences window appears, set to the Window Sizes category **F**.

2. Any of the Width, Height, or Description fields are editable.

   For example, I've changed the 320 x 480 resolution's Description to iPhone, and the 768 x 1024 resolution's Description to iPad.

3. (Optional) If you want to add a window size, click the plus button below the list. Similarly, if you want to remove any of the window sizes from the menu, select that size in the list, then click the minus button below the list.

4. When you're done customizing the window sizes, click OK. The Preferences window closes, and the customizations will appear in the Window Size menu.

F In the Window Sizes category of Dreamweaver's Preferences panel, you can customize the entries that appear in the menu. Here, I've changed the Description field for the iPhone and iPad resolutions from the generic Smart Phone and Tablet to the device's names.

Viewing Pages in BrowserLab

One of the difficulties of browsers is that there are an awful lot of them, and most of us don't have the resources to maintain a lab of computers, operating systems, and different browsers to see how a page will look in the myriad combinations of these environments. A service from Adobe, BrowserLab, is specifically designed to solve this problem. It allows you to see how your pages will render in a variety of browsers by emulating how those browsers render pages.

Adobe BrowserLab displays its page renderings using Flash. You can choose which browsers you are emulating, and you can view rendered pages in a 2-up mode, viewing them side by side to see the rendering differences. There's even an Onion Skin mode that allows you to place one rendered page over another to see how different browsers change the layout of page elements.

Adobe BrowserLab is integrated into Dreamweaver, so you have the benefit of using it as just another preview mode.

To preview a page in Adobe BrowserLab:

1. In Dreamweaver, open the page you want to preview in BrowserLab.

2. Choose File > Preview in Browser > Adobe BrowserLab, or press Ctrl-Shift-F12 (Cmd-Shift-F12).

   The first time you connect to BrowserLab, you'll need to create or enter your Adobe ID, the username and password Adobe requires to access its online services.

   Dreamweaver will also open a Browser-Lab panel .

Ⓐ Choose whether you want to preview the local or server copy of your page from the BrowserLab panel.

3. From the pop-up menu in the Browser-Lab panel, choose Local/Network (if you want to preview the local copy of the page you're working on) or Server (if you want to preview the copy of the page on the server), and then click the Preview button.

Your default browser opens and renders the page as it would appear in BrowserLab's default, which was Internet Explorer 7.0 when we wrote this ⑧.

Browser menu   URL field   Page rendering   Refresh   View menu   Zoom level

⑧ The selected page rendering appears in BrowserLab inside your default browser.

To switch to a different browser rendering:

Click the browser menu in the BrowserLab window, and then choose the browser you want to see **C**.

For example, you could choose a browser that is known for up-to-date CSS rendering, such as Safari for Mac OS X. After a moment, the new rendering appears **D**.

To switch to 2-up or Onion Skin view:

From the View menu in the BrowserLab window, choose 2-up View.

The window splits into two panes to show how the page would render in two different browsers. You can change the browsers you are comparing with the browser menu in each pane **E**.

or

From the View menu in the BrowserLab window, choose Onion Skin View.

The Onion Skin view overlays the two renderings with a 50 percent view of each rendering and a slider above **F**. You can move the slider toward one rendering or the other to make that rendering more visible and get an idea of how that browser is affecting the page elements.

C You can pick from many other browsers and operating systems in BrowserLab.

D If you compare this figure to **B**, you can see how differently a modern, standards-compliant browser (Safari for Mac) renders the page versus an older browser with CSS rendering issues, like Internet Explorer 7. Note the rounded corners of the items in the navigation menu, and the drop shadow on the headline.

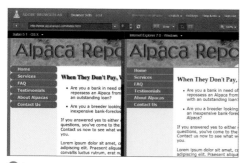

TIP Note that BrowserLab displays static renderings of your pages, so if you have user-interactive elements using JavaScript or Ajax, those won't be shown.

TIP If you make changes to the page in Dreamweaver, you can click the Refresh button in the BrowserLab toolbar to re-render the pages in the displayed browser simulations.

E In the 2-up View, you can compare two different browser renderings. Moving the horizontal or vertical scroll bars in either pane moves the view in both panes simultaneously.

Browser rendering slider

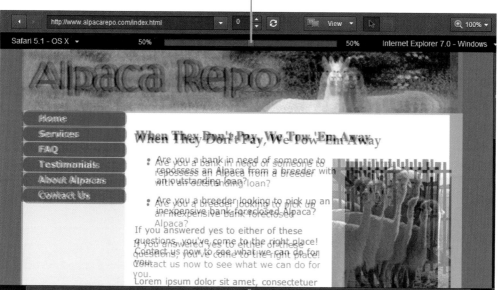

F The Onion Skin view overlays the two page renderings, so you can easily see how page elements are moved on the page. You can use the browser rendering slider to make one of the renderings more visible.

Setting Page Properties

Information that is contained in the **<head>** tag concerns the entire page. These *page properties* include information about the appearance of the page, how links should be displayed, the font settings for headings, and the *encoding* to be used, which is the character set a browser should use to render the page.

For example, Dreamweaver defaults to Unicode (UTF-8) encoding, which can safely represent all characters. Dreamweaver and Web browsers use the encoding to load the appropriate character set for the page. If you set the encoding to, say, one of the Chinese encodings, Dreamweaver and the Web browser will load the appropriate Chinese character set.

Dreamweaver defines CSS rules for properties that you specify in the Appearance (CSS), Links (CSS), and Headings (CSS) categories of the Page Properties dialog. These rules are placed in the **<head>** section of the page.

To set page properties:

1. Choose Modify > Page Properties, or press Ctrl-J (Cmd-J).

   The Page Properties dialog opens Ⓐ.

2. Click the category you want.

   See the following sections for details on each of the categories and their options.

3. Set the options as you like.

4. Click Apply to see the changes on the open document without closing the Page Properties dialog.

   or

   Click OK to save your changes.

TIP Note that the available encodings are different on Windows and Mac. This is not a problem for English, but if you will be working in languages other than English, you should make sure that you use an encoding for that language that will work well across platforms and that you test your site using browsers on Windows and Mac.

Ⓐ Use the Appearance (CSS) category of the Page Properties dialog to use CSS styles to set the page font and size, text and background colors, background images, and margins.

Appearance (CSS)

The Appearance (CSS) category of the Page Properties dialog **A** has the following options that apply CSS styles:

- **Page font** specifies the default font family your Web pages will use. Dreamweaver uses the font family you specify unless the font is overridden by another CSS style. You can also set the font to be bold (strong) or italic (emphasis).

- **Size** sets the default font size. Dreamweaver uses this font size unless the size is overridden by another CSS style. You can choose an absolute size (such as 9, 10, 12, and so forth) or relative sizes (such as small, medium, large, x-large, and so on). Choosing an absolute size allows you to pick any of the measurement units (pixels, points, in, cm, mm, picas, ems, exs, and %).

- **Text color** lets you set the default color for text. Click the color well to bring up a color picker to help you set the color.

- **Background color** lets you set the default color for the page background. Click the color well to bring up a color picker to help you set the color.

- **Background image** allows you to set an image that will appear behind all the text and images on the page. Click the Browse button to bring up the Select Image Source dialog, navigate to the image, and then click OK (Choose). If you set a background image, it overrides the background color.

- **Repeat** sets how the background image will be displayed if it doesn't fill the whole page. You can choose repeat to tile the image horizontally and vertically; repeat-x to tile the image horizontally; repeat-y to tile the image vertically; or no-repeat to display the image only once.

- **Margins** allows you to set the Left, Right, Top, and Bottom margins of the page. You can use any of the measurement systems as units, as you can with text size.

Appearance (HTML)

The Appearance (HTML) category of the Page Properties dialog **B** has the following options, implemented as HTML markup:

- **Background image** allows you to set an image that will appear behind all the text and images on the page. Click the Browse button to bring up the Select Image Source dialog, navigate to the image, and then click OK (Choose). If you set a background image, it overrides the background color.

B The Appearance (HTML) category applies properties to your page using HTML markup.

- **Background** lets you set the default color for the page background. Click the color well to bring up a color picker to help you set the color.

- **Text** lets you set the default color for text. Click the color well to bring up a color picker to help you set the color.

- **Links** sets the color to apply to link text. Click the color well to bring up a color picker to help you set the color.

- **Visited links** sets the color to apply to visited link text. Click the color well to bring up a color picker to help you set the color.

- **Active links** sets the color to apply to link text when you click the text. Click the color well to bring up a color picker to help you set the color.

- **Margins** allows you to set the Left, Right, Top, and Bottom margins of the page. You can use any of the measurement systems as units.

Links (CSS)

You find the following options in the Links category—unsurprisingly, all affect how links are displayed Ⓒ:

- **Link font** specifies the default font family your Web pages use to display links. Dreamweaver uses the font family you specify unless the font is overridden by another CSS style. You can also set the font to be bold (strong) or italic (emphasis).

- **Size** sets the default font size for link text. Dreamweaver uses this font size unless the size is overridden by another CSS style. You can choose an absolute size or a relative size. Choosing an absolute size allows you to pick any of the measurement units (pixels, points, in, cm, mm, picas, ems, exs, and %).

- **Link color** sets the color to apply to link text. Click the color well to bring up a color picker to help you set the color.

- **Visited links** sets the color to apply to visited link text. Click the color well to bring up a color picker to help you set the color.

continues on next page

Ⓒ You can control many aspects of how links display with the Page Properties dialog, which sets the link properties with CSS.

- **Rollover links** sets the color to apply to link text when you place the mouse cursor over the text. Click the color well to bring up a color picker to help you set the color.

- **Active links** sets the color to apply to link text when you click the text. Click the color well to bring up a color picker to help you set the color.

- **Underline style** sets the way links are underlined. Your choices are Always underline, Never underline, Show underline only on rollover, and Hide underline on rollover.

TIP If your page already has an underline style defined through an external CSS style sheet, the Underline style pop-up menu displays Don't change. You can actually change it; the option is there to tell you that there is already a style defined. If you change the underline style in the Page Properties dialog, it overrides the previous underline style definition.

Headings (CSS)

The Headings category **D** has the following options for headings:

- **Heading font** specifies the default font family used for headings. Dreamweaver uses the font family you specify unless the font is overridden by another CSS style. You can also set the font to be bold (strong) or italic (emphasis).

- **Heading 1** through **Heading 6** allows you to set size and color options for each heading size. The size pop-up menus allow you to set absolute sizes (sized with numbers, such as 9, 12, 18, and so on) or relative sizes (such as small, medium, or large); for absolute sizes, you can choose from any of the available measurement units. Click the color well to bring up a color picker to help you set the heading color.

TIP You get more control over the text when you use CSS directly to redefine a Heading style. See Chapter 7 for more information about redefining HTML styles.

D You can set the default font, size, and color for headings in the Headings (CSS) category.

Title/Encoding

The Title/Encoding category allows you to change the title and some of the more arcane items in a Web page **E**:

- **Title** allows you to change the page title. It's equivalent to the Title field at the top of a document window.

- **Document Type (DTD)** allows you to change the **doctype** of the page. When you make a change here, Dreamweaver changes the page's code (if necessary) to make it compliant with the selected DTD.

- **Encoding** sets the text encoding used for the page.

- **Unicode Normalization Form** and **Include Unicode Signature (BOM)** are only enabled when you use Unicode UTF-8 as the encoding. Choose Help > Dreamweaver to learn more.

TIP If you keep the default Unicode (UTF-8) encoding, you should also make sure that from the Unicode Normalization Form pop-up menu you choose C (Canonical Decomposition, followed by Canonical Composition). The exact meaning of this is mostly of interest to true character set geeks. What you need to know is that the C setting is the one used for Web pages.

E Set the title, document type, and encoding for the page in this dialog.

Tracing Image

Some people prefer to design their pages in a graphics tool such as Adobe Photoshop or Adobe Fireworks. They can then export that image and bring it into Dreamweaver as a background image. It isn't a background image for the page; rather, it is a guide that you can use as a reference to re-create the same look in Dreamweaver. This guide is called a *tracing image*. The tracing image appears only in Dreamweaver; it doesn't show up when you preview the page in a browser.

The tracing image category has only two options **F**:

- **Tracing image** has a Browse button that, when clicked, brings up the Select Image Source dialog. Navigate to the image, and then click OK (Choose).

- **Transparency** is a slider that controls the opacity of the tracing image. You can set the image from zero to 100% opacity.

F A tracing image can be a useful guide for re-creating page designs created in a graphics program.

Defining Meta Tags

Information about the page is contained in a kind of HTML tag called a *meta tag*. Meta tags can include a variety of the page's summary information, including keywords to help search engines index the page, a text description of the page, and links to external documents such as style sheets.

When you insert meta information, it appears within the document's `<head>` tag, inside a `<meta>` tag:

```
<meta name="keywords" content=
"HomeCook.info, food, wine, cooking,
home cooking, homecook, dining">
```

You can set six categories of meta tags:

- **Meta** is a general category that allows you to add any information you want. You must give it a name and specify the content.

- **Keywords** adds one or more words to the document for use by search engines to aid them in indexing the page.

- **Description** adds a text description of the site, again for use by search engines.

- **Refresh** reloads the current document after a specified interval of seconds or redirects the document to another URL.

- **Base** sets the base URL for the page. All of the document-relative paths in the page are considered relative to the base URL. For more information about document-relative links, see Chapter 6.

- **Link** adds a link to an external document. It's used most often to define the location for an external CSS style sheet.

To add a meta tag:

1. Choose Insert > HTML > Head Tags, and then choose the tag you want from the submenu (A).

   Depending on the kind of tag you chose, the appropriate dialog appears. For example, if you choose Keywords, the Keywords dialog appears (B). In this dialog, you need to enter the page's keywords, separated by commas.

2. Fill out the dialog, and then click OK.

TIP Don't go overboard with your keywords or description. Search engines have long since figured out that lots of keywords or a very long description are attempts to artificially improve search engine rankings, and sites with excessive keywords or descriptions will be screened out of search results.

(A) Dreamweaver allows you to set many meta tags for your document.

(B) Separate keywords with commas; Dreamweaver turns these keywords into a meta tag for you.

Adding Text to Your Pages

The main message of most Web sites is conveyed by the site's text, and a major part of your job in working with any site will be adding, modifying, and styling that text. Dreamweaver gives you the tools you need to effectively put text on your pages and get your message across.

When you add text, you need to deal with two different aspects of the text: its *structure* and its *presentation*. Structural elements are things like paragraphs, headings, lists, and the like; presentation is how the text looks, including things like the font, font size, text color, and so on. Most sites these days separate the structure and the presentation. Structure is about organizing the content on the page, and presentation involves making the content look good.

In this chapter, we'll concentrate on getting text onto your page and applying structure using headings and lists. We'll also cover using basic HTML text styles to change the look of your text. You'll learn how to more precisely style text and present it using Cascading Style Sheets in Chapter 7.

In This Chapter

Adding Text

Most of the text on a Web page is formatted in *blocks*, which are enclosed by beginning and ending HTML tags. For example, the HTML for a line of text with paragraph tags wrapped around it looks like this:

```
<p>This text is wrapped in beginning and ending paragraph tags.</p>
```

For a browser to understand that this is a paragraph, you (or in this case, Dreamweaver) have to make it one by adding the surrounding **<p>** tags.

Of course, in Dreamweaver's Design view or Live view, you won't see the HTML tags. All of the text contained between the opening **<p>** tag and the closing **</p>** tag is considered by a Web browser to be within the same paragraph, no matter how much text is between the tags. The **<p>...</p>** combination is an example of a *container tag*. Virtually all of the structural formatting that you can apply with Dreamweaver is done with container tags.

Selecting Text

Besides selecting text by dragging over it with the mouse cursor, Dreamweaver also gives you some text selection shortcuts in Design view:

- Double-click a word to select it.
- Move your cursor to the left of a line of text until the cursor changes from an I-beam to an arrow pointing at the text. Then click once to highlight a single line, or drag up or down to select multiple lines.
- Triple-click anywhere in a paragraph to select the entire paragraph.
- For finer control over selecting individual letters, hold down the Shift key and press the left or right arrow key to extend the selection one letter at a time.
- Ctrl-Shift (Cmd-Shift) plus the left or right arrow key extends the selection one word at a time. Ctrl (Cmd) plus the left or right arrow key moves the cursor one word to the left or right but doesn't select any text.
- Press Ctrl-A (Cmd-A) to Select All (the entire contents of the current document).

When you add text to a page with Dreamweaver, the program automatically wraps the text with paragraph tags when you press the Enter (Return) key on your keyboard. You can see this if you switch to Code view by clicking the Code button at the top of the Dreamweaver editing window **A**.

Dreamweaver also has special commands that help you import entire Microsoft Word or Excel documents as Web pages. (See "Using Paste Special," later in this chapter. Also, refer to the bonus chapter "Working with Other Applications" at the end of the ebook edition or download it from **www.dreamweaverbook.com**.)

To insert text:

1. In Dreamweaver's Design view, click in the page where you want to add text.

2. Type the text you want.

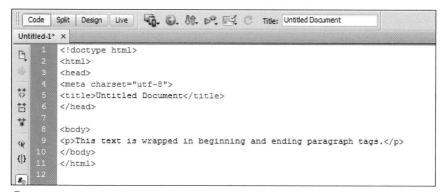

A Dreamweaver adds paragraph tags around text when you press the Enter (Return) key.

Cutting, Copying, and Pasting Text

Just as with a word processor, you can cut, copy, and paste text on a page in Dreamweaver, which shares the same menu commands with virtually all standard Windows and Mac word processors and text editors. When pasting text in Design view from one part of a Dreamweaver page to another or between Dreamweaver pages, text formatting is automatically maintained.

Dreamweaver also allows you to paste text and maintain some or all of the text's formatting. This is especially useful when moving text from applications such as Microsoft Word or Excel to a Web page. See "Using Paste Special," later in this chapter.

To cut or copy text:

1. Select the text you want to cut or copy.

2. To cut the text to the clipboard, choose Edit > Cut or press Ctrl-X (Cmd-X).

   or

   To copy the text to the clipboard, choose Edit > Copy or press Ctrl-C (Cmd-C).

   The text is placed on the clipboard.

TIP When you have text selected, most of the time you can right-click to cut or copy the text using a context menu. You can also right-click to paste text from the context menu. If you have a single-button mouse on the Mac, you can Ctrl-click to bring up the context menu.

To paste plain text:

1. Click to place the insertion point on the page where you want the text to appear.

2. Choose Edit > Paste, or press Ctrl-V (Cmd-V).

TIP If you copy some HTML source code from another program, such as the Source view of a Web browser, and paste it into a Dreamweaver page in Design view, the HTML appears on the page with tags and all. That's because although what you've pasted in is HTML markup, Dreamweaver is trying to be smarter than you—it assumes that markup is what you want to display. If that's not what you want, but rather you want the result of the markup to display in your page, just switch to Code view in Dreamweaver before you paste. The HTML code will paste into the page, and when you switch back to Design view, it will display the proper formatting.

TIP Dreamweaver offers Undo and Redo commands in the Edit menu, which can often be very useful for fixing mistakes or repeating operations. You can also press Ctrl-Z (Cmd-Z) for Undo and Ctrl-Y (Cmd-Y) for Redo.

Dragging and Dropping Text

If all you want to do is move some text from one place on a page to another, it's often faster to drag and drop the text.

To drag and drop text:

1. Select the text you want to move 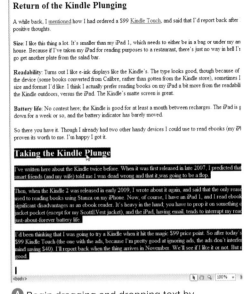.

2. Move the cursor over the selected text.

   The cursor changes from an I-beam to an arrow.

3. Click and hold your mouse button over the selected text, and drag it to its new location, releasing the mouse button when the cursor is where you want the text **B**.

   The text moves to its new home.

TIP To duplicate the text, hold down the Ctrl (Option) key while dragging and dropping. A copy of the text appears when you release the mouse button.

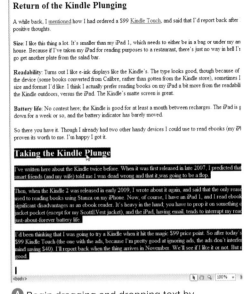

A Begin dragging and dropping text by selecting it.

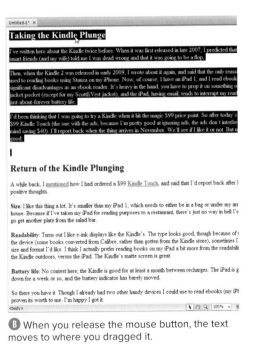

B When you release the mouse button, the text moves to where you dragged it.

Using Paste Special

Dreamweaver's Paste Special command in the Edit menu gives you a variety of options that control the way formatted content is pasted into Dreamweaver's Design view.

You will probably use the Paste Special command most often when pasting in text from Microsoft Word or Excel to maintain the formatting that the text had in those programs . Text pasted in from Excel can appear in Dreamweaver as a formatted table, which saves you a lot of time and effort.

The Paste Special options include:

- **Text only** pastes just the text; paragraph marks and all formatting are stripped from the text 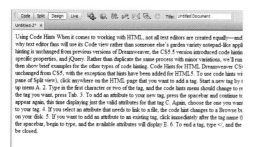.

- **Text with structure** pastes the text and maintains the structure (notably paragraphs, tabs, and lists) but eliminates other text formatting 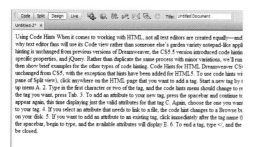.

continues on next page

Ⓐ Paste Special will do a great job of maintaining the formatting from this Microsoft Word document.

Ⓑ This is the "Text only" version of the text from Ⓐ, with paragraph marks and formatting stripped out.

Ⓒ With the "Text with structure" option, the text and paragraph marks are there, but there's no character formatting.

- **Text with structure plus basic formatting** keeps the text and text structure and retains bold and italic formatting .
- **Text with structure plus full formatting** preserves the text, structure, and styles from the original document **E**.

To use Paste Special:

1. Select the text you want to cut or copy.

   The text will usually be in a different application than Dreamweaver.

2. Cut or copy the text.

3. Switch to Dreamweaver, and click to set the insertion point where you want the text to appear.

4. Choose Edit > Paste Special, or press Ctrl-Shift-V (Cmd-Shift-V).

   The Paste Special dialog appears **F**.

5. In the dialog, click the radio button next to the paste option you want.

6. Click OK.

   The text pastes in according to the option you selected.

TIP If you use the "Text with structure plus basic formatting" or "Text with structure plus full formatting" choices, you can also paste graphics into Dreamweaver along with the formatted text.

TIP You can copy and paste graphics from most applications into Dreamweaver, but if you want to paste a graphic along with formatted text, you must use Paste Special.

TIP When pasting from Word and maintaining full styles, Dreamweaver reads the Word styles and creates CSS styles with the same names and attributes. It places the CSS styles in the same document. If you want to use these styles elsewhere on your site, you should move these internal styles to an external style sheet. See "Moving Internal Styles to External" in Chapter 9 to learn how to do that.

D The "Text with structure plus basic formatting" option maintains bold and italic formatting.

E The final option, "Text with structure plus full formatting," maintains all the formatting from the Word document.

F Choose the option you want from the Paste Special dialog.

h1	It doesn't get more important than this.
h2	This is perhaps a bit less important.
h3	This is middling priority.
h4	We'll let you know when you need to pay attention.
h5	Check this out if you really want to.
h6	Hey! Wake up!
paragraph	This is the everyday text that you'll see in most paragraphs.

A Examples of the six heading sizes, plus paragraph, which is usually used for body text.

Applying Headings

After paragraphs, headings are the most important structural element on most Web pages. Headings point your site's visitors to essential information on the page, and they separate sections of the page. Think of headings as being similar to headlines in a newspaper.

Text you enter into Dreamweaver begins with no heading; Dreamweaver refers to this text as None in the Property inspector. As soon as you press Enter (Return), Dreamweaver wraps the text in paragraph tags, and the text becomes paragraph text.

HTML has six sizes of headings, plus paragraph text **A**. These headings don't have a fixed point size, unlike headings in, say, Microsoft Word or Adobe InDesign. Instead, they are sized relative to one another and to the size of the paragraph text, and the size that the user sees depends on the settings in the user's Web browser. By default, headings are usually displayed in boldface.

You can change the look of headings (their size, font, color, and so forth) using CSS, which we'll cover in Chapter 7.

TIP You can have only one size of HTML heading in a particular element. You can work around this limitation with CSS styles.

TIP Headings are also important because they help search engines find and index content on your pages. Google in particular uses headings in this fashion, so it's a good idea to use headings when they are appropriate to your content.

To apply a heading:

1. Click in the line you want to change.

   Note that you don't have to select text; a heading is a block style, so it affects the entire paragraph the cursor is in.

2. Choose Format > Paragraph Format > Heading *x*, where *x* is the heading size you want .

   or

   Press Ctrl-1 for Heading 1, Ctrl-2 for Heading 2, and so on. On the Mac, press Cmd-1 for Heading 1, Cmd-2 for Heading 2, and so on.

   or

   Choose a heading from the Format pop-up menu in the HTML mode of the Property inspector ●.

   or

   Click one of the heading buttons in the Text category of the Insert panel ●.

   There are only buttons for Heading 1, Heading 2, and Heading 3, which are listed as h1, h2, and h3, respectively.

   The text changes to the heading you selected.

B Choose the heading size you want from the Paragraph Format submenu.

C Another way to choose the heading size is to use the Format menu in the HTML mode of the Property inspector.

D The Text category of the Insert panel gives you buttons with many options, including ways to apply three heading sizes.

To turn text into paragraph text:

1. Click in the line you want to change.

2. Choose Format > Paragraph Format > Paragraph.

   or

   Choose Paragraph from the Format pop-up menu in the HTML mode of the Property inspector.

   or

   Press Ctrl-Shift-P (Cmd-Shift-P).

   Dreamweaver changes the text into a paragraph.

To remove heading formatting:

1. Click in the line you want to change.

2. Choose Format > Paragraph Format > None.

   or

   Press Ctrl-0 (Cmd-0). (Those are zeros, not the letter "O.")

   The Format menu of the Property inspector changes to None, indicating that the text has no heading or paragraph style assigned to it.

Applying Character Formats

Character formatting is styling that you can apply to words and individual characters rather than to blocks such as paragraphs. This formatting includes changing the font, font size, and font color.

Beginning several versions ago and continuing through the current version of Dreamweaver, the program dispensed with the old method of applying these sorts of character formatting (which was to use the HTML `<font>` tag) in favor of using CSS styles. This change happened mostly behind the scenes in Code view, so if you have been using Dreamweaver for quite some time, you may not have even noticed the change. Beginning with Dreamweaver CS4, the program enforces the use of CSS for text styling by requiring you to participate in defining CSS rules for changing fonts, font sizes, and font colors.

The reason for the change to CSS is important. Pages styled with CSS are much more flexible than pages that use HTML `<font>` tags, and they can be maintained more easily. For example, when a site is redesigned, every page that uses `<font>` tags must be individually changed to match the new design. If you have hundreds or thousands of pages in your site, that's a lot of work. Sites that use CSS to style text only need to change the style sheet document, and the changes automatically ripple through the whole site. You'll learn more about using CSS to style text (especially for setting font properties) in Chapter 7. Some other formatting operations are still performed using HTML markup, and those are the ones we'll explore in this chapter.

Applying HTML Text Styles

The most common text formatting is to make text bold or italicized, and of course Dreamweaver can do that with either HTML markup or a CSS rule. But it can also apply several other text styles, some of which are for specialized uses, as shown in Ⓐ and **Table 4.1**.

Bold style	~~Strikethrough style~~	`Code Style`	*Citation style*
Italic style	`Teletype style`	*Variable style*	Definition style
<u>Underlined style</u>	*Emphasis style*	`Sample style`	~~Deleted style~~
	Strong style	`Keyboard style`	<u>Inserted style</u>

Ⓐ Dreamweaver offers a number of useful (and not so useful) HTML text styles.

TABLE 4.1 Text Styles

Style	Description
Bold	Makes text boldface.
Italic	Italicizes text.
Underline	Underlines text.
Strikethrough	Text is shown with a line through it.
Teletype	Reminiscent of an old typewriter. Usually shows text in a monospaced font such as Courier.
Emphasis	Italicizes text onscreen. Causes screen readers to stress importance in speech.
Strong	Bolds text onscreen. Causes screen readers to add additional importance to speech.
Code	Depicts programming code, usually in a monospaced font.
Variable	Marks variables in programming code. Usually displayed as italics.
Sample	Meant to display sample output from a computer program or script. Usually displayed in a monospaced font.
Keyboard	Meant to depict text a user would type on the keyboard. Usually displayed in a monospaced font.
Citation	Used to mark citations and references. Usually displayed as italics.
Definition	Used to mark the first, defining usage of a term in a document. Usually displayed as italics (Safari on the Mac displays this as regular text).
Deleted	Marks deleted text. Shown the same as strikethrough.
Inserted	Marks inserted text. Shown the same as underlined.

Many of these text styles are meant for displaying programming or script code, so they won't be used at all on many sites. Others, such as Underline and Strikethrough, are deprecated as of the HTML 4.01 standard, which means that they are obsolete and may not work in future browsers. Instead, you should use a CSS property. See "Dreamweaver CSS Categories" in Chapter 7.

To apply an HTML text style:

1. Select the text you want to change.

2. Choose Format > Style, and then choose the style you want from the submenu.

   The text's appearance changes.

TIP Actually, by default Dreamweaver does not use the traditional `<b>` and `<i>` HTML tags for bold and italic, respectively. Instead it uses `<strong>` and `<em>` (for emphasis). The latter tags are preferred as part of best practices, because they are better handled by the screen readers used by visually impaired users. If you want to switch Dreamweaver back to using `<b>` and `<i>`, choose Edit > Preferences (Dreamweaver > Preferences) and, in the General category of the Preferences dialog, deselect "Use `<strong>` and `<em>` in place of `<b>` and `<i>`."

Planet	Orbital period (years)	Day (days)	Moons
Mercury	0.241	58.6	none
Venus	0.615	-243	none
Earth	1.00	1.00	1
Mars	1.88	1.03	2
Jupiter	11.86	0.414	63
Saturn	29.46	0.426	49
Uranus	84.01	0.718	27
Neptune	164.79	0.671	13
Pluto	248.5	6.5	1

Ⓐ Preformatted text lines up neatly, as in this table.

Ⓑ Apply the style with the Preformatted Text button.

Using Preformatted Text

Browsers usually ignore invisible formatting that doesn't affect page content, such as tabs, extra spaces, extra line feeds, and the like. If you need to display text exactly as entered, however, you can use the Preformatted paragraph format, which wraps the text in the `<pre>...</pre>` tags and makes browsers display all of the text characters.

Originally, preformatted text was meant to display tabular data in rows and columns, as in the output of a spreadsheet. To make the information line up, browsers display preformatted text in a monospaced font such as Courier Ⓐ.

To apply preformatting:

1. Select the text you want to change.

2. From the Format pop-up menu of the HTML mode of the Property inspector, choose Preformatted.

   or

   In the Text category of the Insert panel, click the Preformatted Text button Ⓑ.

   or

   Choose Format > Paragraph Format > Preformatted Text.

   The text changes appearance.

TIP If you want to display tabular data, it often makes more sense to use a table rather than preformatted text. You get much more control over the table style and spacing of the items in the table, and you can add CSS to style the table's contents if needed. See Chapter 10 for information about using tables.

Adding Line Breaks

Just as in a word processor, you press Enter (Return) in Dreamweaver to create a new paragraph. This is fine when you want to actually create a new paragraph, but not so great when you just want to move the cursor down a line, as you might want to do when entering an address. That's because Web browsers (and Dreamweaver) insert a blank line above and below a paragraph, so if you make each line of the address its own paragraph, it looks goofy .

Ⓐ Paragraphs have whitespace before and after them, which isn't really appropriate for things like addresses.

What you want to do is add a *line break*, which moves the cursor down one line without creating a new paragraph. In the code, Dreamweaver adds the HTML `<br />` tag to the end of the line.

Ⓑ After you replace the paragraph tags with line breaks, the address looks better.

To insert a line break:

At the end of the line you want to break, press Shift-Enter (Shift-Return).

or

At the end of the line you want to break, in the Text category of the Insert panel, select Line Break from the Special Characters pop-up menu.

The text changes Ⓑ.

Ⓒ With the appropriate preference enabled, you can see the invisible line break characters.

TIP Line breaks are invisible characters in both Dreamweaver and Web browsers, but you can make them visible in Dreamweaver if you want. Choose Edit > Preferences (Dreamweaver > Preferences), and then click the Invisible Elements category. Select the check box next to "Line breaks," and then click OK. Dreamweaver then displays line breaks in Design view Ⓒ.

Indenting and Aligning Text with HTML

You won't indent or align text in Dreamweaver as you would with a word processor. The most common kind of indenting, indenting the first line in a paragraph, is usually done with a tab in a word processor, but tabs have no effect in HTML. Instead, you can use the **text-indent** CSS style property. Similarly, there are CSS properties for text alignment. See Chapter 7 for more about using CSS.

You can add whitespace to text—and simulate a tab—with non-breaking spaces. See "Inserting Special Characters," later in this chapter.

When you are indenting paragraphs to set them apart from preceding and following paragraphs, Dreamweaver uses the HTML **<blockquote>** tag. This indents both the left and right margins of the block-quoted paragraph. You aren't limited to paragraphs; you can block quote any block element, such as headings.

Dreamweaver can align text with the left margin, right margin, or center of the page. You can also justify text, which adds space as needed between words so that both the left and right margins are aligned.

The method shown here adds alignment attributes to the HTML markup. You can also use Cascading Style Sheets to align text, which is covered in Chapters 7 and 8.

To block quote text:

1. Click in the paragraph or other block element you want to indent.

2. Click the Indent button on the HTML mode of the Property inspector 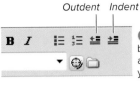.

   or

   In the Text category of the Insert panel, click the Block Quote button.

   or

   Choose Format > Indent or press Ctrl-Alt-] (Cmd-Opt-]).

   The text changes Ⓑ.

> **TIP** To add more indenting, click the Indent button on the Property inspector again. This nests the `<blockquote>` tags.

> **TIP** The CSS `margin` property is a much more flexible way to indent block elements, as described in Chapter 7.

To remove block quoting:

1. Click in the paragraph or other block element you no longer want to indent.

2. Click the Outdent button on the Property inspector.

   or

   Choose Format > Outdent or press Ctrl-Alt-[(Cmd-Opt-[).

   The text changes.

Outdent   *Indent*

Ⓐ Use the Indent button to apply a block quote to your text.

Ⓑ The block quote nicely sets off the sonnet from the commentary text.

C Choose a text alignment from the Format menu.

TABLE 4.2 Alignment Shortcut Keys

Shortcut Key (Windows)	Shortcut Key (Mac)	What It Does
Ctrl-Alt-Shift-L	Cmd-Opt-Shift-L	Left alignment
Ctrl-Alt-Shift-C	Cmd-Opt-Shift-C	Center alignment
Ctrl-Alt-Shift-R	Cmd-Opt-Shift-R	Right alignment
Ctrl-Alt-Shift-J	Cmd-Opt-Shift-J	Full justification

To align text:

1. Click inside the paragraph you want to align.

2. Choose Format > Align, and then choose Left, Center, Right, or Justify from the submenu C.

   or

   Use one of the keyboard shortcuts listed in **Table 4.2**.

TIP Longtime Dreamweaver users may be thrown a bit by the removal of the alignment buttons from the HTML mode of the Property inspector. Those buttons have been moved to the CSS mode of the Property inspector, and Dreamweaver will enforce creating and naming a new style rule if you use the alignment buttons. The program will also alert you if you enter a name for the style rule that is the same as the HTML alignment attributes (left, center, right, or justify). Use different names to prevent confusion.

Working with Lists

Lists are an easy way to organize content on your Web page. Dreamweaver supports three types of lists:

- **Numbered lists or Ordered lists,** for lists with items that need to be in a particular order Ⓐ. List items are numbered and indented from the left margin. If you add or remove items from the numbered list, it automatically renumbers.

- **Bulleted lists or Unordered lists,** for lists of items in no particular order Ⓑ.

- **Definition lists,** where each item has an indented subitem Ⓒ.

Tift Merritt Discography

1. Bramble Rose (2002)
2. Tambourine (2004)
3. Another Country (2008)
4. See You on the Moon (2010)

Tift Merritt Discography

1. Bramble Rose (2002)
2. Tambourine (2004)
3. Home Is Loud (*live recording*) (2005)
4. Another Country (2008)
5. Buckingham Solo (*live recording*) (2009)
6. See You on the Moon (2010)

Ⓐ Numbered lists automatically renumber if you insert a new item between two existing items.

Global Survival Kit

- Metal box
- Survival knife
- Compass
- Fire starter
- Water bag
- Water purification tablets
- Rescue whistle
- Fishing and foraging kit

Ⓑ Bulleted lists are single-spaced and indented.

Excerpts from *The Devil's Dictionary*, by Ambrose Bierce

Originally published 1911 (copyright expired)

CHILDHOOD, *n.*
    The period of human life intermediate between the idiocy of infancy and the folly of youth -- two removes from the sin of manhood and three from the remorse of age.

DAWN, *n.*
    The time when men of reason go to bed. Certain old men prefer to rise at about that time, taking a cold bath and a long walk with an empty stomach, and otherwise mortifying the flesh. They then point with pride to these practices as the cause of their sturdy health and ripe years; the truth being that they are hearty and old, not because of their habits, but in spite of them. The reason we find only robust persons doing this thing is that it has killed all the others who have tried it.

DELIBERATION, *n.*
    The act of examining one's bread to determine which side it is buttered on.

NONSENSE, *n.*
    The objections that are urged against this excellent dictionary.

SCRIBBLER, *n.*
    A professional writer whose views are antagonistic to one's own.

TWICE, *adv.*
    Once too often.

Ⓒ Definition lists have the definitions indented under the definition terms. The definition terms don't have to be all uppercase—they just happen to be in this figure.

To create a list:

1. Type the items for your list into the window. After typing each item, press Enter (Return).

2. Select the items in the list.

3. Choose Format > List, and then choose Unordered List, Ordered List, or Definition List from the submenu.

   or

   Click either the Unordered List or Ordered List button in the HTML mode of the Property inspector.

   or

   Click one of three buttons in the Text category of the Insert panel: *ul* for Unordered List, *ol* for Ordered List, or *dl* for Definition List.

   The text changes to the kind of list you chose.

TIP At the end of your list, you can turn off the list function either by pressing Enter (Return) twice or by clicking the appropriate list button in the Property inspector again.

TIP There are three other buttons in the Text category of the Insert panel that you can use to apply list tags to text. The li button marks text as a list item; the text must be within a bulleted or numbered list. The other two buttons are used for definition lists. The dt button marks text as a definition term, and the dd button marks text as a definition description.

TIP Because the Text category of the Insert panel was originally designed to help you work in Code view, some of the list buttons will cause the Dreamweaver window to change to Split view, so you can see the Code and Design panes at the same time. If you want to avoid code altogether, use the Property inspector or the menu bar to format your lists.

Setting List Properties

You can change numbered list and bulleted list properties in Dreamweaver. Choose between five types of numbering, as shown in **Table 4.3**. For bulleted lists, you can choose either a round bullet (the default) or a square bullet. There are no properties to set for a definition list.

To set list properties:

1. Click in the list you want to change to place the insertion point.

2. Choose Format > List > Properties.

   The List Properties dialog appears **D**.

3. Do one or more of the following:

   ▸ In the List type pop-up menu, select Bulleted List, Numbered List, or Directory List ("definition list" is called "Directory List" in this dialog for some reason).

   ▸ In the Style pop-up menu, select one of the Bulleted List or Numbered List styles.

   ▸ Use the Start count text box to set the value for the first item in the numbered list.

4. Click OK.

> **TIP** You may notice that there is a fourth choice in the List type pop-up menu: Menu List. That choice creates an unusual type of list that is based on the `<menu>` tag. That tag was deprecated (that is, it was recommended that it not be used) when HTML 4.01 was standardized in 1999. We suggest that you avoid the use of the Menu List option. It's one of those little things that should have long since been removed from Dreamweaver, in our view.

D In the List Properties dialog, you can change the way lists are numbered and bulleted.

TABLE 4.3 Numbered List Style Options

List Name	Example
Number	1, 2, 3, 4
Roman Small	i, ii, iii, iv
Roman Large	I, II, III, IV
Alphabet Small	a, b, c, d
Alphabet Large	A, B, C, D

Nesting Lists

You can indent lists within lists to create *nested lists*. Because nested lists do not have to be of the same type, you can create, for example, a numbered list with an indented bulleted list, and you can have multiple levels of nested lists within one overall list **E**.

Solar System Outer Planets and their four largest moons

- **Jupiter**
  1. Ganymede
  2. Callisto
  3. Io
  4. Europa
- **Saturn**
  1. Titan
  2. Rhea
  3. Iapetus
  4. Dione
- **Uranus**
  1. Titania
  2. Oberon
  3. Umbriel
  4. Ariel
- **Neptune**
  1. Triton
  2. Proteus
  3. Nereid
  4. Larissa

E You can nest numbered lists inside bulleted lists.

To create a nested list:

1. Click the end of a line within an existing list to place the insertion point.

2. Press Enter (Return).

   Dreamweaver creates another line of the list.

3. Press Tab.

   Dreamweaver creates a new indented sublist of the same type as the parent list. For example, if the parent list is a numbered list, the new sublist will also be a numbered list.

4. (Optional) If you want the sublist to be a different type of list than the parent list, click the Numbered List or Bulleted List button in the HTML mode of the Property inspector.

5. Type the list item.

6. Press Enter (Return).

   Dreamweaver creates a new sublist item.

7. To return to the original list, use the up or down arrow keys to move the insertion point into one of the items in the original list, or click to place the insertion point where you want it.

TIP You can also click the Outdent button in the HTML mode of the Property inspector to merge the sublist back into the main list.

TIP Use the List Properties dialog to format sublists as well as lists.

TIP If you try to create a sublist within a list that is in a table by pressing Tab, Dreamweaver jumps to the next cell rather than indenting and creating a nested list. One workaround is to create the nested list outside of the table, cut it, and then paste it in the table cell where you want it to go.

Inserting Special Characters

You can add special characters, such as the Euro, copyright, or trademark symbol, to your page in Dreamweaver without having to remember their bizarre HTML equivalents or odd keyboard combinations. In Dreamweaver, relief is just a menu choice away.

About Non-Breaking Spaces

An oddity about HTML is that it ignores multiple spaces. One of the special characters you can insert is the *non-breaking space*, which is useful for adding multiple consecutive spaces and occasionally for nudging text and even images. Dreamweaver uses the HTML code for a non-breaking space (which is ** **) inside paragraph tags so that blank lines appear in Web browsers, like so:

```
<p> </p>
```

If you want multiple spaces between words, insert one or more non-breaking spaces. The easiest way to do this is to press Ctrl-Shift-spacebar (Cmd-Shift-spacebar), but you can also use the Characters pop-up menu in the Text category of the Insert panel or the Insert > HTML > Special Characters submenu.

Dreamweaver by default ignores multiple spaces, but you can change this behavior and force the program to insert multiple non-breaking spaces in the code. Choose Edit > Preferences (Dreamweaver > Preferences), choose the General category, and then select the check box next to "Allow multiple consecutive spaces."

To insert a special character:

1. Click in the page to place the insertion point where you want the special character to appear.

2. In the Text category of the Insert panel, choose the character you want from the Characters pop-up menu **A**.

   or

   Choose Insert > HTML > Special Characters, and then choose the special character you want from the submenu.

   or

   If the character you want doesn't appear in the menu, choose Other Characters from the pop-up menu in the Insert panel or choose Other from the Insert > HTML > Special Characters submenu. The Insert Other Character dialog appears **B**.

3. Click the character you want to use, and then click OK to close the dialog.

   Dreamweaver inserts the special character on your page.

A Insert unusual characters from the Characters pop-up menu in the Text category of the Insert panel.

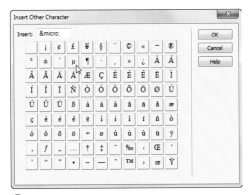

B The Insert Other Character dialog provides the rest of the special characters Dreamweaver can insert.

(A) Dreamweaver lets you insert dates into your pages in a variety of formats.

Adding Automatic Dates

Dreamweaver can insert the current date and time in a variety of formats into your Web page. You can choose whether or not to add the day of the week.

To insert the current date:

1. Click in your page to place the insertion point where you want the date to appear.

2. Choose Insert > Date.

   The Insert Date dialog appears (A).

3. Do one or more of the following:

   ▸ If you want the name of the day to appear, use the Day format pop-up menu to set the appearance of the day of the week.

   ▸ Make a selection from the Date format list.

   ▸ If you want the time to appear, choose the 12-hour or 24-hour format from the Time format list.

   ▸ Select "Update automatically on save," if you want that to happen. This is very useful if you want visitors to your site to know when the page was last updated.

4. Click OK.

   Dreamweaver inserts the date (and any additional items you chose) into your page.

Finding and Replacing

Dreamweaver's Find and Replace feature can save you a lot of time, because you can automatically find and change text on a single page, in pages within a folder, on pages you select, or throughout your site. You can choose to change text in Design view, or you can search and change just in Code view.

Imagine that you have a company's site with dozens of pages devoted to singing the praises of its premier product, the amazing WonderWidget. Then one day you get a call from your client letting you know that because of a trademark dispute, the company has to rename the product WonderThing. Rather than opening each page and making one or more changes on each of them, just put Dreamweaver's Find and Replace feature to work, and you'll be done in just a few minutes.

The Find and Replace window

The Find and Replace window, which you open by choosing Edit > Find and Replace or by pressing Ctrl-F (Cmd-F), will be the tool you use for changing text Ⓐ. Let's look at some of this window's parts.

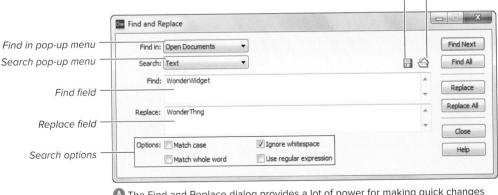

Ⓐ The Find and Replace dialog provides a lot of power for making quick changes on a single page or throughout your site.

- The **Find in** pop-up menu allows you to tell Dreamweaver the scope of the search. You can choose to find text in the Current Document (the default); Selected Text; Open Documents; in a Folder you select; in Selected Files in Site; or in the Entire Current Local Site.

- The **Search** pop-up menu lets you choose what kind of search you want to do. You can choose Text; Text (Advanced), which gives you additional search options; Source Code, which allows you to search in the HTML; or Specific Tag, which searches the contents of HTML tags that you select. The latter two options are covered later in this chapter.

- The **Find** field is where you enter the text you want to find.

- The **Replace** field is where you enter the text you want to use to replace the found word.

- The **Save Query** button allows you to save searches for later use. This is great for instances where you create complex queries, so you don't have to do all the work to set up the search again.

- The **Load Query** button allows you to retrieve a saved search.

- The **Search options** let you constrain your searches. "Match case" returns results with the same uppercase and lowercase letters as the text you entered in the Find field. "Match whole word" finds the text only if it matches one or more complete words. "Ignore whitespace" tells Dreamweaver not to pay attention to additional spaces and non-breaking spaces. It's on by default, and it's usually best to leave it on. Finally, "Use regular expression" (covered later in this chapter) lets you use wildcard characters to construct extremely complex searches.

Finding Text with a Simple Search

Simple searches in Dreamweaver work pretty much the same way that they do in a word processor. Just enter the text you want to find and the text that you want to replace it with, and away you go. Of course, you don't have to replace text; if you want you can just use the Find and Replace dialog to find text in one or more files.

To find text:

1. Choose Edit > Find and Replace, or press Ctrl-F (Cmd-F).

   The Find and Replace dialog appears (see figure **Ⓐ** in "The Find and Replace window").

2. From the Find in pop-up menu, choose one of the options for the scope of your search.

3. From the Search pop-up menu, choose Text.

4. In the Find field, type the word or phrase that you're looking for.

5. Click the Find Next button.

Dreamweaver finds and highlights the found text. If the scope of the search included more than one page, Dreamweaver opens the first file the text was found within and highlights the text. If the text isn't found, you'll get a message to that effect at the bottom of the Find and Replace dialog.

or

Click the Find All button.

Dreamweaver does the search, closes the Find and Replace dialog, and opens the Search tab of the Results panel Ⓐ.

6. If you clicked Find All in step 5, double-click one of the search results in the Results panel to open it and highlight the found text.

TIP You can click the green triangle button in the Results panel to reopen the Find and Replace dialog with the same search terms.

TIP If you have a search that's running for a very long time, you can cancel it by clicking the octagonal red Cancel button in the Results panel (this button is dimmed in figure Ⓐ).

TIP You can clear the search results in the Results panel by right-clicking in the panel and choosing Clear Results.

TIP If you select some text before you bring up the Find and Replace dialog, the text automatically appears in the Find field, as long as you selected fewer than 255 characters.

TIP You can do a quick find on the current page by selecting some text and then choosing Edit > Find Selection or pressing Shift-F3 (Cmd-Shift-G). Dreamweaver highlights the next occurrence of the text you selected.

Reopen Find and Replace with same search items

Cancel currently running search

Search	Reference	Validation	Browser Compatibility	Link Checker	Site Reports	FTP Log	Server Debug

File	Matched Text
samples\tablesorting\script05.html	<script src="jquery/jquery.tablesorter.js"></script>
samples\tablesorting\jquery\jquery.tables...	* TableSorter 2.0 - Client-side table sorting with ease!
samples\tablesorting\jquery\jquery.tables...	* Examples and docs at: http://tablesorter.com
samples\tablesorting\jquery\jquery.tables...	* @example $('table').tablesorter();
samples\tablesorting\jquery\jquery.tables...	* @desc Create a simple tablesorter interface.
samples\tablesorting\jquery\jquery.tables...	* @example $('table').tablesorter({ sortList:[[0,0],[1,0]] })
samples\tablesorting\jquery\jquery.tables...	* @desc Create a tablesorter interface and sort on the fir:
samples\tablesorting\jquery\jquery.tables...	* @example $('table').tablesorter({ headers: { 0: { sorter:

Done. 32 items found in 4 documents.

Ⓐ The Search tab of the Results panel shows you the filename and matched text when you click the Find All button.

To find the next result:

Choose Edit > Find Next, or press F3 (Cmd-G).

Dreamweaver finds and highlights the next result of the search without reopening the Find and Replace dialog.

To find and replace text:

1. Choose Edit > Find and Replace, or press Ctrl-F (Cmd-F).

   The Find and Replace dialog appears.

2. From the Find in pop-up menu, choose one of the options for the scope of your search.

3. From the Search pop-up menu, choose Text.

4. In the Find field, type the word or phrase that you're looking for.

5. In the Replace field, type the replacement word or phrase.

6. Click the Find Next button.

   When Dreamweaver finds the text, it is highlighted.

7. Click the Replace button.

   Dreamweaver replaces the found text with the contents of the Replace field.

   or

   Click Replace All.

   Dreamweaver warns you that you cannot undo changes made in unopened files. Of course, you can undo changes in any open documents by choosing Edit > Undo. If you still want to make the changes, click Yes.

   Dreamweaver searches through the entire scope of the search, replacing all occurrences of the found text. When it is done, you'll see a message telling you how many changes it made.

TIP Use a Replace operation to expand abbreviations and save time while you're creating pages. For example, let's say that you're creating a Web site about JavaScript. Rather than typing JavaScript again and again while writing the site, just type "JS"; then before you upload the site, do a Find and Replace, changing every occurrence of "JS" to "JavaScript." You can do the same thing with company names, people's names, or almost any text that you repeat a lot.

TIP Dreamweaver does not update the Search tab of the Results panel when you perform Replace operations.

TIP If you get a bunch of search results but only want to make replacements in some of those results, you can do that—and save a bunch of time in the process. Rather than opening each page separately and applying the replacement, do it all in one swoop by using the Results panel and the Find and Replace dialog together. First, click the green triangle in the Results panel, which reopens the Find and Replace dialog. In the Results panel, Ctrl-click (Cmd-click) the results where you want to make replacements. Those lines will highlight. Then switch back to the Find and Replace dialog, and click Replace (not Replace All). The files that are modified are marked by a green dot next to their names in the Results panel.

Performing Advanced Text Searches

An advanced text search allows you to do a more precise search by looking for text within (or outside of) particular HTML tags. You can further fine-tune the search by specifying particular attributes of the HTML tags.

Perhaps the most common example of why you would want to use such a search lies in the title of your Web pages. Whenever you create a new page in Dreamweaver, the page automatically gets the title "Untitled Document." If you forget to enter titles, you could end up with a bunch of pages on your site with the same "Untitled Document" name (it's easy to do; while writing this section, I found and fixed a page on my personal site that had been titled "Untitled Document" for four years!). A basic search and replace won't help, because "Untitled Document" is within the `<title>` tag of the pages, and a basic search only searches the body of a document. An advanced text search, which combines text and HTML searches, is the solution.

To perform an advanced text search:

1. Choose Edit > Find and Replace, or press Ctrl-F (Cmd-F).

   The Find and Replace dialog appears.

2. From the Find in pop-up menu, choose one of the options for the scope of your search.

continues on next page

3. From the Search pop-up menu, choose Text (Advanced).

The dialog changes and adds the option to search tags Ⓐ.

4. In the Find field, type the word or phrase that you're looking for.

5. Choose either Inside Tag or Not Inside Tag from the pop-up menu next to the + and – buttons.

Inside Tag refers to text that is enclosed within a container tag, such as `<p>…</p>`.

6. Choose an HTML tag from the Tag pop-up menu.

7. (Optional) If you want to narrow the search further by limiting the search to a particular attribute of the tag you chose in step 6, click the + button. If you do not, skip to step 12.

The attribute line is added to the dialog Ⓑ.

An example of an attribute would be the `class` attribute of the `<table>` tag.

Tag pop-up menu

Ⓐ The Text (Advanced) option allows you to search for text within HTML tags.

8. (Optional) From the first pop-up menu in the attribute line, choose With Attribute or Without Attribute.

9. (Optional) Choose the attribute you want from the next pop-up menu.

   Dreamweaver only shows the attributes for the tag you chose in step 6.

10. (Optional) Set a comparison in the next pop-up menu, choosing from = (equal), < (less than), > (greater than), or != (not equal). These only work if the attribute's value is a numeric amount, such as the **size** attribute of the **<input>** tag—for example, **<input size="4">**.

11. (Optional) In the next field (which is also a pop-up menu), type the value of the attribute. This can be a number or text.

    or

    Choose [any value] from the pop-up menu. This is useful when you want all tags with a particular attribute, but you don't care what the value of the attribute is.

12. If you want to replace the found text, type the replacement word or phrase in the Replace field.

13. Depending on what you want to do, click Find Next, Find All, Replace, or Replace All.

TIP For more information about the different HTML tags and their attributes, choose Window > Results > Reference, click the Results panel, click the Reference tab, and from the Book pop-up menu choose O'Reilly HTML Reference.

Find in:	Entire Current Local Site ▾	Homecook.info
Search:	Text (Advanced) ▾	
Find:	peachpit.com	
	Inside Tag ▾	div ▾
+ −	With Attribute ▾	align ▾	= ▾	center ▾

B You can narrow your search further by adding one or more attributes to the tag search.

Finding and Replacing in Source Code

Dreamweaver's ability to find and replace within the HTML source code is extremely powerful. You can look for text within particular tags, and you can even look within particular tags for specific attributes. You can also find text relative to other tags. For example, you can change specified text within a `<table>` tag and leave everything else alone. If you like, you can even use Find and Replace to replace, delete, or change tags and attributes.

Searching and replacing inside source code is much like regular text searches except you'll be working in Code view. When you perform the search, Dreamweaver automatically changes to Code view, so you don't have to do it manually before you start the search.

To find and replace in source code:

1. Choose Edit > Find and Replace, or press Ctrl-F (Cmd-F).

   The Find and Replace dialog appears.

2. From the Find in pop-up menu, choose one of the options for the scope of your search.

3. From the Search pop-up menu, choose Source Code **A**.

4. In the Find field, type the word or phrase that you're looking for.

5. In the Replace field, type the replacement word or phrase.

6. Depending on what you want to do, click Find Next, Find All, Replace, or Replace All.

A Choose Source Code to search the HTML in Code view.

TIP If you choose Current Document from the Find in pop-up menu, searches will not search related files, such as attached CSS or JavaScript files. To include those in your search scope, choose Open Documents in the Find in pop-up menu.

Finding and Replacing with a Specific Tag

A specific tag search lets you find and modify HTML tags. This has many uses; for example, you may still need to convert old sites that used `<font>` tags to CSS. You can use a specific tag search to strip out all those old tags, replacing them with CSS classes. Or you can change the now-passé `<b>` and `<i>` tags to their more modern equivalents, `<strong>` and `<em>`.

The key to the specific tag search is the Action menu, which specifies what replacement action Dreamweaver will carry out on the tags found in the search. See **Table 4.4** for a list of the actions available.

TABLE 4.4 Action Menu Options

Action	Description
Replace Tag & Contents	Replaces the tag and everything within the tag with the contents of the field that appears to the right of the Action pop-up menu when this action is selected. This can be either plain text or HTML.
Replace Contents Only	Replaces the contents of the tag with the contents of the With field.
Remove Tag & Comments	Deletes the tag and all of its contents.
Strip Tag	Removes the tag, but leaves any content within the tag.
Change Tag	Substitutes one tag for another.
Set Attribute	Changes an existing attribute to a new value, or adds a new attribute.
Remove Attribute	Removes an attribute from a tag.
Add Before Start Tag	Inserts text or HTML before the opening tag.
Add After End Tag	Inserts text or HTML after the closing tag.
Add After Start Tag	Inserts text or HTML after the opening tag.
Add Before End Tag	Inserts text or HTML before the closing tag.

To find and replace within a specific tag:

1. Choose Edit > Find and Replace, or press Ctrl-F (Cmd-F).

   The Find and Replace dialog appears.

2. From the Find in pop-up menu, choose one of the options for the scope of your search.

3. From the Search pop-up menu, choose Specific Tag.

   The Find and Replace dialog changes to show the tag functions Ⓐ.

4. Choose the tag that you want from the tag pop-up menu that appears next to the Search pop-up menu.

   You can either scroll the pop-up menu to find a tag, or you can type the first letter of the tag in the box. Dreamweaver automatically scrolls the list. Depending on the tag you choose, Dreamweaver will change the available actions in the Action pop-up menu, so don't be surprised if the contents of that menu look a bit different from those listed in Table 4.4.

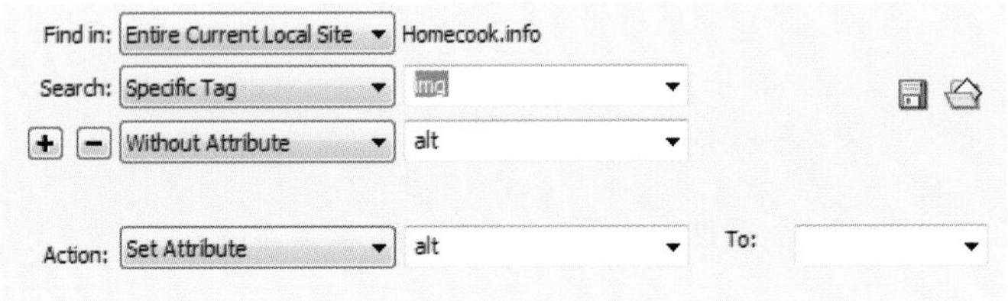

Ⓐ When you are searching within a specific tag, you can add attributes for that tag, and you can also specify actions that you want to perform on the found tag.

5. (Optional) If you want to narrow the search to a particular attribute of the tag that you selected, click the + button and then choose values for that attribute, as discussed previously in this chapter.

    If you want to narrow the search further, you can do so by clicking the + button and adding attributes.

6. Choose from the Action pop-up menu and, depending on the action you chose, set any required values.

7. Depending on what you want to do, click Find Next, Find All, Replace, or Replace All.

Using Regular Expressions for Searching

A *regular expression* is a pattern, written using special symbols, that describes one or more text strings. You use regular expressions to match patterns of text, so that Dreamweaver can easily recognize and manipulate that text. Like an arithmetic expression, you create a regular expression by using *operators*—in this case, operators that work on text rather than numbers.

The operators in a regular expression (see **Table 4.5** on the next page) are like the wildcard symbols that you may have seen in find and replace features in other programs, such as word processors, except that regular expressions are much more powerful. They can also be complex and difficult to learn and understand, so if Dreamweaver's other find and replace methods are sufficient for you, you may not need to bother with regular expressions.

Learning regular expressions is beyond the scope of this book, but we'll show you how to use one in an example. Let's say that you want to find all of the HTML comments throughout your site. You can use this simple regular expression (we know it looks weird, but don't lose heart; all will be explained):

```
<!--[\w\W]*?-->
```

TABLE 4.5 Regular Expression Special Characters

Character	Matches
\	Escape character; allows you to search for text containing one of the below special characters by preceding it with the backslash
^	Beginning of text or a line
$	End of text or a line
*	The preceding character zero or more times
+	The preceding character one or more times
?	The preceding character zero or one time
.	Any character except newline
\b	Word boundary (such as a space or carriage return)
\B	Non-word boundary
\d	Any digit 0 through 9 (same as [0-9])
\D	Any non-digit character
\f	Form feed
\n	Line feed
\r	Carriage return
\s	Any single whitespace character (same as [\f\n\r\t\v])
\S	Any single non-whitespace character
\t	Tab
\w	Any letter, number, or the underscore (same as [a-zA-Z0-9_])
\W	Any character other than a letter, number, or underscore
[abcde]	A character set that matches any one of the enclosed characters
[^abcde]	A complemented or negated character set; one that does not match any of the enclosed characters
[a-e]	A character set that matches any one in the range of enclosed characters
[\b]	The literal backspace character (different from \b)
{n}	Exactly *n* occurrences of the previous character
{n,}	At least *n* occurrences of the previous character
{n,m}	Between *n* and *m* occurrences of the previous character
()	A grouping, which is also stored for later use
x|y	Either x or y

Let's break down that expression. You read a regular expression from left to right. This one begins by matching the beginning characters of the HTML comment, `<!--`. The square brackets indicate a range of characters; for example, `[a-z]` would match any character in the range from a to z. In this case, the range includes two regular expression operators: `\w` means "any single letter, number, or the underscore," and `\W` means "any character other than a letter, number, or underscore." Taken together as a range, `[\w\W]` means "any character."

The `*` means "the preceding character (in this case, everything found by the contents of the square brackets) zero or more times," and the `?` means "the preceding character zero or one time." Taken together, they match a comment of any length. The regular expression ends by matching the closing characters of an HTML comment, `-->`.

To search with a regular expression:

1. Choose Edit > Find and Replace, or press Ctrl-F (Cmd-F).

   The Find and Replace dialog appears.

2. From the Find in pop-up menu, choose one of the options for the scope of your search.

3. From the Search pop-up menu, choose any of the options.

   In this case, since we're looking for HTML comments, you should choose Source Code.

4. Enter the regular expression in the Find field **A**.

5. Select the check box next to "Use regular expression."

   When you choose "Use regular expression," it disables the "Ignore whitespace" search option, because they are mutually exclusive.

6. (Optional) Enter text or a regular expression in the Replace field.

7. Depending on what you want to do, click Find Next, Find All, Replace, or Replace All.

TIP There's a lot to say about regular expressions, certainly enough to fill an entire book or 12. If you're interested in learning more, check out *Mastering Regular Expressions* by Jeffrey Friedl (O'Reilly Media, 2006). For a lighter read, try *Teach Yourself Regular Expressions in 10 Minutes* by Ben Forta (Sams, 2004). There are also many Web sites that provide regular expression tutorials, which you can find with a Google search.

Find in: [Entire Current Local Site ▼] Homecook.info

Search: [Source Code ▼]

Find: `<!--[\w\W]*?-->`

Replace:

Options: ☐ Match case   ☑ Ignore whitespace
         ☐ Match whole word   ☑ Use regular expression

A You can add regular expressions to both the Find and Replace fields.

Checking Spelling

No word processor comes without a spelling checker these days, and Dreamweaver is no different (even though it's not a word processor). You can check the spelling on the currently open page and add words to Dreamweaver's spelling checker in a personal dictionary.

To spell-check your page:

1. Choose Commands > Check Spelling, or press Shift-F7 (same on Windows and Mac).

   If Dreamweaver finds a word it believes is spelled incorrectly, the Check Spelling dialog opens **A**. Otherwise, you'll get a dialog that says "Spelling check completed."

2. Click the Add to Personal button if the word Dreamweaver found is correct and you want to add it to your personal dictionary so that Dreamweaver doesn't flag it as an error again.

   or

   Click Ignore to tell the spelling checker to ignore this instance of the word, or click Ignore All to ignore the word throughout the document.

   or

   Select a replacement from the Suggestions list, or type the replacement in the Change to text box. Then click the Change button, or click Change All to replace the word throughout the document.

3. When the spelling check is finished, click Close.

A Click Add to Personal in the Check Spelling dialog to add an unknown word to the user's personal Dreamweaver dictionary.

Including Images and Media

Image and media files convey much of the message of your Web site. You may even get most of your message across with video and animation, although most sites use images to supplement the text.

Some Web sites suffer from graphic overkill. There's a balancing act between using graphics to enhance the message and using images to bludgeon visitors into submission. Think of sites that use images of green text on a red background, for instance, or sites that are so proud of their "fabulous" graphic look that they relegate text to microscopic type.

Dreamweaver has many ways to place and modify images, as well as to control how text wraps around images. The program does a great job of adding dynamic media to your pages, such as Flash animations and movies, and also other formats such as QuickTime and Windows Media. In this chapter, we'll cover how you can use Dreamweaver to add graphics and media files to your Web pages. You'll get to use your talents to add images to express and enhance your site's message.

In This Chapter

Adding Images

Dreamweaver can place images on your Web page that come from your local hard disk or that are already on your Web site. By default, Dreamweaver prompts you to add *alternate text* to the image, which is text that is read aloud by screen reader software used by the visually disabled. If you have existing images on your pages that don't have alternate text, it's easy to add. You can, of course, easily delete images from your page.

To add an image to your page:

1. Click to place the insertion point in the document where you want the image to appear.

2. In the Common category of the Insert panel, click the Images button **Ⓐ**.

   The Images: Image button is actually a pop-up menu that allows you to add a variety of image types. We'll be talking about these different types later in this chapter.

   or

   Choose Insert > Image, or press Ctrl-Alt-I (Cmd-Opt-I).

   or

   Drag the icon of an image file from the Windows or Macintosh desktop into your document. If you choose this method, skip to step 6.

   The Select Image Source dialog appears **Ⓑ**.

   By default, the dialog will be set to the `images` folder of your local site folder.

3. In the dialog, navigate to and select the file that you want to insert.

   A preview of the image appears in the Select Image Source dialog, with

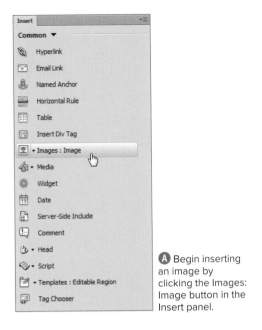

Ⓐ Begin inserting an image by clicking the Images: Image button in the Insert panel.

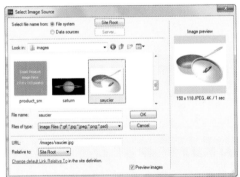

Ⓑ Navigate to the image you want in the Select Image Source dialog.

Ⓒ Dreamweaver lets you know that it will use an absolute file reference rather than a relative reference to the image file until you save the document.

Image Tag Accessibility Attributes

Alternate text: Saucier pan ▼

Long description: http://

If you don't want to enter this information when inserting objects, change the Accessibility preferences.

OK
Cancel
Help

D Enter alternate text for use by screen reader software used by the visually disabled.

Latest Reviews

All-Clad 3 Qt. Saucier
Read our review! »

E The image appears in the document.

Preferences

Category   Accessibility
General
Accessibility
AP Elements   Show attributes when inserting:
Code Coloring
Code Format   ☑ Form objects
Code Hints   ☑ Frames
Code Rewriting   ☑ Media
Copy/Paste   ☑ Images
CSS Styles
File Compare
File Types / Editors
Fonts
Highlighting   ☐ Keep focus in the panel when opening
Invisible Elements   ☑ Offscreen rendering (need to disable when using screen readers)
New Document

F You can set Accessibility settings in Dreamweaver's Preferences dialog.

TIP If you click Cancel in the Image Tag Accessibility Attributes dialog, the image appears on your page without alternate text. You can always add alternate text later using the Property inspector.

information below the image including the image's size in pixels, its graphic format, its file size, and the estimated time for the file to download (based on the Connection Speed pop-up menu in the Window Sizes category of Dreamweaver's Preferences).

4. Click OK (Choose).

If you have not already saved the document, and the Relative to pop-up menu in **B** is set to Document rather than Site Root, Dreamweaver displays an alert letting you know that it can't use a document-relative path, and that it will use an absolute file reference until you save the file **C**.

5. Click OK to dismiss the alert.

The Image Tag Accessibility Attributes dialog appears **D**. This is the dialog you use to add alternate text.

6. In the Alternate text box, type the alternate text you want to use for the image.

7. (Optional) In the Long description text box, add a URL that leads to a page with a detailed description of the image.

8. Click OK.

The image appears on your page **E**.

TIP In some browsers, an image's alternate text appears when you hover the mouse pointer over the image on the page.

TIP The Image Tag Accessibility Attributes dialog only appears if the option for images has been set in the Accessibility category of the Preferences dialog **F**. Because using alternate text is one of the commonly accepted Web best practices, the option is turned on by default. If you don't want Dreamweaver to prompt you for alternate text every time you insert an image, clear the Images check box in Preferences.

To add alternate text to an existing image on your page:

1. Click an image to select it.

2. In the Alt text box in the Property inspector **G**, type the alternate text, and then press Enter (Return).

   Dreamweaver adds the alternate text to the image.

To delete an image:

1. Click an image to select it.

2. Press Backspace (Delete).

   The image disappears from the page.

TIP You can cut, copy, or paste images as you would with text.

G You can also add alternate text in the Alt field of the Property inspector.

About Graphic Formats

There are three main still (as opposed to moving) image formats used on the Web: JPEG, GIF, and PNG. If you are not already familiar with these formats, here's a quick rundown, in the order in which they were originally developed:

- **GIF,** which stands for Graphics Interchange Format, is a lower-resolution graphics format with only eight bits of color information, which means that a GIF file can only contain up to 256 colors. GIFs are usually used for line drawings, flat cartoons, logos, and the like; in other words, images that don't need thousands or millions of colors (as would, for example, a photograph). There are two nice things about the GIF format. One is that it allows for *transparency*, which means you can set one or more colors in the GIF file to be the same as the background color of the page. This allows for irregularly shaped objects to appear on your page and for them to appear to be other than a rectangular image. The other useful feature of this format is the ability to add simple animation to images. A particular GIF file can contain multiple frames, and the file automatically steps through the frames to produce a rudimentary animation, like a flipbook. GIF files are used less frequently than they once were, giving way mostly to PNG files.

- **JPEG,** which stands for Joint Photographic Experts Group, is a format that was developed specifically to handle photographic images. A JPEG file can use 24 bits of color information, which allows it to offer millions of colors. The JPEG format is "lossy," which means that it uses compression to reduce the file size. The look of the image depends on the amount of compression used to record it. High levels of compression will result in noticeable image degradation, because image information is actually being thrown away to reduce the file size. However, you can realize a significant reduction in file size at moderate levels of compression, with little or no visible effect, especially at the relatively low resolutions provided on Web pages. Unlike the GIF format, a JPEG file can contain neither transparency nor animation.

- **PNG,** or Portable Network Graphics, was created to replace the GIF format with an image format that didn't require a patent license to use (the owner of the GIF patent began enforcing the patent in 1995 and demanding royalty payments from software companies whose software created GIF files; those patents have since expired). PNG also improves upon GIF's 256-color limitation; a PNG file supports millions of colors and much better transparency options (but PNG does not offer animation). PNG files are usually smaller than the same file in GIF format, due to better compression. Adobe Fireworks uses PNG as its native file format, and of course Dreamweaver fully supports the PNG format. Some very old Web browsers (for example, Internet Explorer 3) don't support PNG graphics, but there are so few of these browsers still in use that you generally shouldn't worry about it.

Inserting Images from the Assets Panel

Any images that you've used on your site will be listed in the *Assets panel*, which is a tab in the same panel group as the Files panel. The Assets panel has buttons running down its left side that show you different asset categories 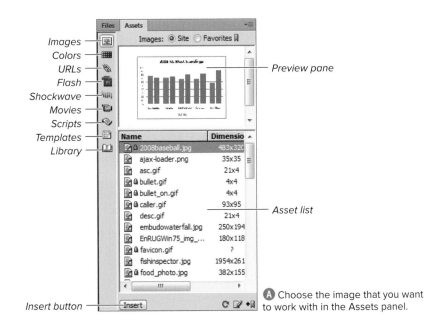. The first of these categories is Images. When you click the Images button in the panel, you get a list of all of the images in your site. Clicking an item in the list shows you a preview of the image in the Assets panel's preview pane, allowing you to easily browse through the images. You can browse any of the other asset categories in the same fashion.

To insert an image from the Assets panel:

1. Click in your document to set the insertion point where you want the image to appear.

2. If it's not already showing, click the tab for the Assets panel, or choose Window > Assets, or press F11 (Opt-F11).

3. Click the Site radio button at the top of the Assets panel.

   The images in your site appear in the asset list.

4. Click the image you want to insert.

   A preview of the image appears in the Assets panel's preview pane.

5. Click the Insert button at the bottom of the Assets panel.

   or

   Drag the image from the asset list into the document.

   or

   Right-click the image you want in the asset list, and then choose Insert from the context menu.

   The image appears in your document.

Labels around figure: Images, Colors, URLs, Flash, Shockwave, Movies, Scripts, Templates, Library, Preview pane, Asset list, Insert button

Ⓐ Choose the image that you want to work with in the Assets panel.

A Use the Images pop-up menu in the Insert panel to insert an image placeholder.

B Use the Image Placeholder dialog to specify the placeholder's parameters.

Adding Image Placeholders

When you first work on a page, you'll often be creating pages without all of the finished elements, such as the text and images. That shouldn't stop you from working on the page's design, of course. You can always copy and paste "The quick brown fox..." or similar text as a placeholder for the text that's to come, and Dreamweaver gives you the ability to insert image placeholders as well. The placeholder lets you allot the space on the page for a future image, allowing you to position and size the placeholder and finish your design before you have all the content. When you are ready to turn the placeholder into the final image, all you have to do is double-click the placeholder.

To insert an image placeholder:

1. Click in your document to set the insertion point where you want the image placeholder to appear.

2. Choose Insert > Image Objects > Image Placeholder.

   or

   In the Common category of the Insert panel, choose Image Placeholder from the Images pop-up menu **A**.

   The Image Placeholder dialog appears **B**.

   continues on next page

3. Fill out the Width and Height fields for the image placeholder (the units are pixels).

The Name and Alternate text fields are optional; if you fill them out, the text will appear in the Property inspector in the Name and Alt text boxes. You cannot use spaces in the Name field.

The default color for an image placeholder is a light gray; if you want to change that color, click in the color well and choose a new color from the resulting color picker.

4. Click OK.

The new image placeholder appears in your document **C**.

To replace the placeholder with an image:

1. Double-click the image placeholder.

The Select Image Source dialog appears (see figure **B** in "Adding Images").

2. Select the file that you want to insert.

3. Click OK (Choose).

The image appears on your page.

TIP If you own Adobe Fireworks, when you select an image placeholder you'll see a button in the Property inspector that has the Fireworks logo and the word Create **D**. Clicking this button launches Fireworks and creates a new image with the same dimensions as the place-holder. After you finish making the image in Fireworks, save the image in your site's images folder. You are then returned to Dreamweaver. The new image is inserted automatically in your document, replacing the image placeholder.

C The image placeholder appears in the document, with its name and size (these are cut off if the image isn't big enough, as shown here).

D Click the Create button in the Property inspector when an image placeholder is selected to launch Adobe Fireworks so that you can replace the placeholder with a finished graphic.

Setting Image Properties

There are several properties that you can set for images using the Property inspector **A**:

- **ID** lets you name the image. This name is used to refer to the image in scripts, and you must enter a name for scripts to be able to manipulate the image, as you might want to do for a rollover. You cannot use spaces or punctuation in an image name. Instead of spaces, we suggest you use the underscore character (_).

- **Src** (for Source) shows the path to the image file on your site.

- **Link** shows the destination if the image has a link to a URL.

- **Alt** shows the alternate text for the image.

- **W** (for Width) is the width of the image in pixels or percent of the image size.

- **H** (for Height) is the height of the image in pixels or percent of the image size.

- **Class** shows the CSS class, if any, that has been applied to the image.

continues on next page

Image map tools   *Image editing and adjustment tools*

A You can make a variety of adjustments to an image in the Property inspector.

- **Edit** includes buttons that allow you to edit the image in an external editor; change image setting, including image file format; and update Smart Objects (more about Smart Objects later in this chapter).

- **Crop**, **Resample**, **Brightness and Contrast**, and **Sharpen** are a group of tools that allow you to make adjustments to the image.

- **Map** is a field and four tools that allow you to name and add an image map to the image. See "Creating Image Maps" in Chapter 6 for more information.

- **Target** specifies the frame or window in which the destination of a link should load. The pop-up menu next to the Target field shows the names of all the frames in the current frameset. There are also five other target possibilities. The **_blank** target loads the linked file into a new browser window. The **_new** target acts like **_blank** the first time it's used, but after that, each time a link using the **_new** target is clicked, it will reuse the same "new" window. We think that **_new** is confusing, and we don't recommend its use. The **_parent** target loads the linked file into the parent frameset, the window of the frame that contains the link, or the full browser window. The **_self** target loads the linked file into the same frame or window as the link. This is the default choice. The **_top** target loads the linked file into the full browser window and removes all frames.

- **Original** shows the location of the original file (usually a Photoshop file) that is the basis of the selected image. This field shows the path to the source of a Smart Object.

To set image properties:

1. Click to select the image to which you want to apply one or more properties.

2. In the Property inspector, apply the property you want.

   The property is immediately applied.

TIP If you don't want to apply an interactive effect (like a rollover) to an image, you can leave its ID field blank.

TIP The pop-up menu next to the Alt field has one choice, <empty>. You can use this attribute for images, such as spacer GIFs, that don't need to be read by screen readers for the visually disabled. Because accessibility guidelines state that all images should have alternate text, it's a good idea to apply this attribute to any images that are literally just taking up space.

TIP If you want to add a border around an image, you can do so using the CSS border properties. Previous versions of Dreamweaver let you set borders in the Property inspector using HTML, but CS6 removes that ability. You'll have more control over the kind and color of the border with a CSS rule. See Chapter 7 for more information.

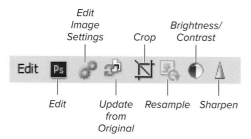

Edit Image Settings · Crop · Brightness/Contrast

Edit · Update from Original · Resample · Sharpen

A The Property inspector gives you access to a variety of image editing tools.

Editing Images

When you're working with images on your site, you'll often want to tweak them to improve their looks. You could use an external image editing program, such as Adobe Photoshop or Adobe Fireworks, to do the job, but it's more convenient to work right in Dreamweaver for simple changes. For extensive modifications, you'll still need an external image editor, however.

The Property inspector gives you seven buttons that allow you to edit an image **A**. Two of the buttons, Edit and Update from Original, hand the image off to Photoshop or another editor for editing and update the Dreamweaver image when the original Photoshop image changes. We cover using these buttons in "Working with Photoshop," later in this chapter.

Edit Image Settings lets you change the file format and optimization of the image. We'll cover this in more detail in "Optimizing Images," later in this chapter.

The other four buttons let you make quick image adjustments right in Dreamweaver. They are Crop, which lets you trim away portions of an image; Resample, which adds or subtracts pixels from an image that has been resized (this reduces the image size for better download performance); Brightness and Contrast, which allows you to correct images that are too dark or too light; and Sharpen, which changes the contrast of the edges inside an image, making it appear to be more in focus.

TIP To halt the editing process after you begin it and leave the image unchanged, press the Esc key.

TIP If you select an image and the image editing tools are grayed out, it's probably because you enabled Check In/Check Out for your site, and you need to check out the file for editing. For more about Check In/Check Out, see Chapter 18.

To crop an image:

1. Select the image that you want to crop.

2. In the Property inspector, click the Crop button.

   or

   Choose Modify > Image > Crop.

3. Dreamweaver puts up an alert dialog letting you know that the changes you will be making to the image are permanent, but that you can still use Undo to back away from the changes. Click OK.

   A crop selection box with eight resize handles appears within the image. Parts of the image outside of the crop selection box are dimmed .

4. Click and drag the crop selection box to move it around the image, and resize the box by dragging any of its selection handles, until you have the portion of the image you want to keep inside the box.

5. To complete the crop, press Enter (Return).

   or

   Double-click inside the crop selection box.

   Dreamweaver trims the image.

B The part of the image outside the selection rectangle will be cropped out.

C Click the Commit Image Size button to accept the new image size.

D Drag the sliders in the Brightness/ Contrast dialog to change the intensity of the image.

To resize and resample an image:

1. Select the image that you want to change.

2. Using the image's resize handles, make the image larger or smaller.

   or

   Use the W and H text boxes in the Property inspector to resize the image numerically.

   The image resizes, and the Resample button in the Property inspector becomes available for use. In the Property inspector, two new buttons appear next to the W and H text boxes: Reset to Original Size and Commit Image Size **C**.

3. Click the Commit Image Size button.

4. In the Property inspector, click the Resample button.

   or

   Choose Modify > Image > Resample.

   Dreamweaver resamples the image. On many images, the effect is quite subtle.

To adjust the brightness and contrast of an image:

1. Select the image that you want to adjust.

2. In the Property inspector, click the Brightness and Contrast button.

   or

   Choose Modify > Image > Brightness/ Contrast.

   The Brightness/Contrast dialog appears **D**.

3. If it isn't already checked, select the Preview check box.

   This makes adjusting the image a little slower, but it allows you to see the effects of your changes on the image as you make them.

continues on next page

4. Move the Brightness and Contrast sliders until the picture looks the way you want it.

or

Enter a numeric value in the text boxes next to Brightness and Contrast. The sliders begin in the middle of the range, and the acceptable range for each slider is from -100 to 100.

5. Click OK.

To sharpen an image:

1. Select the image that you want to sharpen.

2. In the Property inspector, click the Sharpen button.

or

Choose Modify > Image > Sharpen.

The Sharpen dialog appears .

3. If it isn't already checked, select the Preview check box.

This makes sharpening the image a bit slower, but it allows you to see the effects of your changes on the image as you make them.

4. Move the Sharpness slider until the picture looks the way you want it.

or

Enter a numeric value in the text box next to Sharpness. The slider begins at zero and goes to 10.

5. Click OK.

TIP Use a light hand when using the Sharpen tool. Oversharpening an image often makes it look unnatural, with edges in the picture that look too prominent or even oddly outlined **F**.

E Sharpening an image often brings out important detail that isn't as noticeable in the unsharpened image.

F Oversharpening an image (bottom) can make items in the image look weird.

![Image Optimization dialog showing Preset, Format JPEG, Quality 95, File size 317 K]

A You can make a variety of changes in the Image Optimization dialog, including changing the graphics format.

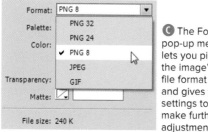

B Use the Preset pop-up menu to apply formats for the image. Each choice includes a bit of information to help you choose the correct format.

Format:	PNG 8
Palette:	PNG 32
Color:	PNG 24
	✔ PNG 8
	JPEG
Transparency:	GIF
Matte:	
File size: 240 K	

C The Format pop-up menu lets you pick the image's file format and gives you settings to make further adjustments.

> **TIP** Keep a close eye on the File size display as you experiment with changes; with some presets, such as PNG 24, you can easily end up making the file size significantly larger, which is usually not what you want.

Optimizing Images

You can *optimize* images that are in a Dreamweaver document. Optimization means that you can change the image from one format to another (for example, from PNG to JPEG), change the quality setting, and more.

To optimize an image:

1. Select the image you want to optimize.

2. In the Property inspector, click the Edit Image Settings button (see figure **A** in "Editing Images").

   or

   Choose Modify > Image > Optimize.

   The Image Optimization dialog appears **A**. The dialog has two pop-up menus (Preset and Format) and a settings area below Format.

   The Preset pop-up menu **B** lets you pick from six different PNG, GIF, and JPEG presets. By default, this menu is set to no value.

   You can use the Format pop-up menu **C** to change the file format to PNG, JPEG, or GIF. Depending on the format you choose, the dialog will change to show the appropriate settings used to modify the parameters of the selected format.

3. Make your choices from the Preset and Format pop-up menus.

   As you make your choices, the File size figure at the bottom of the dialog updates.

4. Click OK.

   The image is saved and updated.

Working with Photoshop

Dreamweaver has built-in integration with Adobe Photoshop CS3 or later. There are two methods of moving Photoshop images into your Dreamweaver document. In the first, you begin in Photoshop by opening an image and copying all or a portion of the image (a portion can be a selected part of the image, or one or more image layers). Then you switch to Dreamweaver and paste. Dreamweaver asks you how you want to save your image, and then places it on your Web page. You can choose the graphic format you want as the object is placed on the Web page.

In the second method, introduced with Dreamweaver CS4, you can choose a Photoshop file in the Select Image Source dialog and then place it into Dreamweaver. It is copied and placed into Dreamweaver in JPEG, GIF, or PNG format as a *Smart Object*, which maintains a link to the original Photoshop **.psd** file. When the **.psd** file is updated and saved, Dreamweaver recognizes the changes and offers to update the copy in the Dreamweaver document. Dreamweaver also remembers the path to the Photoshop source file and allows you to reopen it for modifications in Photoshop.

The benefit of the Smart Object approach is that you can have a single **.psd** file that is used in many different pages of your site. When you update the Photoshop file, you can update any Smart Objects based on that file throughout your site at once.

To copy and paste Photoshop images into Dreamweaver:

1. In Photoshop, open the image you want to bring into Dreamweaver.

2. Select the image or part of the image you want to copy.

   You can select one or more layers in your document, or use one of Photoshop's many other selection tools .

3. If you made a selection from a single layer, choose Edit > Copy.

   or

   If you selected multiple layers, choose Edit > Copy Merged.

4. Switch to Dreamweaver.

continues on next page

A In Photoshop, the background layer and the text layer have been selected in the Layers panel.

5. Choose Edit > Paste.

The image appears on the page full size, along with the Image Optimization dialog .

6. Make any adjustments you want in the Image Optimization dialog:

Using the Preset and Format pop-up menus, you can change the format of the saved image to GIF, JPEG, or PNG and make adjustments specific to each file type. For example, if you choose GIF format, you can set one of the colors in the image to be transparent.

7. Click OK.

The Save Web Image dialog appears .

8. Give the image a name, and navigate to where you want to save it (usually inside your site's **images** folder).

Remember that you can't use spaces in names for images for the Web, and that the only other characters you should use besides letters and numbers are the hyphen and underscore.

9. Click Save.

The Image Description (Alt Text) dialog appears. Alternate text is used by screen reading programs utilized by the disabled.

10. Enter the description for the image, and then click OK.

The image from Photoshop appears on your Web page.

B When the image appears in Dreamweaver, you can see that the image contains both the text and background layers from the Photoshop image. You can also make adjustments to the image optimization settings.

C Give the image a name, and save it in your **images** directory.

Seen in the Healdsburg Plaza

Ramblin' Cow

 After resizing and resampling, here is the image in the finished layout.

From Preview to Optimization

Dreamweaver CS6 changes the workflow of Photoshop integration quite a bit. Previous versions used an Image Preview dialog, which has been replaced by the Image Optimization dialog. In some ways the new workflow is improved, in that there are fewer options and the new dialog encourages you to do your image preparation in a real image editor. But on the other hand, you could do things (like resizing images) in the Image Preview dialog that you can't do in the Image Optimization dialog. So now if you want to import the high-resolution PSD file into Dreamweaver, it comes in at full size. Then you must resize and (sometimes) resample the image in Dreamweaver. That's two separate operations, not just one. In our opinion, that's a step backwards.

11. Use the image editing tools to adjust the image, if needed, to get the final appearance in your layout **D**. For example, you will almost always want to resize and resample the image to fit your Web layout, if you haven't already done so in your image editor.

TIP This copy-and-paste integration process also works with Fireworks.

TIP When images are placed and saved in Dreamweaver, they are flattened and lose their layers. If you want to maintain layers, use the Smart Object method to maintain a link to the original .psd.

TIP Information about the image, such as the optimization settings and the location of the original .psd source file, is saved in a Design Note regardless of whether you have enabled Design Notes for your site.

To edit copy-and-pasted images using Photoshop:

1. Select the image in Dreamweaver.

2. Ctrl-double-click (Cmd-double-click) the image.

   or

   Click the Edit button in the Property inspector (see figure **A** in "Editing Images").

   Dreamweaver opens the source file in Photoshop.

3. Make your changes to the image in Photoshop and save the file.

4. Select all or part of the image and choose Edit > Copy, or if you selected multiple layers, choose Edit > Copy Merged.

5. Switch to Dreamweaver.

continues on next page

6. Paste the image over the image in the Web page. Dreamweaver optimizes the **.psd** image on the clipboard using the original optimization settings and then replaces the image on the page with the updated version.

To place a Photoshop image as a Smart Object:

1. Click to place the insertion point in the document where you want the image to appear.

2. In the Common category of the Insert panel, click the Images button (see figure Ⓐ in "Adding Images").

   or

   Choose Insert > Image, or press Ctrl-Alt-I (Cmd-Opt-I).

   The Select Image Source dialog appears (see figure Ⓑ in "Adding Images").

3. In the dialog, navigate to and select the Photoshop file that you want to insert.

   With Photoshop files, you don't get the usual preview of the image in the Select Image Source dialog.

4. Click OK (Choose).

5. The Image Optimization dialog appears Ⓑ.

6. Using the Preset and Format pop-up menus, select the file format you want to use, and tweak the settings for that format, if needed.

7. Click OK.

   The Save Web Image dialog appears Ⓒ.

8. Give the image a name, and navigate to where you want to save it.

9. Click Save.

   The Image Tag Accessibility Attributes dialog appears.

Smart Object badge

Bacon ipsum dolor sit amet ham hock exercitation nostrud, nisi kielbasa pig consectetur venison sed. Short ribs salami kielbasa, exercitation qui capicola sirloin. Short ribs consequat culpa kielbasa ball tip, chuck enim eu capicola. Tail consequat ribeye hamburger, jerky non laborum ad cow duis eiusmod quis t-bone capicola reprehenderit. Ground round ex t-bone, anim swine corned beef turkey deserunt.

E The road sign has the Smart Object badge in its upper-left corner.

F The bottom arrow in this Smart Object badge has turned red, indicating that the image is out of sync with the original Photoshop file.

G After updating, the image shows the changes that had been made to the Photoshop file.

10. Enter the description for the image, and then click OK.

The image from Photoshop appears on your Web page, with a difference: It has a badge in the upper-left corner, showing that it is a Smart Object **E**.

To update a Smart Object:

1. Click to select the image that you want to change.

If the Smart Object needs updating, the badge will change, with the bottom arrow turning red, indicating that the copy of the image in the Dreamweaver document is out of sync with the original Photoshop file **F**.

2. Click the Update from Original button in the Property inspector (see figure **A** in "Editing Images").

or

Right-click the image and choose Update from Original from the context menu.

The image updates to show the changes in the Photoshop document **G**, and the Smart Object badge shows that it is in sync.

TIP The Smart Object badge appears only in Dreamweaver, not on your published Web pages.

TIP You can have multiple Smart Objects on a single page (perhaps in different sizes, or cropped differently) that all link to the same Photoshop file. You can update each Smart Object independently.

TIP You can update Smart Objects in the Assets panel by right-clicking them and choosing Update from Original from the context menu. The great thing about this method is that if you have used the Smart Object on multiple Web pages, the image is updated on all pages without you needing to open them.

Adding a Background Image

Most pages use a solid color or no color as their background, but sometimes you may want to use an image as the background of your page. This image will underlie all of the text and other images on your page. Though background images are a bit of a dated look, they can still be used on modern pages if you use them well.

Dreamweaver creates background images by creating a CSS rule to redefine the **<body>** tag. You can do this by creating the rule manually (see Chapter 7 for details on how to do that), but it's easier to use the Page Properties dialog.

To add a background image to your page:

1. Open the page to which you want to add the background image.

2. In the Property inspector, click the Page Properties button.

   or

   Choose Modify > Page Properties, or press Ctrl-J (Cmd-J).

   The Page Properties dialog appears Ⓐ.

3. In the Appearance (CSS) category of the dialog, click the Browse button next to "Background image."

   The Select Image Source dialog appears.

4. Navigate to and select the image you want to use as the background image, and then click OK (Choose).

Ⓐ Use the Page Properties dialog to insert a background image.

5. From the Repeat pop-up menu in the Page Properties dialog, choose how you want the image to be repeated on the page (if it is smaller than the page):

- **no-repeat** places the image on the page just once, in the upper-left corner of the page.
- **repeat** tiles the image across and down the page, filling the page.
- **repeat-x** tiles the image across the top of the page.
- **repeat-y** tiles the image down the left edge of the page.

6. To see how the image will appear on the page, click Apply.

The background image appears on the page **B**.

7. Click OK.

TIP Before CSS, designers set background images by adding a `background` attribute to the `<body>` tag. If you are asked to work on older sites, one of the renovations you should make is to remove this old attribute and replace it with a CSS rule.

TIP Be careful when using tiled background images. As you can see from the figure that showcases our cat, it can make the page very hard to read.

B The background image of our cat was repeated endlessly on this page by setting the Repeat field to "repeat." Remember how we said that background images look dated and tacky if you're not careful? This is what we meant.

Adding a Favicon

One of the little touches that will finish up your Web site is the addition of a *favicon*, that little icon that appears in the address bar of a browser when your site loads Ⓐ. A favicon is another way to underscore your site's brand identification, and often represents the logo of the organization that runs the site. Favicons are only 16 by 16 pixels large, and all modern Web browsers support them.

Before you can add a favicon to the index page of your site, you'll need to create one. There are dedicated favicon editing programs available for purchase, but we prefer to use one of the free online tools that convert graphic files into favicons, such as the ones at **favicon.htmlkit.com/favicon/** or **tools.dynamicdrive.com/favicon/**.

Once you have your favicon file, which must be named **favicon.ico** (see the tip at the end of this section for more detail), you'll add it to your site's pages in Dreamweaver. You'll do that with the **<link>** tag, which, while more often used for linking CSS style sheets, works fine for this purpose, too.

Ⓐ Here are the favicons for four different sites, as seen in Mozilla Firefox.

B The Link dialog allows you to add the path to the favicon file.

To add a favicon to your page:

1. Obtain your **favicon.ico** file, and move it into your local site folder.

   Because it's an image, it makes sense to us to put the favicon file into the **images** folder, but you can put it anywhere you want in the local site folder.

2. Open the page to which you want to add the link to the favicon.

3. Choose Insert > HTML > Head Tags > Link.

   The Link dialog appears **B**.

4. In the Href text box, enter the path to the **favicon.ico** file.

   or

   Click the Browse button to open the Select File dialog. Navigate to the **favicon.ico** file and click OK (Choose).

5. In the Rel text box, type **shortcut icon**.

6. Click OK, and then save the page by choosing File > Save.

   After you next synchronize your local site to the remote site, the favicon will show up when you load the page in a Web browser.

TIP You must repeat the process of adding the link to the favicon on every page in your site. If your site uses templates, adding the link to a template file automatically adds it to all the pages based on that template. For more about using templates, see Chapter 16.

TIP The favicon file should be named favicon.ico for the widest compatibility, though it isn't strictly necessary with all browsers. As usual, Internet Explorer is the culprit. It requires the .ico format, while other browsers can use .gif, .png, or .jpg files, as shown in **B**.

Adding Flash and Shockwave

Because Adobe is the maker of the Flash multimedia format, it should come as no surprise that Dreamweaver makes it easy to add many different varieties of Flash objects to your pages. The two kinds we'll discuss here are *Flash animations* and *Shockwave animations*. A Flash animation is a Flash file that has been optimized for playback on the Web. This kind of file has the **.swf** extension. You can play this animation in Dreamweaver or in a Web browser. A Shockwave file is an animation format very similar to a Flash file, but it's created by Adobe Director rather than Adobe Flash. A Flash file can be displayed by any Web browser that has the free Flash Player; Adobe claims that more than 98 percent of Internet users have the Flash Player.

Files with the **.fla** extension are Flash document files that can only be opened in the Flash program. These sorts of files can't be played in Dreamweaver or Web browsers.

To insert a Flash or Shockwave animation:

1. Click to set the insertion point where you want the Flash or Shockwave animation to appear.

2. Choose Insert > Media > SWF, or press Ctrl-Alt-F (Cmd-Opt-F).

   or

   Choose Insert > Media > Shockwave.

   The Select File dialog appears.

3. Navigate to the file you want, select it, and click OK (Choose).

   The Object Tag Accessibility Attributes dialog appears Ⓐ.

Ⓐ Add alternate text for the Flash or Shockwave file in the Object Tag Accessibility Attributes dialog.

Animation placeholder

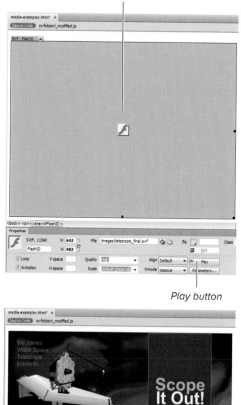

Play button

B To preview your animation, use the Play button in the Property inspector or switch to Live view.

4. Enter alternate text in the Title field of the dialog.

5. Click OK.

Dreamweaver inserts the animation file into your document as a placeholder.

TIP The Access key and Tab index fields in the Object Tag Accessibility Attributes dialog are used with forms. See the "Labeling Your Fields" sidebar in Chapter 11 for more information.

To play the animation placeholder in Dreamweaver:

1. Select the placeholder.

Selection handles appear at the edges of the placeholder.

2. Click the Live View button at the top of the document window.

or

Click the Play button in the Property inspector **B**.

Dreamweaver plays the animation file in the document window.

Adding Flash Video

Flash video is a way of showing video on your Web site. Like other video formats, such as QuickTime, Windows Media, Silverlight, and RealVideo, Flash video can show full-motion video in context on your Web page. But one of the big advantages of Flash video is that most browsers already have the Flash plug-in installed, so your video is likely to be viewable by more people.

Before you can put a Flash video file on your Web page, you must, of course, convert your video to the Flash video format, which has the **.flv** extension. Adobe Flash Professional CS6 includes the Adobe Media Encoder, which can convert Quick-Time, DV, MPEG, AVI, and Windows Media files into Flash video.

To insert a Flash video file:

1. Click to place the insertion point where you want the Flash video file to appear.

2. Choose Insert > Media > FLV.

   or

   In the Common category of the Insert panel, choose FLV from the Media pop-up menu.

   The Insert FLV dialog appears **A**.

3. From the Video type pop-up menu, choose either Progressive Download Video or Streaming Video.

   You will most often choose Progressive Download Video, which downloads the Flash video file to the user's hard disk and then plays it. The Streaming Video choice requires extra server-side software (Adobe Flash Media Server).

A You get a preview of the different media controllers available to you for Flash video directly below the Skin pop-up menu.

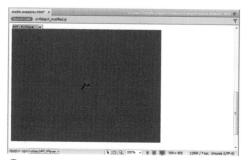

B When you've set all the options in the Insert FLV dialog, a placeholder appears in the document window. When you preview the Flash video in Live view, you can see and hear the video playing.

4. In the URL field, enter the path to the Flash video file. You could also click the Browse button, which brings up the Select File dialog and allows you to navigate to select the video file.

   If the media file is not inside your site folder, Dreamweaver will, as usual, offer to copy it there for you.

5. From the Skin pop-up menu, choose the kind of video controller you want to appear with the video.

   As you choose the skin, the dialog shows you a preview of what the video controls look like for that skin.

6. Enter the Width and Height (in pixels) that you want to use to display the video.

   or

   Click the Detect Size button, which attempts to read the Flash video file and figure out what size it is. Depending on your video, this option sometimes may not work, but it is always worth trying.

7. If you want the video to automatically begin playing when the Web page is loaded, select the Auto play check box.

8. If you want playback control to automatically return to the starting position after the video finishes playing, select the Auto rewind check box.

9. Click OK.

   A placeholder for the Flash video file appears on your page **B**. To play the Flash video file inside Dreamweaver, click the Live View button at the top of the document window.

To edit a Flash video file's properties:

1. Click to select the Flash video file.

2. In the Property inspector, make the changes you want Ⓒ.

TIP There are many variables involved in converting one kind of video file to another, and a complete discussion is way beyond the scope of this book. Instead, we suggest that you begin learning more about Flash video on the Adobe Web site at www.adobe.com/devnet/video/.

TIP Dreamweaver, when purchased as a stand-alone product, doesn't come with Adobe Media Encoder. However, all the Creative Suite 6 bundles that include Dreamweaver include Adobe Media Encoder.

Ⓒ Adjust the settings for a Flash video file in the Property inspector.

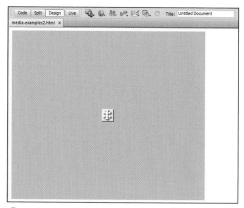

A Dreamweaver puts a placeholder for the plug-in media file in the document window.

Adding QuickTime and Other Media

Video and audio files, with the exception of the various flavors of Flash media, are handled by Dreamweaver as *plug-in media*. That's because these files need plug-in software to be installed in a Web browser to be played. The most common plug-in media are QuickTime, Windows Media, Silverlight, and MP3 audio files.

To add plug-in media files:

1. Click to place the insertion point where you want the media file to appear.

2. Choose Insert > Media > Plugin.

   or

   In the Common category of the Insert panel, choose Plugin from the Media pop-up menu.

   The Select File dialog appears.

3. Navigate to and select the media file you want, and then click OK (Choose).

   A placeholder for the plug-in file appears on your page **A**.

To preview your media file:

1. Select the placeholder for the media file.

2. In the Property inspector, click the Play button.

   This may not work if Dreamweaver can't find the appropriate plug-in on your system. In that case, save the page and preview the file in a Web browser **B**.

TIP Dreamweaver creates the placeholder file as a small square icon on the page. When you preview the file, that icon will be replaced by the media file controller, which has the playback controls. The small size of the icon won't allow you to use the media controller, so before you preview the file, click the placeholder icon and use its selection handles to make it wide enough so that you can see the entire media controller.

TIP For video files, use a video player program, such as QuickTime Player or VLC, to get the dimensions of the video file, and enter those dimensions into the W and H fields in the Property inspector.

TIP If you find that the video playback controls are missing or cut off, increase the value in the H field. For example, I needed to add 20 pixels to the H field to make the controller in **B** appear.

To edit a plug-in file's properties:

1. Click to select the plug-in file.

2. In the Property inspector, make the changes you want **C**.

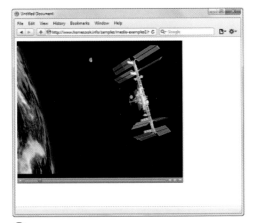

B You usually need to preview media that uses plug-ins, like this QuickTime movie, in a Web browser.

C You can adjust the settings for a plug-in media file in the Property inspector.

6

Working with Links

Links are what make the Web, well, *webby*—the interconnections between pages and sites are a fundamental part of why the Web is different from print. Without links coming in to your site, no one will ever find it. And without links going out from your site, it's a dead end. Dreamweaver makes it easy to add links to your site.

There are a number of different kinds of links: some links are internal to a page, some internal to a site, and some links go to another server altogether. This chapter will cover all of these, along with targets, image links, and email links.

In This Chapter

Creating Text Links

If you can drag your mouse from here to there, you can create a link inside Dreamweaver. All you have to do is decide what on the page you want to turn into the link, and where you want that link to point.

Because creating links is such a large part of developing a Web site, there are multiple ways to create links. You can figure out which method works best for you.

To create a text link:

1. Select some text on the page to be the link. **A** shows that the title "HomeCook.info" has been selected.

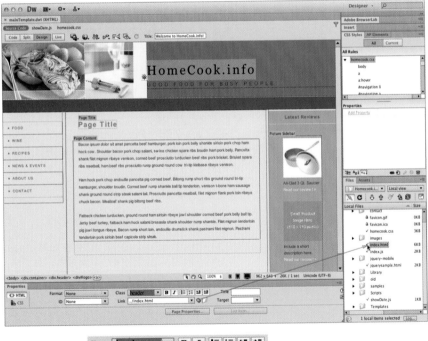

Point to File icon   Browse for File icon

A Drag the Point to File icon, and the arrow will follow to the selected link file.

B You can also select a link file from the Select File dialog.

C Or use this pop-up menu in the Property inspector.

D Finally, you can type the link filename in the Hyperlink dialog.

2. In the HTML tab of the Property inspector, click the Point to File icon immediately to the right of the Link field. An arrow appears, and that arrow can be dragged into the Files panel. Drag it to the file you want, and release the mouse.

or

In the Property inspector, click the Browse for File icon, which looks like a folder, to the right of the Link field. The Select File dialog appears **B**. Choose the file you want and click OK (Choose).

or

In the Property inspector, click in the Link text field and type the name of the file you want to link to.

or

In the Property inspector, click the pop-up menu to the right of the Link text field, and choose from the list of recently used links **C**.

or

In the Common category of the Insert panel, click the Hyperlink button. The Hyperlink dialog appears **D**. Type the name of the file to link to, or click the Browse for File icon to select a file. Click OK when you're done.

TIP If you want to remove a link, click inside the text you want to de-link, click the **<a>** in the tag selector, and then clear the Link text field in the Property inspector.

The Different Types of Links

When you create a link from one Web page to another, there are three possible types of links you can add: *absolute*, *document relative*, or *site root relative*. 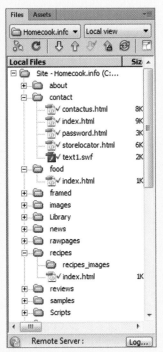 shows the file list from **www.homecook.info**, a fairly typical site, with a number of files in various folders. **F** shows another way of looking at the same information.

- **Absolute:** The **index.html** file contains a link to **http://www.dori.com/index.html**, which is another site altogether. This is an absolute link. The link starts with the explicit name of a server where the file can be found. It's also correct for the link to just go to either **http://www.dori.com/** or **http://www.dori.com**; in both cases, the link takes you to the default file for that domain (in this case, **index.html**).

- **Document relative:** The **index.html** file also contains a link to the **index.html** file in the **about** folder. To tell the browser how to navigate from one to the other, the link is **about/index.html**. That link is *relative* to the document it's being called from: the server knows, based on that link, that it needs to find a folder named **about** at the same level as the **index.html** file, and within that folder, a file named **index.html**.

  If **about/index.html** linked back to **index.html**, it would link to **../index.html**. Once again, the server starts looking for the next file at the same level as the current file, and those two periods tell the server to go *up* a level—back to **www.homecook.info**. And from there, it's easy to find the **index.html** file. A file two levels deep would link to the main index page by linking to **../../index.html**. It goes up two levels of folders before looking for a particular file.

  Document relative links are especially useful when you're testing on your local machine—the browser can get from one page to another just based on the location of the current document.

E Here's a list of folders and files (as seen in the Files panel) from a site of medium complexity.

The Different Types of Links *(continued)*

- **Site root relative:** Another way to reference files within the same site is by referencing them by where they are within the site; that is, relative to the root of the site, not the current document. The root of the site is always identified with a forward slash: **/**. With a site root relative link, the page at **/food/index.html** would link to **/index.html**. You no longer need to tell the server to go up a level or two; instead, you just tell it to start at the root and look for that particular file.

  Site root relative links are useful when you're creating site-wide library items. For instance, the left navigation menu in the document shown in Ⓐ contains links to /recipes/index.html and /food/index.html. With site root relative links, you know that those links work everywhere on the site, no matter what page contains that menu. Library items are covered in Chapter 16.

Links to external sites must be absolute links. Links within a site can use document relative links, site root relative links, or a combination of the two. The kind of link a site uses by default is set in Dreamweaver's preferences (see "Changing Link Relative To").

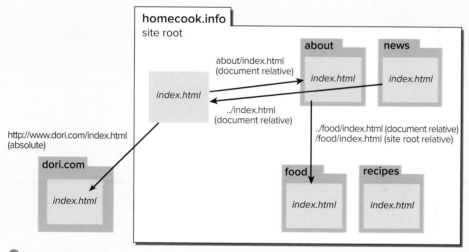

Ⓕ The about, news, food, and recipes folders (or directories) are all contained within the site root folder.

Changing Link Relative To

It's awkwardly named, but it's useful: you can change the *Link Relative To* (that is, whether the link is document relative or site root relative) for either a single file or for the site as a whole. As mentioned in the sidebar "The Different Types of Links," your links can either be document relative or site root relative, or even a mix of the two on each page.

A Use the Select File dialog to make your link site root relative or document relative.

To change the "Link Relative To" for a link:

1. In the Property inspector, click the Browse for File icon. The Select File dialog appears **A**.

2. Near the bottom of the dialog is a pop-up menu labeled "Relative to." From that pop-up, you can switch between Document and Site Root **A**, and the URL for the link will change.

3. Click OK to save your changes.

B Or you can set the "Links relative to" for the entire site.

To change the "Link Relative To" for a site:

1. In the Property inspector, click the Browse for File icon. The Select File dialog appears **A**.

2. Near the bottom of the dialog is a link that says "Change default Link Relative To in the site definition." If you click the link (the part that's blue and underlined), you'll end up in the Advanced Settings category for the Site Setup for your site, with the Local Info category chosen **B**. From here, you can choose either radio button next to "Links relative to," where the choices are Document or Site Root. This changes the link that you're currently modifying, as well as the default for future links, but it will not change any other existing links on the page or site.

3. Click OK to save your changes.

TIP You can also follow the directions found in Chapter 2 for editing the site setup. If you click the Advanced Settings category and then choose the Local Info category, you'll end up in the same place.

Formatting Links

One of the most common uses of CSS is to change the way links are displayed in the browser. Want your links to only be underlined when the cursor is over them? Want the background or text color to change when a visitor clicks? Or maybe you just want something other than your visitor's default colors? That's all CSS, and Dreamweaver can handle that. You'll need to know if your site is going to use internal or external styles (see Chapter 7).

To format links:

1. Click the New CSS Rule button at the bottom of the CSS Styles panel. The New CSS Rule dialog appears.

2. If you want to set a style that will apply to all links (whatever their state) or to set the default appearance for links, in the Selector Type section, choose "Tag (redefines an HTML element)" for the Selector Type, and in the Selector Name section, choose **a**.

   or

   For the Selector Type, choose "Compound (based on your selection)," and for Selector name, choose any option from the pop-up menu: **a:link**, **a:visited**, **a:hover**, or **a:active** Ⓐ. Other CSS rules attached to your document can also appear in this pop-up menu.

   ▸ **a:link** is the default state of the link, seen when none of the other states are in use.

   ▸ **a:visited** is how the link will appear after the link has been clicked and the linked page loaded.

Ⓐ The New CSS Rule dialog lets you choose which rule you're going to define.

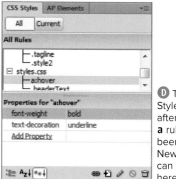

B When you want a new style sheet, you can create that file here.

C After you create the rule, define its values here.

D The CSS Styles panel, after various **a** rules have been defined. New properties can be set from here, also.

- ▸ **a:hover** is how the link will appear while the visitor's cursor is over the link.

- ▸ **a:active** is how the link will appear while the visitor is clicking that particular link.

3. For Rule Definition, there are at least two options: (New Style Sheet File) or (This document only). If the current document links to any style sheets, their names are included in the pop-up menu. Choose whichever is appropriate for this site, and click OK.

4. If you chose to create a new style sheet, you'll see the Save Style Sheet File As dialog **B**. Choose where to save it and what to name it, and click Save. The CSS Rule Definition dialog appears **C**. You can create the specific rules you want for links either here or directly in the CSS Styles panel **D**.

TIP It is important to set styles for your links; otherwise, they are likely to display underlined and blue (unvisited) and purple (visited)—but you can't be sure of that. To control the look of your page, set the link styles.

TIP **D** shows some of the most common rules for CSS-formatted links: bold font weight, and no underline except when the cursor is over the link.

Targeting Links

Sometimes you want a link to go to a new window or to an existing window other than the one you're clicking. That's done by giving the link a *target*—the name of the window in which you want the new page to load.

To give a link a target:

1. Follow the earlier steps to create a link, and then click the `<a>` in the tag selector.

2. Directly next to Link in the Property inspector is a text field named Target where the target is entered. Alternatively, you can click the pop-up menu to the right of the field to choose the target.

3. If you're working on a site without frames, you have five choices: `_blank`, `_new`, `_parent`, `_self`, and `_top` (sites with frames are different and are covered in the bonus chapter on frames). Choose one from the pop-up menu , and the Target field will show your choice.

   ▸ `_blank`: Open a new, blank window.

   ▸ `_new`: Acts like `_blank` the first time it's used, but after that, each time a link using the `_new` target is clicked, it will reuse the same "new" window. We think that `_new` is confusing, and we don't recommend using it.

   ▸ `_parent`: If the current window was opened by a previous link to a blank target (that is, the current window is a newly opened window), open this link in the previous window. If the current window wasn't opened that way, what happens depends on the user's browser—but usually, it just opens in the current window.

   ▸ `_self` and `_top`: For non-framed sites, these are both equivalent to not using any target at all.

A Set a link's target in the Property inspector with this pop-up menu.

TIP To remove a target, just click in the Target text field in the Property inspector and erase its content.

TIP The underscore before the name of a target tells the browser that this is a special type of target, not just the name of another window. You'll learn about named windows in the bonus chapter "Adding Frames" (at the end of the ebook edition or online at www.dreamweaverbook.com).

A The Named Anchor dialog lets you create a new anchor on your page.

Adding Named Anchors

Normally, when a new Web page is displayed, it does so showing the very top of a page. Adding an *anchor* to a link allows you to display the page starting at a given point on a page. To use an anchor, you'll need to create at least two things: the anchor itself and then the link to that anchor.

To create an anchor:

1. Open your document, and click in the spot in the file where you want the named anchor to be.

2. In the Common category of the Insert panel, click the Named Anchor button, and the Named Anchor dialog appears **A**.

3. Choose a name for the anchor that will be unique for this page. Remember that this anchor is going to be part of a URL, so it can contain only characters that are valid: no spaces, ampersands, question marks, and so on.

continues on next page

4. Click OK. In the spot where you created the new anchor, an anchor icon appears 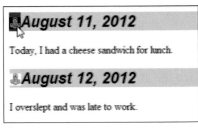. If you click that anchor, the tag selector will show the anchor with its name, and the Property inspector will allow you to modify the name **C**.

TIP Although you do see that anchor on the page in Dreamweaver, it won't be there when you or anyone else views the page in a browser—it's just there for your editing convenience, and it's one of the few ways in which Dreamweaver isn't 100 percent WYSIWYG. Hate seeing them? From the menu bar, choose **View > Visual Aids > Invisible Elements** to toggle the visibility of these icons on or off.

TIP There are many ways to delete a named anchor. One way is to click to select the anchor icon and delete it. Or, in the Property inspector, clear the NamedAnchor Name field. Or, of course, you can do it in Code view.

B The part of the page shown here, part of the world's most boring blog, has two anchors: the selected one is blue, and the unselected one is yellow.

C The Property inspector for a named anchor.

To link to an anchor on the same page:

Follow the directions from "Creating Text Links" earlier in this chapter, but drag the Point to File icon to the Named Anchor icon on the page. The selected text is now linked to the new anchor.

TIP It's possible that the Point to File icon and the Point to File arrow can end up going to different spots on the page. The one that matters, in this case, is the icon itself, not the tip of the arrow.

To link to an anchor on another page:

If you're using Dreamweaver's tabbed interface, you won't be able to see the link source and the destination at the same time, so you'll have to add the anchor part of the link manually. Follow the directions from "Creating Text Links" earlier in this chapter to link to another file, and when that's complete, click in the Link field in the Property inspector and add a **#** followed by the anchor name to the end of the existing link. So if you want to link to the `chap07` anchor on the `dwvqs.html` page, your link would be to `dwvqs.html#chap07`.

or

If the two files are open in different windows, arrange the windows so you can see both the link source and the link destination. Then, follow the directions for linking to an anchor on the same page, but drag the Point to File icon to the anchor on the other page.

Adding Links to Graphics

Making a graphic a link isn't all that different from creating a text link. The main difference is that the Link and Target fields in the Property inspector are in different areas, so you might not see them at first glance. Additionally, you don't get the handy pop-up menu on the Link field, so you can't just reuse one of the links you've recently made.

To add a link to a graphic:

1. Select the image in the document window.

2. Using the Property inspector **Ⓐ**, click the Point to File icon next to the Link field. An arrow appears, and that arrow can be dragged into the Files panel. Drag it to the file you want, and release the mouse.

   or

   Click the Browse for File button next to the Link field; then in the resulting Select File dialog, navigate to and select the file you want as the link's destination, and click OK (Choose).

TIP As mentioned in "Creating Text Links," there are many ways to create links. Over time, you'll find the one that works best for you.

TIP It's very common that images in the upper-left corner of a Web page (usually the site's logo) link back to a site's home page; common enough that if you don't do this, your site's visitors may be confused. Unless there's a good reason why you shouldn't do this for a site, set this up as the default.

TIP You can make individual parts of an image link to different Web pages. That's done with image maps, and they are covered in the next section.

Ⓐ For images, the Link and Target fields aren't where you might expect them to be in the Property inspector.

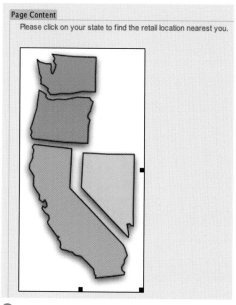

Page Content

Please click on your state to find the retail location nearest you.

Ⓐ We'll turn this map of four Western states into an image map.

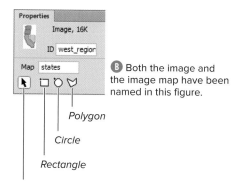

Properties

Image, 16K

ID west_region

Map states

Ⓑ Both the image and the image map have been named in this figure.

Polygon

Circle

Rectangle

Selection

Creating Image Maps

It's easy to add a link to an image: just select the image, and use the Link text box in the Property inspector to define the link's destination. But what if you want different parts of an image to link to different pages? You'll need an *image map*. With an image map, you can define areas of the image as *hotspots*, and each hotspot has its own link.

To create an image map:

1. Select the image you want to turn into an image map.

   In this example, we're using a map of Washington, Oregon, California, and Nevada Ⓐ. We'll add hotspots to each of the states.

2. In the Map text box of the Property inspector, enter a name for the image map Ⓑ.

   The name cannot begin with a number and can contain only letters, numbers, and the underscore character.

   continues on next page

3. Use the Rectangle, Circle, or Polygon tool to draw a hotspot over part of your image.

The tool you use depends on the shape of the area that you want to make into a hotspot. For example, we used the Rectangle tool to create the hotspots for Washington and Oregon, and the Polygon tool to create the hotspots for California and Nevada.

Dreamweaver shows the hotspot as a light blue area overlaid on your image 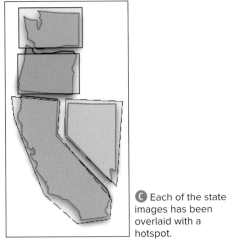. The blue highlighting won't show up on your Web pages.

4. When a hotspot is selected, the Property inspector shows properties for the hotspot . Use the Link field to attach a link to the hotspot.

5. (Optional) Use the Target pop-up menu to target the destination of the link.

If you need more information about the use of the Target control, see "Targeting Links," earlier in this chapter.

6. Enter the alternate text for the hotspot in the Alt field.

7. Repeat steps 3–6 for each of the other areas on the image you want to turn into hotspots.

C Each of the state images has been overlaid with a hotspot.

D Add the link for a hotspot in the Property inspector.

TIP To change the properties of a hotspot, use the hotspot Selection tool to select the hotspot; then make changes in the Property inspector.

TIP You can resize and reshape hotspots; just select the hotspot with the hotspot Selection tool, and then click and drag one of the selection handles that appear at the corners of the hotspot.

TIP Image maps have somewhat fallen out of favor recently; you see more sites using interactive Flash movies to provide users the benefits of clickable images. But they are still perfectly usable and valid ways to make parts of images clickable, and they work on some browsers that don't support Flash, such as the Safari browser on the iPhone, iPod touch, and iPad. Even if your sites use Flash, you can use image maps as a fallback plan, serving a version of the page that uses image maps for browsers that aren't Flash-capable.

A The Email Link dialog lets you set the link (the email address) and the text that will be displayed on the Web page.

Adding Email Links

If you want your site's visitors to be able to contact you, you'll need to add a link that allows people to send you email.

To add an email link:

1. Click the spot on the page where you want to add an email link.

2. In the Common category of the Insert panel, click the Email Link button, and the Email Link dialog appears **A**.

3. Fill in the Text field with the text you want to display in the Web browser, and fill in the Email field with the email address. Click OK when you're done.

TIP Dreamweaver doesn't do any kind of error checking to make sure that the email address is in a valid format, so be careful when you're entering it.

TIP Putting an email address on a Web site can lead to that address getting all kinds of garbage or spam. There are a variety of ways to help protect your email address. The simplest is just to encode—put it into a format that the browser can understand but that a spider sent out by a spammer can't. To learn more about this, search on Google for "email" + "obfuscator." This approach works with some spambots that harvest email links from Web pages, but certainly not all.

7

Styling Page Content

You want your Web site to look inviting, colorful, and organized, right? You need style! With styles, your site doesn't just look good—you get other benefits as well. Compared to older font-tag-based styling, your site is easier to maintain and update, it downloads faster and uses less bandwidth, and it's more accessible to every type of browser. In this chapter you'll get a basic understanding of Cascading Style Sheets, better known as CSS. Then we'll get into the details of how to use Dreamweaver's CSS Styles panel and CSS Rule definition dialog to create and apply styles to your pages.

In This Chapter

Understanding CSS

Cascading Style Sheets are all about style, looks, and presentation. CSS properties and rules give you an amazing array of control over foregrounds, backgrounds, colors, fonts, positions, alignments, margins, borders, lists, and other aspects of presentation.

Dreamweaver organizes the CSS properties it supports (which is most of them) via a couple of manageable interfaces: the CSS Rule definition dialog and the CSS Styles panel. With these two features, you can control every style aspect of every element on your page. From your document's body to its paragraphs, lists, tables, and links, to styling individual words or even individual letters, it's all handled with the CSS Styles panel or the CSS Rule definition dialog.

Content vs. presentation

Content is king, the saying goes, because users seek content when they come to your site. Content is the actual information in the headings, paragraphs, lists, **div**s, tables, forms, images, blockquotes, links, and other HTML elements you use on a page. With no styling, content looks something like an outline Ⓐ.

The unstyled content should be useful and informative, even if it doesn't look like much. That's because some of your visitors get only the text content—for instance, those with screen readers, some mobile browsers, or text-only browsers. Some of these also get images, but not all, so make sure your pages are understandable and navigable even without graphics.

Ⓐ A page with no styles shows content and working links, even though it isn't beautifully arranged.

Ⓑ Add styles to the same page to determine rules for layout, background, fonts, margins, and other presentation features.

Once you add presentation rules, you have the layout, color scheme, font choice, background, and other "pretties" that make a Web page look good in a standard browser **B**. The content itself hasn't changed. What has changed is the way the content is presented on the page. Change the presentation—that is, use different styles—and the same content completely changes its appearance.

The power of CSS derives from the separation of content from presentation. You can make the content look like anything you want simply by changing the way it is styled and presented.

Working with tags

HTML consists of *tags*, and adding tags to your document turns it into something that a computer knows how to handle. A tag is simply a name inside angle brackets, and every browser has certain names (that is, tags) that it understands.

Now, when you look through this chapter, you might be thinking to yourself at first, "Hey, I bought a WYSIWYG tool so I wouldn't have to learn about HTML tags!" That's understandable—but you'll need to learn at least the basics about HTML tags to take full advantage of CSS.

Some tags are *containers*; that is, they can contain content, other tags, or both. Other tags are empty elements; for instance, the `<img>` tag, used for graphical elements, cannot also contain text.

Containers have beginning and ending tags. For instance, each paragraph inside your documents should be inside a `<p>` tag, where `<p>` stands for paragraph. To put some text into a paragraph tag, all you (or more often, Dreamweaver) have to do is add a `<p>` before the text and a `</p>` after (that forward slash is what tells the browser that it's at the end of the paragraph). Makes sense so far?

Next, to apply a style to that paragraph, you apply it to that `<p>` tag. You're not taking anything out of the paragraph or adding anything to the paragraph. It's still a paragraph; but with CSS, you have some say about how that paragraph appears. Each style has instructions that define the style and what it does, and these instructions are called *rules*.

You can learn just enough about HTML tags by looking at the tag selector of your Dreamweaver document. If you find you want to know even more, check out Chapter 17, "Editing Code."

Setting CSS Preferences

When you're first learning CSS, set your preferences so that Dreamweaver gives you the maximum help.

In the CSS Styles category **A**, setting the styles to use *shorthand* is optional. Shorthand omits default values, which saves on bandwidth when downloading style sheets, but it can be confusing to a novice. To make things easier while you're learning, don't enable shorthand.

For the "When double-clicking in CSS panel" preference, select "Edit using CSS dialog" while you're still learning about styles. If you find you prefer to edit using the Properties pane in the CSS Styles panel, you can change it later.

A The CSS Styles preferences should be set based on how you like to work.

Anatomy of the CSS Styles Panel

If you're new to Dreamweaver, start off by taking a long look at the CSS Styles panel—it will become a good friend.

B shows the CSS Styles panel in All mode, with the All Rules and Properties panes displayed. The Properties pane is in Category view.

C shows the CSS Styles panel in Current mode, with the Summary, Rules, and Properties panes displayed. The Properties pane is in Set view.

B The CSS Styles panel in All mode shows the All Rules and Properties panes.

C The CSS Styles panel in Current mode. The Summary, Rules, and Properties panes are visible.

Creating a Style Rule for a Tag

Everything you do to create new styles, apply styles, and edit styles starts with creating a rule. Style rules begin with a *selector*. A selector can be a tag, an **id**, or a **class**.

To create a style rule for a tag:

1. With a page open in Dreamweaver, click the New CSS Rule button in the CSS Styles panel. The New CSS Rule dialog appears **A**.

2. Complete the following:

   ▸ **Selector Type:** Choose Tag (redefines an HTML element).

   ▸ **Selector Name:** Dreamweaver makes its best guess (based on your current selection or cursor placement when you clicked the New CSS Rule button) as to what tag you want this style to apply to. That tag automatically appears in the Selector Name field. If that tag isn't the one you want, choose the correct tag using the pop-up menu **B**.

   ▸ **Rule Definition:** Select "This document only" to add the style to just the document you have open. We'll cover the other options available here later.

3. Click OK, and the CSS Rule definition dialog appears **C**.

4. Set properties in the nine categories as desired. Which category contains which field is covered in "Dreamweaver CSS Categories," next. If you want to see how something looks without dismissing the dialog, click Apply.

5. Click OK, and the new rule takes effect.

A If you select a tag in the document, it may automatically appear in the Selector Name field in the New CSS Rule dialog.

B Any tag can be styled—just select the one you want.

C The Type category is where you set font rules, including your choice of foreground (text) colors.

TIP New rules can also be created by selecting text in the document window and choosing Format > **CSS Styles** > **New**.

TIP There's a lot more to the New CSS Rule dialog, but don't fret—we'll cover its other options later in this chapter.

TIP Not familiar with `class` and `id`? What you need to know is covered in the sidebar "Choosing Between Classes and IDs," later in this chapter.

TIP This example creates an internal style: one where the style information is included inside the Web page. Internal styles are useful for testing, but in the long run, you'll want to make all your styles external—that is, in their own file. We'll cover that in Chapter 9, "Managing Styles."

Choosing Between Divs and Spans

Divs and *spans* are generic containers. A **div**, short for *division*, holds a section of a page that you use and style as a block. Use **div**s to organize content into meaningful containers. You might structure your page with a **div** for the masthead, a **div** for the navigation, a **div** for the content, and a **div** for the footer. Positioning **div**s creates your layout. Blocks of content can then be nested inside other **div**s. In **D**, for example, the highlighted **div #maincontent** is inside another **div**, which is itself inside the **body** tag.

The **span** element is for inline use. A **span** can, for example, enclose a letter, word, or phrase. For example, the word "span" in the previous sentence is in a different font; if this were a Web page, we would achieve that effect by wrapping "span" in a **span** and then applying a style to just that element. With a style rule applied to the **span**, you achieve a distinctive presentation for an inline element.

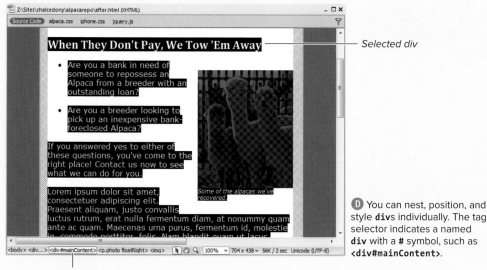

Selected div

Tag selector

D You can nest, position, and style **div**s individually. The tag selector indicates a named **div** with a # symbol, such as `<div#mainContent>`.

Dreamweaver CSS Categories

Dreamweaver uses the CSS Rule Definition dialog to break down CSS into various categories. Below, you'll find each of the categories in the CSS Rule definition dialog, along with what you can find in that category. Each item in the dialog is named according to its CSS property value.

Type Ⓐ

- Font-family
- Font-size
- Font-style
- Line-height
- Text-decoration
- Font-weight
- Font-variant
- Text-transform
- Color

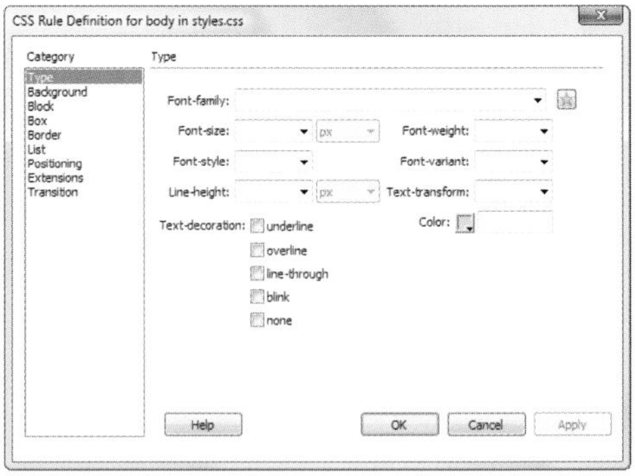

Background Ⓑ

- Background-color
- Background-image
- Background-repeat
- Background-attachment
- Background-position (X)
- Background-position (Y)

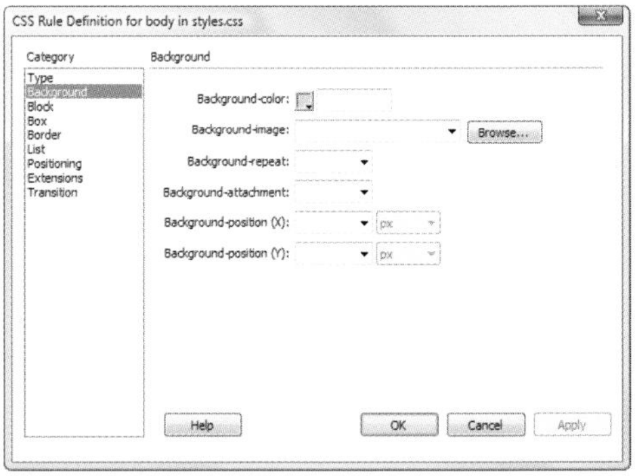

Block Ⓒ

- Word-spacing
- Letter-spacing
- Vertical-align
- Text-align
- Text-indent
- White-space
- Display

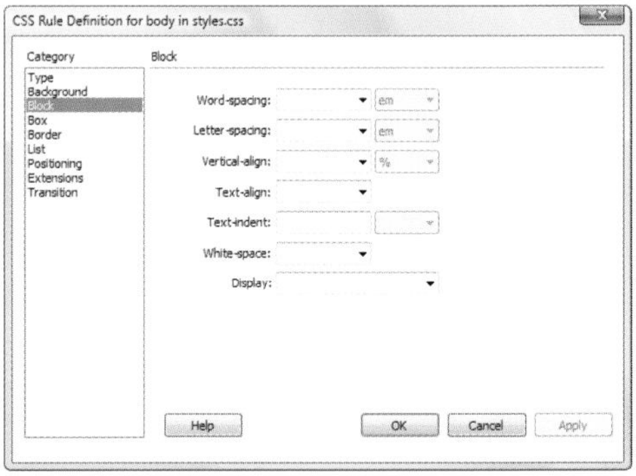

Ⓐ In the Type category, you can set the most common styling properties to text.

Ⓑ Always give a page a background color, even if you're using a background image.

Ⓒ Set rules for spacing and alignment of text in the Block category. Text indent affects the first line only—yes, you can have old-fashioned paragraph indentation with CSS!

D Set rules for width and height in the Box category. Margin and padding are both transparent, which means that a background shows through either.

E Set rules for borders in the Border category. Deselect "Same for all" to style borders individually.

F Set rules for list type and position in the List category. If you want an image instead of a standard bullet, specify it here.

Box **D**

- Width
- Height
- Float
- Clear
- Padding (Same for all, Top, Right, Bottom, Left)
- Margin (Same for all, Top, Right, Bottom, Left)

Border **E**

- Style (Same for all, Top, Right, Bottom, Left)
- Width (Same for all, Top, Right, Bottom, Left)
- Color (Same for all, Top, Right, Bottom, Left)

List **F**

- List-style-type
- List-style-image
- List-style-Position

continues on next page

Positioning

- Position
- Width
- Height
- Visibility
- Z-Index
- Overflow
- Placement (Top, Right, Bottom, Left)
- Clip (Top, Right, Bottom, Left)

Extensions

- Page-break-before
- Page-break-after
- Cursor visual effect
- Filter visual effect

Transition

- All animatable properties
- Duration
- Delay
- Timing function

TIP Page break properties are used in style sheets for print.

TIP The nine categories of style definitions in the **CSS Rule definition dialog cover nearly every CSS property available. What's impressive is that you can apply any of the properties in any of the nine categories to virtually** *any* *element* **in your document. Backgrounds, for example, can be applied not just to the** body **element, but also to the tags** div, table, blockquote, span, acronym, quote, form, **and many others.**

G Set position in the Positioning category. The Z-Index option refers to the stacking order when more than one layer occupies the same position. Clip refers to material that might overflow the size set for width and height.

H Set extensions in the Extensions category. Internet Explorer is the only browser that supports the Filter extensions.

I Set transitions in the Transition category. If you deselect "All animatable properties," you'll see that you can set unique transitions for almost every CSS property.

A A **class** selector name is preceded by a period when creating a new style.

Creating a Custom Class

Redefining the style for a tag gives you considerable control, because HTML has a tag for nearly any type of text you need to format. And yet, there are times when you want to create a style rule for something that doesn't already have a logical tag as a label. You can do that with a **class**. And you get to create a custom name for the style when you create a **class**.

To create a class:

1. With a page open in Dreamweaver, click the New CSS Rule button in the CSS Styles panel. The New CSS Rule dialog appears **A**.

2. Set the Selector Type option to Class (can apply to any HTML element), and set the Selector Name option to a name of your own choosing, preceded by a period (**.**). This is your new **class** name.

3. Click OK, and the CSS Rule definition dialog appears.

4. When you've completed filling out the CSS Rule definition dialog, click OK to accept your changes.

TIP Don't create a **class** to describe text when there is already a logical tag that does the job. For example, don't create a **class** to make text big and bold and use it as a heading. HTML already provides six heading tags (h1, h2, h3, h4, h5, and h6). Simply redefine one of the existing heading tags to suit your purpose. Remember, you want to use HTML to create a logical structure for your content, and CSS to style the structured content.

TIP Pick a **class** name that will serve you over time. A name that describes a purpose rather than a particular property works best. For example, if you wanted to highlight certain vocabulary words in red, you could name a **class** either **.red** or **.vocab**. If you redesign the site later and change the color scheme, the name **.red** might not make sense any longer, but **.vocab** would still have meaning.

Choosing Between Classes and IDs

You can identify any particular element on a page by assigning it a name. Named elements can then be targeted with CSS rules. The two attributes used to assign names in CSS are *classes* and *ids*.

A **class** is reusable. A single **class** can be assigned to many different elements on a page. For example, your blog might have a **class** called **blogentry** applied to every blog entry. Or there might be several vocabulary words on a page that use a common **vocab class**.

An **id**, on the other hand, can only be used once per page. Since each **id** is unique, it can be used for all sorts of tasks in addition to CSS rules, such as link destinations and JavaScript. When working with CSS, it's also useful for a **div** to have an **id**, because it enables you to write rules for that specific block of content with regard to its position, background, margins, and other properties.

In the CSS Styles panel, you see the name of each **id** and **class** style rule you add to your style sheet **B**. In the style sheet, a hash or pound sign (**#**) precedes an **id** selector. A period (**.**) precedes a **class** selector.

B This complete style sheet contains **ids** (**#container**, **#sidebar**), restyled tags (**body**, **h1**), **class**es (**.floatRight**, **.photo**), and pseudo-class selectors (**tr:first-child**).

A The New CSS Rule dialog lets you choose a type, name, and definition for your new rule.

Creating Compound Selectors

Elements in HTML can nest. Inside the **body** might be a **div** named **content**, with a **div** named **newitem** nested inside that. Each of these nested elements exists in a parent-child relationship that allows CSS properties to be inherited. The child elements are *descendants* of the parent elements and inherit properties from them.

You can create extremely selective selectors with descendant elements. Take the lowly list item, or **li**. If you redefine the default **li** style, you style every list item anywhere in the body of your page. However, if you have a **div** named **content** and list items using **li** within that, you can create a rule using the selector **#content li**. Instead of styling every **li** in the document, it will only style each **li** that is inside **content**.

Dreamweaver calls *contextual* selectors like this *compound*. There's more about compound selectors in the "Compound Terminology" sidebar, later in this chapter.

To create a compound style:

1. With a page open in Dreamweaver, click the New CSS Rule button in the CSS Styles panel. The New CSS Rule dialog appears **A**.

continues on next page

2. Set Selector Type to Compound (based on your selection). For Selector Name, one of the pseudo-class selectors may appear in the dialog by default. Select a pseudo-class selector from the pop-up menu or type a selector of your own choosing in this field by doing one of the following:

Type a pound sign (**#**) and an **id** to style a named section of the page—usually a **div** **B**.

or

Type a pound sign (**#**), the **id**, and a space before the pseudo-class selector to style only those navigation links in a particular named section of the page **C**.

or

Type a pound sign (**#**), the **id**, a space, and an HTML tag to style an element found only in the named section of the page **D**.

or

Type a group of selectors, each separated by a comma and a space, to assign the same style properties to every selector in the group with a single rule **E**.

If possible, Dreamweaver will parse your selectors and give you an explanation of them in the dialog (**B** and **D**).

3. Click OK, and the CSS Rule definition dialog appears.

4. When you've completed filling out the CSS Rule definition dialog, click OK to accept your changes.

B A selector based on an **id** must begin with a pound sign (**#**).

C Type in the Selector Name field to create selectors that fit your document.

D A contextual or compound selector lets rules apply only to tags within certain named **div**s.

E Every tag in this group list of selectors will follow the same style rule.

F Dreamweaver politely suggests that you create a new rule for a new **div** as soon as you insert it in your document.

TIP Rules for link pseudo-classes won't work reliably with the cascade unless you define them in the following order: a:link, a:visited, a:hover, a:active. A way to remember the L-V-H-A order is the memory device LoVeHAte.

TIP If you use the Insert Div Tag button in the Insert panel (found in both the Common and Layout categories) to insert a div, Dreamweaver offers you the chance to create a style for the div immediately **F**. Click the New CSS Rule button in the Insert Div Tag dialog to define properties for the new div.

Compound Terminology

Compound selectors are extremely powerful, and they have a specific vocabulary that describes them.

Pseudo-classes are so named because pseudo-states don't actually exist in the document. The user must do something to create the pseudo-class, such as visit a link, hover over a link, or even hover over a visited link.

Comma-separated lists of selectors (**p**, **td**, **li**) are called *group* selectors.

Selectors such as **#nav li** or **#content p** are known as *contextual*, *compound*, or *descendant* selectors. These selectors are the workhorses of CSS because they allow you to write specific rules based on the element in context (or the element from which it descends). For instance, the selector **#content p** styles only the **p** elements in **#content**, and **#footer p** styles only the **p** elements in **#footer**. So while you may have paragraphs in your content area and paragraphs in your footer area, there is no reason why they have to share the same presentation rules.

Working with the CSS Styles Panel

The CSS Styles panel (Window > CSS Styles) shows all the styles affecting a document or a selected style. You can apply, modify, delete, and do other style-related tasks right in the CSS Styles panel without having to open the CSS Rule definition dialog. If you need an overview of what's where in the panel, look back at the "Anatomy of the CSS Styles Panel" sidebar, earlier in this chapter.

To work in All mode:

1. In your document, click All at the top of the CSS Styles panel 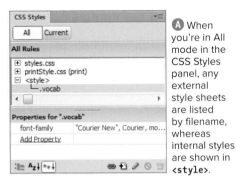. All the styles affecting the document appear: any linked or imported external style sheets as well as any styles only in the open document. An external style sheet is indicated by a filename—for example, **pagestyles.css**. Styles internal to this document are in the **<style>** category.

   Click the plus (+) (Windows) or the disclosure triangle (Mac) to expand a category if it isn't already expanded.

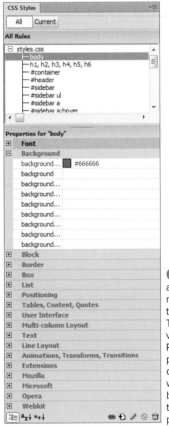

A When you're in All mode in the CSS Styles panel, any external style sheets are listed by filename, whereas internal styles are shown in **<style>**.

B Expand a style sheet name to see all the style rules. The Category view of the Properties pane shows categories, which must be expanded to examine properties.

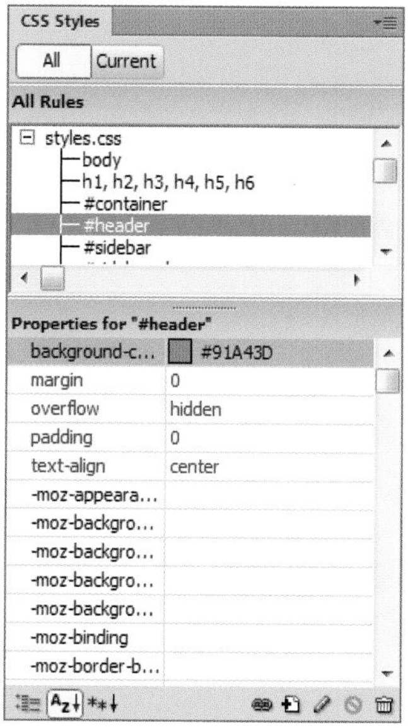

C Pick a specific style from the list, and its properties are shown in the Properties pane. In List view, the Properties pane shows a list of all the properties for a selected style.

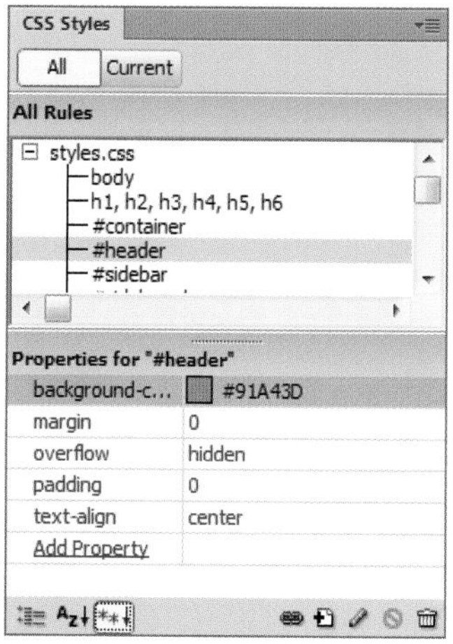

D In Set view, the Properties pane eliminates everything except the set properties for the selected style.

2. Examine the rules for individual styles by highlighting a specific style and doing one of the following:

Click the "Show category view" icon at the lower left of the CSS Styles panel. Properties for the selector appear in categories in the Properties pane at the bottom **B**. Click the plus (**+**) or the disclosure triangle (Mac) to expand any category.

or

Click the "Show list view" icon at the lower left of the CSS Styles panel. Properties for the selector appear as a list in the Properties pane at the bottom **C**.

or

Click the "Show only set properties" icon at the lower left of the CSS Styles panel. Set properties for the selector appear in the Properties pane **D**.

continues on next page

3. To add a new property directly in the CSS Styles panel, click the icon for "Show only set properties" and then click Add Property. An editable field appears with a pop-up menu listing every possible property **E**.

4. To modify a property, click the property value. An editable field appears **F**. Type any change and press Enter (Return).

To work in Current mode:

1. In your document, do one of the following:

Place the cursor in an element in the document window.

or

Select an element using the tag selector at the lower left of the document window **G**.

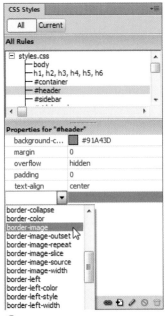

E To set a new property while in the Properties pane, choose from the list.

Tag selector

G Elements you want to style can be selected in the document window with the tag selector.

F Any property value is editable in the Properties pane.

CSS Styles

All | **Current**

Summary for Selection

font-family	Verdana, Geneva, "Bitstre...
color	#000000
text-align	left
float	left
width	12em
font-weight	bold

About "float"

ⓘ float is defined in rule "#sidebar" in styles.css.

Properties for "#sidebar"

float	left
font-weight	bold
width	12em
Add Property	

Ⓗ Current mode focuses on only the currently selected style.

CSS Styles

All | **Current**

Summary for Selection

font-family	Verdana, Geneva, "Bitstre...
color	#000000
text-align	left
float	left
width	12em
font-weight	bold

Rules

body	<body>
#container	<div>
#sidebar	<div>

Properties for "body"

background-c...	#666666
color	#000000
font-family	Verdana, Geneva, "Bitstre...
margin	0
padding	0
text-align	center
Add Property	

Ⓘ You can see information about the selected property or see the cascade of rules that apply to the selected tag.

Properties for "body"

background-color	#666666
color	#000000
font-family	Verdana, Geneva, "Bitst...
margin	0
padding	0
text-align	center
Add Property	

Ⓙ In Current mode, you can see inherited styles affecting a selector. The style is shown with a strikethrough if it doesn't apply to the current selection.

2. Click Current at the top of the CSS Styles panel Ⓗ. The Summary for Selection pane appears.

3. In the middle pane, you can choose whether to show information about the selected property (About, Ⓗ) or show the cascade of rules for the selected tag (Rules, Ⓘ). Click a property highlighted in the Summary for Selection list, and then choose either the About or Rules button on the right.

   At the bottom, the Properties list shows the properties and their values.

4. If properties for the selected element were overridden by rules for other selectors, Dreamweaver indicates this with a strikethrough of the property name Ⓙ. Use the mouse to hover over the property showing a strikethrough, and a pop-up appears explaining why this property is not applied.

TIP Verify how styles are implemented on your pages by previewing them in a variety of browsers, as well as in Dreamweaver's Live view. More than one style rule can affect a particular page element. Sometimes the style rules conflict and you get unexpected results.

TIP When things don't look as expected in the browser, troubleshoot style rules by using Current mode in the CSS Styles panel. The Properties pane provides valuable help to spot style conflicts.

TIP Inheritance information in the About pane of the CSS Styles panel in Current mode is also useful when troubleshooting conflicting style rules.

External, Internal, and Inline: Look Ma, It's the Cascade

Styles can be *external*, *internal*, or *inline*. An external style resides in a separate style sheet file, one with a name that usually ends in .**css**. An internal style lives inside each Web page that needs it and is located within **style** tags inside the document's **head**. And inline styles live within the HTML tags and only apply to whatever's inside that tag.

Style rules *cascade*. This means that although multiple styles can cover a particular element, there are rules to determine which style takes precedence. The order of the cascade is first external, then internal (meaning in the document **head**), and then inline. When style rules conflict, the laws of the cascade determine how the conflict is settled.

In general, the closer a rule is to the element being styled, the more power the rule has in the battle of conflicting style rules. The whole idea is a lot easier to understand with a specific example.

Let's look at the selector **p**. Suppose in your external style sheet you redefined **p** to be black, Arial, and 100% in size. Every **p** element in your document will be black, Arial, and 100%. No conflict there.

Into your conflict-free life comes a need to have *just one document* that uses your attached external style sheet to display paragraphs that are black, Arial, and 90% in size. You know how to create a style for just one document, and you write an internal style making the **p** 90%. Now you have a conflict. Is a **p** element going to follow the rule in the external style or the rule in the internal style? The cascade goes from external to internal, so the internal rule is closer and has the power to overrule the external rule in this conflict. Conflict solved. Any **p** element in this one document will be 90% in size.

But you want one paragraph to be red, not black. So you write a **class** rule and apply it inline to the paragraph. Now you have an inline style and a new conflict. The cascade goes from external to internal to inline, so the inline style has the power to overrule both the external rule and the internal rule. Conflict solved. Any **p** element in this one **class** will be red.

Note that this is the simplest possible case, and there are a number of factors that affect precedence. For instance, the cascade also takes into account how precise one given selector is over another. Many designers have earned gray hairs trying to debug exactly why a particular rule took precedence at a given time, and thankfully, Dreamweaver is a big help in this regard.

Properties for "nav ul a"	
-moz-box-shadow	1px 1px 3px rgba(0,0,0,0.3)
-webkit-box-shadow	1px 1px 3px rgba(0,0,0,0.3)
border	1px solid #618A37
border-radius	8px
box-shadow	1px 1px 3px rgba(0,0,0,0.3)
color	#fff
display	block
margin	5px 0px
padding	10px
text-align	center
text-decoration	none
text-shadow	1px 1px 1px rgba(0,0,0,0.8)
width	140px
Add Property	

offset blur-radius color

Hovering over a property with multiple values gives you a tooltip with the names of those values.

Welcome to RGB and RGBA

Previous versions of Dreamweaver specified colors in hex values; for example, white was **#FFF**. Dreamweaver, as of CS5.5, now supports setting colors in RGB and RGBA, another two CSS3 units for **color** property values. In addition to the red, green, and blue components of the color, in RGBA there is also an *alpha* component that allows you to specify an opacity value for color. Where before you might have needed to create partially transparent images in Adobe Photoshop and then bring those images into Dreamweaver, now you can reduce the opacity of the color through a CSS rule.

The opacity of the alpha value is set as a fourth value in the RGBA declaration. For example, with RGB you would show the color white as **rgb(255, 255, 255)**. If you wanted to use white at 50% opacity, you would set it as **rgba(255, 255, 255, 0.5)**. The range of acceptable values for the alpha value is from 0.0 (completely transparent) to 1.0 (completely opaque).

Adding CSS3 Properties with the CSS Styles Panel

As we just saw, the CSS Styles panel (Window > CSS Styles) shows all the styles affecting a document or a selected style. Dreamweaver CS5.5 brought support for many CSS3 properties and attributes to the CSS Styles panel. And the program's added support for HTML5 tags means that you can target the parts of your document directly. For example, instead of needing to wrap your navigation bar in a **div** and then adding CSS **class**es to that **div**, you can use the HTML5 **nav** tag and then apply styles that modify the tag.

To work with CSS3 properties:

1. In your document, click All at the top of the CSS Styles panel, then click the plus (**+**) (Windows) or the disclosure triangle (Mac) to expand a category if it isn't already expanded.

2. To modify a property, click the property value. An editable field appears. Type any change and press Enter (Return).

   Properties with multiple values display the names of those values in a tooltip when you hover the mouse over the values .

continues on next page

3. To modify a property with multiple values, click the Add Values icon ⬆️ in the values column. A values box will pop up, allowing you to enter the appropriate values for the property **B**. If you're viewing your document in Live view, you'll see the results of your changes in real time.

For more information on which new properties are covered in Dreamweaver, see the "HTML5 and CSS3 Code Hinting Additions" sidebar in Chapter 17.

B Different properties have different acceptable values (and so may look different), but this values box for `text-shadow` is representative.

Working with HTML5

In addition to supporting HTML5 tags as targets for CSS3 rules, Dreamweaver (as of CS5.5) supports HTML5 in a couple of other ways. In the New Document dialog, you can now choose an HTML5 Doc-Type, and Adobe has also provided two HTML5 starter layouts: two-column and three-column fixed layouts. These starter layouts, instead of being made up of **div** soup, use HTML5 semantics to make the structure and meaning of the markup clearer. For example, instead of adding a **div** for a navigation bar and then applying one or more **class**es to it, the starter layouts simply use the **nav** element. Similarly, sidebars use the **aside** element.

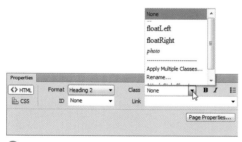

A Use the context menu to apply a **class** style rule.

B Use the Class pop-up menu in the Property inspector to apply a **class** style rule.

Applying Attributes

Most styles take effect immediately in the current document and in any other documents linked to an external style sheet. If you redefine the style for a tag such as **h3**, then any time you use the **h3** tag, the style is applied. Pseudo-class selectors such as **a:link** also are immediately applied to the selected elements in any linked documents.

Other styles are different—they're based on adding a **class** or **id** attribute to an element. For instance, after you create a style rule for a **class**, you must then apply that **class** to text in the document. The same goes for **id**.

To apply a class:

1. In a document, select the text to which you want to apply the **class**.

   or

   Place the cursor anywhere in a paragraph to apply the **class** to the entire paragraph.

   or

   Select a tag with the tag selector at the lower left of the document window.

2. Do one of the following:

   In the CSS Styles panel, select All mode, right-click the name of the **class** you want, and choose Apply **A**.

   or

   In the HTML tab of the Property inspector, choose the **class** you want to apply from the Class pop-up menu **B**.

   or

continues on next page

In the CSS tab of the Property inspector, choose the **class** you want to apply
from the Targeted Rule pop-up menu .

or

In the document, right-click the selected
text, choose CSS Styles, and then
choose the **class** you want to apply.

or

Choose Format > CSS Styles, and in the
submenu choose the **class** you want to
apply .

C You can apply **class**es from either the HTML
tab or the CSS tab of the Property inspector.

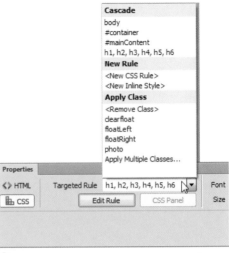

D Another way to apply a **class** style rule is to
choose Format > CSS Styles and then choose from
the submenu.

Selected tag uses a class

E In the tag selector bar, it's easy to identify an element that has a **class** applied to it, because the element has a period in its name—for example, **<div.content>**.

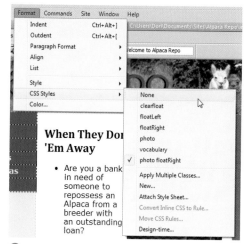

F Removing a **class** is as simple as choosing None from the CSS Styles submenu.

To remove a class:

1. Select the text to which the **class** was applied. The tag selector in the lower left of the document indicates the presence of a **class** with a period; for example, **<p.current>** means that the **class current** was applied to the **<p>** tag **E**.

2. Do one of the following:

   In the HTML tab of the Property inspector, choose None from the Class pop-up menu.

   or

   In the CSS tab of the Property inspector, choose <Remove Class> from the Targeted Rule pop-up menu.

   or

   In the document, right-click the selected text, choose CSS Styles, and then choose None.

   or

   Choose Format > CSS Styles, and in the submenu choose None **F**.

3. The **class** is no longer applied to the selected text. However, the **class** is still available in the style sheet.

To apply an ID:

1. In a document, select the text or tag to which you want to add an **id**.

2. Do one of the following:

   In the CSS Styles panel, select All mode, right-click the **id** you want to apply, and then choose Apply .

   or

   Right-click the element in the tag selector, choose Set ID, and then choose an **id** from the submenu 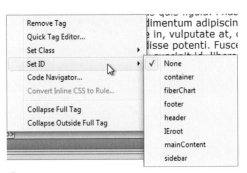.

   or

   Use the HTML tab of the Property inspector to choose an **id** to apply from the pop-up menu .

   or

   Use the CSS tab of the Property inspector to choose the **id** you want to apply from the Targeted Rule pop-up menu .

3. Check the tag selector to verify that the **id** has been applied by looking for the name of the tag followed by a **#** followed by the name of the **id**.

TIP When you remove a `class` from the selected element, it's still available to be applied elsewhere. Removing the `class` attribute from the tag doesn't remove the rule from your page.

TIP If you select some text that isn't inside a container (such as a paragraph or `div`) and apply a `class` or `id`, Dreamweaver wraps a new `span` tag around that text and applies the new attribute to the `span`.

TIP If the pop-up menu in the Property inspector doesn't show the `id` you want, it may be because that `id` is used elsewhere on the page. An `id` must be unique on the page, so if you want to move it from one place to another, remove it from the first place before attempting to apply it to the second.

G Even the tag selector has a context menu, giving you an easy way to add an **id**.

H The Property inspector can also be used to add an **id**.

Multiclass Selection

Click to specify multiple classes:

- ☐ clearfloat
- ☐ floatLeft
- ☑ floatRight
- ☑ photo
- ☐ vocabulary

Type to specify undefined classes:

photo floatRight

Help   OK   Cancel

① If you want to assign more than one **class**, do so in the Multiclass Selection dialog.

To apply multiple classes using the Property inspector:

1. In a document, select the text to which you want to apply the **class**.

   or

   Place the cursor anywhere in a paragraph to apply the **class** to the entire paragraph.

   or

   Select a tag with the tag selector at the lower left of the document window.

2. Do one of the following:

   In the HTML tab of the Property inspector, choose Apply Multiple Classes from the Class pop-up menu **B**.

   or

   In the CSS tab of the Property inspector, choose Apply Multiple Classes from the Targeted Rule pop-up menu **C**.

3. The Multiclass Selection dialog appears **①**, showing all the available **class**es. Choose the ones you want to apply and click OK.

Working with Browser-Specific CSS Properties

Dreamweaver CS5.5 added support in the CSS Styles panel for browser-specific properties, specifically for the Mozilla (Firefox), Microsoft (Internet Explorer), WebKit (Safari and Chrome), and Opera browsers.

To use browser-specific properties:

1. With your document open, click All at the top of the CSS Styles panel.

2. In the All Rules section of the CSS Styles panel, click to select the rule to which you want to apply the browser-specific property.

3. At the bottom of the CSS Styles panel, click the "Show Category view" button.

   In the Properties section of the panel, scroll down until you see the Mozilla, Microsoft, Opera, and WebKit categories **Ⓐ**.

4. Click the plus (+) Windows or the disclosure triangle (Mac) to expand any category.

5. To apply one of the properties, simply add a value in the column next to that property name **Ⓑ**.

   The names of active properties will turn blue.

6. Clicking the "Show only set properties" button at the bottom of the CSS Styles panel shows the browser-specific properties you set **Ⓒ**.

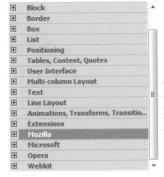

Ⓐ There are four new categories at the bottom of the CSS Styles panel for the browser-specific properties.

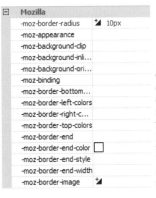

Ⓑ Expanding one of the categories shows you the available properties for that browser. The names of active properties turn blue.

Ⓒ When you view the active properties for the selected CSS rule, you can see the browser-specific properties (in this case, for Mozilla and WebKit browsers).

Creating Styles with the Property Inspector

If you're upgrading from a much older version of Dreamweaver, it's the most natural thing in the world to use the Property inspector to create styles. You can still style text with the Property inspector, but there are a few things to keep in mind.

The old way of using Dreamweaver added dozens, perhaps hundreds, of font tags to a page with the Property inspector. Getting rid of all those bandwidth-eating font tags is a good thing. As of Dreamweaver CS4, you can only apply two HTML styling tags with the Property inspector: `<strong>` and `<em>`. All other style choices create CSS styles, and you're prompted to create a new CSS rule when you try to style text.

Another big change in Dreamweaver CS4 was splitting the Property inspector into two tabs: HTML ⒶA and CSS ⒷB. In the HTML tab, you can apply HTML attributes, such as headings, lists, and indenting. You can also apply CSS **class**es and **id**s. In the CSS tab, you can create CSS rules, apply font families, change the size and color of fonts, and align text.

Ⓐ The HTML tab of the Property inspector allows you to apply HTML tags.

Ⓑ The CSS tab of the Property inspector allows you to apply CSS styles.

To create styles with the Property inspector:

1. Open a new, blank document or a document with content but with no styles yet applied.

2. Click the Page Properties button on either tab of the Property inspector. The Page Properties dialog appears **C**.

   This dialog applies styles and properties that will affect the entire page, and the styles will be written as an internal style sheet. You can move the styles to an external sheet later, if needed; see "Moving Internal Styles to External" in Chapter 9.

3. The Page Properties dialog contains six categories. You can set properties as desired in the following:

   ▸ **Appearance (CSS):** Set appearance properties for the body, including page font, size, text color, background color, and background image. If you use a background image, you should also set how it repeats. Margins are set individually for top, right, bottom, and left.

   ▸ **Appearance (HTML):** Sets HTML appearance properties for the page, including background image, text colors, link colors, and margins **D**. We recommend that you set these with CSS styles instead.

   ▸ **Links (CSS):** Set the font and size, set colors for unvisited, visited, rollover, and active links, and select underline style from the pop-up menu **E**.

   ▸ **Headings (CSS):** Set a heading font, and choose a size and color for each heading **F**.

C Page Properties for Appearance (CSS) determine backgrounds, fonts, colors, and margins, using CSS.

D You can set HTML page properties in the Appearance (HTML) category.

E Page Properties for Links set up fonts, colors, and sizes for links.

F Page Properties for Headings set up fonts, colors, and sizes for headings.

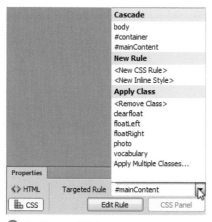

Page Properties for Title/Encoding screenshot.

G Page Properties for Title/Encoding determine title, document type, and language encoding.

Page Properties for Tracing Image screenshot.

H Page Properties for Tracing Image allow you to set an image to trace over when designing your page.

The Targeted Rule pop-up menu screenshot showing:

Cascade
body
#container
#mainContent
New Rule
<New CSS Rule>
<New Inline Style>
Apply Class
<Remove Class>
clearfloat
floatLeft
floatRight
photo
vocabulary
Apply Multiple Classes...

Properties
<> HTML   Targeted Rule   #mainContent
▤ CSS   Edit Rule   CSS Panel

I The Targeted Rule pop-up menu in the Property inspector lists available **class**es and **id**s. Choose one from this menu to apply it.

▸ **Title/Encoding:** Type a page title. Choose the Document Type (DTD) from the pop-up menu. Leave the Encoding and Unicode Normalization Form settings alone unless you know what you're doing and are creating pages in multiple languages **G**.

▸ **Tracing Image:** Browse to locate the tracing image and set the degree of transparency **H**. We discussed tracing images in Chapter 3, "Building Your First Page."

4. Click Apply to see how your changes look, and then click OK to accept your changes.

> **TIP** The styles and properties you set are stored internally in this document only. You can inspect them in Code view. The Document Type appears in the first line of code. The language encoding appears in a meta element in the head. The styles are enclosed in a style element in the head. If you set a tracing image, it appears in Design view.

> **TIP** Names in the Page Properties dialog are not always standard CSS selector or property names. For example, in the Links category, Rollover links correspond to the CSS pseudo-class selector a:hover and Underline style corresponds to the CSS property text-decoration.

To create classes or inline styles with the Property inspector:

1. Open a document and select the text or tag to be styled.

On the CSS tab of the Property inspector, <New CSS Rule> is automatically selected in the Targeted Rule pop-up menu **I**.

continues on next page

If you look in the menu, you'll see that there are other styles you can apply; the Cascade section lists styles available in external sheet(s), the New Rule section allows you to create a new CSS rule or a new inline style, and the Apply Class section allows you to apply existing **class**es.

2. Set new values for any or all of the following settings: Font, Size, and Color. For color, use the color picker to choose a color for the selected text.

   If you're creating a new inline style, the style is created in the document and is applied to the selection. You're done.

   or

   If you're creating a new CSS style, the New CSS Rule dialog appears ⬤.

   (Optional) Instead of applying values in the Property inspector, you can click the Edit Rule button on the CSS tab of the Property inspector ⬤.

3. Choose the selector type, enter the selector name, and choose where you want the new style to reside with the Rule Definition pop-up menu.

4. Click OK. If you formatted the selection with the controls in the Property inspector in step 2, the style is applied. If you used the Edit Rule button, the CSS Rule definition dialog appears. Set the style properties in this dialog, then click OK.

   Dreamweaver creates the **class** with a generic name, and the new **class** appears in the Targeted Rule pop-up menu in the Property inspector. The **class** is applied with a **span** tag to inline text. If the selected text is a complete element, such as a paragraph, the **class** is applied to the element's tag.

⬤ The New CSS Rule dialog appears to help you specify the location for your new rule.

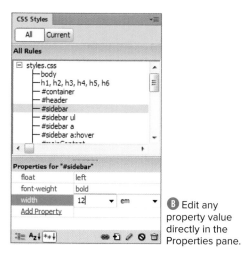

A Right-click any style to reveal the Edit menu.

B Edit any property value directly in the Properties pane.

Modifying a Style

Changing a style is quick and easy. You're already familiar with the CSS Rule definition dialog and the CSS Styles panel, and you can modify styles using either one.

To modify a style with the CSS Rule definition dialog:

1. Open a document. In the CSS Styles panel, click All mode, choose a style, and then do either of the following:

    Right-click the style name and choose Edit **A**.

    or

    Click the Edit Rule button at the lower right of the CSS Styles panel (see **C** in "Anatomy of the CSS Styles Panel").

2. The CSS Rule definition dialog appears. Make changes as desired.

3. Click OK to accept your changes.

To modify a style with the CSS Styles panel:

1. Open a document. In the CSS Styles panel, choose a style in either All or Current mode. Properties for the selected style appear in the Properties pane.

2. Click a value in the Properties pane. An editable field appears **B**.

3. Change as desired, and press Enter (Return) to complete your changes.

Working with Related Files

The vast majority of Web pages you see these days aren't standalone HTML files. Rather, they are HTML files with links to other, related files, including CSS style sheets; external JavaScript files; server-side include (SSI) files; and sometimes even XML and other HTML files.

In pre-CS4 versions of Dreamweaver, it was sometimes difficult to find and get to these related files when you were working on a page. You would have to check the page's source code in Code view or fiddle around in the CSS Styles panel to track down the name of the external style sheets.

Dreamweaver CS4 added the Related Files bar ⓐ at the top of the document window, giving you quick, one-click access to related files.

Related files

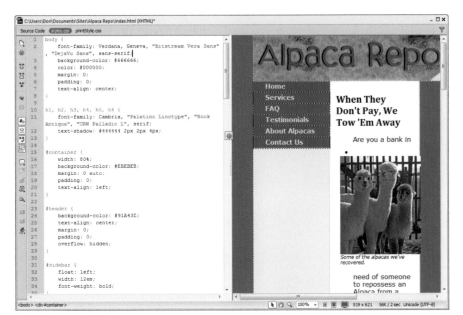

ⓐ The Related Files bar lets you quickly jump to CSS and script files.

ⓑ When you click the name of a style sheet in the Related Files bar, you end up in Split view ready to edit the style sheet.

C You can also see the related files in the View menu.

To use related files:

1. Open a document that uses external files.

   The names of the files appear in the Related Files bar. At the left side of the bar, you will always see the Source Code button, so that you can easily display the source code for the current document after you have opened a related file.

2. Click the name of one of the related files in the Related Files bar.

   Dreamweaver switches to Split view, with the document in the Design View pane, and the related file in the Code View pane **B**.

3. View or edit code in the Code View pane.

   TIP The Related Files feature is enabled by default, but you can turn it off in the General category of Dreamweaver's Preferences panel.

   TIP You can also access related files by choosing View > Related Files and then choosing the file you want from the submenu **C**.

   TIP Dreamweaver will show all linked CSS files in the Related Files bar, even if the CSS files are linked to one another rather than to the current document. In other words, the Related Files bar will show all the style sheets in the cascade. However, it only shows other types of files (such as scripts) when they are directly linked by the current document.

   TIP Related files are especially useful when working with the Code Navigator feature (see "Using the Code Navigator," later in this chapter) and with Dreamweaver's Live view.

Working with Font Groups

Font groups determine which fonts a browser displays on your Web page. A browser uses the first font in the group that is installed on the user's system. If none of the fonts in the group are installed, the browser displays the text as specified by the user's browser preferences.

Ⓐ Use the Edit Font List dialog to create, modify, or remove font groups.

To modify a font group:

1. Open a document in Dreamweaver.

2. Choose Format > Font > Edit Font List.

   or

   Choose Edit Font List from the Font pop-up menu in the Property inspector.

   The Edit Font List dialog appears Ⓐ and displays three categories of information:

   - **Font list:** Displays current font groups.

   - **Chosen fonts:** Displays fonts in the chosen group.

   - **Available fonts:** Displays all the fonts available on your system. The font selected is displayed in the text field below.

Fonts, Browsers, and Operating Systems

Not all computers have the same fonts. For example, a common sans serif font on Windows systems is Arial. A similar sans serif font on Macintosh systems is Helvetica. Many Linux systems have Helvetica, but not all.

But don't assume that you can make generalizations just based on operating system; different versions of operating systems can come with different fonts. And on top of that, different browsers (even on the same operating system) can ship with different defaults for serif and sans serif fonts. All these systems have *some* default fonts, however.

When choosing font groups, select fonts that share similar characteristics and try to cover all the bases in terms of operating systems. Then, add either the generic serif or sans serif choice at the end, just in case none of your preferred choices are available.

Why add a font you don't even have to your font group? One reason is that you expect a lot of your viewers to have a particular font (even though you don't have it). For example, if you are developing pages for a corporate client for use in its intranet, your client may ask for a particular font that is installed on all of the company's machines.

3. Do any of the following:

   ‣ To add or remove fonts from a font group, select the font and click the arrow buttons between the Chosen fonts and Available fonts lists.

   ‣ To add or remove a font group, select it and click the plus (+) or minus (–) button at the top left of the dialog.

   ‣ To add the name of a font that is not installed on your system, type the font name in the text field below the Available fonts list and click the left-facing arrow button to add it to the group.

   ‣ To move a font group up or down in the list, select it from the Font list box and then click the arrow buttons at the top right of the dialog.

4. Click OK to accept your changes.

TIP To avoid surprises, it's good practice to stick with the commonly available fonts for most text. If you really need to use a fancy, decorative font for short bits of text, you may be better off making an image of the text and placing it as a graphic.

TIP We would love to add something here like "You can be assured that people with *this* version of *this* browser on *this* operating system will have *these* fonts"—but we can't. New browser versions get shipped that don't include the same fonts the older versions did. The same goes for operating systems. And then, of course, people can always delete or disable their existing fonts. The font groups that ship with Dreamweaver, as a general rule, are dependable. And of course, always end your font list with either serif or sans serif as fallbacks for best results.

TIP There's one exception to that previous caveat: Web fonts, which are covered in the next task.

Using Web Fonts

One of the big constrictions on the freedom of Web designers has always been the limited range of fonts they could use on pages. Because there are so many browsers running on so many different platforms, designers were more or less forced to use a very restricted set of fonts (often known as Web-safe fonts) that were most likely to appear on Windows, Mac, Linux, and mobile devices. Microsoft's set of Web-safe fonts, including Arial, Verdana, Times New Roman, and Trebuchet, gained widespread use. They're fine, but they're *boring*.

Once again, CSS3 comes to the rescue. The **@font-face** rule allows you to use non-Web-safe fonts by defining the location of a font resource, which can be either local to your machine or external. As of CS 5.5, Dreamweaver supports **@font-face**, and Google now makes a wide selection of attractive fonts available at **www.google.com/webfonts**. At that site, you can create a *collection* of one or more fonts and then either download the collection for use on your own Web server or, even better, use Google-provided code to link to the fonts, which are then served on the fly by Google with minimal impact on page-loading time. Google provides linking code in your choice of HTML, CSS, or JavaScript.

To show you how easy it is to use Web fonts, we've created a simple example based on *Alice's Adventures in Wonderland*. It shows part of a famous conversation between Alice and the White Queen, with different fonts used for each character's dialogue . First, we chose two fonts from Google and used their CSS code as the basis of our CSS style sheet. Then we applied new styles to our text, with one font for each of the two speakers. The following steps explain how the process is done.

Ⓐ In this example, we styled Alice and the White Queen's dialogue differently by using Web fonts.

B Pick two fonts you like, and click Use.

To use Web fonts:

1. Go to Google's Web fonts site, choose the fonts you want to use, and add them to a collection (we picked "Over the Rainbow" and "Redressed"). When you're done, click the Use button to get to the code page **B**.

2. On that page, you have three choices: Standard, **@import**, and JavaScript. We think the simplest is **@import**, so that's what we'll use here. Copy that line of CSS **C**.

continues on next page

C Copy the **@import** line of CSS to paste into your local CSS file.

3. In Dreamweaver, use the Related Files bar to open your CSS file and paste in the **@import** rule you just copied **D**. Save the CSS file and switch back to your Web page; you'll notice that the CSS Styles panel now contains two new rules: one **@font-face** for each of the two fonts we just added **E**.

4. From the CSS Styles panel, select the **.alice class**. In the Properties pane, add the **font-family** property with a value of **Over the Rainbow** (or the equivalent for whatever font you chose) **F**.

D Our CSS file after we added **@import**.

E And suddenly, we've got two **@font-face** rules, bringing in our new fonts.

F To use these new fonts, just type their names into the CSS Styles panel.

CSS Styles

All | Current

All Rules

- alice.css
  - css?family=Redressed|Over+the+Rainbow
    - @font-face
    - @font-face
  - .alice
  - .leftimage
  - .queen

Properties for ".queen"

font-size	24px
font-family	Redressed
Add Property	

G We're nearly done when the queen has her new font.

Alice laughed "There's no use trying," she said "One can't believe impossible things."

"I dare say you haven't had much practice," said the queen. "When I was your age, I always did it for half an hour a day. Why, sometimes I've believed as many as six impossible things before breakfast."

H Switch to Live view, and see your fonts in action.

5. Now, select the `.queen class`, and add a **font-family** property with a value of **Redressed** **G**.

6. At this point, you may be wondering why your Web page still looks the same—just switch into Live view, and you'll see your new fonts appear **H**.

TIP You don't have to use Google to serve your fonts—but why not? They almost definitely have faster download speeds than your server, and there's a slight chance that users may have already downloaded your particular font—both of which make your site appear snappier and more responsive.

TIP Wish you had a wider variety of fonts than just the ones from Google? Here are two more popular resources: Font Squirrel (`www.fontsquirrel.com`) and Typekit (`www.typekit.com`). And given that Adobe recently bought the latter, we won't be surprised to see it integrated into a future version of Dreamweaver.

TIP We're sure *you* know this, so this tip is just for other people: Google has a tendency to change the functionality of their Web sites at the drop of a hat. And if that hat does drop, you might not see screens exactly like the ones in **B** and **C**—but they should be close enough for you to get the idea.

The Not-So-Helpful GUI

You may have noticed that Dreamweaver has a Modify > Web Fonts menu item that brings up the Web Fonts Manager and Add Web Font dialogs ①. We tested it while writing this section, and we found it harder to use than the method we describe in the previous section. Similarly, in the Advanced Settings panel of the Site Setup dialog, you'll find a Web Fonts category where you can set a Web fonts folder ①. We don't recommend that you use that, either—if you do, it makes Dreamweaver act in confusing ways and gives you less flexibility. And worse, once you add it, you can't remove it.

Of course, these are issues that Adobe can choose to address at any time, so keep an eye out for updates.

① The Web Fonts Manager and Add Web Font dialogs. We don't think they're quite ready for prime time.

① Until Adobe says otherwise, this demo site will always have a Web Fonts folder.

If you answered yes to either of these
yo_____t
se_____

Lo_____u
ad_____p
lu_____a
no_____a
pu_____m

Code Navigator indicator

A Click the Code Navigator indicator to open the
Code Navigator window.

Using the Code Navigator

One of the challenges of working with
modern sites is that sometimes it can be
difficult to figure out which of the linked
style sheets or script files is actually being
applied to a given element on your page.
Sure, you can use the Property inspector
or the CSS Styles panel to get the name
of the style that is applied to the element,
but that style could be being modified
by another style sheet elsewhere in the
cascade. What you need is a tool that
shows all of the style sheets and scripts
that are affecting your selection and that
then allows you to easily make changes
to those styles and scripts. That's what the
Code Navigator does.

To use the Code Navigator:

1. Point at the element on your page
   that you want to inspect, then Alt-click
   (Cmd-Opt-click).

   or

   Press Ctrl-Alt-N (Cmd-Opt-N).

   or

   Right-click the selection or a tag in the
   tag selector, and then choose Code
   Navigator.

   or

   Choose View > Code Navigator.

   or

   Click the Code Navigator indicator that
   appears near where you last clicked in
   the document when Dreamweaver has
   been idle for a few seconds **A**.

   continues on next page

The Code Navigator window appears  showing you the script and CSS files associated with the selection. For CSS styles, indented under the name of each style sheet are the names of the CSS rules that apply to the selection.

2. To jump directly to a particular rule, click its name in the Code Navigator window.

   The Dreamweaver window changes to Split view and places the insertion point in the Code View pane ready to edit the style rule you chose.

   or

   To view the properties defined in each of the rules shown in the Code Navigator, hover the cursor over a rule's name. After a moment, a tool tip appears showing you the properties 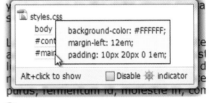.

3. If you ended up in the Code View pane in step 2, edit the style rule. If all you wanted to do was view the rules and properties for the selection, press Esc or click elsewhere in the document to dismiss the Code Navigator window.

TIP You can also invoke the Code Navigator in Code view by placing the insertion point inside a `<script>` or `<link>` tag, or inside a text block that is being styled by CSS, and then clicking the Code Navigator button on the Coding toolbar. See Chapter 17 for more information about working in Code view.

TIP The Code Navigator is incredibly useful, but the Code Navigator *indicator* (Ⓐ) is actually pretty annoying, because it pops up whenever you pause your work. You can (and probably will) turn off the indicator by selecting the "Disable <Code Navigator symbol> indicator" check box at the bottom of the Code Navigator window. You can always bring up the Code Navigator manually, as discussed in step 1.

Ⓑ The Code Navigator window shows the different style sheets associated with the element you selected and also shows which particular rules affect the element.

Ⓒ Hovering over a CSS rule reveals the rule's properties

Using Styles for Layout

In Chapter 7, you saw how to use CSS (Cascading Style Sheets) to style text. CSS can do a whole lot more than just make your words look pretty—style sheets can also be used to lay out the elements on your page.

This chapter covers creating pages using Dreamweaver's CSS layouts, including how to modify them to match your designs.

CSS Layout Basics

When CSS first started becoming popular (that is, when enough browsers supported it consistently), its primary use was for styling text, and Web designers were thrilled to say goodbye to the **font** tag. Besides styling text, it's also possible to use CSS to define how your page is laid out, and thankfully, modern browsers now have sufficient market share that CSS layouts are standard.

The box model

When you lay out a page using CSS, you're using the *box model*—that is, you're creating boxes (almost always done by adding a **div**) and laying them out on your pages. Each box contains several elements 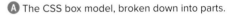: margin, border, padding, and content. Using CSS, you can set rules for each element. If you want, you can (for example) set different rules for the top, right, bottom, and left sides of an element.

Let's say that you want to put a line above and below your text. You can set the border around your text (that is, to the tag that contains your text) to **1px black solid** just for the top and bottom. If you don't set the other sides, they'll be set to 0 by default.

Margin   *Border*   *Padding*   *Content*

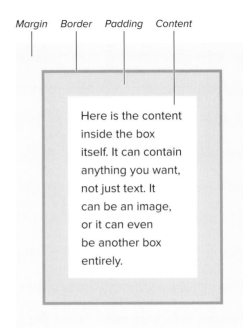

Here is the content inside the box itself. It can contain anything you want, not just text. It can be an image, or it can even be another box entirely.

Ⓐ The CSS box model, broken down into parts.

Source Code styles.css* printStyle.css

```
ID:         header
Class:
Tag:        div
Float:
Position:   absolute
Top:        0px
Right:
Bottom:
Left:
Width:      960px
Height:
Overflow:   hidden (double-click to edit)
```

B An example of an absolutely positioned box with set width.

Positioning your boxes

When you've created boxes on your page, you'll want to place them. To do that, you need to understand two new concepts: *position* and *float*.

The position of a box can be *static, relative, inherit, absolute,* or *fixed* **B**.

- **Static:** The simplest position is static; it just means that the box ends up wherever it would normally end up, all on its own. Any left or top offsets you give it are ignored.

- **Relative:** The next simplest is relative, which is just like static except that you can set its left and top positions.

- **Inherit:** Inherit is used when you want a box to automatically inherit the properties of its parent (that is, its container). Wherever that box happens to be, it just takes on the position rules based on its container.

- **Absolute:** Absolute and fixed are similar in that you can specify exactly where on your page you want the box to appear. The difference between the two involves their frame of reference: an absolutely positioned box is positioned in reference to its container. If you have an absolutely positioned box placed 100 pixels from the top of a page, and another absolutely positioned box inside that box that is also set to be 100 pixels down, the interior box will be 200 pixels down, not 100—because its frame of reference is to the box that it's inside.

- **Fixed:** Fixed positioning, on the other hand, is based on the page itself. If you set a box to be fixed at 100 pixels down, it will always be there, even if you scroll the page. When you scroll, that box will move down with you so that it's always 100 pixels down from the top of the visible page.

Floating your boxes

Alternatively, a box can be set to float, such that its contents stick to one side or the other of its containing element . The values for float are *left*, *right*, *none*, and *inherit*.

- **Left:** A box that is floated to the left causes everything else on the page (everything that isn't explicitly told to be somewhere else, that is) to wrap around it to the right.

- **Right:** A box floated to the right causes everything else to wrap around it on the left.

- **None:** This is the default, but it's sometimes useful to be able to explicitly tell a box not to float (usually when trying to work around browser bugs).

- **Inherit:** If you want a box to inherit the float value of its container, just set float to inherit.

TIP All browsers released in the last several years handle positioning and floating boxes well. Older browsers may have varying degrees of difficulty with these concepts. As always, we recommend testing your site in as many browsers (and versions and platforms) as possible. Adobe's BrowserLab online service is useful if, like most of us, you don't have your own computer lab filled with test machines.

TIP The information about the box model here is just a quick and dirty definition. Many pages (and some entire books) have been written on the intricacies of the box model.

C This **div** (and the navigation area it contains) is floated to the left.

Just Say No to Absolute Positioning

Once upon a time, it was difficult to make a Web page look just the way you wanted it to, because browsers had very little support for layout. Despite the poor browser support, Dreamweaver worked hard to make layout with precise positioning possible through what it (in pre-CS4 versions) called *layers* and now calls *absolutely positioned elements*, or more commonly, *AP elements*.

Given Dreamweaver's capabilities and the commonly used browsers, AP elements are, in our opinion, obsolete. We might seem to be coming off a little heavy-handed here, but it's from experience: don't use AP elements. Just don't. If you have a site that uses AP elements, it's worth taking the time to carefully convert it to use a block-positioned layout with **div**s.

AP elements, along with converting AP elements to tables and vice versa, are remnants of an older, sadder time. Dreamweaver leaves them in for historical reasons, but they're the wrong way to go.

Using the Included Layouts

Initially, you might think that it's difficult to get started using CSS for layout, but fortunately, Dreamweaver has included CSS layouts to make getting started as easy as can be. These files are flexible, professionally developed templates that make a great starting point.

To use the included layouts:

1. From Dreamweaver's menu, choose File > New. The New Document dialog appears .

continues on next page

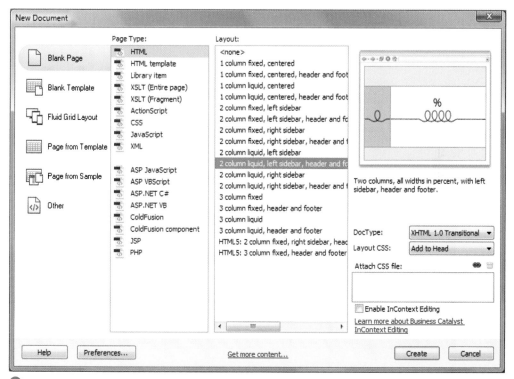

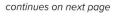 The familiar New Document dialog contains handy CSS-based page designs to get you started. Look at the preview column to decide which of the designs you want to use as the basis for your page.

2. If it wasn't chosen by default, select the category Blank Page, and select HTML from the Page Type menu. You should see 18 designs listed in the center column. Choose any of these to see a preview in the right column. Directly below the preview is a short description of the design.

3. If you see a design you like, click Create. A new, untitled Dreamweaver document opens in the chosen design **B**. You now have a template for your site that's entirely CSS-based. You can modify the page content and its styles.

4. Save the new layout by choosing File > Save or by pressing Ctrl-S (Cmd-S).

TIP Even if none of the included design files suit your taste, take a look at them and check out how they work. They're a good way to learn how to use **CSS** to lay out a page.

TIP When creating a new page based on an included layout, you're given the option of putting the required **CSS** in the head of the document, in a new file, or in an existing file. When you put your site online, your **CSS** should be in an external file, but it's easier to test and debug when it's in the head of the document. If you decide to start with it in the head, you'll want to check out Chapter 9, which covers moving internal styles to an external file.

TIP Don't forget to add a title to your page in the Title field of the Document toolbar.

TIP If you previously used a much older version of Dreamweaver, you might be wondering where some of its included layouts went. The answer is that while it was great that there were so many options, the sheer number of them (elastic, fixed, liquid, hybrid, and so on) ended up confusing people. Some of them, sadly, were so complex that they were brittle—that is, they could break when new browser versions shipped. Back in CS5, Adobe pruned the list, keeping only those that are commonly used and rock solid. They also rewrote the templates to use cleaner code and to include instructions in the layouts that make it easier for you to understand how the different parts of the layouts work.

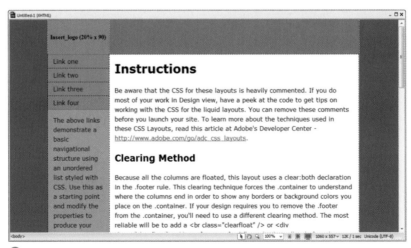

B Here's your new page, ready to receive your content.

Laying Out Your Page

Here's where things get interesting: now that you've got the theory, it's time to put it into practice. With the included CSS layouts, it's straightforward.

Before you start laying out your page, you need to think about what you want on that page and where you want it to go. As discussed in Chapter 2, the best way to do that is with pencil and paper. That should tell you what styles you'll need—for instance, a header, footer, content area, and navigation area. Once you have a design in mind, look through the included CSS layouts to see which best fits your idea .

Now you're ready to start. In this case, we'll start with the 2-column liquid layout, with a left sidebar, header, and footer . The *liquid* part of the name means that the page content expands and contracts to fit the width of the browser window.

Ⓐ You'll want to have a plan before you start laying out your page; here's our planned design.

Ⓑ Start by selecting a new blank page with a new layout.

To lay out your page:

1. Choose the "2-column liquid, left sidebar, header and footer" layout, and Dreamweaver gives you a bare-bones page to start 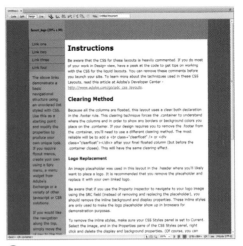.

2. Almost all your work will be done in the CSS Styles panel **D**. Here the **body** styles are all fine except for the background color—we want it to be gray instead of the default blue, so we changed its value to **#666666**.

3. Next is the **.container** rule, which applies to the one large **div** that contains all the content on the page. Again, we only want to change the background color; now it will be a lighter shade of gray, **#EBEBEB** **E**.

C This page doesn't just contain dummy text—it also contains many helpful tips.

D Start your new page by changing the styles for the **body** tag.

E Next, change the styles for the **class** named **.container**.

F The **.content** style needs a white background, which we added here.

4. The **.content** area is the section that will contain (as you might guess) the bulk of the page content. For easy readability, we want its background to be **#FFFFFF** (that is, white). This section doesn't have a default background color, so we have to add it **F**.

5. The default page assigned a background color to the sidebar, which we don't want. To remove the default, select the **background-color** property (found under **.sidebar1**) and click the trashcan icon **G**.

6. Our page header has two parts: the foreground banner and the background color. The banner image is named **header.jpg**, and it simply needs to be dragged into the **.header div**. Next, delete the dummy logo image placeholder that came with the layout, and change the blue background to a green that blends into the header graphic (**#91A43D**). And finally, add a **text-align** style declaration with a value of **center** to center the banner horizontally within the header area **H**.

7. All that's left to change is the background color of **.footer** to another shade of gray, **#DDDDDD** **I**.

G Click the trashcan icon in the CSS Styles panel to delete a property and its value.

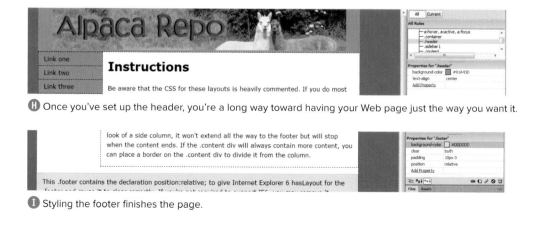

H Once you've set up the header, you're a long way toward having your Web page just the way you want it.

I Styling the footer finishes the page.

TIP Setting the background color for `.sidebar1` by letting the background color for `.container` show through is a technique called faux columns. To produce the desired effect (a sidebar with a background color going from the header to the footer), each page needs to have enough content so that the main content area is longer than the sidebar's content. Thankfully, our navigation needs here are minimal enough that that isn't a problem.

TIP You don't really need to know that white is #FFFFFF—you can just select the color you want from the color well in the panel.

Using CSS Shorthand

Chapter 7 mentioned CSS shorthand properties, and here you can see them in action.

If you're used to colors in HTML always having six hexadecimal digits, you may initially be confused when you see values like **#03F** or **#C96**. Three-digit color values are just shorthand; to translate one to its six character version, just double each digit—for instance, the colors just mentioned are actually **#0033FF** and **#CC9966**, respectively. Keep in mind, though, that you can only use the three-digit version when all the digits are doubled; there are no shorthand versions of **#91A43D** or **#EBEBEB**.

Properties for "ul.nav"	
border-top	1px solid #EBEBEB
list-style	none
margin-bottom	15px
Add Property	

A Here you've changed the standard **ul.nav** rule.

Properties for "ul.nav a, ul.nav a:visited"	
background-color	#336666
border-bottom	1px #EBEBEB solid
color	#EBEBEB
display	block
font-weight	bold
padding	5px 5px 5px 15px
text-decoration	none
Add Property	

B Once you've changed the rule for your links, you can see how the navigation will look.

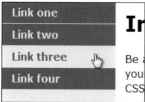

C The almost-completed navigation section before styling the rollovers.

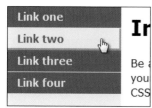

D Swapping the color scheme from gray on green to green on gray means you're almost there.

E Adding a border to the right and bottom makes your links look like 3D buttons.

Laying Out Your Navigation

The previous task laid out the entire page except for one small section: the navigation menu. While the menu is only a small section of the Web page, it's a vitally important part to your visitors. Here's how to personalize it to match the rest of your design.

1. Start by removing the one unwanted style rule: the **border-bottom** on the **ul.nav li** rule.

2. The only change the **ul.nav** rule needs is to the top border's color, and that's done by changing the value of **border-top** to **1px solid #EBEBEB** **A**.

3. The changes to the **ul.nav a, ul.nav a:visited** rule are a little more complex. Start by changing **color** to **#EBEBEB** and **background-color** to **#336666**. Then add two new properties: **font-weight**, which should be set to **bold**; and **border-bottom**, which should be set to **1px #EBEBEB solid** **B**.

4. You may think you're done **C**, but you still need to handle rollovers. That's where users get feedback so they know where to click.

   The rule to change is **ul.nav a:hover, ul.nav a:active, ul.nav a:focus**. Change the color to **#336666** and the background color to **#EBEBEB**: the same colors you used in the last step, just reversed. When you roll the cursor over a link, it will go from gray text on a green background to green on gray **D**.

5. Make the links look like buttons by setting their padding and border values **E**. To achieve the desired button-like effect, you have to do a little bit of calculating.

continues on next page

For each side of the button, add together the width of the padding and the width of the border for the non-hovering (inactive) version of the button. Then for the hover state, the width of the padding added to the width of the border must be the same sum as the non-hover version.

In this example, look at the bottom of any navigation link: when inactive, the padding is **5px** and the border is **1px**, for a total of 6 pixels. So when you're hovering, the sum of the padding and the border must also be 6 pixels—if not, the button will appear to jump around. With the border and the padding each set to **3px**, you get the effect you want.

Now look at the right side. The inactive state has **5px** padding and no border, for a sum of 5 pixels. To get a nice even button when hovering, set the right border to **3px**, which means the padding needs to be **2px**.

Now that you have the values you need, all you have to do is add them to the **ul.nav a:hover, ul.nav a:active, ul.nav a:focus** rule. Set both the **border-bottom** and **border-right** properties to **3px #999999 solid**. And finally, add **padding-bottom** with a value of **3px** and **padding-right** with a value of **2px** ⑤.

Don't forget that you can inspect any element on the page by Alt-clicking (Opt-clicking) to show the Code Navigator, including the rules that apply to that element. Hovering over a rule, as in ⑥, shows all the declarations that make up the rule. The tool tip also shows the values (if any) of float, position, top, right, bottom, left, width, height, and overflow. See Chapter 7 for more about using the Code Navigator.

⑤ Here you've set the necessary properties to make the rollover happen.

⑥ Hovering over a style in the Code Navigator gives you useful information about that element.

TIP If you're trying to find the padding width for a particular side, you might be thrown off by padding having a value of 5px 5px 5px 15px—which is the one you want? When you see four values like this in CSS, they're always in the order top, right, bottom, left (a clockwise direction). So with that value, the bottom and right sides each have 5 pixels of padding.

TIP Not seeing the rollovers? Turn on Live view, which shows your site the way a browser would display it. And if you're trying to track down a layout issue and want the hover effect even when you aren't actually hovering, choose View > Style Rendering > Show :hover Styles—but don't forget to set it back again afterwards.

Modifying Your Navigation

You have your page now just the way you want it—or so you think. After working with it, you realize that the left sidebar needs to be used for other purposes, and you want the navigation horizontally along the top. Back to the drawing board to start all over again, right? Nope; here's where the power of CSS really comes through.

To modify your navigation:

1. Using the tag selector, select **ul.nav** , and then drag the selection to just after the header and before the sidebar. This can be a little tricky, so use Edit > Undo until you get it right. The result should look like **B**. But don't panic because of the way it looks—you're not done yet.

continues on next page

A Select the **ul.nav** element from the tag selector, and then carefully move it to its new home.

B Now the navigation is above the content, but every button goes clear across the page.

2. Now you just need to modify the CSS, so you start by changing the **ul.nav** rule **C**:

   - ▸ Delete the **margin-bottom** and **border-top** properties.
   - ▸ Add the property **height** with a value of **1.8em**.
   - ▸ Add the property **background-color** with a value of **#336666**.
   - ▸ Add the **border-left** and **border-bottom** properties with values of **1px #EBEBEB solid**.
   - ▸ Add the property **padding-bottom** with a value of **3px**.

3. Make these changes to the **ul.nav a, ul.nav a:visited** rule **D**:

   - ▸ Delete the **border-bottom** property.
   - ▸ Add the property **float** set to **left**.
   - ▸ Add the property **border-right** with a value of **1px #EBEBEB solid**.
   - ▸ Change the width of the **padding-bottom** property from **5px** to **3px**.
   - ▸ Add the property **width** set to **22%**.

   As shown in **E**, the navigation has now taken shape. Floating each link to the left caused them to display in a single horizontal line.

Properties for "ul.nav"	
list-style	none
height	1.8em
background-color	■ #336666
border-left	1px #EBEBEB solid
border-bottom	1px #EBEBEB solid
padding-bottom	3px
Add Property	

C A few modifications to the **ul.nav** rule fix some of the issues.

Properties for "ul.nav a, ul.nav a:visited"	
background-color	■ #336666
color	□ #EBEBEB
display	block
font-weight	bold
padding	5px 5px 3px 15px
text-decoration	none
border-right	1px #EBEBEB solid
float	left
width	22%
Add Property	

D Tweaking the link rule takes you most of the way there.

E Looks good—all that's left to do are the rollovers.

Properties for "ul.nav a:hover, ul.nav a:activ...	
background-color ☐	#EBEBEB
border-bottom	3px #999999 solid
border-right	3px #999999 solid
color ■	#336666
padding-bottom	0px
padding-right	3px
Add Property	

F The rollover rule needs some changes to the right and bottom padding.

4. Make these changes to the **ul.nav a:hover, ul.nav a:active, ul.nav a:focus** rule **F**:

   ▸ Change the **padding-bottom** property from **3px** to **0px**.

   ▸ Change the **padding-right** property from **2px** to **3px**.

   Your menu should now look like **G**, with button-like links spread evenly across the page under the header.

G And here's the finished product.

TIP We gave the buttons a width of 22% to spread them out. You could also have done this by setting the width to a specific pixel size, but using a percentage makes them expand and contract with the rest of the liquid layout. However, you'll need to remember to lower that number if you want to add another navigation button.

TIP We did the same calculation here as in the previous task to make sure that the bottom and right sides appear button-like. The bottom has 3 pixels of padding and no border when inactive, and no padding and a 3-pixel border when active. The right has 5 pixels of padding with a 1-pixel border when inactive, and 3 pixels of padding and a 3-pixel border when active.

TIP You might be wondering if you could have just left out the declaration setting `padding-bottom` to 0px. In this case, no—you need that declaration of zero pixels of padding to explicitly override the three pixels of padding set in the previous step. If you left out the declaration, the browser would use the inherited padding, throwing off your button layout.

Managing Styles

The two previous chapters covered CSS and how it works with your Web pages. After you've gotten the hang of CSS, though, you may find that you're spending too much time trying to figure out which styles affect which sections of the page. Or maybe you'll find that you're trying to keep track of where your styles are (inline? internal? external?) and in what order they apply to your site. Or maybe it'll be that you are testing styles but don't want to change your entire site yet.

No matter what your particular issue, Dreamweaver has made it simple and straightforward to manage moving, duplicating, debugging, and deleting styles.

Renaming Styles

It's a good idea to give styles a descriptive name of your choosing. You may want to rename a style because your site has changed, or maybe you just don't like the style names in the default CSS layouts. Whatever the reason, they should have meaningful names.

To rename a style for a class:

1. In the HTML tab of the Property inspector, choose Rename from the Class pop-up menu **A**. The Rename Style dialog appears **B**.

   or

   In the CSS Styles panel, find and select the rule you want to rename **C**. Right-click the rule name and select Rename Class from the context menu **D**. The Rename Class dialog appears **E**.

A Choose Rename from the Class pop-up menu to give a style a new name.

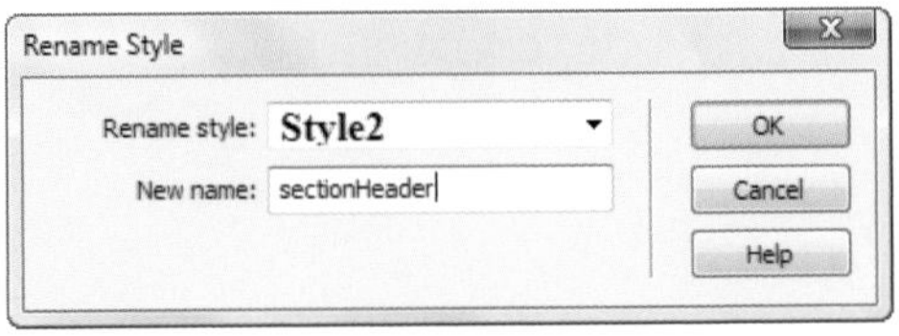

B Type the new name in the field to rename your style.

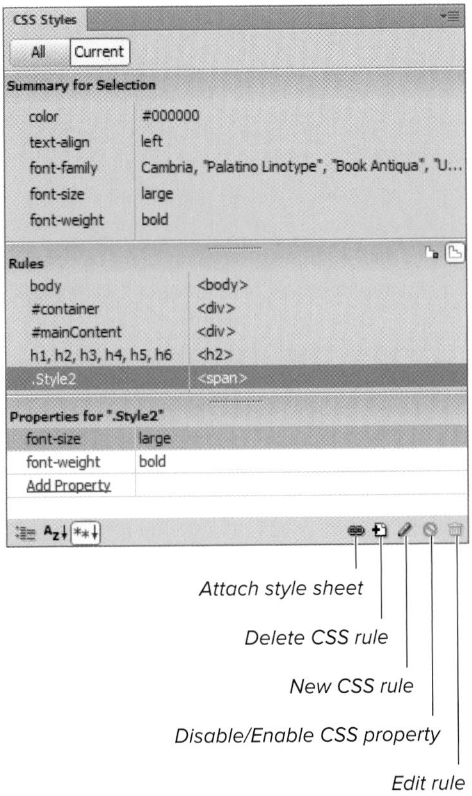

Attach style sheet

Delete CSS rule

New CSS rule

Disable/Enable CSS property

Edit rule

C You can also rename styles from the CSS Styles panel.

Go to Code	
New...	
Edit...	
Duplicate...	
Rename Class...	
Edit Selector	
Move CSS Rules...	
Disable	
Enable All Disabled in Selected Rule	
Delete All Disabled in Selected Rule	
Apply	
Cut	Ctrl+X
Copy	Ctrl+C
Paste	Ctrl+V
Delete	Del
Site	▶
Use External Editor	
Attach Style Sheet...	
Design-time...	
Media Queries...	

D In the CSS Styles panel, choose your style, right-click, and choose Rename Class.

Rename Class

Rename class: **Style2** ▾   OK

New name: [＿＿＿＿＿＿]   Cancel

Help

E They may have different names, but the Rename Style dialog and the Rename Class dialog do the same thing.

Dreamweaver

⚠ This style is defined in an external stylesheet, and may affect multiple documents.

Use Find & Replace to fix the documents that use this style?

Yes   No   Cancel

F If you want, Dreamweaver will update the name everywhere in your site after you rename a style.

2. If the class you want to rename isn't already selected, use the pop-up menu to choose it. Type a name in the New name field, and click OK.

3. If the style you chose is used in multiple places or it's in an external style sheet that can affect multiple pages, you'll be prompted as to whether you want to make this change everywhere **F**. If you want this (you usually will), click Yes.

   If you click Yes, the Find and Replace dialog appears, with the parameters you need to search for and replace already filled in, and with the scope of the search set for your entire site. See the section "Finding and Replacing with a Specific Tag" in Chapter 4 to learn more about using this dialog.

   If you click No, the Find and Replace dialog does not appear, and you will need to make any updates manually.

TIP The two dialogs have different names, but they do identical tasks.

Deleting Styles

When you delete a style from a style sheet, the formatting of any element using that style immediately changes.

To delete a style:

1. Open a document, and in the CSS Styles panel, choose the style name to delete.

2. Click the Delete CSS Rule button in the lower right of the panel. Note that you don't have to click OK or accept anything—it just disappears immediately.

TIP **Even though you've deleted the style, any references to it will still exist in the document. That is, classes and ids aren't removed from your pages when you delete rules that apply to those classes and ids.**

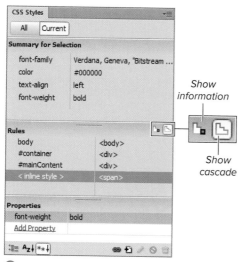

Creating Rules from Inline Styles

Inline styles (first covered back in Chapter 7) are a handy way to test properties to see if using a particular bit of CSS does what you want it to do. However, remember that the main power of CSS is being able to apply it in many places in a document and many documents in a site—and if you're only applying it to a single tag, you're missing out on all that power. So while inline styles are great for quick tests, once your CSS has passed the test, it's time to turn it into a rule.

Show information

Show cascade

Ⓐ To turn an inline style into a rule, first find the `<inline style>` rule in the CSS Styles panel.

Ⓑ One way to convert the style to a rule is with Convert Inline CSS to Rule, found under the Format menu.

Ⓒ The Convert Inline CSS dialog lets you set all the options for your new rule.

To create a rule from an inline style:

1. In your document, click anywhere within the area where the inline style is applied. In the CSS Styles panel, make sure that you're in Current mode and that the Rules pane is visible by clicking the Show cascade button. You should see a rule called `<inline style>` Ⓐ.

2. Right-click the `<inline style>` rule and choose Convert to Rule from the menu.

   or

   Choose Format > CSS Styles > Convert Inline CSS to Rule Ⓑ.

   The Convert Inline CSS dialog appears Ⓒ.

continues on next page

3. The first choice in that dialog is what type of rule you want to end up with D:

   ▸ A new CSS class, where you get to choose the class name.

   ▸ A rule that applies to all tags of the given type; that is, if the inline style is applied to a `<p>` (paragraph) tag, you can apply that style to all paragraphs.

   ▸ A new CSS selector, where the default is a rule based on the location of the inline style.

   The last two are context-sensitive, so your defaults change depending on your inline style selection.

4. Next, you have a choice of creating the new rule in an external style sheet or in the head of the current document. Any currently linked external style sheets will be in the pop-up menu. If you don't have any external style sheets, you can either create one here or put the new rule into the head of the current document (you'll see how to move the internal rule to an external style sheet later in the chapter). Choose an option, click OK, and your new rule will be created.

TIP It's possible for the Rules pane to show more than one style named `<inline style>`, so make sure you're choosing the correct one.

TIP Dreamweaver CS5 added the ability to create a new external style sheet from the Convert Inline CSS dialog. If you want your new rule to be in a new external style sheet, you can either:

Follow the preceding steps to create a new rule, and then in the Convert Inline CSS dialog, enter a name for your new file. A dialog appears telling you it doesn't exist and asking if you want to create it. If you do, click Yes and your new CSS file is created (containing your new CSS rule) and attached to the HTML page.

or

Follow the preceding steps to create a new internal rule, and then follow the steps in "Moving Internal Styles to External," later in this chapter.

or

Follow the steps in the next task, "Creating a New External Style Sheet," and then use the steps in this task to put the new rule into that style sheet.

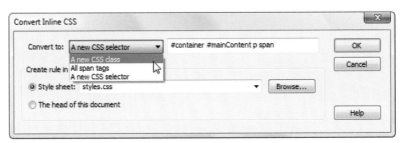

D You can make a new class, a new selector, or a new rule that applies to all instances of a certain tag.

Creating a New External Style Sheet

Up to now, we've covered how to create internal styles, but we also mentioned that internal styles may not always be the right choice. Here's how to create a new external style sheet, either from scratch or using one of the many sample files that are included in Dreamweaver as a starting point.

To create a new external style sheet based on a sample file:

1. From Dreamweaver's menu, choose File > New. The New Document dialog appears.

2. If it wasn't chosen by default, select the category Page from Sample. Under Sample Folder, select CSS Style Sheet to display a list of style sheets in the center column Ⓐ. Choose any of them to see a preview and description in the right column.

continues on next page

Ⓐ Dreamweaver comes with plenty of CSS designs for you to use as starting points.

3. If you see a design you like, click Create. A new untitled style sheet document opens in Code view that contains the rules defined in the style sheet you selected. Save this file with a name that ends in **.css**.

To create a new external style sheet from scratch:

1. Choose File > New. The New Document dialog appears **A**.

2. In the New Document dialog, select Blank Page for the Category, select CSS for the page type, and click Create. A new blank style sheet opens in Code view **B**. Save this file with a name that ends in **.css**.

or

1. With a document open, click the Insert Div Tag button in the Common or Layout category of the Insert panel, and the Insert Div Tag dialog displays **C**. Click New CSS Rule, and the New CSS Rule dialog opens **D**.

B A blank CSS document, ready for you to add your rules.

C Use the Insert Div Tag dialog to open the New CSS Rule dialog.

D Enter the selector information you need for the new rule, and set the Rule Definition pop-up menu to New Style Sheet File.

E If you said you wanted a new style sheet file, here's where it's actually created.

F Now that you've created a new style sheet file, you need to add rules to it.

G The new style sheet appears in the related files at the top of the document window.

2. Enter any **class**, tag, **id**, or pseudo-class selector that you'd like in your new CSS file. Set the Rule Definition pop-up menu to (New Style Sheet File) and click OK. The Save Style Sheet File As dialog appears **E**.

3. Choose a filename that ends in **.css**, and click Save. The CSS Rule Definition dialog appears **F**. Add the rules you want (as described in Chapter 7), click OK, and you'll return to the Insert Div Tag dialog, with your new style sheet (including any rules you set) available as a related file in the bar at the top of the current document **G**.

4. If you created a new style sheet using the Insert Div Tag dialog and don't actually want to insert a new div, click Cancel to dismiss the dialog.

TIP If you've created a new style sheet using the Insert Div Tag dialog, your new style sheet is automatically attached to your document. If you created the new style sheet any other way, you'll have to attach it manually. That's covered in "Attaching a Style Sheet," later in this chapter.

Moving Internal Styles to External

There are a number of reasons why your pages might have internal styles instead of using an external style sheet: possibly they're from an older site (when that was more common), or possibly you used internal styles to test your layout. But now your internal style sheet is ready to live on its own, so your styles need to come out of your Web page and into a stand-alone file, because external style sheets are much easier to maintain and a single sheet can apply to many different HTML pages in your site.

To move styles:

1. Open the Web page that contains the style (or styles) you want to move. In the CSS Styles panel, make sure that you're in All mode. Select the rules that you want to move, right-click, and choose Move CSS Rules from the context menu. The Move To External Style Sheet dialog appears **Ⓐ**.

Ⓐ To move a rule to an external style sheet, bring up the Move To External Style Sheet dialog.

2. If you are moving the rules to an existing external style sheet (the default), choose it from the pop-up menu and click OK. If the sheet you want isn't listed, click Browse, find the sheet in the resulting Find Style Sheet File dialog, and click OK.

or

If you want to move the rules to a new style sheet, click "A new style sheet" and then click OK. You should be prompted with the correct place to save your file. Come up with a good, descriptive name (ending in **.css**) and click Save.

Your rules will be moved to the style sheet, and the style sheet will be attached to the current page (if that's not already the case).

TIP When you moved internal styles to external in versions of Dreamweaver prior to CS3, the styles were only copied, not moved. You no longer have to manually attach the style sheet and then delete the styles from the current document, because Dreamweaver does it all for you.

TIP If your external style sheet already contains any rules with the same name as the rules you're moving, Dreamweaver displays a dialog **B**. You can choose if you want both rules in the style sheet or just the previous version.

B If you're moving a rule that might cause a collision, Dreamweaver warns you about the problem.

Attaching a Style Sheet

It doesn't do you any good to create a style sheet if your Web pages don't know about it. For a Web page to use an external style sheet, that style sheet must be *attached* to the Web page.

To attach a style sheet:

1. Click the Attach Style Sheet icon at the bottom of the CSS Styles panel (see figure **C** in "Renaming Styles").

   or

   Right-click in the CSS Styles panel and choose Attach Style Sheet **A**.

   or

   From the HTML tab of the Property inspector, choose Attach Style Sheet from the Class pop-up menu (see figure **A** in "Renaming Styles").

2. The Attach External Style Sheet dialog appears **B**. Click the Browse button to bring up the Select Style Sheet File dialog **C**. Navigate to an existing style sheet, select it, and click OK.

3. Back in the Attach External Style Sheet dialog, select Add as Link if it isn't already chosen, and click OK to attach the style sheet. If your style sheet includes any rules that affect the active document, you'll see those changes reflected immediately.

A There are at least two ways to attach a style sheet from the CSS Styles panel.

B Choose which style sheet you want to attach to your Web page and how you want to attach it.

C Choose which style sheet file to attach by browsing for it.

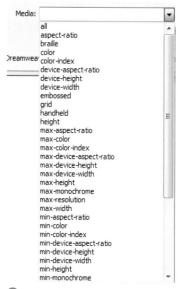

D Media options are set here. For instance, if you want your style sheet to apply only when the page is printed, choose the print media type.

TIP Take a look at the All Rules pane of the CSS Styles panel. Notice that your style sheet is now included, and all of its properties can be viewed.

TIP You're offered a choice of using *link* or *import* to attach your style sheet. Each has its advantages: link, the default choice, works in more browsers, whereas import allows you to nest style sheets (that is, you can attach a style sheet using import, and then that style sheet can include an import of another style sheet, and so on).

TIP You can use both link and import in the same document. That's a handy way to use two style sheets, where the link attaches a bare-bones style sheet and the import attaches a more complex style sheet that very old browsers (such as Netscape 4.*x*) can't handle.

TIP When attaching a style sheet, you're also offered a choice of media in the Attach External Style Sheet dialog. Among the choices included in the Media pop-up menu are all, handheld, print, projection, and screen **D**. It's also acceptable to use no media type at all; in that case, the style sheet applies to all media types. And finally, you can also enter a list of media types (comma-separated) if you want your style sheet to apply to some media types but not others.

TIP If you set the media type for your style sheet, you can test it by choosing View > Style Rendering and picking which media type to view. When you do this, though, remember that few browsers offer full support for media types.

Using Drag-and-Drop Styles

If you've found all the methods so far for dealing with style management to be somewhat complicated, then here's what you've been wishing you could do: drag and drop styles.

Moving styles inside a document

As mentioned in the Chapter 7 sidebar "External, Internal, and Inline: Look Ma, It's the Cascade," where style rules are physically located determines which rules take precedence when there's a conflict. If you have two rules that conflict inside a document (either a Web page or a style sheet) and you want the one that's currently being overridden to dominate, all you have to do is drag that rule below the other.

To move a style inside a document:

1. Open the Web page or style sheet that contains the style (or styles) you want to move. In the CSS Styles panel, make sure that you're in All mode, select the rules that you want to move, and drag them to their new location **Ⓐ**. A blue line (a black line on the Mac) appears showing where the rules will be relocated.

   On the Mac, a ghostly version of the style name moves with the cursor. On Windows, a small document icon appears instead.

2. When you're happy with the new location, release the mouse, and Dreamweaver moves the rules for you.

Ⓐ You can see which style it is you're dragging while you're dragging it.

B On either platform, you can drag multiple style rules at one time.

Moving styles from one document to another

Not only can you move styles inside a document, but you can also move them from document to document—whether the documents are style sheets or Web pages.

To move a style from one document to another:

1. Open a Web page that either links to two style sheets or that contains the style (or styles) and also links to an external style sheet. In the CSS Styles panel, make sure that you're in All mode and that both files are displayed (if no external style sheet is displayed, follow the directions in "Attaching a Style Sheet"). Select the rules that you want to move, and drag them to their new location **B**. A line appears showing where the rules will be relocated.

2. When you're happy with the new location, release the mouse, and Dreamweaver moves the rules for you.

TIP If you want to copy a style rule (that is, you want it to end up in both the original document *and* the target document), hold down the Ctrl (Opt) key while dragging the rules.

TIP If you're moving a style rule into a document that already contains a rule with that name, you'll get a warning dialog like the one in figure **B** in "Moving Internal Styles to External."

Using CSS Inspection

Laying out pages with CSS can be frustrating because it can be difficult to tell which elements are where and why. Thankfully, Dreamweaver has a few clever features that make creating CSS-based layouts much simpler. CSS inspection, added in CS5, is one of the handy ways to tell you just what's going on in a selected area.

CSS inspection works with Live view mode to visually display the box model for an element. Hover over an element on your page, and it displays with an aqua background, yellow margins, lavender padding, and gray borders **A**. But that's not all—as you hover over various parts of your document, the CSS Styles panel (in Current mode) dynamically updates to display the rules currently in effect.

Turning on Inspect mode:

Click the Live view button and then the Inspect button in the Document toolbar to enable both CSS inspection and Live view **B**.

or

Choose View > Inspect to enable both CSS inspection and Live view.

or

Press Alt-Shift-F11 (Opt-Shift-F11) to enable both CSS inspection and Live view.

or

While in Live view mode, right-click the document and choose Inspect from the context menu **C**.

A Inspecting an element shows the margins, padding, and borders.

B Click the Live View button, and the Inspect Mode button appears.

C When in Live view, you can inspect any element by right-clicking it.

TIP To leave both Inspect mode and Live view, just click the Live View button. You can't be in Inspect mode if you aren't also in Live view.

TIP Dreamweaver has definite opinions about how you ought to work with CSS inspection, and it says so every time you turn it on **D**. If you click More Info, you'll see **E**, which says that if you're in CSS Inspect mode, you should also be in Split view with Live Code view on, and that the CSS Styles panel should display Current mode. If you get tired of seeing this, just select "Don't show me this message again."

Modifying styles with CSS inspection:

1. While in Inspect mode, hover over any section of your document **A** to display the box model for that element.

2. If you have a problem with how an element displays, click the element, *freezing* Inspect mode. When CSS inspection is frozen, the colors remain visible and don't change when you move the cursor.

3. In the CSS Styles panel, change a rule, and the colored borders around the element update to match your change.

4. Click anywhere in your document to get rid of the colors.

ⓘ Inspect mode is most useful with certain workspace settings. Switch now | More Info...

D Dreamweaver wants you to know the right way to use Inspect mode.

Dreamweaver

ⓘ Inspect mode works best with the following:
* CSS Styles panel open in Current mode
* Enable Split Code/Live View
* Enable Live Code

Switch to these settings?

☐ Don't show me this message again.

[Switch] [Cancel]

E But if you don't want to see this suggestion again, you can turn it off.

Using the Visual Aids

If you've tried CSS Inspection and wished you could apply it to an entire page, you want what Dreamweaver refers to as *visual aids*.

 shows our example CSS-based page with all visual aids turned off, which is fine. But if we had a problem, it would be difficult to tell where each **div** begins and ends. That's where the visual aids shine.

The Visual Aids menu is found in the Document toolbar. Although it looks like a button, that little downward facing arrow means that it's actually a pop-up menu. If you click it, you'll see the options shown in Ⓑ. Or, you can choose View > Visual Aids and then select any of the submenu options Ⓒ.

To turn each visual aid on or off, choose it from the menu to toggle its check mark, or you can choose Hide All (Ctrl-Shift-I or Cmd-Shift-I) to turn them all off temporarily. For day-to-day use, we keep CSS Layout Backgrounds turned off and CSS Layout Box Model and CSS Layout Outlines turned on.

Ⓐ Here's our standard page.

Ⓑ Here's the Visual Aids menu in the Document toolbar.

Ⓒ You can also access the Visual Aids menu via the menu bar.

D CSS layout backgrounds are gaudy but useful.

E The CSS Layout Box Model option shows you the exact limits of the currently selected element.

F CSS layout outlines give you a subtle way of telling your elements apart.

Here's a rundown of the CSS-related items in these menus:

- **CSS Layout Backgrounds:** Put on your sunglasses and turn on CSS Layout Backgrounds **D**. With this aid, Dreamweaver assigns a different background color for every layout block. If you've already set a background color, that will go away, as will background images—note that you can see the header logo, but you can't see the header background color.

   Dreamweaver's documentation describes the color choices as "visually distinctive," but we prefer to not beat around the bush: we just call them loud and bright. Sorry, but there's no way to change the color choices. On the other hand, the garishness makes it very clear which **div** is which.

- **CSS Layout Box Model:** You've seen the Layout Box Model aid **E** used previously. When enabled, it shows just the selected element, including its margin, borders, and padding. Here, the **a** tag has varying amounts of padding on each side. When this visual aid is enabled, each is shown visually on the document along with the dimensions of the element.

- **CSS Layout Outlines:** The CSS Layout Outlines option simply puts a dashed line around the border of each layout block **F**. It can be tricky to see what your borders are set to when this is on, and you should also keep in mind that the dashed line includes the padding but excludes the margins.

Experimenting with CSS Enable/Disable

Another way to debug CSS is to enable and disable rules. Adobe made this easy to do in CS5 with CSS Enable/Disable, which is available on the CSS Styles panel.

To use CSS Enable/Disable:

1. In the Properties pane of the CSS Styles panel, move your cursor just to the left of a property name. You should see a gray Disable CSS Property icon appear (it looks like the universal sign for "No": the circle with the diagonal slash through it) **A**. Click the icon, which will turn it red. If you are in Current mode, a red Disable CSS Property icon also appears next to the property name in the Summary pane **B**.

   or

   In the Properties pane of the CSS Styles panel, select a property. Underneath the Properties pane, in the bottom part of the panel on the right side, click the gray Disable button **C**, which turns the CSS Property icon to the left of the property red. If you are in Current mode, a red Disable CSS Property icon also appears next to the property name in the Summary pane.

   or

   With the CSS Styles panel in Current mode, find a property in the Summary pane that you want to disable. Click the gray Disable CSS Property icon to its left, which turns it red. In the Properties pane, the selected property will also display the red Disable CSS Property icon.

   or

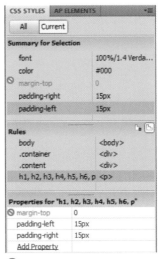

A Hover just to the left of a property, and the Disable CSS Property icon appears.

B Disabling in either pane shows the result in both.

C You can also disable a property via the button at the bottom of the CSS Properties pane.

TIP If you select a property or disable a property from the Summary pane, the Rules and Properties panes update to show the affected rule.

TIP If the open document is an HTML file in Code or Split view, and the rule you disabled is in an external CSS file, the commented-out code doesn't automatically display.

TIP Disabled rules aren't only disabled within Dreamweaver. If you disable a rule, save the file, and then upload your changes to the live server, the rule stays disabled until you enable it again. If you want similar functionality that only applies while testing, use design-time style sheets (described in the next task) instead.

With the CSS Styles panel in Current mode, find a property in the Summary pane that you want to disable. Select the property, click the gray Disable button under the Properties pane, and the red Disable CSS Property icon appears next to the property name. In the Properties pane, the selected property will also display the red Disable CSS Property icon.

2. If your document is open in Design view, Dreamweaver displays the page without that rule. If you are in Code view, Dreamweaver scrolls the source to show the rule commented out. If you're in Split view, you'll see both **D**.

3. To re-enable a disabled rule, click the red Disable CSS Property icon in either the Properties pane or the Summary pane **E**.

D Disable rules in the CSS Styles panel, and you'll see changes in both the page display and the CSS source code.

E To re-enable a property, simply toggle the icon.

Using Design-Time Style Sheets

It's common when working with CSS-based layouts to want something to display in a particular way while you're designing, but *only* while you're designing—that is, during *design time*. You can tell Dreamweaver to use certain style sheets only at design time, and even to turn off certain style sheets only at design time.

As with the previous visual aids, you wouldn't want your real Web site to look like that, but it's handy while trying to do those last few tweaks or track down a problem. If you want something that Dreamweaver's built-in visual aids don't provide, design-time style sheets allow you to create your own.

To show a design-time style sheet:

1. Create and save a new style sheet containing the style rules that should display only inside Dreamweaver.  shows an example that contains two simple rules: **p** is set to **display:block**, and **h1** gets a background color of **orange**. See the "CSS Layout Blocks" sidebar for an explanation of why you'd want to modify the **p** tag.

2. To choose a design-time style sheet, either choose Format > CSS Styles > Design-time **B** or right-click inside the CSS Styles panel and choose Design-time from the context menu **C**. The Design-Time Style Sheets dialog appears **D**.

A This very simple style sheet gives you extra information in Dreamweaver.

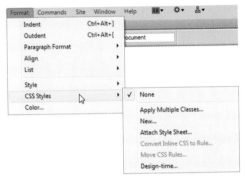

B Design-time style sheets can be chosen from the Format menu.

C Or they can be chosen from the CSS panel.

D But either way, you end up at the Design-Time Style Sheets dialog.

E The Select File dialog lets you choose your design-time style sheet.

3. To add a style sheet that shows only at design time, click the upper plus button. The Select File dialog appears **E**. Navigate to your new style sheet, choose it, and click OK.

4. Back in the Design-Time Style Sheets dialog, your new style sheet is now listed next to "Show only at design time." If it's correct, click OK.

5. The Web page now appears with some slight changes **F**: the **h1** title has an orange background, and paragraphs can be identified using the CSS Layout Box Model visual aid. If we use the CSS Layout Backgrounds visual aid **G**, paragraphs are now clearly distinct from other elements on the page.

F Now the **h1** is all lit up.

G Paragraphs are delineated when the background visual aid is used.

CSS Layout Blocks

Dreamweaver uses what it refers to as *CSS layout blocks,* which are:

- A **div** without `display:inline`
- An element with `display:block`
- An element with `position:absolute`
- An element with `position:relative`

CSS layout blocks are used by the visual aids and design-time style sheets to help designers understand how the parts of a CSS-based layout work together on your page.

For instance, say you have a design-time style sheet that assigns `position: relative` to all of your links (that is, to all **a** tags). When you then turn on CSS Layout Backgrounds, all of your links will be their own bright color, allowing you to easily pick them out.

To hide a style sheet at design time:

Follow steps 2 through 4 from "To show a design-time style sheet," but click the lower plus button instead. Select a style sheet to hide, and click OK.

In , the main style sheet for the page has been hidden. This allows you to see the page without the effect of styles or to see the page with some styles but not others. This can be a big help when trying to track down CSS-related issues.

To remove a design-time style sheet:

1. Bring up the Design-Time Style Sheets dialog, as described earlier. Select the style sheet to remove, and click the minus button above the style sheet name in either box of the dialog. If you have multiple style sheets to remove, continue to delete them in this way.

2. Click OK, and your Web page displays closer to the way it will appear on the Web.

H Style sheets can also be hidden, as shown on this plain page.

TIP When used in conjunction with Dreamweaver's **CSS** layout blocks, design-time style sheets are an extremely powerful tool.

TIP Despite how it looks, your document is not actually being changed—only the way the page is displayed is being changed. Design-time style sheets are not really added to or removed from your Web page: Dreamweaver handles it all internally.

TIP Don't forget that you also have the Style Rendering toolbar (covered in Chapter 1), which you can use to display your page as it would appear with print style sheets, hand-held style sheets, projection style sheets, and so on. You can also use the Style Rendering toolbar to turn off the display of style sheets altogether.

TIP It's worth noting that when you remove design-time style sheets from your document, you're not actually deleting the style sheet—you're just removing the relationship between your page and the style sheet.

10

Inserting Tables

You will often use tables on Web pages to present tabular information—that is, data best presented in the form of rows and columns. It's also possible to use tables for layout—that is, to align text and images on the page—but as you'll see later in the chapter, in most cases you should be using CSS for layout instead.

In this chapter, you'll learn how to create and format tables, ensure that tables and their content look the way you intend, work with Dreamweaver's many table tools, and save time when you're using tables.

Moving Away from Tables for Layout

In previous years, one of the most wide-spread uses for a table was as a layout device (sometimes called *layout tables*). You can create tables on your page and then use the table cells to contain the text and images on the page. Because you have good control over the size of the cells and the position of their boundaries, you can line up and lay out elements on the page with precision, though it often requires some extremely complex tables. By hiding the borders of the table cells, the site visitor doesn't notice the tables. This, up until the last several years, is how most nicely designed Web pages were created.

However, there are many problems with using tables for layout. First of all, the table has nothing to do with the *content* of the page (the information your visitor sees); all it does is affect the *presentation* of the content. One of the biggest benefits of CSS is that it *separates* content from presentation. As a result, you can completely redesign CSS-based sites largely by changing one file, the style sheet. If your presentation is mixed with your content, as it is with a table-based layout, it makes site redesigns difficult and expensive. Similarly, tables make it difficult to maintain visual consistency throughout a site (because the layout tables on different pages may not be the same).

So that's what is wrong with tables from the standpoint of the Web designer, but there are problems for the site visitor, too. Tables make the size of an HTML page unnecessarily large (costing you extra bandwidth charges), and site visitors must download the layout tables on every page they visit in the site (ditto). Pages load more slowly than with a CSS-based layout, and slow page loads drive visitors away. Table-based pages are also much more difficult to read by users with disabilities and by visitors using mobile devices, such as cell phones and tablets.

Tables were necessary for good-looking Web sites back in 1997 because the Web browsers of the day had many limitations, not the least of which was that none of them supported the then-emerging CSS standards for layout. But all modern browsers have good support for using CSS for layout (including browsers such as Internet Explorer 8 and 9, Mozilla Firefox, Google Chrome, Apple Safari, and Opera). The vast majority of users of the Web now use Web browsers that can handle CSS-based layouts just fine. And most mobile device browsers are based on the WebKit framework (also used by Safari and Chrome), so they display CSS well.

As a result, you can (and should!) use Dreamweaver to build great-looking, CSS-based sites that are faster to load, accessible for everyone, and easier for you to redesign and maintain. To learn more about laying out your pages with CSS, see Chapter 8.

Table-based layout was pervasive for most of the first decade of the Web, and Dreamweaver can still be used to create page layouts with tables. But Dreamweaver CS4 removed a set of tools, called Table Layout Mode, that made it easier to use tables for layout. The page templates that come with Dreamweaver were completely revised with CS5 to use CSS layout rather than tables. Adobe has clearly—and correctly—endorsed CSS for layout, and it keeps adding CSS features to Dreamweaver to support that direction.

By the way, even with sites that use tables for layout, you can still use CSS to style the text inside the tables. Some CSS markup is devoted to styling text, and some is devoted to positioning elements on the page. You can use the styling kind of CSS to make your text look good, even inside a table. You just shouldn't mix the positioning elements of CSS with tables; choose one method or the other for positioning elements on your pages.

By using CSS for layout, tables can go back to what they were originally intended to do—namely, to display tabular information that lines up in neat rows and columns. Think of a baseball box score or a timetable showing a bus schedule—both perfect candidates for tables.

Creating a Table

Tables typically consist of one or more rows and one or more columns. Each rectangular area at the intersection of a row and column is called a *cell*. Cells contain the page's text or images, and items within a cell can't extend past the cell's boundaries.

You can insert a table anywhere on a page, even within another table (this is called *nesting* a table). By default, Dreamweaver creates tables with three rows and three columns, but you can easily change that format during the process of inserting the table. After you do make changes, Dreamweaver remembers them and uses them as the defaults for the next table you create.

To add a table to your page:

1. Place the insertion point where you want the table to appear.

2. In the Layout category of the Insert panel, click the Table button 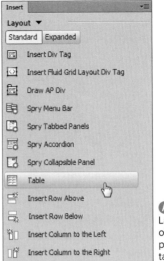.

   or

   Choose Insert > Table, or press Ctrl-Alt-T (Cmd-Opt-T).

   The Table dialog appears **B**.

3. Enter the number of rows you want in the table, and press Tab.

4. Enter the number of columns you want in the table, and press Tab.

5. In the Table width text box, enter a number that will be either in pixels or a percentage of the page width, and then choose the units from the pop-up menu to the right of the text box **C**.

A You'll use the Layout category of the Insert panel to add tables to your pages.

B The Table dialog lets you get started building a table.

C You can set the width of your table either in pixels or as a percentage of the browser page width.

D The green dimension lines tell you the width of the table in pixels. The dimension lines above each column do not show pixel widths in this figure because the columns are set to be a percentage of the table width.

6. Set one or more (or none) of the following (see the "Anatomy of a Table" sidebar for explanations of the settings):

   ▸ Enter a figure in the Border thickness text box to set the size of the border, in pixels, that will be displayed between cells.

   ▸ Enter a figure in the Cell padding text box to set the amount of space, in pixels, between the content in the cells and the cell border.

   ▸ Enter a figure in the Cell spacing text box to set the number of pixels of space between cells.

7. In the Header section, choose the kind of header you want: None, Left, Top, or Both. The icons for the headers tell you what each choice looks like.

8. (Optional, but recommended.) In the Accessibility section, enter a caption for the table. Caption text appears in all browsers. If you enter text in the Summary text box, that text appears only in screen readers for the visually disabled.

9. Click OK.

   The table appears in your page **D**. When a table is selected, as in the figure, or when the insertion point is in a table cell, Dreamweaver shows green dimension lines above or below the table. The top dimension line shows the width of the table in pixels. Each column also has a dimension line, which shows the width of the column in pixels if you have set a fixed width for the column. Columns with widths relative to the table width show dimension lines (so you can easily see each column) without pixel values. These dimension lines appear only in Dreamweaver's Design view, not in a Web browser.

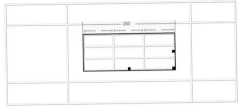

E You can nest a second table inside any cell of an existing table.

TIP To insert a table within a table, place the insertion point inside a cell of an existing table and then choose either of the methods in step 2. The new table appears inside the first table **E**.

TIP You don't have to get the number of rows and columns right the first time; you can always add or subtract them later. See the sections "Adding Rows and Columns" and "Deleting Table Elements" later in this chapter.

TIP If you don't want to see the dimension lines above tables, you can turn them off by choosing View > Visual Aids > Table Widths, which removes the check mark from the menu item.

TIP Captions are actually part of the table. When you move the table, the caption moves with it. Table captions appear above the table by default, but you can change that in the code. Switch to Code view, and then find the table's `<caption>` tag. Click inside the tag to put the insertion point after the word, and then press the spacebar. A pop-up menu appears with the `<caption>` tag's possible attributes. Choose `align` (which inserts `align=""` into the code and gives you another pop-up menu with the alignment values); then choose one of the five possible alignments (`bottom`, `center`, `left`, `right`, `top`) from the pop-up menu.

TIP To edit a caption, select it in Design view and type over the existing text. To change the horizontal alignment of the caption in relation to the table, place the insertion point in the caption and then right-click and pick one of the choices (`left`, `center`, `right`, or `justify`) from the Align submenu in the context menu.

Anatomy of a Table

Besides rows and columns, tables have several other attributes that affect how they look. You'll find controls for these items in the Property inspector when you select a table.

- **Border thickness** is the width of the border around the table, in pixels **F**. Dreamweaver sets it to 1 pixel by default, which results in a thin border. If the border thickness is set to a nonzero amount, you will also see a border between table cells. You'll often see the border thickness set to 0 on pages that are using tables for page layout and the designer doesn't want you to see borders. Borders with 0 thickness appear in Design view with dotted borders.

- **Cell padding** is the amount of space, in pixels, between a cell's borders and its content **G**. Use this setting to give cell content more breathing room within cells. If you don't specify a number here, most browsers use a default value of 1 pixel.

- **Cell spacing** is the amount of space between each table cell, also measured in pixels **H**. If you don't specify a number here, most browsers use a default value of 2 pixels. Wide cell spacing gives the table a look that is very 1996, so use this setting with care.

The following table attributes can't be set in the Property inspector, but can be changed in Code view:

- **Table header** tags part of the table as a header. The header is formatted as bold and centered, but more important, it has the `<th>` HTML tag, which allows screen readers used by visually disabled users to correctly read the table. It's better to use a table header tag in Dreamweaver than to manually make cells bold and centered.

- **Border color** is the color of the border around the table and between the table's cells. This gives a dated look, so use with care.

Sales Territory	1st Quarter	2nd Quarter
North	$2,700	$2,850
East	$3,700	$4,200
South	$2,200	$2,100
West	$2,900	$3,200

Sales Territory	1st Quarter	2nd Quarter
North	$2,700	$2,850
East	$3,700	$4,200
South	$2,200	$2,100
West	$2,900	$3,200

Sales Territory	1st Quarter	2nd Quarter
North	$2,700	$2,850
East	$3,700	$4,200
South	$2,200	$2,100
West	$2,900	$3,200

F The same table with a border thickness of 0 pixels (top), 1 pixel (middle), and 10 pixels (bottom). Cell padding and cell spacing are set to zero.

Sales Territory	1st Quarter	2nd Quarter
North	$2,700	$2,850
East	$3,700	$4,200
South	$2,200	$2,100
West	$2,900	$3,200

G Cell padding has been set to 5 pixels, which gives more whitespace around the table contents.

Sales Territory	1st Quarter	2nd Quarter
North	$2,700	$2,850
East	$3,700	$4,200
South	$2,200	$2,100
West	$2,900	$3,200

H Cell spacing of 7 pixels creates a wide border between cells—a dated look.

Selecting Table Elements

To work effectively with a table, you'll need to know how to select its elements. You can select an entire table; one or more rows and columns; an individual cell or multiple cells; and nonadjacent cells, rows, or columns.

To select the entire table:

Click the table's upper-left corner.

or

Click the bottom or the right edge of the table.

or

Click in the table, and then choose Modify > Table > Select Table.

A border with resize handles appears around the table Ⓐ. Dimension lines also appear.

Clicking any interior cell border also selects the entire table.

To select an entire row:

1. Place the pointer at the left edge of a row.

   The pointer becomes an arrow.

2. Click to select the entire row Ⓑ.

   You can click and drag to select multiple rows.

   The cell borders for the selected row highlight.

To select an entire column:

1. Place the pointer at the top edge of a column.

   The pointer becomes an arrow.

Ⓐ You can tell this table is selected because it has a thick border around its edges with resize handles.

Ⓑ When you move the cursor to the left edge of a table and the pointer changes to an arrow, you can click to select the whole row.

C The pointer also changes to an arrow above columns. Click to select the column.

D If you prefer, you can use the pop-up column menu to select the column.

E By Ctrl-clicking (Cmd-clicking), you can select nonadjacent cells.

2. Click to select the entire column **C**.

You can click and drag to select multiple columns.

or

Click the triangle in the dimension line above any column to display a pop-up menu, then choose Select Column **D**.

The cell borders for the selected column highlight.

To select a single cell:

Click and drag in the cell.

or

Click in the cell, and then choose Edit > Select All or press Ctrl-A (Cmd-A).

or

If the cell is empty, triple-click inside the cell.

The cell highlights to show it has been selected.

To select multiple adjacent cells:

Click in the first cell you want to select, and drag to the last cell.

or

Click in the first cell you want to select, hold down Shift, and then click in the last cell. All the cells in between will also be selected. You can also Shift-click in this manner to select rows or columns.

To select nonadjacent cells:

Ctrl-click (Cmd-click) in the first cell, hold down Ctrl (Cmd), and then click the other cells you want to select **E**. You can also Ctrl-click (Cmd-click) to select nonadjacent rows or columns.

Making Table Selections Easier

When you're selecting tables and table elements, it can sometimes be difficult to select the particular part you're after, especially if some of the table cells are narrow horizontally or vertically Ⓐ. To make things easier on you, Dreamweaver offers *Expanded Tables mode*, which temporarily adds a border (if there is none) and increases the cell padding and cell spacing. These changes aren't permanent and don't show up in a Web browser.

Sales Territory	Q1	Q2	Q3	Q4
North	$2,700	$2,850		
East	$3,700	$4,200		
South	$2,200	$2,100		
West	$2,900	$3,200		

Ⓐ Because they are so small, it could be difficult to select the cells under Q3 or Q4.

B Click the Expanded button in the Layout category of the Insert panel to enter Expanded Tables mode.

C Expanded Tables mode makes all the tables in the document bigger, so you can select table elements more easily. Note the indicator bar at the top of the document window that tells you that you're in a special mode.

To enter Expanded Tables mode:

1. Choose View > Table Mode > Expanded Tables Mode.

   or

   In the Layout category of the Insert panel, click the Expanded button **B**.

   or

   Press Alt-F6 (Opt-F6).

   The Design view switches to Expanded Tables mode **C**, changing the appearance of all the tables in the document.

   An indicator bar appears at the top of the document window to let you know you're in the Expanded Tables mode.

2. Select and edit table elements as you like.

TIP Remember that Expanded Tables mode is not a WYSIWYG (What You See Is What You Get) view, as is the standard Design view. Always switch out of Expanded Tables mode before you do any serious table formatting. When you are in Expanded Tables mode, you cannot use Live view.

To exit Expanded Tables mode:

Choose View > Table Mode > Expanded Tables Mode.

or

In the Layout category of the Insert panel, click the Standard button.

or

Click the [exit] link in the Expanded Tables mode indicator bar at the top of the document window.

or

Press Alt-F6 (Opt-F6).

Adding Rows and Columns

You may find you need to add additional content to your table. Dreamweaver allows you to add rows or columns to your table, either singly or in multiples.

To insert a single row in a table:

1. Place the insertion point in a table cell.

2. In the Layout category of the Insert panel, click either the Insert Row Above or Insert Row Below button **A**. A new row appears above or below the row where the insertion point is.

   or

   Choose Insert > Table Objects > Insert Row Above, or press Ctrl-M (Cmd-M).

   or

   Choose Insert > Table Objects > Insert Row Below.

   or

   Right-click in the cell, and choose Table > Insert Row from the context menu. This adds a row above the row where the insertion point is.

   The row appears in your table **B**.

> **TIP** If the insertion point is in the last cell of the table, pressing Tab adds a row to the bottom of the table.

To insert a single column in a table:

1. Place the insertion point in a table cell.

2. In the Layout category of the Insert panel, click either the Insert Column to the Left or Insert Column to the Right button. A new column appears to the left or right of the column where the insertion point is.

Insert Row buttons

Insert Column buttons

A You'll use the Layout category of the Insert panel to make changes to tables.

Sales Territory	Q1	Q2	Q3	Q4
North	$2,700	$2,850		
East	$3,700	$4,200		
South	$2,200	$2,100		
West	$2,900	$3,200		

B A new row has appeared in the middle of this table.

C Use the Insert Rows or Columns dialog to add multiple rows or columns to a table in one operation.

or

Choose Insert > Table Objects > Insert Column to the Left.

or

Choose Insert > Table Objects > Insert Column to the Right.

or

Right-click in the cell, and from the context menu choose Table > Insert Column. This adds a column to the left of the column where the insertion point is.

The column appears in your table.

To insert multiple rows or columns into a table:

1. Place the insertion point in a table cell.

2. Right-click, and then choose Table > Insert Rows or Columns from the context menu.

   or

   Choose Modify > Table > Insert Rows or Columns.

   The Insert Rows or Columns dialog appears C.

3. Select either the Rows or Columns radio button.

4. Enter the number of rows or columns you want to add. To increase or decrease the number, you can either type a number into the text box or use the arrow buttons next to the text box.

5. Next to Where, click the appropriate button to select the location of the new rows or columns.

6. Click OK.

   The rows or columns appear in your table.

Merging and Splitting Cells

Dreamweaver lets you combine two or more adjacent cells into one larger cell (called *merging*) or split a single cell into two or more cells.

To merge cells:

1. Select the cells you want to merge.

2. Choose Modify > Table > Merge Cells, or press Ctrl-Alt-M (Cmd-Opt-M).

   or

   Right-click, and then choose Table > Merge Cells from the context menu.

   The cells merge Ⓐ.

   You can merge an entire row or column into one cell.

To split cells:

1. Place the insertion point in the cell you want to split into two or more cells.

2. Choose Modify > Table > Split Cell, or press Ctrl-Alt-S (Cmd-Opt-S).

   or

   Right-click, and then choose Table > Split Cell from the context menu.

   The Split Cell dialog appears Ⓑ.

3. Choose whether to split the cell into rows or columns.

4. Enter the number of new rows or columns for the split.

5. Click OK.

   The cell divides into two or more cells Ⓒ.

> **TIP** Even if you select multiple cells, Dreamweaver can split only one cell at a time. If you try to split multiple cells at once, the Split Cell menu item will be unavailable.

Ⓐ The four cells at the left edge of this table (top) have been merged into one cell (bottom).

Ⓑ You can use the Split Cell dialog to divide cells into multiple rows or columns.

Ⓒ In this example, the center cell has been split into four cells.

A Use the Property inspector to change the width of a table numerically.

Resizing Table Elements

You can resize tables horizontally or vertically, and also make columns wider and rows taller. You can resize table elements by clicking and dragging, or you can specify the width of tables numerically, and numerically specify the width and height of rows and columns.

To resize an entire table:

1. Click the bottom or the right edge of the table. The table will be selected, and a border with resize handles appears around it.

2. Drag one of the resize handles. To widen the table, drag the handle on the right edge of the table; to make the table taller, drag the handle on the bottom edge of the table; and to make the table grow in both directions simultaneously, drag the handle at the bottom-right corner of the table. Holding down the Shift key as you drag maintains the proportions of the table.

To resize a table numerically:

1. Click the bottom or the right edge of the table to select it.

2. In the Property inspector, enter a number in the W (for width) field A. In the pop-up menu next to the field, choose either %, which makes the table width a percentage of the overall width of the page, or pixels, to set an absolute size for the table width.

3. Press the Tab key or click in the document window to apply your changes.

To resize columns:

1. Select the column you want to resize.

2. Drag the column's right border to make the column wider.

   or

   In the Property inspector, type a number in the W (for width) field **B**. The width unit is in pixels. Alternatively, in the document window, click the triangle in the dimension line above the column and choose Clear Column Width from the pop-up menu; this makes the column resize to fit the contents.

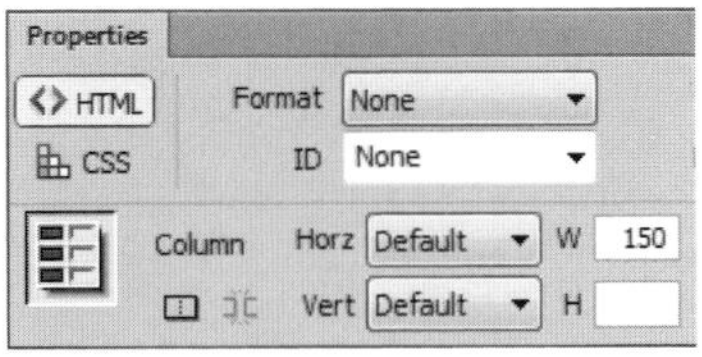

To resize rows:

1. Select the row you want to resize.

2. Drag the bottom border of the row to make the row taller.

   or

   In the Property inspector, type a number in the H (for height) field **C**. The height unit is in pixels.

   If you set a width in percentage for a table, the table resizes based on the width of the user's browser window. This may really change the look of your table. Be sure to preview the page in a Web browser and resize the browser window to see the effect.

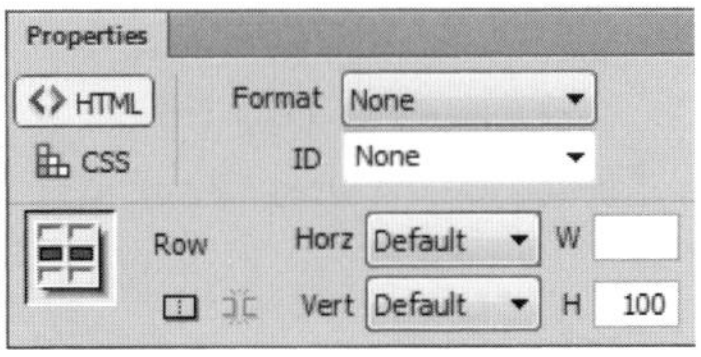

B When you select a column, the Property inspector changes and you can numerically set the column's width.

C Selecting a row allows you to numerically set the row's height.

Clearing and Converting Table Values

When you have a table selected, there are four buttons in the Property inspector that can be very handy and save you a bunch of time **D**. These buttons clear the width and height values for the table, or convert table units from percent to pixels or vice versa.

Clear Column Widths and Clear Row Heights are great for collapsing a table to fit its contents. Convert Table Widths to Pixels lets you change widths from relative to fixed measurements. Convert Table Widths to Percent does the opposite, converting a fixed-size table to a relative one.

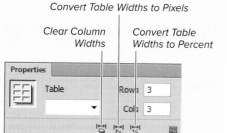

Convert Table Widths to Pixels

Clear Column Widths

Convert Table Widths to Percent

Clear Row Heights

D Use these four buttons in the Property inspector to quickly clear width and height values or to convert tables to and from fixed widths.

TIP Tables always stretch to fit the content inside the table.

TIP Text inside cells usually wraps to fit the width of the cell. To force the cell to expand to the width of the text, you can turn off text wrapping on a cell-by-cell basis. Click in the cell, and then in the Property inspector, select the "No wrap" check box.

TIP Don't be misled into thinking you have ultimate control over row height and column width and therefore control over what your site visitor sees. Different browsers display content differently, and short of previewing your site with every browser ever made on every computer platform, there's no way to be absolutely certain that your site visitor will see exactly what you intended.

TIP Older versions of Dreamweaver had an H (Height) field in the Property inspector for the entire table. That is an invalid property for current HTML, so the field was removed in Dreamweaver CS3.

Deleting Table Elements

If you want to remove tables, rows, or columns, you can make short work of the task.

To delete a table:

1. Select the table by clicking its right or bottom edge. A border with resize handles appears around the table.

2. Press Backspace (Delete).

To delete rows:

1. Select one or more rows.

2. Press Backspace (Delete).

   or

   Choose Modify > Table > Delete Row, or press Ctrl-Shift-M (Cmd-Shift-M).

   or

   Right-click the row, and then choose Table > Delete Row from the context menu.

   The row disappears from the table.

To delete columns:

1. Select one or more columns.

2. Press Backspace (Delete).

   or

   Choose Modify > Table > Delete Column, or press Ctrl-Shift-minus key (Cmd-Shift-minus key).

   or

   Right-click the row, and then choose Table > Delete Column from the context menu.

   The columns disappear from the table.

Sales Territory	1st Quarter	2nd Quarter	3rd Quarter	4th Quarter
North	$2,700	$2,850	$2,800	$2,975
East	$3,700	$4,200	$4,000	$4,750
South	$2,200	$2,100	$2,300	$2,350
West	$2,900	$3,200	$3,800	$5,100

Sales Territory	1st Quarter	2nd Quarter	3rd Quarter	4th Quarter
North	$2,700	$2,850	$2,800	$2,975
East	$3,700	$4,200	$4,000	$4,750
South	$2,200	$2,100	$2,300	$2,350
West	$2,900	$3,200	$3,800	$5,100

Sales Territory	1st Quarter	2nd Quarter	3rd Quarter	4th Quarter
North	$2,700	$2,850	$2,800	$2,975
East	$3,700	$4,200	$4,000	$4,750
South	$2,200	$2,100	$2,300	$2,350
West	$2,900	$3,200	$3,800	$5,100

Sales Territory	1st Quarter	2nd Quarter	3rd Quarter	4th Quarter
North	$2,700	$2,850	$2,800	$2,975
East	$3,700	$4,200	$4,000	$4,750
South	$2,200	$2,100	$2,300	$2,350
West	$2,900	$3,200	$3,800	$5,100

(A) The effects of different types of table alignment. From top to bottom: Default, Left, Center, and Right alignments.

Specifying Table Alignment

When you have a table and text together, you can set the alignment of the table, in some cases wrapping the text around the table (A). You can choose from four different alignments:

- **Default** uses the browser's default alignment for tables (usually it places the table to the left side of the page). This setting prevents text from wrapping around the table to the right.

- **Left** places the table to the left side of the page and allows text to wrap around the right side of the table.

- **Center** centers the table on the page with no text wrapping.

- **Right** places the table to the right side of the page and allows text to wrap around the left side of the table.

You can use the Property inspector to set table alignment. This applies HTML attributes to the `<table>` tag, which is acceptable but not really compliant with best practices. Instead, you should specify table alignment with a CSS style. See Chapter 7 for more information.

To set table alignment:

1. Select the table you want to align.

2. In the Property inspector, choose the alignment you want from the Align pop-up menu.

   The table moves to the alignment you selected.

Setting Cell Properties

Alignment of the text or images inside a cell requires using the Property inspector to set *cell properties* for each cell. You can use these alignment cell properties to set both the horizontal alignment and the vertical alignment. You can also set cell properties for the background color of the cell, and set the color of the cell border.

To set cell alignment:

1. Place the insertion point in the cell you want to format.

2. In the Property inspector, from the Horz pop-up menu choose Default, Left, Center, or Right 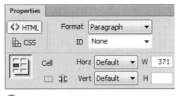 **A**.

   The Default choice usually gives the same visual result as Left **B**.

3. From the Vert pop-up menu, choose Default, Top, Middle, Bottom, or Baseline.

   The Default choice usually gives the same visual result as Middle. Baseline sets the cell alignment to match the baseline of the text within the cell and is usually used to align images and text that are inside the same cell. Baseline usually gives the same visual result as Bottom **C**.

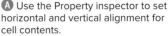

A Use the Property inspector to set horizontal and vertical alignment for cell contents.

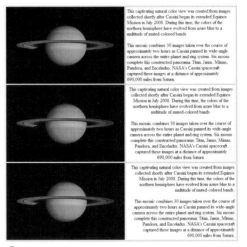

B Horizontal text alignment within a cell. From top to bottom: Left, Center, and Right text alignment.

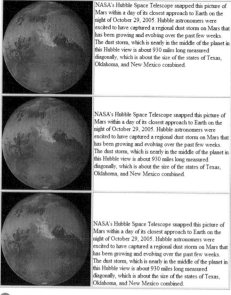

Each of the three cells contains:

NASA's Hubble Space Telescope snapped this picture of Mars within a day of its closest approach to Earth on the night of October 29, 2005. Hubble astronomers were excited to have captured a regional dust storm on Mars that has been growing and evolving over the past few weeks. The dust storm, which is nearly in the middle of the planet in this Hubble view is about 930 miles long measured diagonally, which is about the size of the states of Texas, Oklahoma, and New Mexico combined.

C Vertical text alignment within a cell. From top to bottom: Top, Middle, and Bottom alignment.

To set a cell background color:

1. Place the insertion point in the cell you want to format.

2. In the Property inspector, click the color well next to Bg to bring up the color picker and select the cell's background color.

   The cell's background color changes.

   Dreamweaver accomplishes this color change by adding an HTML attribute to the table cell, which is not considered a current best practice. Instead, you should apply table cell background color changes via CSS. See "Formatting Tables," later in this chapter, for more information.

Sorting Table Content

It's not uncommon to enter data into a table, add more data, and then want to sort the whole thing. You asked for it, Dreamweaver can do it. The program sorts by the content of any column in your table, either numerically or alphabetically, in ascending or descending order, and it can sort on two successive criteria.

There are some limitations to Dreamweaver's sorting abilities. You cannot sort merged cells, and Dreamweaver doesn't have the ability to sort part of a table, so you can't, for example, have the program ignore the merged cells you used for your table's title (though you can have the program include or ignore header rows). Dreamweaver displays an error message if you try to sort a table containing merged cells.

Another problem is that the sorting algorithm Dreamweaver uses isn't terribly smart. For example, you can sort numerically, but Dreamweaver doesn't understand dates in tables, so you're liable to get sorts like this:

> 3/19/99
>
> 3/25/77
>
> 3/3/02

Dreamweaver sorted the dates numerically, reading left to right, which resulted in an incorrect sort.

Despite these restrictions, table sorting in Dreamweaver is useful—you just have to be aware of the limitations.

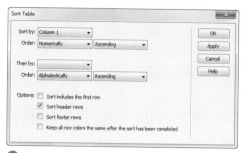

A The Sort Table dialog lets you sort the contents of your table either alphabetically or numerically.

To sort a table:

1. Place the insertion point in any cell of the table you want to sort.

2. Choose Commands > Sort Table.

   The Sort Table dialog appears **A**.

3. From the Sort by pop-up menu, choose the column you want to use to sort the table.

4. In the Order pop-up menu on the left, choose whether to sort the column alphabetically or numerically.

5. In the Order pop-up menu on the right, choose whether to sort the column in ascending or descending order.

6. If you want to sort on a second set of criteria, repeat steps 3 through 5 and use the Then by set of pop-up menus.

7. Make any selections from the Options list.

   By default, the "Sort includes the first row" option is not selected, because the first row of a table is frequently a header row. If your table doesn't seem to be sorting properly, select this option.

8. Click OK.

   Dreamweaver sorts your table according to the criteria you selected.

   Dreamweaver can't sort by rows, just columns.

TIP If you want a merged row at the top of your table, do the sort first and then merge the cells.

TIP Be careful when you're sorting numbers. If you accidentally leave the sort on Alphabetically, you'll get an alphanumeric sort (1, 10, 2, 20, 3, 30) instead of a numeric sort (1, 2, 3, 10, 20, 30).

Formatting Tables

You can apply a CSS style to an entire table (which can change the look of the table), or you can apply a CSS style to selected table cells, which can change the look of the table contents.

When you use a CSS style to format a table, the table's look is defined by instructions in a CSS style sheet. You can choose to have the table style apply to all tables in your document (if you use the style sheet to redefine the `<table>` tag), or you can create a custom CSS class for a particular kind of table you want to use, and apply the style to the table with the Property inspector.

To apply a CSS style to a table:

1. Select the table or table cells you want to format.

2. In the Property inspector, choose the style you want from the Class pop-up menu .

   The selection takes on the formatting from the CSS style you chose.

   You can create, format, and save an empty table for later use. Just create and format the table, select it, and then save it as a snippet. See Chapter 16 for more about creating snippets.

Ⓐ Apply a CSS style to a table in the Property inspector.

A	B	C	D	E
1				
2 **2011 National League Standings**				
3				
4 **East**	W	L	PCT	
5 Philadelphia	102	60	.630	
6 Atlanta	89	73	.549	
7 Washington	80	81	.497	
8 NY Mets	77	85	.475	
9 Florida	72	90	.444	
10				
11 **Central**	W	L	PCT	
12 Milwaukee	96	66	.593	
13 St. Louis	90	72	.556	
14 Cincinnati	79	83	.488	
15 Pittsburgh	72	90	.444	
16 Chicago Cubs	71	91	.438	
17 Houston	56	106	.346	
18				
19 **West**	W	L	PCT	
20 Arizona	94	68	.580	
21 San Francisco	86	76	.531	
22 LA Dodgers	82	79	.509	
23 Colorado	73	89	.451	
24 San Diego	71	91	.438	
25				

Ⓐ Tabular data to be imported into Dreamweaver often starts out as a Microsoft Excel worksheet.

Importing and Exporting Tabular Data

Because tables are best used for tabular data, it stands to reason that Dreamweaver has an easy way to import such data (from database programs or Microsoft Excel, for example) and turn it into a table. This data needs to be in the form of a *delimited text file*—that is, a file that includes the data, separated by some character, such as a tab, a comma, or another delimiter.

To explain how a delimited file works, imagine that you have some data that would be displayed well in a table, such as baseball standings. Each row of the table with the standings contains information on a team, and the different columns of the table contain the team's name, number of wins, number of losses, and winning percentage, as in the example (shown in Excel) in Ⓐ. To use this Excel data in Dreamweaver, you first need to export the data out of Excel as a delimited file, which is easy: You simply save a copy of the file in the "Text (Tab delimited)" format. This saves the data in the Excel worksheet as a plain text file. Each column of data is separated by a tab character, and each row of the data ends with a return character. Dreamweaver can then read this delimited text file and convert it into a table.

Dreamweaver can also do the reverse trick of turning the data in a table into a delimited text file. This allows you to export table data to Excel or a database program for further processing, or you can take a table on a Web page and move it to a word processor or page layout program such as Adobe InDesign.

To import tabular data into a table:

1. Place the insertion point where you want the table to appear.

2. Choose File > Import > Tabular Data.

   or

   Choose Insert > Table Objects > Import Tabular Data.

   The Import Tabular Data dialog appears **B**.

3. Click the Browse button to select the delimited data file.

   The Open dialog appears.

4. Navigate to the data file, select it in the Open dialog, and then click Open.

   The name of the data file appears in the Import Tabular Data dialog's Data file text box.

5. From the Delimiter pop-up menu, choose the delimiter character used in the data file.

   Your choices in this pop-up menu are Tab, Comma, Semicolon, Colon, and Other. If the data file uses an unusual delimiter character, choose Other and type that character into the text box next to the Delimiter pop-up menu.

B Use the Import Tabular Data dialog to select the delimited text file and format the table you are about to create.

2011 National League Standings			
East	W	L	PCT
Philadelphia	102	60	.630
Atlanta	89	73	.549
Washington	80	81	.497
NY Mets	77	85	.475
Florida	72	90	.444
Central	W	L	PCT
Milwaukee	96	66	.593
St. Louis	90	72	.556
Cincinnati	79	83	.488
Pittsburgh	72	90	.444
Chicago Cubs	71	91	.438
Houston	56	106	.346
West	W	L	PCT
Arizona	94	68	.580
San Francisco	86	76	.531
LA Dodgers	82	79	.509
Colorado	73	89	.451
San Diego	71	91	.438

C The unformatted table, built from the imported data, appears in your document. You can use Dreamweaver's tools to style the table as you like.

6. In the Table width section, choose "Fit to data" if you want the table width to be just as wide as the data, or choose "Set to" if you want the table to be a fixed width. If you choose the latter option, enter a number in the text box and choose the units from the pop-up menu (either percent or pixels).

7. You can enter values for cell padding, cell spacing, and the table border. You can also choose to format the text in the top row of the table (which is usually a header of some sort). Your choices are No Formatting, Bold, Italic, or Bold Italic.

8. Click OK.

   Dreamweaver reads the delimited text file and inserts it into your page as an unformatted table C.

TIP If the table imports incorrectly, chances are that the data file uses a delimiter different from the one you chose in step 5. You have to delete the incorrect table and import it again with the correct setting.

TIP If you are importing tabular data from Word or Excel, consider copying and pasting the data using Edit > Paste Special. Dreamweaver understands Office program formatting, and you'll save time because you won't have to reformat in Dreamweaver. See Chapter 4 for more about using Paste Special.

To export a Dreamweaver table's data to a delimited file:

1. Place the insertion point in any cell of the table.

2. Choose File > Export > Table.

   The Export Table dialog appears .

3. From the Delimiter pop-up menu, choose the delimiter character you want to use in the exported text file. Your choices are Tab, Space, Comma, Semicolon, or Colon.

4. From the Line breaks pop-up menu, choose the operating system that is the destination for the text file. Your choices are Windows, Mac, or UNIX.

   The reason for this option is that each of the platforms has a different way of indicating the end of a line of text.

5. Click Export.

   The Export Table As dialog appears.

6. Give the file a name, navigate to where you want to save it, and click Save.

   Dreamweaver saves the table data as a delimited text file.

TIP If you want to export only a portion of a table (for example, the top ten rows), select those rows, copy them, and then paste them into a different part of the document, where they will create a new table. Export the new table as a delimited text file, and then delete the new table.

D Use the Export Table dialog to save the data from a Dreamweaver table as a delimited text file.

Using Forms and Fields

A lot of Web sites exist just to provide information and entertainment to site visitors. But if you want your site to get information back from your visitors, you'll need some way to let them interact with you and your site. To do that, you'll need to add a form.

A form contains fields, and those fields can be anything from a simple check box to a group of radio buttons or a single or multi-line text entry area. And of course, you'll want some sort of "OK" or "Submit" button so that your visitors know how to send you their completed form. Look at the Forms category of the Insert panel Ⓐ, and you'll see that it contains everything you need to add any kind of form and field to your site.

The Uncovered Fields

There are nine items in the Insert panel that aren't covered in this chapter:

- **Jump Menu:** We cover jump menus in Chapter 13, "Using Behaviors and Navigation Objects."

- **File Field:** If you need to upload a file to a server, you'll want to use this type of form field. It's fairly self-explanatory, but you'll need to talk to your server administrator about how they've set up their server to accept files.

- **Spry Validation:** These seven buttons help you use Spry, Adobe's Ajax user interface library, to validate form entries. We cover Spry in Chapter 14, "Building Pages with Dynamic Elements."

Insert

Forms ▼

▢	Form
▯	Text Field
▨	Hidden Field
▢	Textarea
☑	Checkbox
▤	Checkbox Group
◉	Radio Button
▤	Radio Group
▤	Select (List/Menu)
↗	Jump Menu
▣	Image Field
▤	File Field
▭	Button
abc	Label
▯	Fieldset
▯	Spry Validation Text Field
▨	Spry Validation Textarea
☑	Spry Validation Checkbox
▤	Spry Validation Select
▨	Spry Validation Password
▯	Spry Validation Confirm
▤	Spry Validation Radio Group

Ⓐ The Forms category of the Insert panel contains all the items you might want to add to your form.

Adding a Form to a Page

You could start creating a page by throwing fields onto it, but when your visitor clicks Submit, the browser won't know what to do with the data. That's where you need a form—it tells the browser that all this information is part of one package, and it tells the browser what it should do with all of the information that it has gathered.

A form is made of a number of different elements, but not all of them need to appear on every form. **A** shows the form we'll be creating in this chapter. This form, which for layout purposes is created within the main page content **div**, contains a nested **div** that includes the First Name and Last Name text fields and the comments text area.

Text fields

Text area

Radio button group

Fieldset with check boxes

List/Menu

Buttons

A The completed form, with its components, as it appears in a browser.

To add a form to a page:

1. Choose where on your Web page you want your form, and click the Form button on the Insert panel. A red dashed box appears on your page .

   The red box is the form area, and behind the scenes in the code, Dreamweaver has added a `<form>`...`</form>` container tag.

2. If that box isn't automatically selected, select it, and you'll see the options you can change for your new form in the Property inspector **C**. The ones that apply solely to forms are:

   ▸ **Form ID:** If you're going to be doing any JavaScript validation of your form, it's a requirement to give it a name. In addition, some CGI protocols need their associated forms to have a particular name. (CGI stands for Common Gateway Interface—a server program that interprets the data sent by your form.)

   ▸ **Action:** This is the program on the Web server that is executed when the form is submitted. You'll need to get the name of this from your system administrator or hosting provider. It's also commonly referred to as a System CGI.

Form area

B A form looks bare until you add the form fields.

C The Property inspector is where you set a form's name, action, and method.

- **Method:** The most common options are GET and POST. POST passes the form data as part of the header of the request to the server. GET passes the data as part of the URL of the request to the server. Because of this, and because GET has a length limitation, POST is what you'll usually want. Dreamweaver also has a Default choice in the Method pop-up menu, which allows the form to be submitted using the browser's default setting. This is usually a GET method, and we don't recommend it.

- **Enctype:** This field describes the enclosure type being sent to the server. The default is `application/x-www-form-urlencoded`. The only time you'll want to use `multipart/form-data` is if you're asking your visitors to upload a file.

TIP Make sure that all your form fields are inside your form; if they are not, their contents won't be sent to the server.

TIP If you try to add a form field to a page that doesn't have a form, you'll be asked if you want to add a form tag. You might think from this that it's not worth bothering to add a form tag manually first, but it is. You'll have better control over where the form is placed, and what ends up going inside it.

TIP No, that red border around the form won't actually display on your site. It's just there in Dreamweaver's Design view so that you'll know where the form begins and ends. If you turn on Live view, the red outline disappears.

Adding Text Fields

The simplest type of form field you can have is a single-line text field. Your average form will have several of them, allowing people to enter anything from their name to their phone number to their shoe size.

A The first text entry field added to the form.

To add text fields:

1. Choose where in your form you want your text field to appear (by clicking in the document), and click the Text Field button on the Insert panel. The Input Tag Accessibility Attributes dialog may appear, depending on the settings in Dreamweaver's Preferences. If it does, see how to handle it in the "Labeling Your Fields" sidebar, later in this chapter, and then return to this point. The new text field appears on your page **A**.

2. If the text field hasn't been automatically selected, select it, and you'll see the options you can change for your new field in the Property inspector **B**. From there, you can change the fields:

   ▸ **TextField:** This field contains the name of the field, which can be used by JavaScript behaviors and by scripts on the server.

B Set a text field's properties using the Property inspector.

- **Char width:** The width of the text input area on your page. The larger this number, the wider the space it needs. And because it's the number of characters allowed, the larger the font you've set (usually with CSS), the wider the space will be.

- **Max chars:** The maximum number of characters that a user can enter into this field. For instance, you could limit a credit card to 16 characters.

- **Type:** This has three values: *Single line*, *Multi line*, and *Password*. Multi line is covered in the next section, "Adding a Text Area." The only difference between Single line and Password is what users see when they enter something into this field: if the type is Password, no matter what your visitor types, it will appear as black dots. The correct value will be sent back to the server, though.

- **Init val:** This is the initial value of the field. This text is displayed when the page is loaded.

- **Class:** This is the CSS class, if any, applied to the field.

TIP A *hidden field* is similar to a text field. It's used when there's information that a script needs from a form, but which a user doesn't enter—so the field contains a value but isn't seen in the document. Adding a hidden field is virtually identical to adding a text field: just click the Hidden Field button in the Insert panel (obviously, where it's put on the Web page doesn't matter), and then set the value and unique field name in the Property inspector.

Labeling Your Fields

When you click a button in the Insert panel to add a form field to your page, the Input Tag Accessibility Attributes dialog may appear Ⓐ. This dialog allows you to set certain attributes that can enhance accessibility for people with disabilities. These fields are:

Ⓐ To enable your site to be accessible for people with disabilities, set the label attributes here. The default position for a text field label is before the form item.

- **ID:** This is the same as the field name in the Property inspector. It's used by scripts (both client-side and server-side) to manipulate the contents of fields and process the form.

- **Label:** Ⓐ shows a label of "First Name:" being entered. Figure Ⓐ from "Adding Text Fields" shows the result: that text is displayed just to the left of the new text field.

- **Style:** There are three style options: *Attach label tag using 'for' attribute*, *Wrap with label tag*, and *No label tag*. If you choose *Wrap with label tag*, Dreamweaver surrounds your new **<input>** tag with a **<label>** tag:

```
<label>First Name: <input type="text" name="textfield" /></label>
```

If you choose *Attach label tag using 'for' attribute*, Dreamweaver writes the **<label>** tag based on what you enter for *Position* (covered below):

```
<label for="textfield">First Name: </label><input type="text"
name="textfield" id="textfield" />
```

Unfortunately, Dreamweaver doesn't offer full WYSIWYG support for this option— you can change the **name** and **id** attributes of your new text field (by changing the TextField field), but the **label**'s **for** attribute, which should change to match, doesn't. There isn't any way to change it short of going into the markup and changing it by hand.

If you choose *No label tag*, the text you enter appears, but it'll be just that: text.

The **<label>** tag helps make your site more accessible in two ways: it tells voice browsers that this is the text associated with this field, and it allows users with certain browsers (such as Firefox) to click the text label as an alternative to only clicking inside a check box. This gives your visitor a larger space in which to click. Accessibility is important, and using the **<label>** tag helps make your site more accessible—but if you want to use it with Dreamweaver's Design view, stick with the *Wrap with label tag* option.

Labeling Your Fields (continued)

- **Position:** The label for a form field can be either before or after the field. For text fields, you'll usually see the label before the field. For check boxes and radio buttons, you'll usually see the label afterwards. The default value of the position changes depending on the type of field **B**.

- **Access key:** Some browsers allow users to enter keyboard shortcuts to select form fields. If you want this option, enter the keyboard shortcut for the field here. For instance, if I entered *g* in figure **B**, a user with Internet Explorer for Windows could click that check box by pressing Alt-G.

- **Tab Index:** If you want users to be able to tab from form field to form field in a particular order, you'll want to assign each field a tab index. This is the numbered order in which the user can tab through your form's fields. It's especially useful to set this when your form fields are inside table cells, as the default can be quite different from what you actually want to occur. The numbers need to be between 0 and 32767, and they don't have to be in sequence: you can make your fields be (for instance) 100, 200, and so on, leaving room for future changes to your form.

B For a check box, the label's default position is usually after the form item.

If you don't use labels, access keys, or tab indices and are annoyed at seeing this dialog come up every time you add another form field, you can get rid of it by clicking the link at the bottom. This opens Dreamweaver's Preferences, and turning off "Show attributes when inserting Form objects" makes the dialog go away for good. If you later decide you want it back, go back into Preferences, choose the Accessibility category, and you can turn it on again.

You can also add a label afterwards by clicking the Label button on the Insert panel, but it doesn't do what you expect. Instead of bringing up the Input Tag Accessibility Attributes dialog, Dreamweaver adds a `<label>` tag around whatever you selected and throws you into Split view. If you are markup-phobic, stick with adding labels along with their associated fields.

Adding a Text Area

It's possible that you want your visitors to enter more than just a single line of text—maybe they have a lot to say, or you just want them to have a free-form area in which to enter their comments. If that's the case, you'll want to use a text area.

To add a text area:

1. Choose where in your form you want your text area to appear, and click the Textarea button on the Insert panel. The new text area appears on your page **A**.

2. If the text area isn't automatically selected, select it, and you'll see the options you can change for your new field in the Property inspector **B**. From there, you can change the same values that you could for text fields, with some small differences:

   ▸ **Num Lines:** This is the number of lines that you want the field to take up on the page. If you only want a single line, use a text field instead.

   ▸ **Disabled** and **Read-only:** These check boxes do similar but not identical things. Disabled displays the text area, but doesn't let users select or change it. You might use this with a script that enables the text area if the user performs a particular action. Read-only makes the text area unchangeable by users, but they can still select and copy the field's contents.

A A text area lets your visitors enter multiple lines of text, and it will scroll when necessary.

B Use the Property inspector to set the dimensions and initial value of the text area.

I am interested in learning more about:

☐ Recipes

☐ Wine

☐ Cookware

☐ Cooking News

☐ Deals

A Check boxes are an easy way to get exact information from your site's visitors.

Adding Check Boxes

Check boxes are one of the most commonly used form fields, and you're likely to want several on your forms. They're particularly useful when you want specific responses from your site visitors and you don't want them to have to enter data into text fields (and possibly misspell their entry).

To add a check box:

1. Choose where in your form you want your check box to appear, and click the Checkbox button on the Insert panel. A new check box appears on your page **A**.

2. If the check box isn't automatically selected, select it, and you'll see the options you can change for your new field in the Property inspector **B**:

   ▸ **Checkbox name:** This is the name of the field, and it's used by JavaScript validation as well as server-side scripts.

   ▸ **Checked value:** This is the value that's passed to the server (and JavaScript client-side code) when the user has checked the check box.

   ▸ **Initial state:** This refers to the appearance of the check box when the page is first loaded—is the box checked or unchecked?

TIP Just a reminder: the difference between check boxes and radio buttons is that for a group of radio buttons, only a single option can be picked. When you have a group of check boxes, however, the state of each check box is not dependent on the other check boxes, so you can select multiple check boxes.

Properties			
Checkbox name	Checked value recipes	Initial state ○ Checked
recipes		⦿ Unchecked

B Set the name and value of the check box in the Property inspector along with the checked status of the box when the page is loaded.

Adding a Fieldset

A *fieldset* is HTML's way of grouping fields on your form to add additional meaning for the user. How a fieldset displays on a Web page depends on the browser being used, and you can't control that: Dreamweaver's Design view shows a thin gray line around a fieldset's contents. Compare figure 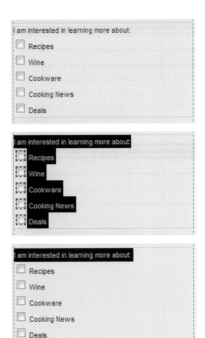 in "Adding Check Boxes" with **A**: it's easier to see that those check boxes are grouped together and that all have a similar function.

To add a fieldset:

1. Choose where in your form you want your fieldset to appear, and click the Fieldset button on the Insert panel.

2. The Fieldset dialog appears **B**, asking you to enter a *legend*—that's the text that appears at the beginning of the fieldset **A**. Enter that text, click OK, and the fieldset box appears in the document.

3. If you're adding a fieldset to an existing form, drag the related fields into the fieldset. If it's a new form, click inside the fieldset and create its fields.

> **TIP** If the fieldset contains no form fields, the legend appears inside the box. When form fields are added, the legend is displayed as part of the box.

> **TIP** If you're dragging fields inside the fieldset, be careful when selecting—make sure (for example) that all of a label is selected.

> **TIP** You can't change a fieldset or a legend using the Property inspector. You can change the legend by modifying the text in the document window, and you can change the fieldset by going into Code view.

> **TIP** A fieldset can contain any form fields, not just check boxes.

A Adding a fieldset to your form helps group related form fields, making your form easier for your visitors to understand. Dreamweaver puts a thin gray line around the fieldset in the document (top). Selecting the `<fieldset>` tag in the tag selector shows you the items in the fieldset (middle), and selecting the `<legend>` tag in the tag selector highlights the fieldset's legend (bottom).

B Enter the legend text in the Fieldset dialog.

A The Radio Group dialog lets you enter all of your radio buttons in a single dialog.

Adding a Radio Button Group

Radio buttons don't exist by themselves—they always come in a group. And of that group, only one option can be chosen: your visitors can pick rock *or* paper *or* scissors.

To add a radio button group:

1. Choose where in your form you want your radio button group to appear, and click the Radio Group button on the Insert panel.

2. The Radio Group dialog appears **A**, asking you to enter several fields:

   ▸ **Name:** A radio group needs a name that associates all of the radio buttons together. In this example, your visitor is choosing whether or not to subscribe to a newsletter, so the name is "newsletter." This name will not appear in the finished form.

   ▸ **Label:** Each radio button needs a label to distinguish it from its neighbors. In this example, the labels are "Yes" and "No."

   ▸ **Value:** Each radio button needs a value, which will be passed back to the server, to JavaScript, or to both. The example values here are, again, "yes" and "no."

   ▸ **Lay out using:** Radio buttons are normally aligned vertically, so here you make your choice of how you want that layout to be done in the HTML markup. Your choices are "Line breaks" and "Table." Line breaks will almost always be sufficient.

continues on next page

The Radio Group dialog starts with two fields, which you can overwrite to say whatever you want. If you want to add more radio buttons, click the **+** on the left side. If you want to delete buttons, in the list, select the one you want to remove, and click the **–**.

To rearrange the order of buttons, in the list, select the name of the button to move, and then click the up/down arrows to move that button.

3. Click OK to accept your entries, and your new radio button group is added to your document **B**.

> Would you like to subscribe to our newsletter?
> ○ Yes ○ No

B Here's your radio group. Only one item can be selected.

TIP If you want your buttons to all be on the same line (as in this example), select "Lay out using: Line breaks," and then remove the line breaks. Sadly, Dreamweaver doesn't include an option of "just leave them on the same line, OK?"

TIP There's also an option on the Insert panel to add a single radio button (Radio Button): It's unlikely, though, that you'll ever want to have only a single radio button on a page. If you add a single radio button to an existing radio group, be sure to copy the name of the group exactly into the Property inspector **C**. In fact, your best bet is to click one of the existing radio buttons, copy the name from the Property inspector, click the new radio button (if it already exists; add it if it doesn't), and then paste the name in from the clipboard.

TIP If you want one of your radio buttons to be set as selected, click that button in your document and then change the Initial state in the Property inspector from Unchecked to Checked.

TIP Dreamweaver will happily let you set multiple radio buttons with their initial state checked even though browsers won't display it that way. Each kind of browser may display this error in a different fashion, so don't make the mistake in the first place. Be careful that you're only setting one (or no) radio button to be checked.

Properties					
○	Radio Button	Checked value	yes	Initial state	○ Checked
	newsletter				⊙ Unchecked

C When setting the properties for an individual radio button, set the name of the group carefully—it has to match other radio buttons to work correctly.

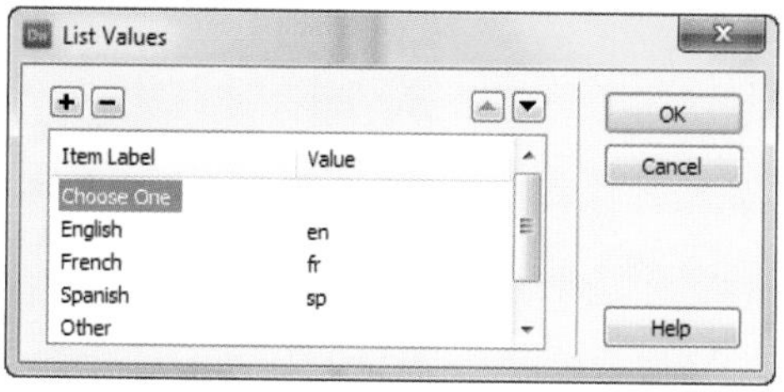

Ⓐ You'll enter all the values for pop-up menus and scrolling option lists in the List Values dialog.

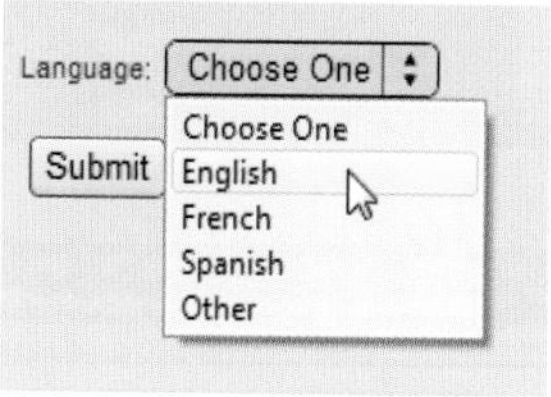

Ⓑ The new pop-up menu is now on your form (shown here in Live view to display the menu in action).

Adding a List/Menu

Another common form element is what's referred to in the Forms category of the Insert panel as *Select (List/Menu)*. It's actually the two forms of the HTML `<select>` tag: either a pop-up menu or a scrolling list of options. If it's the latter, you can decide whether the user can click a single option or multiple options.

To add a pop-up menu:

1. Choose where in your form you want your pop-up menu to appear, and click the Select (List/Menu) button on the Insert panel. The Input Tag Accessibility Attributes dialog may appear. If so, fill it out as described earlier in this chapter.

   The empty list appears in your layout, with a downward-pointing triangle indicating the future pop-up menu.

2. Make sure the empty list is selected in the layout; then, in the Property inspector, click the List Values button. The List Values dialog appears **Ⓐ**. Enter your desired options. The Item Label is what appears in the pop-up, and the Value is what's sent to the server/JavaScript.

3. Click OK, and your new pop-up appears on your page **Ⓑ**.

continues on next page

4. If the pop-up menu isn't automatically selected, select it, and you'll see the options you can change for your new field in the Property inspector ⓒ:

▸ **Name:** This text field at the left side of the Property inspector contains the field name that will be passed back to the server-side CGI/JavaScript when it processes the form.

▸ **Type:** The choices are Menu or List; for a pop-up menu, choose Menu.

▸ **Initially selected:** You can choose one of the menu options to be the default that's shown when the page loads.

▸ **List Values:** Clicking this button causes the List Values dialog ⓓ to reappear, so you can easily change the list contents.

ⓒ You can change the existing pop-up menu into a scrolling option list by clicking the List button in the Property inspector.

ⓓ You can return to the List Values dialog to view or change the items by clicking the List Values button in the Property inspector.

To add a scrolling option list:

1. Follow steps 1–3 in the previous exercise to create a pop-up menu, and select the pop-up menu.

2. In the Property inspector ⑤, change Type to List. You'll notice that even though you've changed the type to list, your field still displays as a pop-up menu.

3. Change the Height field to show the number of items you want displayed at any one time in the scrolling list. Changing this causes the field to display as a scrolling list ⑥.

4. If desired, change the Selections option to allow multiple choices. When you do this, visitors to your site will be able to pick several options in the scrolling list at one time.

TIP If you leave the Height set to 1 and change Selections to "Allow multiple," you'll also see your pop-up menu change to a scrolling list. But a scrolling list with a height of one isn't much of a scrolling list—it's too difficult for your users to see what's available.

⑤ If you change from a pop-up menu to a scrolling list, you'll get a couple of new options in the Property inspector.

⑥ Here's what a scrolling list looks like.

Adding a Button

A form on your site doesn't do you much good unless you can get the information that's entered into it, and that's the primary use of buttons. A Submit button triggers the action specified in the form tag (described earlier in this chapter). Another type of button is the Reset button, which allows a user to go back to a form's original state.

To add a button:

1. Choose where in your form you want your button to appear, and click the Button icon on the Insert panel. The default value—the Submit button—appears on your document **A**.

2. If the button isn't automatically selected, select it, and you'll see the options you can change for your new button in the Property inspector **B**:

   ▸ **Button name:** This is the name of the button; generally, you'll use "submit" to specify that it's a Submit button, and "reset" or "cancel" to show that it's a Reset button **C** (from a user interface standpoint, "Cancel" is

A Add a Submit button to your Web form so you can receive your visitor's completed form.

B The buttons you'll usually use are Submit and Reset; this one's a Submit button.

C A button can be changed to a Reset button using the Property inspector.

preferable as the button name in the Value field). Note that the value in this field is what will be used by the code processing the form (the user doesn't see it), so lowercase is generally preferable; by standardizing on all lowercase for code names, you lessen the possibility for errors if you modify the code by hand. You should use the properly capitalized name for the Value field.

▸ **Value:** This is the message that is displayed on the Submit button itself. It's common for it to say "Submit," but it can also say, "Place order," "OK," or whatever you think your users will understand.

▸ **Action:** There are three possible actions. *Submit form* and *Reset form* do what you'd expect. *None* creates a generic button, which can later be set to trigger a JavaScript action (covered in Chapter 13).

TIP There is actually one other type of button: an image button. It is created by clicking the Image Field button on the Insert panel. You'll be prompted to browse for an image file in your site, and the image then appears in your document. When a visitor comes to your site and completes the form, clicking that image triggers an immediate submission of the form.

Submit/Reset or Reset/Submit?

If you want to start a fight in a group of designers, just ask which order your Submit and Reset buttons should be in. There are two vocal schools of thought, and they tend to break down into Windows advocates versus Mac advocates.

In a nutshell, Windows users expect to find the OK/Submit button as the first button in a group, whereas Mac users are accustomed to always seeing it as the rightmost button. As shown in **D** and **E**, interface designers who work on cross-platform applications are able to change the order depending on the user's platform. While this is the same General Preferences dialog on both platforms, notice that where Mac and Windows users click to accept their changes is very different.

If you're working on a Web site, you don't have that flexibility, but you should be aware that visitors to your site will have expectations about how your forms should work—and at least some of those expectations may be different than yours. We're not going to make the call here as to which is preferable; that call should be made based on your visitor logs and your personal preferences.

D Dreamweaver's General Preferences panel on Windows shows the buttons as OK and Cancel at the bottom right and Help at the bottom left.

E The General Preferences panel on the Mac also has Help at the bottom left, but uses the order Cancel and OK at the bottom right.

Using Dreamweaver's Layout Tools

The layout of elements on your pages is key to the usability of your sites, and Dreamweaver has many tools that help you view and work with your page layouts. These tools fall into two main areas: tools that help you work within your document window to align and view page elements, and tools to help you visualize your CSS-based layouts.

The document window tools will be familiar from image editing programs, and include an onscreen grid, page guides, and rulers. Because it's often useful to get a closer look at your work, you also have the ability to zoom the document window.

CSS-based layouts allow you to create Web pages that look good on computers, tablets, and smart phones, and Dreamweaver gives you two ways to do the trick. One is to create and add separate media query style sheets and swap out the style sheet for the page to match the screen size that is calling for the page. Another way is to create a single grid-based layout that builds and includes the media queries in the same style sheet and automatically switches screen sizes as needed. Dreamweaver CS6 handles both approaches, and we'll see that in this chapter.

In This Chapter

Using the Grid

If you want items on a page to line up, a handy way to make sure they're aligned is to use the grid—a feature you may well be familiar with from other applications, such as Photoshop. If you're used to it elsewhere, it's easy; if you're not, here's a quick overview.

The grid overlays graph-paper-like lines on your Web page, making it easy to see if elements on the page are horizontally or vertically aligned. Nothing on your page is actually changed, and the lines are only visible inside Dreamweaver. If you choose to have elements on your page *snap to the grid*, whenever you move an element close to a grid line, it will "jump" (or snap) to match up with it. That way, you know for sure that your elements are perfectly aligned.

To turn the grid on or off:

To toggle the grid display, choose View > Grid > Show Grid 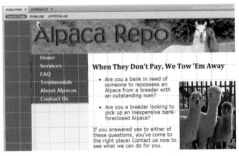.

or

Press Ctrl-Alt-G (Cmd-Opt-G).

Your document displays the grid if it wasn't already displayed **B**, and vice versa.

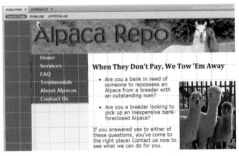

A You can get to all the grid options from the menu.

B Here's the page with the grid visible.

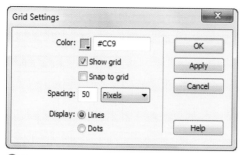

C If you don't like the grid defaults, you can change the settings.

To change the grid settings:

1. Choose View > Grid > Grid Settings **A**. The Grid Settings dialog appears **C**.

2. From this dialog, you can change the color, the spacing, and whether the grid displays as lines or dots. You can also use this as a way to set the Show Grid and Snap To Grid options at the same time. If you want to check how a setting looks, click Apply. When you like your results, click OK, and if the grid is set to show, your document appears with your chosen grid style. If the grid is not set to show, the settings will still be changed and will display their new values the next time you show the grid.

To make elements snap to the grid:

1. Choose View > Grid > Snap To Grid **A**.

   or

   Select the "Snap to grid" check box in the Grid Settings dialog **C**.

   or

   Press Ctrl-Alt-Shift-G (Cmd-Opt-Shift-G).

2. Move an absolutely positioned page element. It snaps to line up with the grid if you move the element within a few pixels of a grid line.

Using Rulers and Guides

Rulers and guides are also tools commonly found in other design applications. Dreamweaver has both horizontal and vertical rulers, which can use pixels, inches, or centimeters as units.

Guides can do almost everything grids can and a whole lot more. For instance, guides can be locked into place, guides can be set to percentages of the page, and not only can elements snap to guides, but guides can be set to snap to elements.

To turn rulers on or off:

To toggle the display of rulers, choose View > Rulers > Show Ⓐ. You can also choose the ruler units in this menu.

or

Press Ctrl-Alt-R (Cmd-Opt-R).

To turn guides on or off:

To toggle the display of guides, choose View > Guides > Show Guides Ⓑ.

or

Press Ctrl-; (Cmd-;).

Ⓐ You can turn rulers on and off in the View menu.

Ⓑ As you could with the grid options, you can get to many guide options in the View menu.

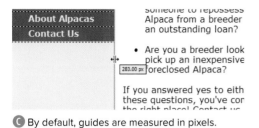

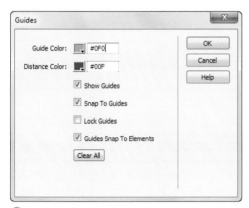

someone to repossess Alpaca from a breeder an outstanding loan?

• Are you a breeder look pick up an inexpensive 283.00 px foreclosed Alpaca?

If you answered yes to eith these questions, you've cor the right place! Contact us

C By default, guides are measured in pixels.

D Use the Guides dialog to change any of its settings.

To add a guide to your page:

1. Click in either the horizontal or vertical ruler, and then drag into the document. The guide appears along with a tip that displays the number of pixels that the guide is currently away from the edge of the document **C**.

2. When the guide is where you want it, release the mouse button. The line remains, but the tip goes away.

To edit guide settings:

1. Choose View > Guides > Edit Guides, and the Guides dialog appears **D**.

2. From here, you can set:
   ▸ The guide and distance colors
   ▸ Whether guides should show
   ▸ Whether elements should snap to guides, guides snap to elements, both, or neither
   ▸ Whether guides are locked

   You can also use it to clear all the current guides by clicking the Clear All button.

3. When your changes are complete, click OK.

TIP To move a guide, move the mouse over the guide. When the cursor changes, click the guide and drag it to its new location.

TIP To remove a guide from your page, move the guide off the document. Mac users will see a little "puff of smoke" animation—sorry, Windows users! You can also remove all the guides at once (without the animated effect) by choosing **View > Guides > Clear Guides** or by clicking Clear All in the Guides dialog **D**.

TIP To inspect the current position of a guide, hover the cursor over the guide, and a tip showing the position appears.

TIP To position a guide based on the percentage distance of the document rather than pixels, hold down the Shift key while moving the guide **E**. The tip displays the current location in both pixels and percentage when you're moving it and also when you check the guide's position later.

TIP To see how far a guide is from the sides of your document, hold down the Ctrl (Cmd) key. Lines appear showing the distance in pixels (and percentage, if set in the previous tip) to the edges of the document **F**. If you have multiple guides on your page, the distance shown will be from guide to guide or from guide to edge.

TIP Guides can be locked on your page so that they can't be moved. To do this, choose View > Guides > Lock Guides **B** or use the Guides dialog **D**. It's a toggle, so just do it again to unlock your guides.

TIP Rulers have to be visible for you to add guides, but you can view, move, and delete guides even when the rulers are hidden.

TIP Guides can be used to simulate dimensions of standard browsers. Choose View > Guides and pick one of the standard sizes from the bottom of the menu **B**. This creates both vertical and horizontal guides on your page. Be careful, though, because you can still move them accidentally, and then they aren't much use for providing dimension hints. This is the one exception to the previous tip: you can create guides with this method even when the ruler is hidden.

TIP As with the grid, you can choose to snap elements to your guides—but you can also choose to snap guides to your elements. Choose View > Guides > Snap To Guides, or View > Guides > Guides Snap To Elements, or even both **B**. Or, you can set them in the Guides dialog **D**.

TIP If you double-click a guide, the Move Guide dialog appears **G**. Use this dialog to set the guide to a precise position in pixels, inches, centimeters, or percentages.

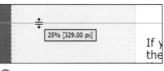

E If you want a percentage instead of pixels, hold down the Shift key.

F Holding down the Ctrl (Cmd) key gives you the distance between the document edge and the guide.

G Double-click a guide to get to the Move Guide dialog.

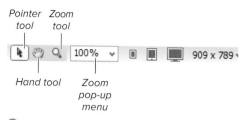

Pointer   Zoom
tool   tool

Hand tool   Zoom
             pop-up
             menu

A The magnification tools in the Status bar are especially useful when making detailed changes to your pages.

Some of the alpacas we've

B You can zoom in on a particular part of the screen.

Zooming In on Your Page

Yes, it's another feature borrowed from standard design applications, just like the grid and guides. The Zoom feature lets you design your pages more precisely. And as with the grid and guides, you'll need to be in Design view to use it.

To zoom in on your page:

Select the Zoom tool from the Status bar at the bottom right of your document **A** and your cursor changes to a magnifying glass with a plus. While in Zoom mode, you can do either of two things:

- Click and drag to draw a box over the area you want to zoom in on. That rectangle expands to take up the entire document window **B**.

- Click the spot on the page you want to magnify. Continue to click it until you get the magnification level you want.

  or

  Press Ctrl-= (Cmd-=) until you've reached the level you want.

  or

  Select a magnification level from the Zoom pop-up menu in the Status bar.

  or

  Type your desired magnification level into the Zoom text box in the Status bar.

  or

continues on next page

Select View > Magnification and pick a magnification level **C**.

or

Select an element on the page, and then choose View > Magnification > Fit Selection **C**.

or

Select an element on the page, and then choose Fit Selection from the Zoom pop-up menu in the Status bar.

To zoom out from your page:

Select the Zoom tool from the Status bar at the bottom right of your document. Press Alt (Opt) and the cursor changes to a magnifying glass and a minus. Click the page to zoom out.

or

Press Ctrl-– (minus key) (Cmd-– [minus key]) until you've reached the level you want.

or

Select View > Magnification and pick a magnification level **C**.

or

Choose View > Magnification > Fit All or View > Magnification > Fit Width **C**.

or

Choose Fit All or Fit Width from the Zoom pop-up menu in the Status bar.

TIP To edit your page in Zoom mode, select the pointer in the Status bar and click inside the page.

TIP To pan your page after you've zoomed in, select the hand icon in the Status bar, and then drag the page to move around.

C You can also access the magnification levels from the menu.

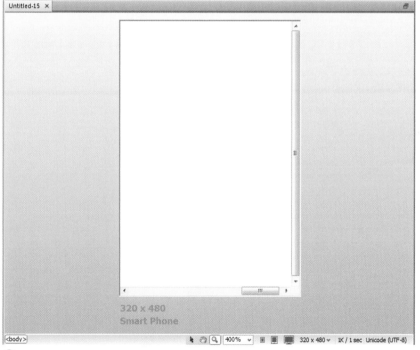

240 × 320	Feature Phone
320 × 480	Smart Phone
480 × 800	Smart Phone
592w	
768 × 1024	Tablet
1000 × 620	(1024 × 768, Maximized)
1260 × 875	(1280 × 1024, Maximized)
1420 × 750	(1440 × 900, Maximized)
1580 × 1050	(1600 × 1200, Maximized)
✓ Full Size	
Edit Sizes...	
✓ Orientation Landscape	
Orientation Portrait	
Media Queries...	

Ⓐ Dreamweaver comes with preset window sizes for the most commonly used monitors.

Setting Page Dimensions

It's handy to be able to easily set guides to show the dimensions of common browsers, but it's not quite the same as seeing how your design actually appears in a window of that size. That's where setting page dimensions comes in.

To resize the window to a preset size:

Click the Window Size pop-up menu in the Status bar, and select one of the listed sizes Ⓐ. Your document window resets to that size. If the new size fits within the document window, you see a view of the selected size Ⓑ.

Ⓑ If the window size you set fits in the document window, Dreamweaver shows it to you as a view.

To edit the preset window sizes:

1. Click the Window Size pop-up menu in the Status bar, and select Edit Sizes. The Window Sizes Preferences pane appears **C**.

   or

   Open Dreamweaver's Preferences panel and select the Window Sizes category.

2. Click in any of the fields and write over the current value to replace it. To add a value, click in the first unfilled line **D**. To delete a value, clear the entire line by deleting the contents of each field.

3. Click OK to accept. The new size now appears in the Window Size pop-up menu **E**.

TIP You can resize the window to a fixed width (leaving the height as is) by entering only a width value. To make the window resize to a fixed height, enter only the height.

TIP Although it looks like you can sort the values in the Window Sizes Preferences pane, you actually can't.

TIP Sadly, if you enter a new window size, it doesn't get added as a new possible value for creating guides—it's only for resizing.

TIP While you're in the Window Sizes Preferences pane, take the chance to reset the Connection speed if it's not appropriate for you or your audience. Dreamweaver uses that number to calculate page download time, which is shown on the far-right end of the Status bar.

C You can view or edit the window sizes in the Window Sizes category of Dreamweaver's Preferences panel.

D New sizes can be added just by clicking in the first unused line and typing the appropriate dimensions.

E And here's the new window size.

Using Multiscreen Preview

Not too long ago, it was perfectly reasonable to create a Web page that was simply meant to be viewed in a browser. We didn't ask, "What kind of machine will this browser be running on?" We had browsers running on computers, darn it, and we liked it! But this Cranky Old Man approach doesn't work with today's clients. Clients these days think it's perfectly reasonable to request that their Web pages look good on computers, tablets, and smart phones. Those Web pages don't have to look the *same* on every device, but they do have to render gracefully no matter the size of the screen, preferably using HTML5 and CSS to make the pages look good at any resolution. Happily, these client requests are also ushering out the era of execrable restaurant Web sites created entirely in Flash.

Dreamweaver CS5.5 introduced a new feature, Multiscreen Preview, that works with Live view to show you simultaneous views of three different screen sizes, for Phone, Tablet, and Desktop. Multiscreen Preview makes it much easier to make your Web pages multi-device aware.

In this section, you'll see how to bring up the Multiscreen Preview panel and change the size of its viewports. In the next section, you'll see how to really put Multiscreen Preview to work, by creating and linking in a media queries CSS file that can work site-wide and change the display of your sites on the fly, according to the screen size of the device that is viewing your page.

To activate Multiscreen Preview:

1. Open the page you want to view in multiple resolutions.

2. In the Document toolbar, click Design view.

   It doesn't matter if you have Live view turned on or off.

3. Click the Multiscreen button in the Document toolbar .

   or

   Choose Window > Multiscreen Preview.

   or

   Choose File > Multiscreen Preview.

   The Multiscreen Preview panel appears **B**. Note that in this screenshot, the viewports all show the same layout, beginning with the upper-left corner of the page. That's because we have yet to implement media queries, which will be covered later in this chapter. The viewports are also all in Live view; you can tell because in the screenshot the Menus button under the hand cursor is animated.

   Each of the three viewports shows its pixel dimensions (horizontal and vertical), and each has independent scroll bars. Because you're looking at a live rendered view of the page, you can click links (to go to another page in your site, for example) and all three viewports will update.

4. (Optional) Navigate within your site. The Multiscreen Preview window has a toolbar with the familiar browser controls of Back, Refresh, Home, and an address bar that shows the URL **C**. You can't type in the address bar; instead, you're meant to open a document in the main Dreamweaver window, then invoke the Multiscreen Preview panel.

Multiscreen button

A Click the Multiscreen button in the Document toolbar to activate the Multiscreen Preview panel.

B The three viewports of the Multiscreen Preview panel: Phone, Tablet, and Desktop.

C Use the familiar browsing controls to change the pages you're looking at in the Multiscreen Preview panel.

View	Width	Height
Phone	320	300
Tablet	768	300
Desktop	1126	

Viewport Sizes

OK

Reset to defaults

Cancel

D Change any of the values to change the width or height of any of the viewports (you can only change the width of the Desktop viewport, because its height automatically resizes along with the Multiscreen Preview panel).

E In this example, we added 150 pixels to the height of the Tablet viewport.

TIP The Multiscreen Preview panel doesn't sync automatically with Design view or Live view, so if you make changes in one of those views, you need to click the Refresh button in the Multiscreen Preview panel. Similarly, if you switch between different top-level document tabs in Dreamweaver, you will also need to click the Refresh button in the Multiscreen Preview panel in order to render the newly selected file.

TIP By default it opens as its own window, but the Multiscreen Preview panel is just like other Dreamweaver panels, and you can treat it as such, docking it with the rest of your panels or even collapsing it to an icon. Just use the regular panel controls in the upper-right corner of the panel.

TIP If you don't have a browser-renderable document open (for example, a CSS or JavaScript file), the Multiscreen button in the Document toolbar will be disabled. It is also disabled when you click on tabs for related files at the top of the Dreamweaver document window.

To set viewport sizes:

1. On the right end of the toolbar in the Multiscreen Preview panel, click Viewport Sizes.

   The Viewport Sizes window appears **D**.

2. Change the values (in pixels) for any of the three viewports (Phone, Tablet, or Desktop).

3. Click OK.

   The viewport changes you made are reflected in the Multiscreen Preview window **E**.

TIP Note that you can't change the Height value of the Desktop viewport. That's because the Multiscreen Preview panel can't show the full size of today's desktop screens, and the important value to target for the desktop is the Width. You can always scroll the Desktop viewport if needed.

Adding Media Queries

It's not enough to simply design your pages for the desktop; now any designer worth his or her salt needs to design with the mobile Web in mind. Using *media queries*, a part of the CSS3 specification, you can automatically link your HTML pages to different CSS style sheets that rearrange the layout of your pages for given screen sizes. The reason to rearrange the layout is simple: a page layout that looks great and is perfectly functional on a desktop browser may initially look fine on a smaller screen (such as an iPad, iPhone, or Android device), but chances are the browser on the mobile device will automatically zoom the page out to fit as much of it as possible on the device's screen. Making the user pinch, scroll, and zoom the screen just to see your content isn't a good user experience. It's better to anticipate and adapt the page for the smaller screen size. You're not changing the *content* of the page for different screen sizes; instead you're changing the *presentation* of that content for a better user experience.

Dreamweaver's Media Queries dialog allows you to insert a link to a media query CSS style sheet, and helps build that style sheet for you. You can choose to insert the link to the media query style sheet on just the page that you're working on, or you can create a site-wide media query style sheet.

It's important to note that although you can use Dreamweaver to create a style sheet optimized for a given screen size, the program can't create it for you automatically. You'll need to make your layout decisions and create the alternative style sheets yourself, though they will usually be able to inherit many properties from the main desktop style sheet.

A The Media Queries dialog allows you to easily make media queries for multiple screen sizes.

B Browse to or create the site-wide media query file.

To create a media queries style sheet:

1. Open (or create) the HTML document you want to style.

2. Choose Modify > Media Queries.

   or

   More often, you'll want to begin working from the Multiscreen Preview panel, so click the Multiscreen button in the Document toolbar, then click the Media Queries button in the Multiscreen Preview panel.

   The Media Queries dialog appears **A**.

3. If you want to create a site-wide media queries style sheet, in the "Write media queries to" section of the dialog, click Site-wide media queries file.

   or

   If you want the media queries to apply only to the current document (though most of the time it's better to reuse media queries throughout the site), click the "This document" button, then skip to step 5.

4. Continuing with the process of creating a site-wide media queries file, click Specify.

   In the resulting dialog **B**, choose either Use existing file or Create new file from the pop-up menu. If you choose the former, click the folder icon at the right side of the dialog to browse to the existing file. Of course, if you choose to create a new file, you should also click the folder icon at the right side of the dialog to specify the name and location of the new style sheet. Click OK.

   continues on next page

Behind the scenes, Dreamweaver has added the path to the site-wide media query file to the Local Info subcategory of Advanced Settings for the site setup ⒸC. You won't see this unless you go looking for it.

5. Because some devices (notably Apple's iPhones with the high-resolution Retina displays) play tricks when reporting their screen size, you should select "Force devices to report actual width" in the Media Queries dialog ⒹD.

6. Chances are you're going to want to create media queries for smart phones and tablets, so click the Default Presets button in the Media Queries dialog.

   In the list, Dreamweaver creates defaults for Phone, Tablet, and Desktop ⒺE. If you want to create additional media queries for other devices you specifically want to target, click the plus button at the bottom of the list.

Ⓒ If you created a site-wide media query file, Dreamweaver records it in the site setup's Advanced Settings.

☑ **Force devices to report actual width**

> *Inserting a special meta tag in your document will force certain devices to report their actual width instead of reporting a false width and then scaling the page.*

Ⓓ It's a good idea to always force devices to report their actual screen width.

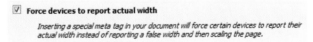

Description	Media Query	CSS File
Phone	only screen and (max-width:320px)	
Tablet	only screen and (min-width:321px) and (max-width:768px)	
Desktop	only screen and (min-width:769px)	
⊞ ⊟		Default Presets

Ⓔ Clicking Default Presets creates three media queries.

Properties

Description: Phone

Min Width: ___ px   Max Width: 320 px

CSS File: [Use existing file: ▾] css/phone.css   📁

F Specify the destination CSS file for the Phone preset.

Properties

Description: Tablet

Min Width: 321 px   Max Width: 768 px

CSS File: [Use existing file: ▾] css/tablet.css   📁

G The Tablet preset has both Min Width and Max Width values.

H After setting the media queries, the Multiscreen Preview panel shows you the result of the different style sheets at each screen resolution.

7. Change the defaults to target particular screen sizes, and to point at appropriate CSS style sheets for each media query. When Dreamweaver creates the default presets, the first one, for Phone, is selected. In the Properties section below the list **F**, you can change the description. For a phone, you can leave the Min Width blank (implying zero pixels), but you should specify the largest width in Max Width (the default is the iPhone's 320 pixels). In the CSS File field, create or browse to the CSS style sheet you want to use for this preset.

8. Click the Tablet preset. This style sheet's properties **G** include a Min Width—which starts at 1 pixel wider than the Phone style sheet's Max Width—and a Max Width of 768 pixels (corresponding to the iPad in portrait mode). Browse to the **tablet.css** style sheet.

   The final preset, Desktop, has a Min Width of 769 pixels and leaves the Max Width field blank. It uses the style sheet **desktop.css**.

9. Click OK.

   The Media Queries dialog disappears. In the **<head>** section of the document's HTML, Dreamweaver has now created a link to the site-wide media queries file (in this example, because we're using the Adobe demo assets, the code was **<link href="css/citrus_mq.css" rel="stylesheet" type="text/css">**). In the **citrus_mq.css** style sheet, there are **@import** rules pointing to the three style sheet files, with the media query rule for each preset you see in the Media Query column in **E**.

   Back in the Multiscreen Preview panel, the display for each viewport changes to reflect the style sheet associated with each viewport size **H**.

Using Fluid Grid Layouts

Years ago, it was common for Web designers to look forward to the day when everyone would have big displays and could see their works as intended. In recent years, that goal has become obsolete—sure, you have a big screen on your desk, but you've also got a small screen in your pocket and a medium-sized screen in your bag. You want your site to look its best on all of them, but you don't want to have to create multiple sites. And that's why Dreamweaver now has fluid grid layouts.

Fluid grid layouts let you design your site based on grids with rows and columns: using one layout for smart phones, another for tablets, and a third for computer monitors—and which layout is displayed is based on the width of the browser window. As our example, we'll use the good old Home Cook site you've seen before—but now it will work on a variety of screen sizes **A**. For our purposes here, we're using Dreamweaver's terminology of *Desktop* for computer monitors, but of course that also covers laptop screens.

To create a fluid grid layout:

1. Choose File > New Fluid Grid Layout **B**.

   The New Document dialog appears, with the Fluid Grid Layout tab selected **C**. This is where we create our grids for the three screen sizes: Mobile, Tablet, and Desktop.

A We like the way this site looks—but not on mobile devices.

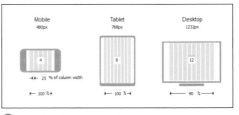

B Both File > New and File > New Fluid Grid Layout take you to the New Document dialog.

C The New Document dialog is where you set up the grid for each of the three screen sizes.

D Start off by saving your fluid grid layout style sheet and giving it a meaningful name.

E Dreamweaver starts off on the Mobile layout; the theory being that you should design for the smallest size first, and then add the extras on to the larger versions.

F Here are the two files that Dreamweaver requires you to have: one is a style sheet, and the other is a collection of JavaScripts.

2. In this example, for mobile devices (such as smart phones) we've entered 4 columns, and for tablets, we'll say 8. For either kind of device, given their limited space, we want to use 100% of the screen. For desktops, we can use 12 columns, but we'll leave some space for margins on either side, so we've entered 90% as the page width in **C**. When done, click Create. The Save Style Sheet File As dialog appears.

3. Dreamweaver requires you to start off by saving a style sheet **D**, and we've called ours **fluidgrid.css**. Enter the name for your style sheet, and then click Save.

Your screen will look like **E** after you create your style sheet; this example shows the smart phone (four-column) layout.

To build your fluid grid layout, you'll lay out the **div**s separately on each of the three screen sizes. Dreamweaver automatically starts you on the Mobile size layout.

4. Save the page by choosing File > Save, and Dreamweaver lets you know that you'll also need a couple of dependent files **F**. Click the Copy button to copy them (they're required). That puts us back to **E**, and now it's time to start building our layout grid.

If you can't read the fine print in the figure, it says, "Use Insert Panel for additional Fluid Grid Layout Div tags. Note: *All Layout Div tags must be inserted directly inside the* **gridContainer** *div tag*. Nested Layout Div tags are not currently supported." The italicized part is what you need to keep in mind; normally, you can insert **div**s anywhere you want, but not when you're working with fluid grid layouts.

continues on next page

5. To add new elements to the page, follow the onscreen directions: go to the Insert Panel, and choose Insert Fluid Grid Layout Div Tag ⒢. The Insert Fluid Grid Layout Div Tag dialog appears ⒣.

6. Enter the name of your new **div**; we've called ours **navbar**. Once we add that **div** and a couple of others we need for the layout we've designed (in this case, **contentArea** and **reviews**), the page now looks like ⒤.

7. Now that we've created the **div**s, we're ready to do some layout work. Select the **navbar div** ⒥, and then move the right handle to make the **div** thinner. One column is enough for the **navbar** on smart phones, and the result is shown in ⒦.

8. The content area can fit into three columns, so resize the **div** to be three columns, as shown in ⒧.

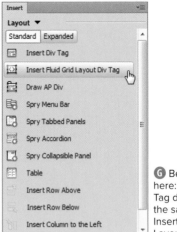

⒢ Be careful here: Insert Div Tag doesn't do the same thing as Insert Fluid Grid Layout Div Tag.

⒣ It's OK to leave "Start New Row" selected, as you'll have plenty of chance to change it later.

⒤ Here are the four **div**s: the three just created plus the one that was automatically generated.

⒥ Drag the right handle to resize the **div**. in this figure, we're in the middle of the drag, so the **div** hasn't visually updated its size yet, though you see the onscreen tip showing the **div**'s current size.

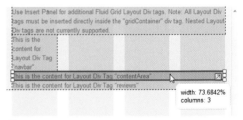

⒦ Here's the **div** after it's been resized.

⒧ Again, here the right handle is being dragged, giving the content area the remaining three columns.

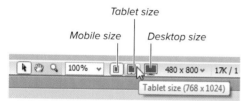

M All that's left to do now is click the arrow button to move the **div** into position.

N And here's our navigation and content **div**s, just the way we want them to appear on smart phones.

Mobile size

Tablet size

Desktop size

O Click these icons to switch between the different layouts.

P All the **div**s we added are full width again when we switch to Tablet layout.

9. Of course, you'll want that three-column content area to be to the right of the navigation, and clicking the "Move Up a Row" arrow on the right side of the selected **div** **M** gives you **N**.

10. Switch between the different layouts by choosing between the Window Size icons at the bottom of the document window **O**. You'll notice (possibly to your surprise) that when you changed the smart phone layout, the others didn't change **P**. That's because although each layout shares the same files, their designs are independent.

11. For the eight-column tablet view, give the **navbar** and **reviews div**s two columns each, and the main content area four columns **Q**.

12. The 12-column desktop view **R** gets two columns for the navigation, three for the reviews, and seven for the main content.

continues on next page

Q We can choose to lay out our **div**s any way we wish; here, we've chosen a simple 2-4-2 column design.

R On the desktop we have all the room we need, so we're going for an asymmetrical 2-7-3 column layout.

13. Next up is the easy part: copying and pasting the content from our old Home Cook page Ⓐ into our new fluid grid layout. Once that's accomplished (plus a little bit of CSS tweaking), you can see the results in Ⓢ (Mobile size), Ⓣ (Tablet size), and Ⓤ (Desktop size).

Ⓢ The Mobile layout has a header (with site name and tagline below the graphic) above the navigation and content areas.

Ⓣ The Tablet layout has the header (with site name and tagline in a condensed font) above the navigation, content, and reviews areas.

TIP In order to make the most of the limited space on a smart phone, set the reviews column to have a style of `display:none`. It's a handy way to hide less-important content when there just isn't room.

TIP Wondering how to get rid of those annoying pink bars and green highlights when you actually want to see how your page looks? Refer back to "Using the Visual Aids" in Chapter 9 for how to toggle them on and off.

TIP Dreamweaver started us off with one default grid div **E**. Here, we've repurposed it as the header for our pages.

U And finally, the Desktop layout has the header (with expanded font) above the navigation, content, and reviews areas—and there's still room for left and right margins.

Using jQuery for Layout

Since Dreamweaver 5.5, the program has allowed you to create layouts for mobile devices using the jQuery Mobile JavaScript framework. You'll find jumping-off points for these layouts in the Page from Sample tab of the New Document dialog. In the Mobile Starters sample folder, there are three kinds of jQuery Mobile layouts:

- **jQuery Mobile (CDN)** uses **.css** and **.js** files directly from jQuery's Content Delivery Network (CDN). That's another way of saying that the jQuery files are hosted on servers spread across the Internet and are often going to be served to your user more quickly than they would be if they were hosted on your own server.

- **jQuery Mobile (Local)** uses the same files as the CDN choice, but now they're hosted on your server.

- **jQuery Mobile with Theme (Local)** again uses the same files, but with the addition of your own jQuery theme file, so you can specify the look of the resulting layout.

All of this is just to provide a mobile site using standard user interface widgets—which is nice, but your smart phone site will then look like a standard smart phone site. And it doesn't help the non–smart phone versions at all. Making pretty much any kind of modification involves diving into and modifying the HTML, CSS, and JavaScript in Dreamweaver's Code view, which puts it outside the scope of this book.

Our opinion is that it's a bad idea for designers to create multiple versions of the same site. And this—*unless all you want is a mobile site*—forces Dreamweaver users into exactly that situation.

Using Behaviors and Navigation Objects

Dreamweaver provides a number of built-in JavaScript actions you can easily add to your pages. No prior knowledge of JavaScript is required to use them. Adobe calls these JavaScript actions *behaviors*. Behaviors can add interactivity to your site. Many times the behavior is triggered by a user's action; for example, the behavior will happen when the user clicks a link or hovers over a link. Other behaviors happen without any overt user action, such as when a browser checks for a needed plug-in as a page loads.

In Dreamweaver, you add many behaviors with the Behaviors tab of the Tag Inspector panel. Some behaviors are also available in the Insert panel. In addition, Dreamweaver imports behaviors from other Adobe software, such as Fireworks.

In this chapter, you'll learn how to use behaviors to add rollovers, open new windows, check for plug-ins, validate forms, and insert jump and pop-up menus. **Table 13.1** lists some of the available behaviors.

TABLE 13.1 Dreamweaver Behaviors

Behavior	Description
Call JavaScript	Specify that a custom JavaScript should execute for a specific event. You can write the custom JavaScript yourself or use one from the many available JavaScript libraries.
Change Property	Change the value of an object's properties. Only certain properties can be changed, and only in certain browsers.
Check Plugin	Send visitors to specific pages based on whether they have certain plug-ins installed. This works only in certain browsers.
Drag AP Element	Set up movable elements that users can drag. Attach this behavior to the document to make interactive puzzles, games, or sliders.
Effects	Add one of seven visual effects: Appear/Fade, Blind, Grow/Shrink, Highlight, Shake, Slide, and Squish.
Go To URL	Open a new page in a specified window or frame, or change the contents of two or more frames with one click.
Jump Menu	Create or edit a jump menu. Normally, you create a jump menu using Insert > Form Objects > Jump Menu, and merely use the Behaviors panel to edit it.
Jump Menu Go	Like Jump Menu but adds a Go button to the menu to activate or reactivate the menu choice.
Open Browser Window	Open a URL in a new window. You can set the properties for the new window.
Popup Message	Create a JavaScript alert with the message you specify, usually a brief informative statement.
Preload Images	Preload images that won't be seen right away (for example, images for rollovers). That way, there's no wait to see the image when the action is triggered.
Set Text of Container	Replace the content and formatting of an existing absolutely positioned element with new content. The new content can include text, HTML, and JavaScript functions.
Set Text of Frame	Change the text display in a frame to the new content and formatting you specify. The new content can include text, HTML, and JavaScript functions.
Set Text of Status Bar	Put a message in the browser's status bar.
Set Text of Text Field	Replace the content of a form's text field with new content. The new content can include text or JavaScript functions.
Show-Hide Elements	Show, hide, or restore the default visibility of one or more absolutely positioned elements.
Swap Image	Swap one image for another to create rollover effects or even swap more than one image at a time.
Swap Image Restore	Restore the last set of swapped images to their previous source files. If you leave the Restore option selected when you attach a Swap Image action, this action gets automatically added.
Validate Form	Check the contents of specified text fields to be sure the user has entered the proper type of data. You can also check whether the user entered something in a required field.

A Behaviors are shown in black if they are available for the particular element you chose, and in gray if they aren't. You can't select a grayed-out behavior.

Using the Behaviors Panel

To add interactivity to your site, you'll want to add behaviors to the objects on your pages, such as images and links. To add, modify, and remove behaviors, you'll use the Behaviors tab of the Tag Inspector panel (in this chapter, we'll just refer to the "Behaviors panel"). Objects can have multiple behaviors attached, so you'll also need to know how to rearrange their order.

To add a behavior:

1. If the Behaviors panel is not visible, choose Window > Behaviors (Shift-F4).

2. Select an object on the page, such as an image or a text link.

3. Click the plus button on the Behaviors panel to see the list of available actions for the selected object **A**. If a choice is grayed out, that action is not available for the selected object. Click to choose an action.

4. The dialog for the chosen action opens **B**. Enter the requested information in the dialog.

continues on next page

B The Go To URL dialog is nice and simple. If you're using frames, frame names appear in the "Open in" box.

5. The default event for that action is displayed in the events column on the left side of the Behaviors panel ⓒ. If you want a different event, select it from the pop-up menu in the events column ⓓ by clicking the default.

To edit a behavior:

1. Select an object with an attached behavior.

2. Double-click the behavior name in the behaviors column of the Behaviors panel.

   or

   Select the behavior name and press Enter (Return). The dialog for the behavior opens.

3. Change any parameters and click OK.

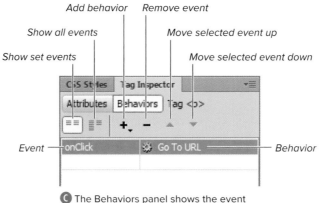

Add behavior   Remove event

Show all events

Move selected event up

Show set events

Move selected event down

Event

Behavior

ⓒ The Behaviors panel shows the event handler and the behavior name.

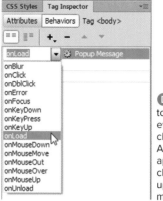

D If you want to change the event handler, click the event. An arrow appears, and clicking it brings up the pop-up menu.

E Behaviors attached to an element execute in the order in which they are listed in the Behaviors panel.

To change the order of behaviors:

If more than one behavior is attached to an object, the behaviors run in the order listed in the Behaviors panel, from the top to the bottom **E**. Select an event and use the up or down arrow to change the order.

To delete a behavior:

1. On your Web page, select an object with an attached behavior.

2. In the Behaviors panel, select the name of the behavior you want to delete.

3. Click the minus button.

   or

   Press Delete.

TIP You can extend Dreamweaver by adding additional behaviors from the Adobe Dreamweaver Exchange. Download the bonus online chapter "Customizing and Extending Dreamweaver" (www.dreamweaverbook.com) for more information about extending Dreamweaver.

TIP JavaScript you write yourself can be inserted in Dreamweaver. To learn more about JavaScript, check out another of our books: *JavaScript: Visual QuickStart Guide* (Peachpit, 2011).

TIP You might be wondering about those behaviors in the Effects submenu. We'll cover them in Chapter 14, "Building Pages with Dynamic Elements."

Events and Browsers

JavaScript includes many *event handlers*, such as **onClick** or **onDblClick**, as seen in figure Ⓓ of "Using the Behaviors Panel." The name of the event handler is usually pretty descriptive of the user event involved.

Not every browser understands every event. Dreamweaver previously gave you a say as to the browsers you could choose events for, but as part of Adobe's embrace of standards-compliant browsers, that ability was removed in Dreamweaver CS5. Now, the only behaviors in Dreamweaver are those that work in modern browsers.

Events can be applied only to certain tags. **Table 13.2** shows specific event names and associated tags. Not all events available in Dreamweaver are listed here, and some event handlers available in JavaScript are not available in Dreamweaver.

TABLE 13.2 Dreamweaver Event Handlers

Event	Triggered when	Associated with
onAbort	The user stops the browser from completely loading the object	documents, images
onBlur	A field loses focus	form fields
onChange	The user changes a default value on the page	form fields
onClick	The user clicks an object	links, forms
onDblClick	The user double-clicks an object	links, images
onFocus	A field gains focus	form fields
onHelp	The user clicks F1 or something labeled Help	links, images
onKeyDown	The user presses a key on the keyboard	form fields
onKeyPress	The user presses any key	form fields
onKeyUp	The user releases a key	form fields
onLoad	When a page, frameset, or image finishes loading	documents, images
onMouseDown	The user presses the mouse button	links, images
onMouseMove	The user moves the mouse	links, images
onMouseOut	The user moves the mouse off a selected object	links, images
onMouseUp	The user releases the mouse button	links, images
onMouseOver	The user points the mouse at an object	links, images
onReset	The user clicks a form reset button	forms
onResize	The user resizes the browser window	documents
onScroll	The user scrolls up or down	documents
onSelect	The user selects text in a form field	form fields
onSubmit	The user clicks the Submit button in a form	forms
onUnload	The user leaves a page	documents

A An example of an Up state image.

B An example of an Over state image.

C The Images icon in the Common category of the Insert panel has a pop-up menu with several options.

Adding Rollovers

Web users love *rollovers*, sometimes called mouseovers. There's something endlessly pleasing about running a mouse over a page and watching things change. A color changes, an image changes, or an image somewhere else on the page changes or pops up. Web users also expect rollovers—if they move their mouse over an image and nothing happens, they'll assume that it's not a link and move on to something else.

To add a rollover:

1. Prepare two images, such as those in **A** and **B**, for the rollover's Up and Over states.

2. Position the insertion point in the document where you want the rollover to appear.

3. Select Insert > Image Objects > Rollover Image.

   or

   In the Common category of the Insert panel, click the arrow beside the Images icon and select Rollover Image **C**.

continues on next page

4. The Insert Rollover Image dialog appears **D**. Fill out the fields:

▸ **Image name:** This is the name that JavaScript uses internally to refer to this image.

▸ **Original image:** The path to the Up state of the image, which is what displays when the page is loaded.

▸ **Rollover image:** The path to the Over state of the image, which is what displays when the user's cursor is over the image.

▸ **Preload rollover image:** This should be selected so the Over version of the image is in the browser's cache when it's needed. Don't make users wait for the Over image to download—they might think the page isn't working and give up on your site.

▸ **Alternate text:** This is the alternate information for users with nongraphical browsers.

▸ **When clicked, Go to URL:** This is the URL of the Web page you want to open when the user clicks the image.

D Specify both the Up and Over images to insert a rollover image.

E Be sure the Swap Image Restore behavior is added along with the Swap Image behavior.

Image States

To understand rollovers, buttons, and navigation bars, you need to know something about image states. An image state corresponds with a mouse event. The most common image states are:

- **Up:** This image appears when the page first loads. It's the default image, in that it's what is displayed unless the user is interacting with this image.

- **Over:** This image appears when the user moves the mouse over the image.

- **Down:** This image appears when the user clicks the image. Down state images are often used in navigation bars to indicate the current page.

- **OverWhileDown:** This image appears when the user moves the mouse over an image after clicking.

Most rollovers use only the Up and Over states.

5. Click OK to accept the changes.

6. Check the newly created events in the Behaviors panel to be sure they're what you want **E**.

Note that if your rollover is within an HTML tag, that tag appears in the Behaviors panel. In this case, the rollover is within the **a** tag.

TIP To preview the rollover, click the Live view button at the top of the document window and then roll over the image with your cursor. You can also preview the page in a browser to see the rollover.

TIP Select the behavior in the Behaviors panel if you want to change the mouse events or edit the parameters of the Insert Rollover Image dialog.

TIP Adding a single rollover adds two events to the Behaviors panel: one for the action of moving the mouse over the image (Swap Image) and one for the action of moving the mouse off the image (Swap Image Restore). Check to make sure that both parts are added, or your rollover won't work the way you expect it to.

Opening a New Browser Window

It isn't a good idea to open a new browser window unless you really, really need one. Some users may not realize that a new window opened. Users may become lost or confused by the grayed-out Back button. Users may not realize they must close the new window to get back to the original page. Certain browsers, particularly those used by people with accessibility needs, may not deal with new windows in a way that helps the user understand what's happening. Depending on the action you use to trigger the opening of the new window, some users may not see it at all. For example, setting a new window to open during an **onLoad** event is the trick to getting a pop-up or pop-under ad in a user's face, so many users set their browsers so that pop-up windows won't open, ever.

Given all that, when is a new browser window justified? Consider it when the content of the new window is a small example or elaboration of one idea. Small means smaller than a normal-sized browser window. Small also means small in concept: if the main content of your page is already clear, a new window can add a little something that people can check if they're interested. For instance, a reasonable use of a new window is to show an enlarged image of a product.

You should explicitly tell users that their click will cause a new window to open: "Click the image to see a larger view— opens in new window." Leave the decision about whether to click up to your users— don't blindside them with windows that automatically open without warning.

To add the Open Browser Window action:

1. Prepare an HTML page or image that will appear in the new window.

2. Select an object, such as a link or image, in the document window.

3. In the Behaviors panel, click the plus button to add a new behavior. Choose Open Browser Window from the pop-up menu, and the Open Browser Window dialog appears **A**.

continues on next page

A When you open a new browser window, you have all kinds of control over how it will appear.

4. Fill out the following fields:

- ▸ **URL to display:** This is the HTML page or image that will appear in the new window.

- ▸ **Window width** and **Window height:** Set an exact pixel size for the new window.

- ▸ **Navigation toolbar:** Selecting this adds Back, Forward, Home, and Reload buttons.

- ▸ **Location toolbar:** Selecting this adds a location text box with the page URL showing.

- ▸ **Status bar:** Selecting this adds a display at the bottom of the browser window showing status information.

- ▸ **Menu bar:** Selecting this adds browser menu items, such as File, Edit, View, Go, and Help. This option applies only to Windows users; Mac users always have access to the menu.

- ▸ **Scrollbars as needed:** Selecting this adds scrollbars (horizontal or vertical) only if needed. If deselected, there will be no scrollbars. It's a good idea to always select this attribute.

- ▸ **Resize handles:** Selecting this adds a gripper in the lower-right corner of the window for the user to drag, and a maximize button at the top of the window. If deselected, the user can't resize the window by either method. This is another good attribute to routinely include.

- ▸ **Window name:** This is a required identifier needed by JavaScript. Remember, no spaces are allowed in this name.

5. Click OK to accept.

6. Check the default event. If it isn't the event you want, select another event from the pop-up menu.

TIP If the new window contains only an image, the pixel dimensions of the image and the pixel dimensions of the window won't be an exact match. For better control, many designers put the single image on an HTML page and link to the HTML page.

TIP Dreamweaver can be extended with an action to add a "Close Window" script to an HTML page. It's a good idea to give users an obvious way to close the new window. See Appendix B, "Customizing and Extending Dreamweaver" for more information.

TIP Though it's certainly reasonable to use Dreamweaver's built-in behaviors to work with opening windows, you might instead want to use a widget based on jQuery or Spry to do the job, especially if you're displaying something like an image gallery. A widget is likely to be more flexible to use. See Chapter 14 for more.

Checking for Plug-ins

The Check Plugin behavior sends users to different pages depending on whether they have particular plug-ins. For example, if a user has Flash installed, you might send them to one page; otherwise, you might send them to a page where they get the same information but without Flash.

You can depend on most Dreamweaver behaviors to work on a wide variety of browsers, but the Check Plugin action smacks into some browser issues. You can't detect plug-ins in Internet Explorer for Windows using JavaScript.

In general, plug-ins are on their way out, driven in large part by Apple's refusal to support Flash on their mobile devices and Adobe's subsequent abandonment of its mobile Flash development, but also because HTML5 can now handle displaying rich media content natively. Plug-in detection is still useful for desktop browsers, but it's rapidly becoming yesterday's technique.

To add the Check Plugin action:

1. In the document window, use the tag selector to select either the document (the **body** tag) or a link (the **a** tag).

continues on next page

2. In the Behaviors panel, click the plus button and select the Check Plugin action from the pop-up menu. The Check Plugin dialog opens Ⓐ and shows the following:

   ▸ Choose a plug-in from the pop-up menu: Flash, Shockwave, Live Audio, QuickTime, or Windows Media Player.

   or

   ▸ Click the Enter radio button and type the name of a plug-in in the text box. The name must be exactly the same as the name in bold on the Enabled Plugins page in a Mozilla-based browser such as Firefox. To see the Enabled Plugins page, enter **about:plugins** in the Firefox address bar.

   ▸ **If found, go to URL:** Enter the URL in this text box. This field is optional; if you leave it blank, the user stays on the same page if the plug-in is detected.

   ▸ **Otherwise, go to URL:** Enter the alternate URL in the text box. If you leave this field blank, users *without* the plug-in stay on the same page.

   ▸ **Always go to first URL if detection is not possible:** When detection is impossible, the user is normally sent to the URL in the "Otherwise, go to URL" box. But if you select this check box, the user instead goes to the first URL (the one labeled "If found, go to URL"). If this is selected, users may be prompted by the browser to download the plug-in.

3. Click OK to accept changes.

4. Check the default event in the Behaviors panel to be sure it's the one you want.

Ⓐ You can check for any plug-in if you know the correct name for it. In this case, we're looking for the Flash plug-in, which is in the pop-up menu.

TIP All Netscape browsers since version 2.0 can detect plug-ins. By "Netscape browser," we mean Netscape Navigator, Netscape Communicator, Mozilla Firefox, and other browsers based on any of these.

Here's a brand-new Insert Jump Menu dialog, ready for you to add as many items as you want.

Using Jump Menus

A jump menu is a pop-up menu listing links to documents or files. When users choose an item, they "jump" directly to the new URL.

Jump menus save space on the page. For example, to find a retailer in your area, you might be asked to select your state or country. A list of states or countries could be very lengthy. Putting the links in a jump menu saves you from listing them in full as part of the page layout.

In addition to the required list of linked items, a jump menu can optionally include a menu selection prompt, such as "Select one," and a Go button.

To insert a jump menu:

1. Place the insertion point in the document.

2. Select Insert > Form > Jump Menu.

   or

   In the Form category of the Insert panel, click the Jump Menu button.

   The Insert Jump Menu dialog appears Ⓐ. Fill it out as follows:

   ▸ **Menu items:** Don't type anything in this list. As you add items to the menu, they automatically appear.

     Move items up or down in the list by selecting one and using the up or down arrow to change its order.

   ▸ **Text:** Type the text you want for the menu item. You can type a prompt such as "Choose one" here. For text to be a prompt, leave the URL blank.

   ▸ **When selected, go to URL:** Browse for or type the URL to go to here.

continues on next page

- **Open URLs in:** Select the window where you want the URL to display.

- **Menu ID:** Type a name here for JavaScript to use; as always, it cannot contain any spaces.

- **Insert go button after menu:** Select this if you want a Go button. The Go button isn't required to make the menu work for users with JavaScript enabled in their browsers. If the user's browser doesn't use JavaScript, the Go button is needed.

- **Select first item after URL change:** If you entered a prompt in the Text field, select this.

3. Click OK to accept your changes, and the jump menu appears on your page.

To edit a jump menu:

1. Double-click the behavior name in the Behaviors panel. The Jump Menu dialog opens **B**.

2. Make any changes needed.

3. Click OK to accept the changes, and the revised jump menu appears in your document.

B When you edit a jump menu, some of the original options are missing, particularly the "Insert go button after menu" choice.

C Make sure your new button has a value and that it doesn't have an action.

D The Jump Menu Go dialog attaches a Go button to an existing jump menu of your choice.

E The finished jump menu, with a Go button.

To insert a jump menu Go button:

1. Select an insertion point in the document window. A jump menu must already exist in the document.

2. Insert a button from the Forms category of the Insert panel. In the Property inspector, set the button's Action to None and its Value to Go (or something similar), as in **C**.

3. In the document, select your new button. In the Behaviors panel, click the plus button and select Jump Menu Go. The Jump Menu Go dialog opens **D**.

4. Select a jump menu for the Go button to activate. A Go button needs to be associated with a jump menu to work. If you have only one jump menu on the page, you can take the default.

5. Click OK to add the behavior to the button. The finished menu appears on the page **E**.

TIP A jump menu requires a form, which Dreamweaver adds automatically. You'll notice the red form indicator bordering the jump menu in the document window, and you'll see a `form` tag in the tag selector bar.

Validating Forms

Dreamweaver behaviors can check up on how users complete forms. You can require certain fields, check to make sure that a user has entered a value in a required field, or check to make sure that the user entered the correct type of information in a field.

With the Validate Form behavior, you can set parameters for an entire form. You can also use the Validate Form behavior on individual fields. See Chapter 11, "Using Forms and Fields," for more information about making a form with Dreamweaver, and Chapter 14, "Building Pages with Dynamic Elements" for form validation routines using the Spry or jQuery JavaScript frameworks.

To validate a form:

1. In the document window, select the Submit button.

   or

   Select the `form` tag from the tag selector at the bottom of the document window.

2. In the Behaviors panel, click the plus button and select Validate Form. The Validate Form dialog opens Ⓐ:

- ▸ **Fields:** Select a field in the box.
- ▸ **Required:** Select this if the user *must* enter data in this field for the form to be accepted.
- ▸ **Anything:** Select this radio button if any combination of text and numbers is acceptable.
- ▸ **Number:** Select this if you want the user to enter a zip code, phone number, or other strictly numerical data.
- ▸ **Email address:** Select this if you want to check for an @ symbol within the entered data.
- ▸ **Number from:** Select this if you need to check for a number within a specified range.

3. Select the remaining fields in the Fields box and set the parameters for each until you have completed the dialog for each field in the form.

4. Click OK to accept your changes.

Ⓐ One form validation option is to require an email address from the user. You can also see here why you should always name your form fields: it makes it easier to know which field is which in this dialog.

TIP You can also select an individual form field and add a Validate Form behavior. The dialog is the same, but the event handler (that's the real name for those fields on the Behaviors panel) is different. Check the Behaviors panel to be sure it's the correct event (onBlur or onChange) when setting validation parameters field by individual field. Be careful with this method, because it can get annoying to a user who wants to skip certain questions and come back to them later. Saving the validation for last, when the user finally clicks the Submit button, is a better idea.

TIP When a user enters something incorrectly or neglects to fill in a required field, a JavaScript alert box similar to **B** pops up with a message about the error.

TIP It's good practice to give users an explicit cue when a field is required. An asterisk next to a required field is a common visual cue, along with a note to the user that the asterisk denotes a required field. You may have color-blind users, so merely formatting the required field labels in a different color isn't considered adequate.

TIP The Dreamweaver behaviors for validating forms are different from server-side scripts used to handle submitted information. The same validity checks on user data you add with Dreamweaver should also be done with server-side scripts. Why both? The server-side checks are necessary because not all users have JavaScript enabled in their browser (some mobile browsers may lack JavaScript altogether). The client-side JavaScript checks added here are also useful because they give faster feedback to users.

The page at www.homecook.info says:

The following error(s) occurred:
- lname is required.
- email is required.

OK

B The user sees an alert if the form validation requirements aren't met.

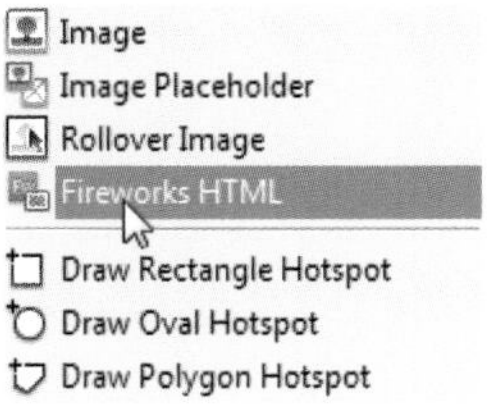
Image
Image Placeholder
Rollover Image
Fireworks HTML
Draw Rectangle Hotspot
Draw Oval Hotspot
Draw Polygon Hotspot

Ⓐ You can choose to add Fireworks HTML from the Images icon in the Common category of the Insert panel.

Inserting Fireworks Pop-Up Menus

If you own Adobe Fireworks, you can use it to create a pop-up menu. When you insert a Fireworks pop-up menu into a Dreamweaver document, it's best to use the round-trip editing feature to edit the menu in Fireworks. You will be able to edit the pop-up menu in Dreamweaver, but if you do, you lose the ability to edit it in Fireworks later. Stick with Fireworks.

When you have the Fireworks pop-up menu completed, simply export it. Fireworks creates all the image and HTML files for you and adds them to the Dreamweaver site root folder. With the files in your site folder, you're ready to insert the menu in Dreamweaver.

To insert a Fireworks pop-up menu:

1. Place the insertion point in the document where you want the menu.
2. Choose Insert > Image Objects > Fireworks HTML.

   or

   In the Common category of the Insert panel, click the pop-up menu by the Images icon and select Fireworks HTML Ⓐ.

   The Insert Fireworks HTML dialog opens Ⓑ.

continues on next page

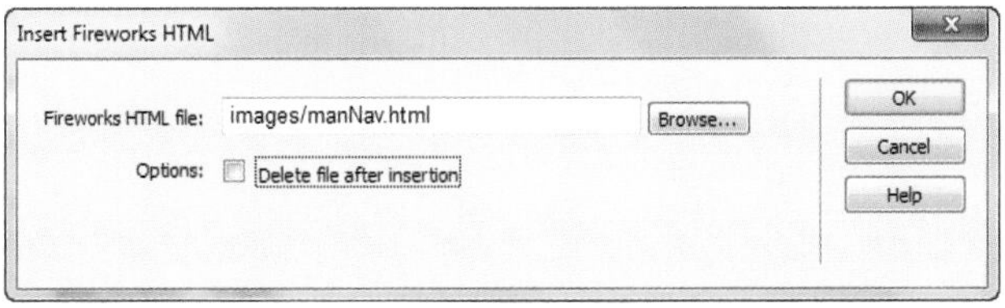
Insert Fireworks HTML
Fireworks HTML file:
images/manNav.html
Browse...
Options:
Delete file after insertion
OK
Cancel
Help

Ⓑ Getting Fireworks HTML into Dreamweaver is as easy as pointing to the HTML file.

3. Browse for or type the name of the Fireworks HTML file.

4. (Optional) Select the "Delete file after insertion" option if you no longer want the Fireworks HTML to be stored as a separate file. Selecting this option won't affect the source PNG file associated with the HTML file or your ability to use round-trip editing to edit the pop-up menu in Fireworks.

5. Click OK to insert your menu. All the HTML, image links, and JavaScript connected to the pop-up menu are inserted in the appropriate areas in the document.

TIP Deleting the HTML file after insertion has its pros and cons. You might want to keep it around to use elsewhere, or you might want to delete it to clean up after yourself. Either way, you can re-create it inside Fireworks, so if you delete it accidentally, it's not the end of the world.

Building Pages with Dynamic Elements

A common feature of modern Web sites is widespread user interactivity enabled by extensive use of CSS and JavaScript. This allows applications that run inside a Web browser to offer the kind of responsiveness that was once reserved for native applications.

In Dreamweaver CS3, Adobe added a library of widgets to enable Web builders to make their sites look like cutting-edge destinations. This library—also referred to as a *framework*—is named Spry. In Dreamweaver CS5, Adobe expanded the program's ability to use other, more popular frameworks (Spry never really caught on outside Dreamweaver), such as jQuery. No matter the framework, you don't need to know anything about CSS or JavaScript to use widgets.

In this chapter, we'll take a quick look at the Spry elements that come with Dreamweaver, but we'll focus on working with jQuery and using the Adobe Widget Browser to use elements from other frameworks in your pages. And we'll end the chapter with one of Dreamweaver CS6's new features: CSS3 transitions, which allow fancy effects without any JavaScript at all.

What Are Spry and jQuery?

Before you start using jQuery and Spry widgets, it helps to know a little bit more about the frameworks and how they work behind the scenes.

A (brief) history of frameworks

When people first started adding JavaScript to pages, they quickly realized that a lot of the work they were doing was the same stuff, over and over and over again. In recent years, it's become common to let JavaScript handle more and more of the user interface (UI) duties. This means that Web sites have become smarter and more flexible, but it's also been a lot more work for people who write code. Programmers tend to hate writing new code when they know someone else has already solved that particular problem. Instead, they go looking for free code offered by others, and in return offer their own solutions. The result is shared libraries of code that can handle most of the usual user interface requirements.

However, programmers also tend to have definite (and idiosyncratic) opinions about the "right" way to write code, and the result of that has been the creation of many different frameworks. If you've ever heard of libraries such as Dojo, YUI, or Prototype, they're all more or less the same thing, built by developers who thought that *their* way of doing things was better than what already existed.

Spry is Adobe's answer to this challenge, geared to work with Dreamweaver. It's not an application; instead, it's a collection of code snippets (both CSS and JavaScript) that when added to your pages creates some standard effects.

What's in Spry

Spry contains three types of components:

- **Widgets:** These elements let you create a more interactive Web site. There are two main types of widgets: UI widgets (such as the accordion, menu bar, and collapsible panel) and form validation (such as text fields and text areas).

- **Effects:** Unlike widgets, effects don't so much interact with the user as just look good on their own. You can use effects to visually highlight transitions or to emphasize elements on your page. Some examples of effects are highlight, shrink, and squish.

- **XML data sets:** If you want data on your page that's read from an external file, or you want users to be able to sort displayed information without having to reload the page, or you want to show some detailed information when the user selects various options, then you're looking at using Spry data sets.

About jQuery

The jQuery framework (**jquery.com**) is a freely downloadable, open-source set of utilities and controls that help you build interactive Web applications. We think it's one of the best, and since it's become the most popular framework, it appears most other folks agree. These are some of jQuery's strengths:

- **Lightweight:** It's considerably smaller than many of its competitors, which means sites using it load more quickly.

- **Ubiquitous:** It's very easy to integrate jQuery into your Web sites. You can host it on your own server, but many people prefer to use a link to jQuery hosted on one of the content delivery networks (CDNs), which are systems of servers spread throughout the Internet's infrastructure, connected by fast pipes. When the user needs jQuery, the CDN serves it up from the closest server to them, making the page more responsive. Google and Microsoft both host the latest version (and some older versions) of jQuery on their CDNs. Best of all, if the user has recently visited a page that uses jQuery, they may already have some of the jQuery files cached, making your site appear to be amazingly fast.

- **Active development community:** If you have a question, you can ask it in their forum and get a fast response, or you can search the archives to see if it's a FAQ.

- **Plug-in architecture:** If you need a feature that isn't in jQuery, there's a good chance that someone's written it as a plug-in. An additional benefit of plug-ins is that you're only adding them to your site when they're needed—that is, you don't have their added weight on every page.

- **Speed:** Even in tests created by its competition, jQuery comes out ahead (see **http://mootools.net/slickspeed**, for instance).

- **Ease of use for non-geeks:** Because its selection queries are based on CSS, someone who isn't a full-time professional programmer can easily drop into jQuery, add some functionality to their site, and have it work the way they expect.

For all of the above reasons, jQuery has become one of the—if not *the*—most popular JavaScript frameworks available.

TIP If after working with jQuery and Spry you decide that you want to learn more about JavaScript, we recommend another book we've written: *JavaScript: Visual QuickStart Guide, Eighth Edition* (Peachpit, 2012).

Adding Spry Elements

By now, you've surely noticed the Spry category 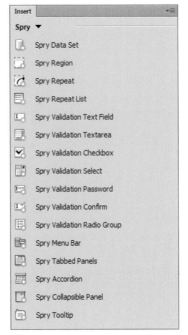 in the Insert panel. It's just one of the many places where you can find Spry elements to add to your page.

This section shows you how to insert Spry elements on your pages. To learn much more about working with Spry and how you configure Spry widgets, see the bonus chapter "Using Spry Widgets." Bonus chapters are included in the ebook edition of this book, and they are freely downloadable from **www.dreamweaverbook.com** for readers of the paper edition.

Ⓐ Spry widgets are found in the Spry category of the Insert panel.

To add a Spry element:

For widgets and data objects: With the Spry category showing in the Insert panel, choose where on your page you want to add the element, and then click the desired Spry button.

or

For widgets and data objects: Choose Insert > Spry from the menu bar, and then choose which Spry element you want to add from the submenu Ⓑ.

or

For form validation widgets: Choose Insert > Form from the menu bar, and then choose which Spry widget you want to add from the submenu Ⓑ.

or

For UI widgets: Choose Insert > Layout Objects from the menu bar, and then choose which Spry widget you want to add from the submenu Ⓑ.

or

For effects: Select the element on the page you want the effect to affect, click the plus button on the Behaviors tab of the Tag inspector, and choose an action from the Effects submenu Ⓒ.

> **TIP** If you've added a widget, you'll see the object on the page outlined with a bright blue border and the name of the widget. If you've added an effect, you'll see it listed in the Behaviors tab of the Tag inspector.

> **TIP** Believe it or not, these aren't all the places where you can find options to add Spry elements in Dreamweaver.

Tag...   Ctrl+E
Image   Ctrl+Alt+I
Image Objects   ▶
Media   ▶
Media Queries...

Table   Ctrl+Alt+T
Table Objects   ▶
Layout Objects   ▶
Form   ▶

Hyperlink
Email Link
Named Anchor   Ctrl+Alt+A
Date
Server-Side Include
Comment

HTML   ▶
Template Objects   ▶
Recent Snippets   ▶

Widget...
Spry   ▶
jQuery Mobile   ▶
InContext Editing   ▶
Data Objects   ▶

Customize Favorites...
Get More Objects...

Form

Text Field
Textarea
Button
Checkbox
Radio Button
Select (List/Menu)
File Field
Image Field
Hidden Field

Radio Group
Checkbox Group
Jump Menu

Fieldset
Label

Spry Validation Text Field
Spry Validation Textarea
Spry Validation Checkbox
Spry Validation Select
Spry Validation Password
Spry Validation Confirm
Spry Validation Radio Group

Div Tag
Fluid Grid Layout Div Tag
AP Div

Spry Menu Bar
Spry Tabbed Panels
Spry Accordion
Spry Collapsible Panel

Spry Data Set
Spry Region
Spry Repeat
Spry Repeat List

Spry Validation Text Field
Spry Validation Textarea
Spry Validation Checkbox
Spry Validation Select
Spry Validation Password
Spry Validation Confirm
Spry Validation Radio Group

Spry Menu Bar
Spry Tabbed Panels
Spry Accordion
Spry Collapsible Panel
Spry Tooltip

Ⓑ Spry commands can be found in several locations in the Insert menu, as shown in this composite illustration.

Tag Inspector
Attributes | Behaviors | Tag <body>

Call JavaScript
Change Property
Check Plugin
Drag AP Element
Effects   ▶
Go To URL
Jump Menu
Jump Menu Go
Open Browser Window
Popup Message
Preload Images
Set Text   ▶
Show-Hide Elements
Swap Image
Swap Image Restore
Validate Form

Get More Behaviors...

Appear/Fade
Blind
Grow/Shrink
Highlight
Shake
Slide
Squish

Ⓒ Spry effects are considered behaviors, so they're found in the Behaviors tab of the Tag inspector.

Using the Adobe Widget Browser

There are many JavaScript frameworks, not just jQuery and Spry, and it would be useful if developers could integrate components written in any of them into Dreamweaver for easy use by Web designers. Recognizing this fact, Adobe added the Adobe Widget Browser to Dreamweaver CS5. The Widget Browser is an Adobe AIR application that makes it easy to browse and download *widgets* (which Adobe is defining as small collections of JavaScript, CSS, and HTML packaged together to form a complex Web component) from the Adobe Exchange, a Web site that contains extensions for many Adobe programs (**www.adobe.com/ exchange/**). In Dreamweaver CS5.5, Adobe added the ability to launch the Widget Browser from Dreamweaver and to drag-and-drop widgets from the Widget Browser directly into Dreamweaver's Design view.

The problem that the Widget Browser solves is that while there are many widgets that are freely available on the Web, it can be difficult for designers to customize and configure the code for their particular needs. For example, while a widget may allow you to change its colors and fonts, it may not be easy to do so without digging into the code. The Widget Browser provides a user interface for this configuration. However, for the Widget Browser to use a widget, the widget must be specially packaged for use by the Widget Browser and added to Adobe Exchange. The nice thing for the Web designer is that it doesn't matter if the widget developer's favorite JavaScript framework is jQuery, Spry, or others; as long as it is packaged as a widget, Dreamweaver will be able to use it.

A The Extend Dreamweaver menu looks like a gear in the menu bar.

With the Adobe Widget Browser, you can look through the available choices, preview them to see if they'll do what you want, download widgets, and configure a widget to set its properties. After you have downloaded and configured a widget, the Widget Browser makes it available for use in Dreamweaver.

To browse and download widgets:

1. Choose Extend Dreamweaver > Widget Browser **A**.

2. The first time you launch the program, you'll have to sign in to the Adobe Exchange using your Adobe ID. When you are signed in, the browser window appears **B**.

continues on next page

B The Adobe Widget Browser allows you to pick from a variety of new widgets for your pages.

3. Click a widget in the browser window to get more information on it .

4. To see the widget in action, click the Preview button in the Widget Browser's toolbar. The widget preview is displayed **D**.

Depending on the widget, you may be able to click the preview to try it out. Also, presets may appear on the left side of the window, allowing you to change the parameters of the widget.

C Clicking a widget gives you details about it.

D Click the Preview button in the Widget Browser's toolbar to take the widget for a spin.

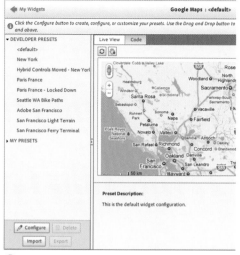

After you download the widget and add it to My Widgets, you can begin to configure it.

Widgets allow you to configure and save your own presets.

5. When you find the widget you want, click the Add to My Widgets button to download it to your computer and make it available for Dreamweaver's use.

The widget downloads, and the Widget Browser displays a dialog that tells you that you can change the presets for the widget and that it has been added to Dreamweaver.

To configure a widget:

1. In the Widget Browser's toolbar, click My Widgets.

The program shows you the widgets you have downloaded.

2. Click to select the widget you want to configure.

The widget appears in the Widget Browser window with the default presets. New features include a My Presets section in the preset area and a Configure button below **E**.

3. Click Configure.

The window changes to show you the available parameters for the widget **F**.

4. Make any changes you want in the properties area on the left side of the window, and then enter a name for the preset in the Name field (you may also add an optional description).

5. Click Save Preset.

The new preset appears in the presets list.

Using Widgets

Widgets that have been downloaded into the My Widgets panel of the Adobe Widget Browser and configured by you are available for use in Dreamweaver. You insert them into your pages as you would other Dreamweaver elements.

You can export presets as an XML file from your widgets, so you may share with other people a custom preset that you create for a widget. Of course, there is a matching import preset feature.

To insert a widget:

1. In Dreamweaver's Design view (make sure that Live view is turned off), click in the document to place the cursor where you want the widget to appear, and then choose Insert > Widget.

   or

   From the Common category of the Insert panel, click Widget.

   or

   Drag-and-drop the widget you want from the My Widgets panel of the Widget browser into the Dreamweaver document window.

   The Widget dialog appears **A**.

2. From the Widget pop-up menu, choose the widget you want to use.

   The widget must have been made available to Dreamweaver by the Adobe Widget Browser to appear in this menu. Or to put it another way, you must have first added the widget to the My Widgets section of the Widget Browser.

3. Choose the preset you want from the Preset pop-up menu.

4. Click OK.

   The widget appears in the document **B**.

A Choose the widget, and then choose the preset you want for it; clicking OK inserts it on your page in Dreamweaver.

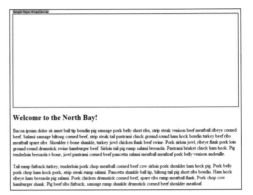

B The widget appears on the page, shown here in Design view. With this Google Maps widget, you can configure many aspects of the map, including the starting location, the map type, and more. Because we're in Design view, the widget appears here as a placeholder.

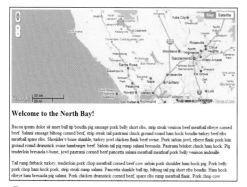

 C The inserted and configured maps widget, as shown in Live view.

D The Adobe Widget Browser now has the ability to export and import widget presets.

Because the widget is a dynamic element, if you're in Design view, it appears as a placeholder. To see it working, click the Live View button.

5. If appropriate to the widget you are using, edit the widget's settings, place-holder text, or graphics to customize the widget's contents for your page **C**.

TIP Sometimes it is easier to change a widget's text information in Code view than in Design view, because you can see with more precision where the text needs to go inside a `div`.

To export and import widget presets:

1. Switch to the My Widgets view of the Adobe Widget Browser.

2. Click the widget for which you want to export presets.

3. At the bottom of the left column of the Widget Browser, click the Export button **D**.

   A Save File dialog appears, asking you to name the preset file and save it in a particular place. Do so, then click Save.

   If you have not created any custom presets, the Export button may not be active. Also, *all* of the presets will be exported, not just the preset that's currently selected in the Widget Browser. There isn't any way to export a single preset.

4. Those who import the presets will need to have added the same widget that the presets were exported from to their copy of the Widget Browser, and of course they will need a copy of the exported XML file from step 3. To import the presets, they should click the widget they want to import the presets from, click the Import button, and then select the XML file with the presets.

Adding CSS3 Transitions

You've seen how you can change a CSS property when the user performs some action. For example, in Chapter 8, you saw how to use CSS to make navigation menus without needing JavaScript. In that case, when the user hovered the cursor over a menu, the CSS property was changed instantly and the menu appeared or disappeared. But what if you wanted to have the CSS change from one property to another over time, creating an animation effect? You can do that with a CSS3 feature that is new to Dreamweaver CS6: *CSS transitions*. Transitions are designed to smoothly change properties when triggered by the user's interactions (hovering, clicking, and the like), and you have a lot of control over the effect's duration and how the effect changes over time.

Here's a page with a lovely gallery of alpacas, but we'd like to allow viewers to see an image at a larger scale when they hover the cursor over it. The image smoothly grows from its initial size to its final size. Here's how to make it happen.

To add a CSS3 transition:

1. Open the gallery page in Dreamweaver, and choose Window > CSS Transitions.

   The CSS Transitions panel appears Ⓐ. It may appear as a floating panel. You can use it in this way, or you can drag it into the same tab group as CSS Styles, as we've done here.

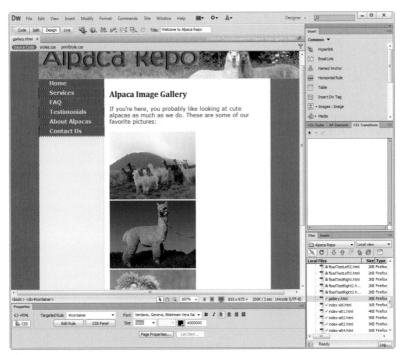

Ⓐ Begin with CSS transitions by opening the panel of the same name, which we've docked in a tab group with the CSS Styles panel.

B The CSS transition is created entirely in this dialog.

C You first need to specify the target rule, either by choosing it from the pop-up menu or by typing it into the Target Rule field. Because we've chosen a compound rule here, we needed to type it in.

D Pick the event that will trigger your CSS transition.

2. In the CSS Transitions panel, click the + to bring up the New Transition dialog, which is where all the work gets done **B**.

3. As always with CSS, start by figuring out the target rule. In this case, the action should happen on all images that are inside paragraphs, so the target rule is **p img** **C**.

4. Transition On is the pop-up menu where you set when you want your transition to occur **D**:

▸ **active** is triggered when an element is engaged or activated.

▸ **checked** is triggered when an element (such as a check box or radio button) is selected.

▸ **disabled** is triggered when a UI element is disabled.

▸ **enabled** is triggered when a UI element is enabled.

▸ **focus** is triggered when an element on the page is given focus.

▸ **hover** is triggered when a user moves the cursor over an element but has not yet clicked it.

▸ **indeterminate** is triggered when the browser can't tell if a UI element has been enabled or disabled.

▸ **target** allows one element on the page to modify another.

We want things to happen when users hover over the images, so we set Transition On to hover.

continues on next page

5. We could make the image's height and width expand and shrink at different rates, but that would be obnoxious, so we'll leave the default, "Use the same transition for all properties," selected **E**.

6. The Duration setting is how long an effect takes to complete, and the Delay setting is how long the browser should wait before beginning the effect. Either can be set in seconds or microseconds; we'll set Duration to 2 seconds and leave Delay alone **F**.

7. Unless you can handle how Bezier curves work in your sleep, the Timing Function setting can be a little complex **G**. Here's a high-level cheat sheet:

▸ **cubic-bezier(x1,y1,x2,y2):** Allows more technical users to set their own values.

▸ **ease:** Transition starts moderately slowly, picks up speed, and then slows down gradually. Equivalent to **cubic-bezier(0.25, 0.1, 0.25, 1.0)**.

▸ **ease-in:** Transition starts slowly, then speeds up at the end. Equivalent to **cubic-bezier(0.42, 0.0, 1.0, 1.0)**.

▸ **ease-in-out:** Transition starts slowly, speeds up in the middle, and then slows down again at the end. Equivalent to **cubic-bezier(0.42, 0.0, 0.58, 1.0)**.

▸ **ease-out:** Transition starts quickly, then slows down at the end. Equivalent to **cubic-bezier(0.0, 0.0, 0.58, 1.0)**.

▸ **linear:** Transition occurs at a steady rate. Equivalent to **cubic-bezier(0.0, 0.0, 1.0, 1.0)**.

The default is ease, so that's what we'll stick with.

E You have the choice of using the same or different transitions for each property.

F Enter the duration and delay of the transition effect.

G The choices in the Timing Function pop-up menu describe the speed of the transition effect over time.

 Pick the property you want to modify with the CSS transition. If you have more than one property you want to modify, you'll be using this pop-up menu for each property.

8. Property is where you choose the properties that you want to modify. Click the + button under Property to select your choice from the pop-up menu . Dreamweaver lets you set each property's end value, so the choices available on the right will vary depending on which property you're changing (for example, the **visibility** property has the end values shown in the pop-up menu in ).

Here, we're going to set two properties (**height** and **width**), and our end values will be three times the size of the current value. That is, our image width of 256 pixels and image height of 192 pixels become 768 and 576, respectively .

Repeat this step for each property of the target rule that needs a transition.

continues on next page

Property:
visibility

End Value: visible
visible
hidden
collapse
inherit

 The choices available for End Value change to match the allowable values for the selected property. For the **visibility** property, for example, the End Value choices are included in a simple pop-up menu.

Property:
height
width

End Value: 576   px

 Here, we are setting the end value of the **height** property to 576 pixels. As usual in Dreamweaver, you can choose different units from the pop-up menu, such as points, ems, percentage, and the like.

9. Finally, decide where you want to create the transition—in the current page, or in a new or existing external style sheet **K**. When you're done, click Create Transition.

10. Switch into Live view, or load the page in your browser **L**, and view the resulting beauty of the gentle members of the *camelid* family **M**.

TIP If you're not sure about which Timing Function setting to use, play around with them! The best way to decide is to just try different values and see which one works best for you.

TIP If you want a rule that applies to a particular ID or class and you're having trouble remembering the name, click the Target Rule pop-up, and you'll get a list of every CSS property currently in use.

TIP The end values of properties aren't always sizes. Because of the varying nature of properties that support transitions, you can have anything from color pickers on up. The choices for `text-shadow`, for instance, are fairly complex **N**.

K Choose whether you want the transition to be saved in an existing style sheet or a new one.

L When the page loads, all three images are the same size.

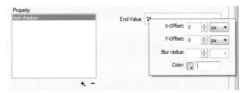

M Hovering over one of the images applies the CSS transition, zooming the image to three times its original size.

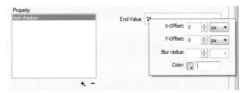

N Depending on the property, there will be a variety of possible settings. For example, the `text-shadow` property allows you to set horizontal and vertical offsets and the amount of blur for the text shadow, and it includes a color picker so you can set the shadow's color.

Working with Content Management Systems

A particularly powerful feature in Dreamweaver CS6 is the ability to work with sites that are built upon the foundation of a *content management system* (CMS). There are many types of CMSs, but the ones we (and Dreamweaver) focus on are Web content management systems, which are applications that run on a Web server and create and manage Web content. The CMS manages and controls a dynamic collection of Web material and usually (but not always) assembles and creates Web pages that are served to the user "on the fly"; that is, the page is built and sent to the user when the user requests the page. Unlike the static HTML pages we discuss creating in most of the rest of this book, pages that come out of a CMS often don't exist at all before the CMS software puts together the HTML, CSS, images, and scripts and squirts them over the Internet to a user's waiting Web browser.

Dreamweaver CS6 supports three of the most popular Web CMSs: WordPress, Joomla, and Drupal. You can use Dreamweaver to author and test content from any of these systems.

About Content Management Systems

Dreamweaver supports the three most popular PHP-based CMSs: WordPress, Joomla, and Drupal. (PHP is a programming language that typically is installed and run on Web servers.) These systems have several things in common. They are all open-source projects and can be downloaded from their respective project Web sites at no cost. Many Web hosting companies make it easy to install these CMSs from their hosting control panel, often with only a few clicks, demystifying what was previously a complex process. Installations generally (but not always) use a MySQL database to store and manage their data. As noted, Web pages and their elements are assembled by the CMS upon request, with text, images, and other content drawn from the database. The CMS takes content out of the database and serves it up as a Web page.

Pages generated by a CMS are based on templates that control the site's look and feel. Because the content of the site is separate from its presentation, you can easily change the entire look of the site by modifying or switching the set of templates used by the site. A CMS can accommodate multiple users, with an administrator assigning different roles to particular users (for example, subscriber, contributor, editor, and so on). All of the systems provide plug-in architectures that make it easy for developers to extend the features of the core software.

Each CMS has its own passionate adherents. Imagine that a group of Web geeks walk into a bar. After a few rounds of drinks, the conversation turns to an apparently simple question: Which is the best CMS? The discussion goes on for a while, becoming more spirited, and, as more drinks are consumed, people's opinions are expressed with more emphasis. Finally, the frank exchange of views ends when the bouncers break up the fistfight and turn everyone out into the street.

Let's leave the sound and fury behind and just talk a bit about each of the three.

WordPress

In contrast with the other two systems, WordPress is primarily known as weblog creation software, though it is certainly not limited to creating weblogs. By far the most popular blog software, WordPress was in use by more than 70 million Web sites worldwide as of 2011. WordPress blogs are based on sets of templates called *themes* and can include widgets that add extra features to a site, such as Twitter integration, easy access to the site archives, and much more. One of the reasons for its popularity is that it has an installer program that makes setting up WordPress relatively easy for the novice. You can use a single installation of WordPress to run multiple sites. WordPress's home can be found at **www.wordpress.org** Ⓐ. WordPress has a very active developer community, providing free and paid themes, widgets, and other plug-ins. These extensions add an incredible range of capabilities to the base WordPress installation.

A The WordPress Web site has launched a zillion blogs.

B The Joomla site lets you download the CMS and boasts extensive documentation to help you get started.

C Like the sites of the other two systems, the Drupal site provides news about the platform.

Joomla

Joomla excels at creating larger sites, such as corporate Web sites, e-commerce sites, online newspapers and magazines, community sites, and government sites. Joomla is fairly easy to install and set up for the novice user. Many Web hosting services offer easy installs that help you get your site up and running with little effort. Web designers can create sites in Joomla, and then turn the sites over to clients to add and manage content. Joomla's user management system can be configured to give different user groups varying levels of permissions for editing and publishing. Joomla allows the administrator to easily set up polls and provides extensive template management features. You can get started with Joomla at **www.joomla.org** **B**.

Drupal

Well known as a workhorse for sites with heavy traffic, Drupal is in use at many large corporate and government sites, including Sony Music, *Popular Science* magazine, and **whitehouse.gov**. The CMS makes it easy to create a static Web site, a single or multiuser blog, online forums, or a community Web site that can accept user-generated content. Drupal sites also boast advanced search features, a robust commenting system, a multilevel menu system, and the ability to host multiple sites from a single installation. Drupal is widely considered to have a steep learning curve for new administrators but makes up for it in part by having excellent performance in delivering pages and being scalable when your site becomes popular. Drupal's home is at **www.drupal.org** **C**.

In this chapter, we'll use a WordPress blog in our examples. There are only minor differences in the way that Dreamweaver interacts with each of the three CMSs.

Connecting to Your CMS

To get started working on your site, you'll need to make the initial connection to the CMS in Dreamweaver. You can work with a testing server (preferred) or directly on your live server.

You need to let Dreamweaver know where each of the servers resides. If you have a local testing server (see the "Using XAMPP, MAMP, and LAMP for Local Testing Servers" sidebar), you need to make sure that it is installed, configured, and running.

To connect to your CMS:

1. If you have not already done so, define the local and remote sites. See Chapter 2 for more information, if necessary.

2. In the Files panel, open the folder that contains your dynamic site and double-click the index file (usually called `index.php`).

   Dreamweaver opens the file, but you don't see any content. Instead, in a status bar at the top of the document window, Dreamweaver tells you that you need to set up a testing server Ⓐ.

3. Click the Setup link in the status bar.

   Dreamweaver opens the Site Setup dialog, which is set to the Servers category Ⓑ.

Ⓐ Before you can discover dynamically related files, you have to set up a testing server.

Ⓑ You define the testing server in the Site Setup dialog.

C Enter the testing server configuration information in the server definition dialog.

D You can tell at a glance which server is the remote server and which is the testing server.

4. (Optional: Perform this step only if you want to use the live remote server as the testing server, which we do *not* recommend.) Select the Testing check box next to the previously defined remote site, and then skip to step 10.

5. Click the plus button at the bottom left to add a server.

6. In the resulting dialog C, enter a name in the Server Name field (we recommend Testing Server).

7. Choose Local/Network from the Connect Using menu.

8. Click the folder icon next to the Remote Folder field, and navigate to the local copy of your site that is inside the appropriate Web directory on your testing server.

   Depending on the testing server software you're using, this folder could be named **/www/** or **/htdocs/**.

9. Click Save.

   You return to the Site Setup dialog, and now you can see that a testing server has been added and selected as the Testing server D.

10. Click Save to close the Site Setup dialog.

TIP It's possible for you to use the same server as both the remote server and the testing server. You'll have to decide if you are comfortable with the risk of messing up your live site as you make changes to it.

Using XAMPP, MAMP, and LAMP for Local Testing Servers

A CMS needs a server to run on, and the CMSs supported by Dreamweaver need a server that must be running at least three programs: a Web server program, such as Apache; the database program MySQL; and the programming language PHP.

Most professional sites use at least two servers: a server on which content is developed and tested (called a local, testing, or staging server) and the server that the site's users interact with (the live or production server). In many situations, the testing server is on a machine elsewhere on a company intranet, or even on the Internet (suitably access-protected, of course; you probably don't want people looking at your site while it's under construction). You might, for example, create a subdomain at your Web hosting company for your testing server. So the main, live site would be at **www.domain.com**, and the testing server could be at **test.domain.com**.

If you don't have a handy intranet, you can run the testing server on your own machine with the help of three freely downloadable packages: XAMPP for Windows (**www.apachefriends.org/en/ xampp.html**), MAMP for Mac (**www.mamp.info**), and LAMP for Linux (many possibilities, because of the sundry Linux distributions; Google the LAMP package for the Linux distro you use). These packages make it easy to install an instance of Apache, PHP, and MySQL on your machine; installing these programs can otherwise be frustratingly complex and difficult. In contrast, installing and using XAMPP, MAMP, or LAMP is a simple process, like working with any other program.

The Mac and Windows packages have a control panel Ⓐ from which you can access the Web-based configuration tools for the running server programs (the Linux version is controlled from the command line in a terminal application). You will also have to create a local installation of your preferred CMS. Once you have local and remote versions of your site, you can work with the different files on your machine and use Dreamweaver's synchronization tools to upload changes from the testing server to the live remote server.

Ⓐ The MAMP control panel gives you the server status and lets you start and stop the Apache and MySQL servers.

Using XAMPP, MAMP, and LAMP for Local Testing Servers *continued*

If you do a lot of WordPress development, there's an excellent paid ($50) alternative to the open-source testing servers called DesktopServer (**www.serverpress.com**) **B**. It's based on MAMP and XAMPP, but it has many specialized features for WordPress developers (not to mention that it is considerably easier to set up for use with Dreamweaver). DesktopServer includes a preconfigured copy of WordPress, so you don't need to install it separately. It automatically creates a testing server with your site name mapped to the pseudo top-level domain **.dev** (for example, **www.yoursite.dev**), so it's easy to tell the live version of your site from the local testing server when previewing in a browser. The program allows you to import live WordPress sites, and it creates a local testing server and then a Dreamweaver Site Definition file that you import into Dreamweaver. You can work on the local testing copy of your WordPress site and then export and deploy it to your live server.

B DesktopServer allows professional WordPress developers to easily create local testing servers, experiment with site design changes, and then deploy to live servers with a few clicks.

Using Dynamically Related Files

As mentioned earlier in this chapter, Web pages served by a CMS are assembled on the fly from many different elements (often dozens or hundreds of PHP, JavaScript, CSS, and other types of files), so you often have no idea exactly what the page will look like until you preview it in a Web browser. Each CMS has a back-end administrative interface where you enter content and control the elements of the site, but they all rely on browsers to view the final output.

As you might guess, this presents a challenge for a tool like Dreamweaver. It requires the CMS to put together the page you want to work with before Dreamweaver can show it to you. Then Dreamweaver can display the page to you in Live View.

Dreamweaver knows how to work with the supported CMSs so that it can discover

all of the files that go into building the page you want to work with in the document window. Once Dreamweaver has discovered all the files that make up the document, it lists them in the Related Files toolbar. You can then open any of the related files and edit them using Dreamweaver's tools. Dreamweaver makes it relatively easy to do something that was previously quite difficult and required serious expertise in a particular CMS: find the particular related files you need.

To discover dynamically related files:

1. In the Files panel, double-click a file you want to view (you will usually start with `index.php`).

   Dreamweaver displays a status bar under the document toolbar letting you know that "This page may have dynamically-related files that can only be discovered by the server" 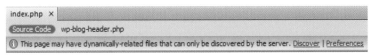.

A Dreamweaver lets you know that you need to discover the dynamically related files.

B This alert dialog lets you know that to discover the dynamically related files, Dreamweaver must execute the scripts included in the page.

2. Click the Discover link in the status bar.

Depending on the CMS, Dreamweaver may display a Script Warning dialog **B**.

3. Click Yes to dismiss the Script Warning dialog.

Dreamweaver begins discovering the dynamically linked files and displays them in the Related Files toolbar.

4. If you're not already in Live View, Dreamweaver may use the status bar to alert you that you need to switch to that view. Click the Live View link in the status bar.

Dreamweaver displays the rendered page in the document window **C**.

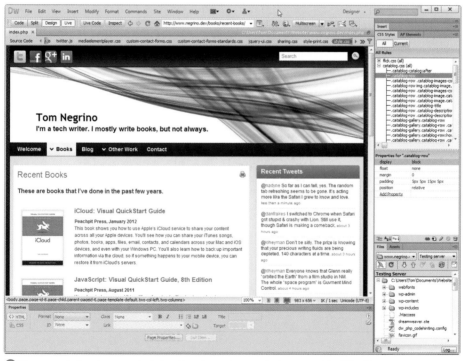

C The page in the document window is a dynamic page being served by WordPress.

To work with dynamically related files:

- Clicking any of the files in the Related Files toolbar will change the document window into Split view, displaying the file in the Code pane .

- You can click the Inspect button in the document toolbar to turn on CSS Inspect mode, so you can see the box model for elements on the page . Just hover over an element on your page, and it displays with different colors for the background, margins, padding, and borders. For more information about CSS Inspect mode, see "Using CSS Inspection" in Chapter 9.

- Nobody's monitor is wide enough to display all of the dynamically related files, so the Related Files toolbar now supports scroll arrows on either end when there are too many related files to display 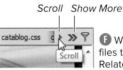. Scroll as needed to find the files that you want to work with. Click the Show More button next to the right scroll arrow to display the related files in a menu **G**.

D Clicking this CSS file in the Related Files toolbar displays it in Split view.

E In CSS Inspect mode, you can see the box model for elements on the page, with **divs** and padding in different colors.

Scroll   Show More

F When there are too many files to fit in the window, the Related Files toolbar scrolls.

G The Show More menu displays all of the related files.

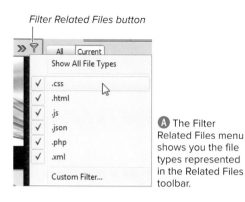

Filter Related Files button

A The Filter Related Files menu shows you the file types represented in the Related Files toolbar.

B Enter your custom filter criteria.

C After filtering, the Related Files toolbar (or, if there are enough files, the Show More menu) displays considerably fewer files.

TIP You can filter the results in the Related Files toolbar at any time, not just when you are viewing dynamically related files.

Filtering Related Files

One of the problems with discovering the dynamically related files in a CMS-backed site is that you can get an embarrassment of riches. There can be so many files that it can be difficult to scroll through them in the Related Files toolbar or find them in the Show More menu. Dreamweaver allows you to filter the related files to show only the file types you want. That lets you easily work on just the CSS files, for example, or those and the JavaScript files, hiding all the PHP files. You can also customize the filter to show only the files you want.

To filter related files:

1. At the right edge of the Related Files toolbar, click the Filter Related Files button.

   Dreamweaver shows that the button is actually a menu that contains the file types in the Related Files toolbar **A**.

2. In the menu, deselect the file types you do not want to view. To go back to viewing all file types, choose Show All File Types.

To create a custom filter:

1. From the bottom of the Filter Related Files menu in the Related Files toolbar, choose Custom Filter.

   The Custom Filter dialog appears **B**.

2. In the dialog, enter the filenames or file extensions you want to display in the Related Files toolbar. Separate different names or extensions with a semicolon. You can also use asterisks as wildcard symbols. For example, in **B** we used `jquery*` to create a filter that captured jQuery-specific files, producing the result shown in **C**.

3. Click OK to put your filter into action.

Using Live View Navigation

Live view, introduced in Dreamweaver CS4, renders pages in the Dreamweaver document window by using WebKit (the same page rendering engine found in several standards-compliant browsers; WebKit is constantly being improved, so the version of WebKit included in Dreamweaver has been updated in each successive version of Dreamweaver). This greatly speeds Web development, because designers don't always have to resort to previewing in a separate browser. But because Live view originally couldn't follow links, you couldn't easily explore your sites. Now that Dreamweaver can work with dynamically based sites, the ability to follow links is vital, so it was added in Dreamweaver CS5.

Live view navigation allows you to interact with server-side applications and dynamic data. In addition, *Live Code view* highlights changes as they happen, allowing you to quickly locate the dynamically loaded data or code changes triggered by JavaScript. You can also enter a URL in the Browser Navigation toolbar to inspect pages from a live Web server and edit pages you've browsed to, as long as they exist in one of your locally defined sites.

To use Live view navigation:

1. Open a document that contains links and elements that are updated via JavaScript—for example, a navigational menu.

2. Click Live Code in the Document toolbar.

   or

   Choose View > Live Code.

   The document window splits to display both the Live Code and Live View panes Ⓐ. As usual with Live Code, the Code pane isn't editable but will show how the code changes as you interact with the document in the Live View pane.

3. Use the menu. As you do, note how the code changes in the code pane.

4. Click one of the links in the menu.

   Notice that the link is *not* followed, as it would have been in a browser. Dreamweaver does this purposely so that you can create, style, and modify active links.

Code added by JavaScript

Ⓐ Live Code view shows you the code as it is being rewritten by JavaScript.

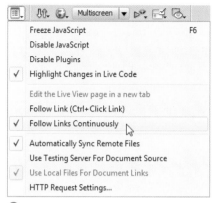

Freeze JavaScript   F6

Disable JavaScript

Disable Plugins

✓ Highlight Changes in Live Code

   Edit the Live View page in a new tab

   Follow Link (Ctrl+Click Link)

✓ Follow Links Continuously

✓ Automatically Sync Remote Files

   Use Testing Server For Document Source

✓ Use Local Files For Document Links

   HTTP Request Settings...

Ⓑ Choosing Follow Links Continuously makes Dreamweaver's Live view treat links the same way a Web browser would.

5. To follow the link, Ctrl-click (Cmd-click) the link.

   Dreamweaver follows the link.

6. To follow links as you would in a browser, choose Follow Links Continuously from the Live View Options menu in the Browser Navigation toolbar Ⓑ. You can then click a link in the Live View pane, and it will change to the link's destination.

TIP You can enter any URL in the address field of the Browser Navigation toolbar, and Dreamweaver will display the page in Live view and list its associated files in the Related Files toolbar Ⓒ. If you click one of the files in that toolbar, Dreamweaver switches to Split view and displays the code, but it will also show a status bar telling you that you cannot edit the remote file.

Ⓒ You can enter any URL you want in the Browser Navigation toolbar, and Dreamweaver will display that URL in Live view.

Freezing or Disabling JavaScript

When you are working with interactive elements, it can be very useful to freeze the action when it is in a particular state. You can then inspect the code in that state without worrying that a stray movement of your mouse will change the state (and therefore the code you're trying to inspect). Dreamweaver allows you to freeze JavaScript as it is executing. You can then edit your CSS or JavaScript and then refresh the page to see the effect of your changes. You can also disable JavaScript altogether, which re-renders the page to show how it would appear in a browser that has JavaScript disabled.

To freeze JavaScript:

1. Click the Live View button in the Document toolbar.

2. (Optional) Click the Live Code button in the Document toolbar.

3. Interact with the document in the Live View pane until the page is in the state you want.

4. Press F6.

   or

   Choose Freeze JavaScript from the Live View Options menu in the Browser Navigation toolbar (see figure ⑧ in "Using Live View Navigation").

   Dreamweaver displays a status bar telling you that JavaScript is frozen ⓐ.

5. (Optional) Edit your JavaScript or CSS. Save your changes, and then press F6 to resume JavaScript rendering. Click the Refresh Design View button in the Document toolbar (or press F5) to see your changes.

To disable JavaScript:

Choose Disable JavaScript from the Live View Options menu in the Browser Navigation toolbar.

ⓐ Dreamweaver lets you know when you freeze JavaScript.

Making Life Easier: Using Templates, Libraries, and Snippets

The first thing you do when you begin a site in Dreamweaver is define a site root folder, as discussed in Chapter 2. You tell Dreamweaver where you're keeping all your site files, and Dreamweaver rewards you for sharing the information by making all sorts of cool site-wide tools available to speed up your workflow and make your life easier. In seconds, Dreamweaver's site management tools can make changes to every file in your local site root folder—changes that would take you much longer done one file at a time.

We'll cover two of those timesaving whole-site tools—templates and library items—in this chapter. In addition, you'll learn how to create time-saving bits of reusable code called *snippets*. You access templates and library items from the Assets panel. Snippets have a separate panel.

Before getting into the details, some brief definitions are in order. *Templates* are like master page designs. They create a uniform page design for a site while allowing certain material on each page to be customized for individual pages. *Library items* are not full pages, but reusable objects with text, code, images, or other elements that you insert in documents; for example, you can create a navigation bar as a library item. Updating either a template or a library item results in the automatic updating of any page in the entire site that is attached to the template or library. *Snippets* are custom-built code samples that you save for quick insertion. Changing a snippet doesn't have any site-wide effects.

They Can't Break Your Sites!

Pages made from templates are perfect for use in organizations that want relatively inexperienced people to be able to make changes and updates to sites without the possibility of accidentally "breaking" the site. In fact, Adobe has a program, Adobe Contribute (part of Adobe Creative Suite Web Premium and Master Collection, also available separately and as part of the subscription-based Adobe Creative Cloud), that works hand in hand with sites built using Dreamweaver templates to allow people to add content and make changes to Web sites without being able to mess up the site's design elements. With Contribute, the site designer can assign site contributors to *user roles*, which specify the editing tasks the user is allowed. For example, you can specify that a user can add text and change text on a page but can only style that text with CSS styles you supply, or you can prevent the user from styling text at all. You can also require that users send their changed pages to a supervisor for review before making the page live on the site. Many other permissions and restrictions are possible if people who work on your site use Contribute.

With the launch of the CS4 suite, Adobe introduced a hosted service called InContext Editing that worked entirely in a Web browser. With InContext Editing, inexperienced users could make simple changes to Web sites, again without the possibility of breaking the site. The separate InContext Editing service was discontinued in 2010 and rolled into a paid, more full-featured service called Business Catalyst, which is supported in Dreamweaver CS5 and later. To get more information about using Dreamweaver to work with Contribute and Business Catalyst, download "Working with Other Applications," part of the bonus material from **www.dreamweaverbook.com**.

Creating a Template

Templates are perfect for many situations. For example, let's say you have a large site where many different individuals change content and add pages. Using a template provides control over the page layout and design by restricting changes to only certain *editable regions* on a page. Other areas on the page are *locked regions*, which can't be changed by people working on an individual page. Locked regions can be edited only in the original template file. This kind of control guarantees a consistent look and feel for a site and prevents any accidental changes to locked regions.

When a change is made to a template, every page made from, or *attached* to, the template is automatically updated throughout the entire site. You can create a template from scratch, but it is simpler to use an existing page as a model for the template, and that's what we'll explain here.

Before you save a document as a template, make sure you've already included any needed `<meta>` tags, style sheets, behaviors, or other underlying parameters. These page elements are located in the locked regions of a template. There's no way to add things like style sheet links to individual pages made from a template—they must exist in the template already.

To create a template from an existing page:

1. Open the document you want to turn into a template.

2. Choose File > Save as Template.

   or

   Choose Make Template from the Templates pop-up menu in the Common category of the Insert panel 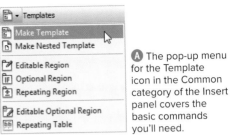.

   The Save As Template dialog appears with the Site pop-up menu set to the current local site **B**.

3. Enter the requested information in this dialog.

   ▸ **Existing templates:** You don't enter anything in this field. Dreamweaver lists any existing templates for the site automatically.

   ▸ **Description:** Type a brief description of the template. This is optional but recommended.

   ▸ **Save as:** Type the name of the template. You can omit the file extension; Dreamweaver takes care of that for you, as described next.

4. Click Save.

   If it doesn't already exist, Dreamweaver adds a **Templates** folder to your site files. Your new template will be inside this folder, with the file extension **.dwt**, which indicates that the document is a Dreamweaver template.

> **TIP** It's possible to create a template from scratch. Choose File > New and select Blank Template in the New Document window. Or you can start one using the New Template button in the Templates area of the Assets panel.

A The pop-up menu for the Template icon in the Common category of the Insert panel covers the basic commands you'll need.

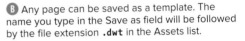

B Any page can be saved as a template. The name you type in the Save as field will be followed by the file extension **.dwt** in the Assets list.

> **TIP** Templates are for local use; they're never loaded in a browser. The Templates folder and its **.dwt** files don't need to be uploaded to the server. Just upload the individual HTML pages made from the template. To make this easier, you can cloak the Templates folder, which prevents Dreamweaver from uploading it to the remote server. See "Cloaking Files and Folders" in Chapter 2 for more information. On the other hand, you might choose to upload your Templates folder to the server so that you always have a handy backup of your templates.

> **TIP** There is still an InContext Editing category of the Insert panel. Though the standalone InContext Editing service has been discontinued, the functions in that panel still work with Business Catalyst.

Make Template
Make Nested Template
Editable Region
Optional Region
Repeating Region
Editable Optional Region
Repeating Table

**A** Use the pop-up menu for the Template icon in the Common category of the Insert panel to designate editable regions in the template.

New Editable Region

Name: Main_Content

This region will be editable in documents based on this template.

OK
Cancel
Help

B A short, descriptive name is best for a template region. It's best not to use spaces in the name; instead, use the underscore character, as shown.

Adding Editable Regions

Once you've saved the **.dwt** file, you will want to open it and define any regions you want to be editable. Regions on the page that you don't specifically mark as editable will be locked and can't be changed by anyone who is using Contribute or Business Catalyst and working on pages made from your template—hey, that's the whole point!

To add an editable region:

1. Open the template document.

2. Select the element to make editable (for example **<div>**, **<img>**, or **<td>**) with the tag selector in the document window.

   or

   Select the text to make editable. This choice is most useful when the text is within a **div**. Selecting the entire **div**, rather than just the text within it, makes everything about the **div** editable, including its position. You probably don't want your users to be able to change anything other than the text, so select just that text and it will be the only editable part of the **div**.

3. Choose Editable Region from the Templates pop-up menu in the Common category of the Insert panel **A**.

   or

   Choose Insert > Template Objects > Editable Region.

   The New Editable Region dialog appears **B**.

4. Type a name for the region.

continues on next page

5. Click OK.

The editable region will be outlined in green in the document window. A tab at the upper-left corner of the region displays the region name **C**.

6. (Optional) Delete the text that was in the region and replace it with some general instruction regarding the region—for example, "This region is for main content." If you don't do this, it's OK—anyone making a page from the template can replace the text later.

TIP You can make any of the following editable: an entire table, the table header, a table row, or individual cells within a table. But you can't put a table column or multiple noncontiguous table cells in a single editable region.

TIP Don't use special characters in region names: no ampersands (&), single quote marks ('), double quote marks ("), or angle brackets (<) and (>). You can use spaces, but we recommend you use the underscore character (_) instead to match the naming conventions of other items in Dreamweaver, such as form elements and CSS IDs.

TIP Page titles (the title that appears at the top of a Web browser window, defined by the `<title>` tag) are editable by default on pages that are created from templates.

TIP When you name your editable regions, give them region names that make their purpose clear for the people who will eventually be entering content into the region, such as Main_Content in this example.

Region name

Main_Conttent

C In the document window, the editable region is indicated by a visible tab giving the region name.

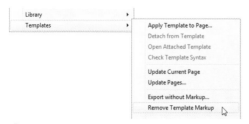

A To remove an editable region from a template, choose Remove Template Markup.

Removing Editable Regions

If you make a region editable and later decide you want to lock it instead, it's easy to remove the editable region. This doesn't remove the content within the region; it removes the ability of the user to edit anything in the region. As the designer, you can still put any content you want in the region. But that content won't be editable by the user.

To remove an editable region:

1. Click the tab in the upper-left corner of the region to select the region.

2. Choose Modify > Templates > Remove Template Markup A.

3. The region is locked.

Other Kinds of Template Regions

Dreamweaver can create more complex editable areas in addition to the basic editable region. These kinds of editable regions are used less frequently, but they're still useful when you need them. You probably noticed the options in the Templates pop-up menu in the Common category of the Insert panel (see figure A in "Creating a Template" and figure A in "Adding Editable Regions"). They are:

- **Repeating Region:** Repeating regions can be duplicated by the user as often as needed. They're useful for things that vary from page to page— for example, a chart of product colors or sizes or a list of recipe ingredients. Repeating regions aren't editable until you define the editable areas of the region.

- **Optional Region:** You set conditions for optional regions, indicated by the word *if* in the tab showing the region name. Optional content can be either hidden or displayed, depending on whether the conditions are met. For example, let's say that you have a page of upcoming events. You have an image that says "Coming Soon!" that you want to appear next to events that will occur in the next month. You can write code that checks the date and then displays the "Coming Soon!" image in an optional region when the code expression is true.

- **Editable Optional Region:** As with optional regions, you can decide whether or not to display content in these regions. Editable optional regions are, well, editable.

- **Repeating Table:** Repeating tables are actually repeating regions, but they automatically include table tags, so you can easily use them for tabular data.

Building Pages Based on a Template

Most of the time, you will create new pages based on your template. This is the easiest and least confusing way to make templates work. It's also possible to take an existing page, say from an older site that you're completely redesigning, and apply a template to that page. That method is a bit trickier.

To make a new page from a template:

1. Choose File > New.

   The New Document dialog appears.

2. Click the Page from Template tab, and then click the site you are working on in the Site column.

   The existing templates for that site appear in the Template for Site column.

3. Select the template you want from the Template for Site column.

   A preview of the template appears in the dialog .

4. Click Create.

   A new page, based on the template, appears.

5. Add content to the editable regions, and save the new document with an appropriate filename and location on your site.

> **TIP** You can create a new page from a template faster once you get used to working with templates. In the Assets panel, click the Templates category, and then right-click the template name and choose New from Template from the context menu 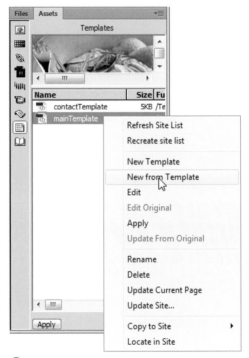.

Ⓐ If you begin a new page from a template with the File > New command, you must choose the site and then the template.

Ⓑ Fewer steps are involved in starting a new page from a template if you right-click the template name in the Assets panel.

Apply button

C Modify an existing page to fit into a template page by selecting the template and clicking the Apply button.

D When retrofitting an existing page to work with a template, you must decide where to put the content. The pop-up menu shows possible regions.

TIP Dreamweaver expects the `Templates` folder to be at the top level of your site structure. Don't move it into a subfolder. If you do, Dreamweaver won't display the template files in your Assets panel or in the New Document template list.

To apply a template to an existing page:

1. Open the existing document to which you want to apply the template.

2. In the Assets panel, select the template you want and click the Apply button (in the lower-left corner) **C**.

   or

   Drag the template from the Assets panel to the document window.

   or

   Choose Modify > Templates > Apply Template to Page. The Select Template dialog appears. Click a template in the list to choose it.

   The Inconsistent Region Names dialog appears **D**. This dialog allows you to tell Dreamweaver in which region of the new page it should place the document's existing content.

3. In the Inconsistent Region Names dialog, do the following:

   ▸ In the scrolling list, select an unresolved region.

   ▸ Use the "Move content to new region" pop-up menu to select an editable region for the content.

   If you choose Nowhere from the pop-up menu, the content is removed from the document. If you click the "Use for all" button, all the unresolved content is moved to the selected region.

4. Click OK.

5. The resulting document probably needs some cleaning up to work seamlessly with the template. For example, you may need to restyle some text or move a bit of content manually. After that is completed, save as usual.

Modifying a Template

Templates give you tons of control over what can be edited and what can't. Sure, that's important. But what happens if you make lots of pages from your template and then something changes? Maybe you need to add a new item to the menu, or you need a new editable region on the page. The answer is that something really cool happens when a Dreamweaver template is modified: Dreamweaver automatically changes all the pages you've already made using that template. So you can make changes to just one page (the template) and have those changes automatically ripple through the site.

Normally, you'd start your modification directly in the template file. But you can also start from any document that is attached to the template. You can pick and choose the attached pages to which you want the changes to apply.

To modify a template file:

1. In the Assets panel, click the Templates button to display the templates, and then double-click the template file you want to edit.

   or

   In the Assets panel, click the Templates button to display the templates, and then highlight the template file and click the Edit button at the bottom of the panel.

   The template file opens in the document window.

2. Edit as desired, and then choose File > Save or press Ctrl-S (Cmd-S).

   The Update Files dialog appears. Each file attached to the template is listed in the dialog .

Ⓐ Here's the powerful part of using templates: Dreamweaver offers to update template-based pages when you change a template.

B If you allow Dreamweaver to update template-based pages, it reports the results when it's finished.

3. (Optional) Select one or more of the files in the dialog. To select a single file, click its name. You may also select noncontiguous files in the list by holding down the Ctrl (Cmd) key and then clicking the files you want. Surprisingly, selecting *no* files in this dialog is the same as selecting them *all*.

   If you click Update, every selected file attached to the template will update. If you click Don't Update, none of the files attached to the template will update.

4. Click Update.

   The Update Pages dialog appears **B**. Dreamweaver sorts through all the files in your site and makes the updates, showing you the progress in the Update Pages dialog.

   This dialog also allows you to update all the pages in the site to their corresponding templates, or to just update files based on a specific template. If you don't need any additional updates other than the ones Dreamweaver already made, go to step 8.

5. (Optional) From the "Look in" pop-up menu, choose Entire Site, Files That Use, or Selected Files.

   The first choice reapplies all the templates in the site to files made from those templates. The second choice, which is what you will want most of the time, updates only the pages that are based on the template you just edited. Selected Files applies changes only to the pages that you selected in step 3.

   When you make a choice from the "Look in" pop-up menu, the inactive Done button becomes active and its label changes to Start.

   continues on next page

6. (Optional) Make sure the Templates check box is selected.

7. (Optional) Click Start.

   When the process is complete, the Start button changes to Done and becomes inactive.

8. Click Close to dismiss the Update Pages dialog.

9. Close the template file.

To modify a template attached to a current document:

1. With a document based on a template open, choose Modify > Templates > Open Attached Template.

   The template opens in a separate window.

2. Make your modifications as described in the previous section.

   When you save the template, you'll be prompted to update pages attached to that template, including the page you started with.

To modify an individual template-based page:

1. Change a template file, as described previously. In the Update Files dialog **A**, click Don't Update.

2. Open a document attached to the same template.

3. Choose Modify > Templates > Update Current Page.

   The page updates with the changes you made to the template. No other pages on the site will update.

TIP When your template links to a CSS file, all your template-based pages link to it as well. If you change your CSS rules, the pages created from the template automatically reflect those changes in exactly the same way non-template-based pages reflect CSS changes.

TIP HTML pages changed by the update of a template file need to be uploaded to the server for the change to be visible to your site's visitors. The easiest way to do this is to synchronize the local and remote sites. See "Synchronizing the Local and Remote Sites" in Chapter 2 for more information.

Creating a Library Item

For someone working alone, the restrictions imposed by using a template may be unnecessary or even annoying. For example, when you use templates, you have to set up the editable and locked regions, and then when you go to modify a page based on the template, you don't have access to page elements in the locked regions. These restrictions are great if you're a designer who is giving pages to co-workers to modify. But on sites where you want to exercise total control over editing every page, library items offer some of the same time-saving abilities as templates, including the ability to update pages and maintain consistency, but with far fewer restrictions.

Library items aren't full pages. They're small bits of text, images, or code that you insert when needed. Good material for a library item might be a navigation bar, a copyright notice, a list of links, a graphic masthead, or perhaps a search box. If you want to use something frequently, have it display consistently on any page, and update all instances of it at one time, a library item fits the bill. And library items are easy to create and use.

To create a library item:

1. Open a document.

2. Select an element in the document **body**. It can be anything you want to reuse: text, tables, forms, navigation bars, images, or other elements.

3. Do one of the following:

   Choose Modify > Library > Add Object to Library.

   or

   In the Library category of the Assets panel, click the New Library Item button.

   or

   Drag the selection into the Library category of the Assets panel.

4. The item appears in the Library category of the Assets panel 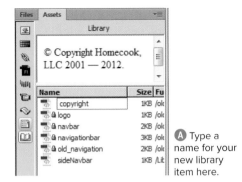. Type a name for the item.

   In the document window, the item will be highlighted with a color, indicating that it's a library item.

   TIP The default color used to highlight a library item is yellow. If desired, you can change this color in the Highlighting category of Dreamweaver's Preferences panel.

   TIP If it doesn't already exist, Dreamweaver creates a `Library` folder at the top level of your site. Library items are stored in this folder, with the file extension `.lbi`. The folder is for local use and doesn't need to be uploaded to the server.

A Type a name for your new library item here.

(A) A quick way to insert a library item into a document is to use the Insert button in the lower-left corner of the Assets panel.

Insert button

Using a Library Item

All you have to decide is where you want to use your library items on your pages. The rest is easy.

To insert a library item:

1. Position the insertion point in the document.

2. Drag the library item from the Library category of the Assets panel into the document.

   or

   Highlight the library item and click the Insert button in the lower-left corner of the Assets panel (A).

   The library item appears in the document.

To delete a library item:

- **From a document:** Select the library item in the document window and press Backspace (Delete).

- **From a site:** Choose the library item in the Library category of the Assets panel and press Backspace (Delete). This step cannot be undone.

TIP Library items become part of the page's code and are subject to any CSS rules in style sheets linked to the page. For example, if your library item contains a paragraph and you have a CSS rule for the p selector, the inserted item will reflect the rule.

Editing a Library Item

You need to be a bit careful when you edit library items, because when you change a library item, Dreamweaver changes all instances of that item throughout all the pages of your site, except any documents that are currently being edited. This can take some time if you have a large site, and you have to edit the item again to undo a mistake; the Undo command won't save you in this case. It's nothing to worry about; just be aware that changes can have far-reaching effects.

To edit a library item:

1. Do one of the following:

Double-click the item in the Library category in the Assets panel.

or

Highlight the item in the Library category in the Assets panel, and then click the Edit button in the lower-right corner of the Assets panel.

or

Highlight the item in the document window. The Property inspector shows information for the library item **Ⓐ**.
Click Open.

Ⓐ When you select a library item in the document window, you can use the Property inspector to open the library item.

B An open library item window is rather like a normal document window, except there's nothing there but the library item.

Update Library Items

Update library items in these files?

index.html

Update

Don't Update

C If you update library items, Dreamweaver reports on what will happen.

2. A window much like a document window appears, but it contains only the library item **B**.

3. Edit the item as needed.

4. Choose File > Save, or press Ctrl-S (Cmd-S). The Update Library Items dialog appears.

   ▸ **Update:** Updates every instance of the library item used in your site.

   ▸ **Don't Update:** No library items are updated.

   See the following section, "To update a library item only in the current document," if you want to select individual pages to update.

5. Click Update to have Dreamweaver open the Update Pages dialog, run through all the files containing the library item, update them, and report "Done" to you in the dialog when it's finished **C**.

6. Click Close to dismiss the Update Pages dialog.

To update a library item only in the current document:

1. Edit the library item, and then click Don't Update in the Update Library Items dialog (see the previous section, "To edit a library item").

2. Open a document containing the library item.

3. Choose Modify > Library > Update Current Page. The library item on this single page updates.

4. Save the document.

To rename a library item:

1. Highlight the name of the library item in the Library category of the Assets panel. Do one of the following:

   Right-click and choose Rename from the context menu.

   or

   Click the item name, wait a second, and click it again.

   The library item's name is selected and becomes editable .

2. Type the new name for the item.

3. The Update Files dialog appears **E**. Click Update to change the name of the library item on every page where it is in use.

> **TIP** Library items can't contain any head elements, so you don't have access to the CSS panel when editing a library item (internal CSS style sheets appear within the <head> tag).

> **TIP** Library items can't contain a <body> tag, so you don't have access to the Page Properties panel when editing a library item.

> **TIP** HTML pages changed by the update of a library item need to be uploaded to the server for the change to be visible to your site's visitors.

> **TIP** If a document is open when a library item updates, you'll have to save the document manually. Updates save automatically in a closed document.

D Need a better name for a library item? You can change it here.

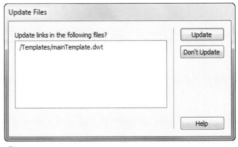

E When you change a library item name, Dreamweaver asks you if you want to change all the instances of the item in the site to reflect the new name.

Working on Library Items with the Property Inspector

As we mentioned in the previous section, "Editing a Library Item," the Property inspector offers some options for working on library items. You saw how to edit the library item using the Open button, but there are two as yet unexplained buttons on the Property inspector: "Detach from original" and Recreate.

Detaching a library item doesn't remove the item from the page. It breaks the connection between the copy of the library item on the current page and the original source in the site's `Library` folder. If you later update the original library item, the current page's code won't be changed by the update. You might want to do this if you have a library item that you want to be based on, but slightly different from, the original library item.

Sometimes you can have a page that contains the code from a library item that was removed from the site's `Library` folder (or never existed there). For example, let's say that you copied a page (that contained a library item) from one of your sites to a different site. The site that now contains the page will not, of course, have a corresponding library item in its `Library` folder. You can use the code in the current document to re-create the library item in the new local site.

To detach the library item:

1. Select a library item in the document window.

2. In the Property inspector, click "Detach from original" Ⓐ. Dreamweaver displays a dialog asking if you're sure you want to detach the item. Click OK. The link between the item on the page and the original in the **Library** folder is broken.

To re-create a missing or deleted library item:

1. Open a document containing code for a library item that is missing from the Library category of the Assets panel.

2. Highlight the item. The tag selector should display `<mm:libitem>`.

3. In the Property inspector, click Recreate. The item is re-created using the name it has on this page. The re-created item appears in the Library category of the Assets panel.

TIP If you detach a library item from a page, the highlighting in the document window that indicated that the element was a library item disappears along with the broken connection to the library item source. But the detached library item still remains on the page; all you've done is sever its link to the original item.

TIP Right-clicking a library item in the document window reveals a context menu with the same options available on the Property inspector: Open, Detach, and Recreate.

Ⓐ The Property inspector can be used to detach a library item from the source or to re-create a library item that's lost or missing.

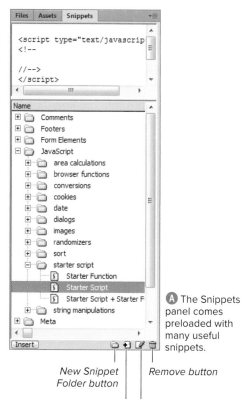

<A> The Snippets panel comes preloaded with many useful snippets.

New Snippet Folder button

Remove button

New Snippet button   Edit Snippet button

<B> There's a brief description of the snippet to the right of its name.

Using Dreamweaver Snippets

The Snippets panel is used to store useful bits of code, or *snippets*, that can be inserted any time, any place. In that way, snippets are like library items. But there's a big difference between snippets and library items. If you change or update a snippet, there's no sitewide update to previously inserted versions of the snippet. There's no connection between the code in an inserted snippet and the original snippet.

Dreamweaver comes with many useful prebuilt snippets already loaded and ready to use. You'll find them in the Snippets panel. If the Snippets panel is not already visible, choose Window > Snippets to bring it forward.

In the Snippets panel <A>, the snippets that come with Dreamweaver are nicely organized into folders for you. Inside the folders you find individual snippets. Click an individual snippet to see a preview in the preview pane at the top of the panel. You can also see a description of the highlighted snippet. If you work with a narrow window, as in <A>, you may have to scroll to the right with the horizontal scrollbar at the bottom of the Snippets panel to see the description. Expand the width of the panel <B> to read the description without scrolling.

You've probably already figured out that any custom snippets you save appear in the Snippets panel, too. Your snippets and Dreamweaver's snippets are used in the same way. We'll explain how to save a new snippet first, and then how to use it.

To save a snippet:

1. Open a document containing the material you'd like to make into a snippet. Select the snippet . Be sure you get all the surrounding material needed by clicking the tag in the tag selector.

2. Click the New Snippet icon in the lower-right corner of the Snippets panel. The Snippet dialog appears ⓓ. Complete the following fields:

   ▸ **Name:** Type a name for the new snippet. See the tip at the end of this section regarding rules for naming snippets.

   ▸ **Description:** Type a description. This is helpful, but optional.

   ▸ **Snippet type:** Select "Wrap selection" if the snippet is meant to wrap around a selection. Select "Insert block" if the snippet is meant to be inserted as a block.

ⓒ Select something on a page to save as a snippet.

ⓓ When you save your own snippets, you decide on a name, a description, and other basics.

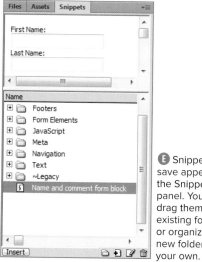

E Snippets you save appear in the Snippets panel. You can drag them into existing folders or organize new folders of your own.

If you choose "Wrap selection," you will be asked to choose the parts of the snippet to insert before or insert after the wrapped selection.

▸ **Insert code:** The code you selected in the document is displayed here. This is an editable field.

▸ **Preview type:** Choose either Design or Code.

3. Click OK.

4. The snippet appears in the Snippets panel **E**. The preview displays in the preview pane.

To use a snippet:

1. Position the insertion point in the document.

2. Highlight the snippet in the Snippets panel and do one of the following:

   Click the Insert button in the lower-left corner of the Snippets panel.

   or

   Double-click the snippet name.

   or

   Drag the snippet from the Snippets panel onto the document.

3. The snippet appears in the document. Replace any dummy text with the correct content 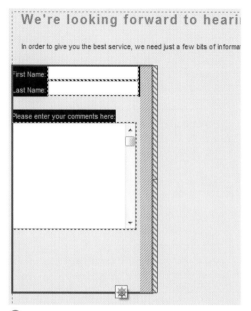.

TIP The snippet preview pane won't display the snippet with any CSS shown. The snippet must be on a page before CSS rules take effect.

TIP Delete or modify snippets by highlighting them and using the Edit Snippet or Remove buttons in the lower-right corner of the Snippets panel.

TIP Organize your snippets by dragging them into preexisting folders or by creating new folders of your own naming.

TIP Don't use any special characters, such as ampersands (&) or angle brackets (< and >), in snippet names.

F When you insert a snippet into a document, the text or other element the snippet contains appears on your page.

17

Editing Code

Dreamweaver is a WYSIWYG (What You See Is What You Get) application. Given Dreamweaver's design strengths, why would you ever bother looking at code, much less editing it?

Believe it or not, there are people who purchase Dreamweaver and then spend most of their time in Code view. There are a number of reasons why; some of the more common we hear are

- "It's perfect for control freaks like me who just want to change that one character or move things one pixel."

- "I learned tags before good WYSIWYG editors existed, so it's faster for me to make changes this way."

- "There are things I can do this way that can't be done any other way in Dreamweaver."

These are all perfectly valid reasons to want to use Code view (and there are plenty of other reasons). If you haven't before, check it out. You might find that Code view works best for you or that it's useful when you simply want to tweak one small thing on your page.

In This Chapter

Using the Coding Toolbar

Yes, it's another toolbar in Dreamweaver, but the Coding toolbar is a little different: it only shows up when you're in Code view, and it only acts on those things that you would deal with when you're in Code view.

To use the Coding toolbar:

1. If you're in Design view, click the Code button in the Document toolbar. This switches you into Code view, so you'll now see the tags (instead of the WYSIWYG appearance of your page) and the Coding toolbar. For instance, 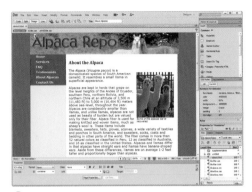 shows a page in Design view, whereas 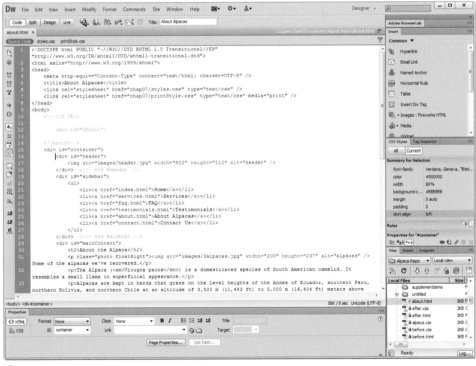 shows the same page in Code view.

Ⓐ Here's the familiar Design view that you've grown to know and love.

Ⓑ The Code view shows the exact same page but in a whole new light.

Open Documents

Show Code Navigator

Collapse Full Tag

Collapse Selection

Expand All

Select Parent Tag

Balance Braces

Line Numbers

Highlight Invalid Code

Word Wrap

Syntax Error Alerts in Info Bar

Apply Comment

Remove Comment

Wrap Tag

Recent Snippets

Move or Convert CSS

Indent Code

Outdent Code

Format Source Code

C The Coding toolbar provides everything you need to manage text and tags.

2. On the left side of the document window, you'll see the Coding toolbar **C**. Let's review its buttons, from top to bottom:

▸ **Open Documents:** The name of this button might make you think that it's a way to open documents, but that's incorrect; it actually offers a pop-up menu of all the items that are currently open.

▸ **Show Code Navigator:** Displays the Code Navigator window. Code Navigator is covered in Chapter 7.

▸ **Collapse Full Tag:** Collapsing code (and why you'd want to do it) is covered later in this chapter. For now, it's enough to know that this button will do it. Holding the Alt (Option) key while clicking this button collapses everything outside the current tag.

▸ **Collapse Selection:** This button collapses the current selection of code, and holding down the Alt (Option) key while clicking this button collapses everything outside the selection.

▸ **Expand All:** If any code on the page is collapsed, clicking this button expands it again.

▸ **Select Parent Tag:** This button causes the selection area to change to include the parent tag, based on the current cursor position.

▸ **Balance Braces:** If your current cursor position is inside a `<script>` or `<style>` container, clicking this button causes the innermost set of braces—( ), { }, or [ ]—to be selected. This also works inside external JavaScript and CSS files.

continues on next page

- ▸ **Line Numbers:** Toggles the display of line numbers in the current document. If they're currently displayed, they'll be hidden, and if they're currently hidden, they'll display.

- ▸ **Highlight Invalid Code:** If you enter tags that Dreamweaver doesn't like and you've chosen this option, your mistake will be highlighted in yellow. If you click in the highlighted area, the Property inspector will tell you more about the error **D**.

- ▸ **Word Wrap:** Toggles between wrapping code to the window (on) and allowing long lines to scroll horizontally off the screen (off).

- ▸ **Syntax Error Alerts in Info Bar:** Turns on or off an information bar that appears at the top of the page if Dreamweaver detects a code syntax error. The program also highlights the line of code containing the error.

- ▸ **Apply Comment:** The pop-up menu on this button gives several choices, each of which wraps comments around the selected text:

  - ▪ **Apply HTML Comment:** Inserts `<!--` and `-->` before and after the selection, respectively.

  - ▪ **Apply /* */ Comment:** Wraps this type of comment around the selected CSS or JavaScript.

  - ▪ **Apply // Comment:** Inserts this type of comment at the beginning of each selected line of CSS, JavaScript, or both.

  - ▪ **Apply ' Comment:** Inserts this type of comment at the beginning of each selected line of VBScript.

  - ▪ **Apply Server Comment:** If you're working on a server-side file such as PHP, JSP, or ColdFusion, Dreamweaver automatically detects the file type and inserts the correct type of comment.

- ▸ **Remove Comment:** Removes comment tags from the selected code.

- ▸ **Wrap Tag:** Opens the Quick Tag Editor (described later in this chapter), allowing you to wrap a tag around the selection.

- ▸ **Recent Snippets:** Allows you to insert a recently used snippet. Snippets are covered in Chapter 16, "Making Life Easier: Using Templates, Libraries, and Snippets."

- ▸ **Move or Convert CSS:** Here you can either convert inline CSS to a rule or move CSS rules. CSS is covered in Chapters 7–9.

D It's always a good idea to tell Dreamweaver to highlight invalid code, so you see problems at a glance.

E The Code View Options choice in the View menu contains some very useful settings.

F If you have too many buttons for your screen size, you'll find they're still accessible once you learn where they're hiding.

- ▶ **Indent Code:** Takes the selection and moves it to the right, based on your chosen indentation preference in the Code Format settings (covered in the sidebar "Text Editing Tips," later in this chapter).

- ▶ **Outdent Code:** Takes the selection and moves it to the left.

- ▶ **Format Source Code:** From this pop-up menu, you can choose whether to apply formatting to the file as a whole or to just the current selection. Whichever you choose will be formatted as specified in the Code Format settings, which can also be accessed via this pop-up menu.

TIP Some of these options can also be set from View > Code View Options **E**. There are a few extra ones there, also: Hidden Characters, Syntax Coloring, and Auto Indent. In earlier versions of Dreamweaver, you could get to this from the View Options button in the Document toolbar, but that's gone away as of CS5.

TIP If you appear to be missing a button or two, don't fret—your document window may just be smaller than the Coding toolbar. If that's the case, you'll see a couple of downward-facing arrows at the bottom of the toolbar. Click those arrows, and the missing buttons appear off to the side **F**.

TIP If for some reason you don't like this toolbar and just want to make it go away, you can do that just as you would with other Dreamweaver toolbars: choose View > Toolbars > Coding. And if you change your mind, that same command brings it back.

TIP Dreamweaver opens files in Design view by default. If you want all your HTML files to open in Code view instead, open the Preferences panel and choose the File Types/Editors category. In the "Open in Code View" text box, add a space followed by `.html`. You can add any other file types where you want to use Code view by default by adding those file extensions, too.

Layout for Coders

If you've chosen to use the Coder layout, rather than the Designer layout, your screen will look a little different than our screenshots. You may also check out Coder layout because you decide, after using Code view for a bit, that it's the way you want to work in the future. 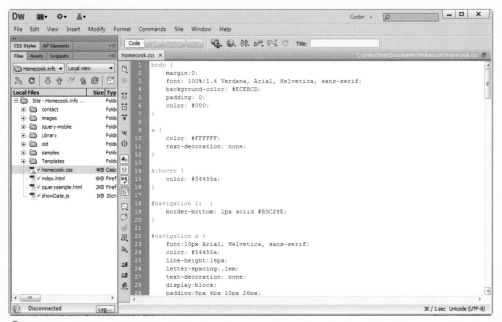 shows you how a CSS style sheet appears if you change the Workspace Switcher menu to Coder layout 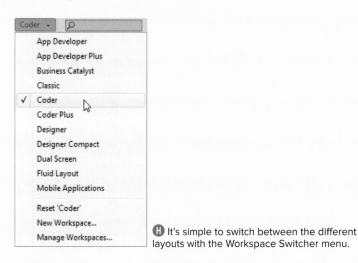.

G Coder layout is for those who want to see lots of code with as few distractions as possible.

H It's simple to switch between the different layouts with the Workspace Switcher menu.

Layout for Coders *continued*

Other preset workspaces of interest to codeheads include Coder Plus, which adds an icon bar to the right of the document window, providing easy access to the Insert, CSS Styles, and AP Elements panels; and App Developer and App Developer Plus, which are useful for people setting up database-backed Web sites 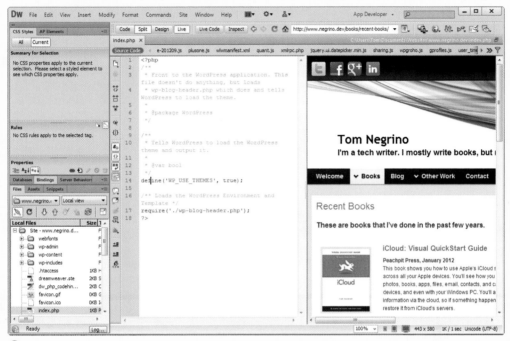. The latter two workspaces display the document window in Split view and show the Databases, Bindings, and Server Behaviors panels.

I If you're setting up a database-backed Web site, check out the App Developer workspace.

Text Editing Tips

When you start using Code view and see tags and markup for the first time, you'll find that there are a lot of things that Dreamweaver assumes you already know. In case you don't, here are a few handy tips:

- **Word Wrap:** You may want all of your paragraphs to be one long string of text, but if you have Word Wrap turned off, all your long lines will go off the right side of the document. You can turn Word Wrap on in the Coding toolbar ⓒ.

    When you're entering code, be careful about putting in hard returns (where you press Enter/Return) versus the soft returns that Dreamweaver displays even though you didn't type anything in. If you want soft returns, just keep typing and Dreamweaver will handle it for you. If you want hard returns, you might as well turn off Word Wrap.

- **Syntax coloring:** At first, you might wonder why the text in the code editor is *so* many different colors. Even if all the colors confuse you and make you think about turning off syntax coloring, give it a try with colors first. Syntax coloring is one of the best ways to learn what's what in code, because similar elements will have identical coloring.

    Wish there were fewer colors all at once? In the Code Coloring category of the Preferences panel, you can change any color to any other color. And if for some reason you want to make things even more tasteless, you can add unique background colors to each different foreground color. But you shouldn't.

- **Line numbers:** These are another matter of personal preference. Some people love them, whereas other people find them terribly annoying. What you'll want to note is how they work in conjunction with Word Wrap: soft-wrapped lines only get a single line number ⓓ.

- **Indentation:** If you haven't worked with code before, you might not immediately get why indentation is so useful. But if you're trying to figure out where your **div**s begin and end, you'll get it quickly when you can see them lined up with each other, with their contents indented.

    There's no single "right" way to indent code. What we've found works best is to find one style that works for you and then *stick to it*. It's the consistency that matters most, especially when you have multiple people working on a site.

    If you want to manually indent/outdent your code, you can (with the Indent Code and Outdent Code buttons on the Coding toolbar ⓒ), but we recommend instead turning on Auto Indent by choosing View > Code View Options ⓔ.

Text Editing Tips *continued*

- **Code formatting:** The last button on the Coding toolbar (actually a pop-up menu) lets you format your source code ⓒ. If your tags are all over the place because your code came from here and there (as happens to all of us), the Apply Source Formatting option can be found in that pop-up menu. If you don't like the way Dreamweaver formats your code by default, you can choose the Code Format Settings option from the pop-up menu, and you'll be presented with the Code Format category of the Preferences panel. Even if you don't know much about tags, it's easy to use this to put your text just where you want it Ⓙ.

Ⓙ Dreamweaver lets you format your code precisely the way that you want it.

Using Split View

Does losing your WYSIWYG view freak you out a little? Wish you had a way to see Code view and Design view at once? Well, that's exactly what Split view is about. It splits the document window into two separate panes, so you can see both code and WYSIWYG simultaneously.

Dreamweaver adds two enhancements to the basic split idea:

- A Split Code view, where both panes show code. This is very useful when you want to copy and paste code from one section of your page to another part of the same page.

- An option to split the pane vertically rather than horizontally. In both horizontal and vertical split modes, you can choose which panes contain the Code and Design views.

To use Split view:

1. Whether you're in Design view or Code view, click the Split button in the Document toolbar. Your document window splits into two: one part for Design view and one for Code view. By default, the split is vertical **Ⓐ**.

2. If you want to reverse the two (you prefer Code view on the right instead of Design view, or vice versa), use the Layout button pop-up menu on the Application bar **Ⓑ**. When you're in Split view, you can choose whether Design view should go on the top (when split horizontally) or left (when split vertically).

3. (Optional) If you want to use the horizontal Split view, toggle Split Vertically from the View menu or the Layout button. The display changes from the vertical split to the horizontal split **Ⓒ**.

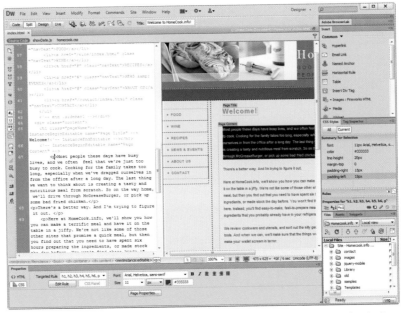

Ⓐ Split view is like training wheels for code—it lets you see how changing the design changes the code, and vice versa.

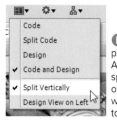

B The Layout button pop-up menu on the Application bar lets you split your view horizontally or vertically and then pick which view goes on the top or left.

TIP If you've never looked at HTML tags before, Split view can be a great way to familiarize yourself with which tags go with which elements of your design.

TIP You can change the size of the panes by pointing at the border between them. When the cursor changes into a two-headed arrow, you can drag the border to resize the panes.

4. (Optional) If you want the Code view in both panes, so that you can look at different parts of the same page in each pane, choose Split Code from the View menu or the Layout button. Your display changes to reflect your choice.

TIP When you update your page in Design view, Code view automatically updates in response. But when you update in Code view, the Property inspector displays the message "You have made changes to the code. To edit selection properties, click Refresh or press F5."

TIP When you're in vertical Split view, the Coding toolbar only extends down the left side of the Code pane, not down the full document window.

TIP If you select anything in one view, the document automatically scrolls to show and highlight the same selection in the other view.

C Depending on your working style, you may prefer the horizontal Split view instead of the vertical Split view.

Using Live Code View

Live Code view is a version of Split view that complements Live view (see Chapter 1 for more about using Live view). Normally, when you're in Split view, you see the Design view in one pane and the Code view in the other. If you then click the Live view button, Dreamweaver changes the rendering in the Design pane to show how the contents of that pane would look in a Web browser. The underlying code in the Code View pane remains the same. But what if your Web page uses JavaScript for visual effects such as rollovers? As the script executes, it's actually changing the HTML on the page, rewriting it under script control. Live Code view allows you to see how the HTML in the Code View pane changes as you interact with the page in the Design View pane. This is especially useful if you're trying to debug a script because it is not producing the effect that you want.

To turn on Live Code view:

1. In any view, click the Live view button on the Document toolbar.

   The page rendering changes to show what the Web page would look like in a Web browser **A**.

2. Click the Live Code button on the Document toolbar.

   The document changes to Split view, with the code in the Code View pane highlighted to indicate that it is live **B**. As you interact with the page in the Design View pane, the code in the Code View pane is updated.

TIP There are useful options for Live Code view, found in the Live View Options menu in the Browser Navigation toolbar. We discuss these options in more detail in Chapter 15, "Working with Content Management Systems."

script05.html
Source Code script04.css jquery.js jquery.tablesorter.js script05.js

Beatles Discography

Album	Year	Label
Please Please Me	1963	Parlophone
With The Beatles	1963	Parlophone
A Hard Day's Night	1964	Parlophone
Beatles for Sale	1964	Parlophone
Help!	1965	Parlophone
Rubber Soul	1965	Parlophone
Revolver	1966	Parlophone
Sgt. Pepper's Lonely Hearts Club Band	1967	Parlophone
Magical Mystery Tour	1967	Capitol
The Beatles	1968	Apple
Yellow Submarine	1969	Apple
Abbey Road	1969	Apple
Let It Be	1970	Apple

script05.html
Source Code script04.css jquery.js jquery.tablesorter.js script05.js

Beatles Discography

Album	Year	Label
Please Please Me	1963	Parlophone
With The Beatles	1963	Parlophone
A Hard Day's Night	1964	Parlophone
Beatles for Sale	1964	Parlophone
Help!	1965	Parlophone
Rubber Soul	1965	Parlophone
Revolver	1966	Parlophone
Sgt. Pepper's Lonely Hearts Club Band	1967	Parlophone
Magical Mystery Tour	1967	Capitol
The Beatles	1968	Apple
Yellow Submarine	1969	Apple
Abbey Road	1969	Apple
Let It Be	1970	Apple

A In Design view, Dreamweaver shows you the usual view (top). In Live view (bottom), you can see the application of the CSS styles and the highlighting of the row under the cursor thanks to JavaScript.

Live Code script04.css jquery.js jquery.tablesorter.js script05.js

```
<tr class="even">
        <td>Please Please Me</td>
        <td>1963</td>
        <td>Parlophone</td>
</tr><tr class="odd">
        <td>With The Beatles</td>
        <td>1963</td>
        <td>Parlophone</td>
</tr><tr class="even">
        <td>A Hard Day's Night</td>
        <td>1964</td>
        <td>Parlophone</td>
</tr><tr class="odd">
        <td>Beatles for Sale</td>
        <td>1964</td>
        <td>Parlophone</td>
</tr><tr class="even">
        <td>Help!</td>
        <td>1965</td>
        <td>Parlophone</td>
</tr><tr class="odd">
        <td>Rubber Soul</td>
```

Beatles Discography

Album	Year	Label
Please Please Me	1963	Parlophone
With The Beatles	1963	Parlophone
A Hard Day's Night	1964	Parlophone
Beatles for Sale	1964	Parlophone
Help!	1965	Parlophone
Rubber Soul	1965	Parlophone
Revolver	1966	Parlophone
Sgt. Pepper's Lonely Hearts Club Band	1967	Parlophone
Magical Mystery Tour	1967	Capitol
The Beatles	1968	Apple
Yellow Submarine	1969	Apple
Abbey Road	1969	Apple
Let It Be	1970	Apple

Live Code script04.css jquery.js jquery.tablesorter.js script05.js

```
<tr class="even over">
        <td>Please Please Me</td>
        <td>Please Please Me</td>
        <td>1963</td>
        <td>Parlophone</td>
</tr><tr class="odd">
        <td>With The Beatles</td>
        <td>1963</td>
        <td>Parlophone</td>
</tr><tr class="even">
        <td>A Hard Day's Night</td>
        <td>1964</td>
        <td>Parlophone</td>
</tr><tr class="odd">
        <td>Beatles for Sale</td>
        <td>1964</td>
        <td>Parlophone</td>
</tr><tr class="even">
        <td>Help!</td>
        <td>1965</td>
        <td>Parlophone</td>
</tr><tr class="odd">
```

Beatles Discography

Album	Year	Label
Please Please Me	1963	Parlophone
With The Beatles	1963	Parlophone
A Hard Day's Night	1964	Parlophone
Beatles for Sale	1964	Parlophone
Help!	1965	Parlophone
Rubber Soul	1965	Parlophone
Revolver	1966	Parlophone
Sgt. Pepper's Lonely Hearts Club Band	1967	Parlophone
Magical Mystery Tour	1967	Capitol
The Beatles	1968	Apple
Yellow Submarine	1969	Apple
Abbey Road	1969	Apple
Let It Be	1970	Apple

B In Live Code view, the HTML code changes under JavaScript control as you interact with the page in the Design pane (bottom).

Using the Quick Tag Editor

If you prefer Design view (as do most people who've bought a WYSIWYG editor, after all) but wish you could type a little bit of HTML now and then without switching back and forth between modes, there's an answer: the Quick Tag Editor.

To use the Quick Tag Editor:

1. With your page in Design view, put the cursor in the place where you want to add a tag, or select the tag you want to change, or select the element you want to wrap a tag around.

2. Press Ctrl-T (Cmd-T).

   or

   Click the Quick Tag Editor button at the right edge of the Property inspector.

3. The Quick Tag Editor appears, in one of its three modes: Insert, Edit, or Wrap. In any of these modes, start typing, and the possible options appear in the code hints menu below.

   ▸ **Insert HTML:** This mode allows you to place a new tag on the page Ⓐ.

   ▸ **Edit tag:** This allows you to modify an existing tag, either to change it or to add attributes to it Ⓑ.

   ▸ **Wrap tag:** In this mode, you can wrap a new tag around an existing element Ⓒ.

Ⓐ With the Quick Tag Editor, you can easily insert a new tag on the page.

Ⓑ The Quick Tag Editor also lets you edit existing tags.

Ⓒ And lastly, you can tell the Quick Tag Editor that you want to wrap a tag around existing page elements.

4. To accept your changes and leave the Quick Tag Editor, press Enter (Return). To leave the Quick Tag Editor without making any changes, press Esc.

TIP Dreamweaver tries to guess which Quick Tag mode you want to be in. If it guesses incorrectly, you can cycle through the three modes by pressing Ctrl-T (Cmd-T) again. Be careful about what's actually chosen when you do that, though—sometimes, the selected area can expand. For instance, if you've selected the text of a link with the goal of modifying that link, but you've also (accidentally) selected something outside the <a> (link) tag, you can find that you're modifying the <p> (paragraph) around the text instead of the link itself.

TIP If the Quick Tag Editor appears but is covering an area you want to see, you can move it. Just click and drag in the area that displays the mode name to put it in the location you want.

Using the Tag Editor

You've seen the Quick Tag Editor; now here's the Tag Editor itself. It's not really slower than the Quick version, and it's handy for when you want more control than you can get in, say, the Property inspector but don't want to deal with actual HTML tags.

To use the Tag Editor:

1. With your page in Design view, select an element where you want to edit an existing tag. For instance, you can select an image or the text of a link.

2. Right-click, and choose Edit Tag.

   or

   Press Shift-F5.

   or

   From Dreamweaver's menu, choose Modify > Edit Tag.

3. The Tag Editor dialog for that particular tag appears. Every tag has a custom dialog of its own, with a variety of categories in the left column. shows the Tag Editor dialog for an `<img>` tag, and shows the Tag Editor dialog for an `<a>` tag. Make any desired changes.

4. Click OK when complete.

> **TIP** Near the bottom right of the Tag Editor dialog is the Tag info disclosure arrow. Click it, and the dialog size increases to include a description of the tag you're modifying. For more information about this description, see "Using the Tag Chooser" and "Using the Code Reference," later in this chapter.

> **TIP** You can also access the Tag Editor from Code view by right-clicking a tag .

Ⓐ The Tag Editor for images lets you modify every possible image attribute and event.

Ⓑ The Tag Editor for the **a** tag allows you to change attributes and events for links.

Ⓒ Right-click a tag, and this menu appears with the available options.

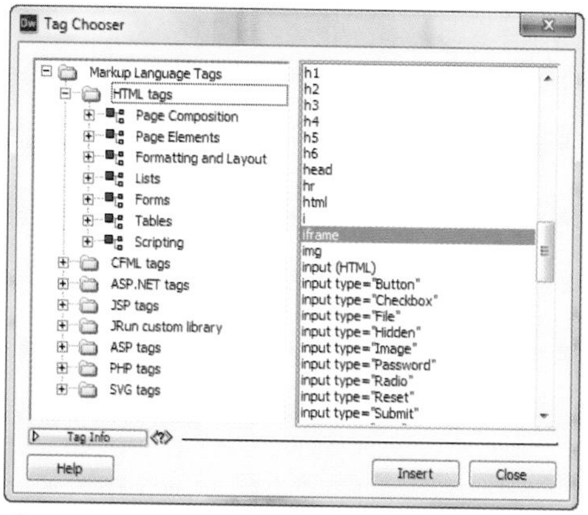

A The Tag Chooser lets you insert tags.

Using the Tag Chooser

If you're beginning to think that there are a lot of different ways to insert elements into a Dreamweaver page, you're right—except that you haven't even seen many of them yet. Here's a tool you might not have run across yet—Dreamweaver's Tag Chooser.

To use the Tag Chooser to insert tags:

1. With your page in Code view, put the cursor into the section of the document that you want to add to or edit.

2. Right-click, and a menu of the available options appears. Choose Insert Tag (see figure **C** in "Using the Tag Editor"). The Tag Chooser dialog appears **A**.

3. Click any of the icons or tag categories on the left side, and the matching tags will appear on the right.

4. Select one of the tags on the right, and click Insert. If the tag you chose contains angle brackets (< >), it will be inserted into the page. Otherwise, a Tag Editor dialog appears, allowing you to enter the required information. For more about the Tag Editor dialog, see "Using the Tag Editor."

5. When you are done with the Tag Chooser dialog, click Close.

To use the Tag Chooser to get tag information:

1. With the Tag Chooser open **Ⓐ**, select a tag on the right side.

2. Click the Tag Info button that's just above the Help button on the bottom left. The Tag Info reference area appears, along with useful information about the tag you selected **Ⓑ**.

   or

   Click the **<?>** button directly to the right of the Tag Info button. The same information appears, but in the Code Reference panel. For more information about the Code Reference panel, see "Using the Code Reference," later in this chapter.

   You can also open the Tag Chooser by clicking the bottommost icon in the Insert panel when you're in the Common category. If you do this in Design view, Dreamweaver automatically switches to Split view.

Ⓑ When you select a tag and then click the Tag Info button, Dreamweaver displays a reference guide to that tag.

Collapsing Code

If you spend much time working with tags and code, you'll often find yourself in a situation where you wish you could hide just some of it. Thankfully, that's something you can do with Dreamweaver.

To collapse code:

1. In Code view, select the code that you want to collapse Ⓐ. The simplest way to do this is to click somewhere inside the area and then click the Select Parent Tag button on the Coding toolbar (see figure Ⓒ in "Using the Coding Toolbar").

continues on next page

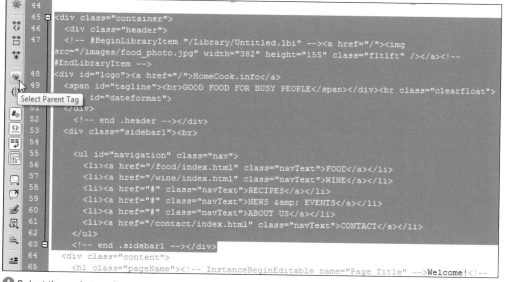

Ⓐ Select the code to collapse, and then look for the vertical line on the left.

2. Just to the left of the code, you'll see a vertical line that goes from the beginning of the selected area to the end. Windows users will see a white box with a minus sign on each end; Mac users will see two gray triangles, the top one facing down and the bottom one facing up. Click one of these endpoints, and the selected code collapses ⓑ. You'll now see the first part of the first line inside a highlighted box, plus a white box with a plus sign (Windows) or a right-facing gray arrow (Mac).

or

Click anywhere inside the tag you want to collapse, and click the Collapse Full Tag button on the Coding toolbar.

or

Select the code you want to collapse, and click the Collapse Selection button on the Coding toolbar.

or

Click in a particular location on the page, and press the Alt (Option) key while clicking the Collapse Full Tag button on the Coding toolbar. This collapses everything *but* the full tag around your particular cursor position.

or

Select a segment of code, and press the Alt (Option) key while clicking the Collapse Selection button on the Coding toolbar. This collapses everything *but* the current selection.

or

Right-click inside a tag on the page, and choose Selection ⓒ. From there, you can choose Collapse Selection, Collapse Outside Selection, Collapse Full Tag, or Collapse Outside Full Tag.

ⓑ Click one of the icons on the endpoints of the line, and the selected text collapses to a single line.

C You can also collapse code by right-clicking the selection and choosing one of the collapse options.

To work with collapsed code:

- Put your cursor over the highlighted box, and a tool tip appears displaying all of the collapsed code D.

- Collapse a section of code if you need to move it from one area of the page to another. You'll know that you're moving exactly what you want to move and no more.

- If you collapse a section of code and then save and close the page, the next time you open the page that section will still show as collapsed.

To expand code:

Click the collapsed code symbol (the white box with a plus sign [Windows] or the right-facing gray arrow [Mac]) to the left of the code you want to expand.

or

Double-click the highlighted box.

or

Click the Expand All button on the Coding toolbar, which expands *all* the collapsed code on the page.

or

Right-click on the page, and choose Selection C. From there, you can choose Expand Selection or Expand All.

D If you want to know what's collapsed, this tool tip gives you the info without actually expanding the code.

Using Code Hints

When it comes to working with HTML, not all text editors are created equally—and Dreamweaver's code hints are one reason why text editor fans will use its Code view rather than someone else's garden variety notepad-like application. While the basic process of code hinting is unchanged from previous versions of Dreamweaver, the CS5.5 version introduced code-hinting features for HTML5, CSS3, browser-specific properties, and jQuery. Rather than duplicate the same process with minor variations, we'll run through the entire process for HTML and then show brief examples for the other types of code hinting.

Code Hints for HTML

Dreamweaver CS6's code hints for HTML are largely unchanged from CS5, with the exception that hints for HTML5 have been added.

To get hints for HTML:

1. In Code view (or the Code pane of Split view), click anywhere on the HTML page that you want to add a tag. Start a new tag by typing <, and the code hints appear in a pop-up menu Ⓐ.

2. Type the first character or two of the tag, and the code hints menu should change to reflect your typing Ⓑ. When the hinted value is the tag you want, press Tab.

3. To add an attribute to your new tag, press the spacebar and continue to type. The code hints pop-up menu will appear again, this time displaying just the valid attributes for that tag Ⓒ. Again, choose the one you want and press Tab to get the full attribute added to your tag.

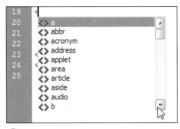

Ⓐ Start typing, and the code hints pop-up menu appears.

Ⓑ As you continue to type, the code hints narrow down your choices.

Ⓒ Code hints work for attributes as well as tags. Note that Dreamweaver is smart enough to find all of the instances in which the typed letters (**sr**) appear.

D Code hints can tell you when the attribute needs a URL as its value.

E You can add an attribute to an existing tag—just click inside the tag and start typing.

F Dreamweaver lets you make code hints work just the way you choose.

TIP Dreamweaver CS5 introduced improved code hinting for PHP, including custom class hinting, integrated documentation, and site-specific code hinting for **CMS** and application frameworks. To control the site-specific code hinting, choose **Site > Site-Specific Code Hints.** The resulting dialog has presets for the three **CMS** platforms that Dreamweaver supports, allowing you to control how code hints are provided for **WordPress, Joomla,** and **Drupal** sites.

4. If you select an attribute that needs to link to a file, the code hint changes to a Browse button **D**. Click the button to browse to the file on your disk.

5. If you want to add an attribute to an existing tag, click immediately after the tag name (for instance, right after the **g** in **<img>**), press the spacebar, and begin to type. The available attributes will display **E**.

6. To end a tag, type **/>**, and the most recently opened tag will automatically be closed.

TIP If the code hints pop-up menu doesn't appear, press Ctrl-spacebar (Cmd-spacebar) to make it display.

TIP You can use the arrow keys on your keyboard to move up and down through code hints to choose the tag or attribute you want.

TIP If you're using XHTML and you end a tag with > rather than />, code hints will automatically change it to the proper format.

TIP You can't modify an attribute with code hints; instead, delete the attribute and re-create it.

TIP If you want a special character but can't remember its exact name (such as   for non-breaking space), just type the first letter or symbol (&, in this case) and you'll get a code hint that lists all the possible characters you can enter.

TIP If there's anything you don't like about how code hints work, you can change them to suit your taste by modifying the values in the Code Hints category of Dreamweaver's Preferences panel **F**.

Code Hints for CSS

You'll find code hints for CSS3 and the browser-specific properties in Dreamweaver CS6.

To get hints for CSS:

In a CSS style sheet, begin creating a rule and then simply start typing a CSS property. Properties matching what you type will appear in the pop-up menu ⒢.

or

To get a browser-specific property, create a rule and then type the dash (–). Dreamweaver will pop up a menu containing the four types of browser-specific properties ⒣. Choose from the pop-up menu, or keep typing to continue narrowing your choices until you have inserted the property you want.

```
.style {
    font-
        ◈ font-family
        ◈ font-size
        ◈ font-size-adjust
        ◈ font-stretch
        ◈ font-style
        ◈ font-variant
        ◈ font-weight
```

⒢ In CSS files, the code hints work when you're adding properties to a rule.

```
.style {
    -
        ◈ moz-
        ◈ ms-
        ◈ o-
        ◈ webkit-
```

⒣ To get the browser-specific code hints, begin by typing the dash.

HTML5 and CSS3 Code Hinting Additions

Dreamweaver has code hinting support for the following HTML5 elements and their associated attributes: **<article>**, **<aside>**, **<audio>**, **<canvas>**, **<command>**, **<datalist>**, **<details>**, **<embed>**, **<figcaption>**, **<figure>**, **<footer>**, **<header>**, **<hgroup>**, **<keygen>**, **<mark>**, **<menu>**, **<meter>**, **<nav>**, **<output>**, **<progress>**, **<rp>**, **<rt>**, **<ruby>**, **<section>**, **<source>**, **<summary>**, **<times>**, **<video>**, and **<wbr>**.

For CSS3, there are too many properties to list, but they include properties and attributes from the following W3C categories: Border and Background, User Interface, Multi-column Layout, Line Layout, Text, Marquee, Ruby, Transitions, and Animations 2-D and 3-D. Because CSS3 is still very much in a state of flux (there's no final standard, just a bewildering array of Working Drafts, Candidate Recommendations, Proposed Recommendations, and Recommendations for each category listed), you can expect that future versions of Dreamweaver will support newer versions of the many parts of CSS3 when those parts are supported by more browsers. Historically, the browsers with the most up-to-date support for CSS3 rules are Safari and Chrome.

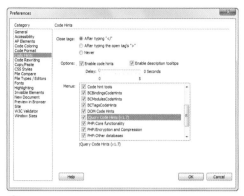

I Confirm that jQuery code hinting is turned on in Dreamweaver's Preferences panel.

Code Hints for jQuery

Before you start using code hinting for jQuery, you should confirm that it is turned on in the Code Hints category of Dreamweaver's Preferences panel **I**. jQuery code hints are on by default, and they will work in any **.js** file. You have the option of turning them off if you prefer to work with a different JavaScript framework.

To get hints for jQuery static methods:

In a JavaScript document, type either **jQuery.** or its more common shortcut, **$.**. Dreamweaver will pop up a list of static methods **J**.

To get hints for jQuery non-static methods:

In a JavaScript document, type either **jQuery() or $().** Dreamweaver will pop up a list of non-static methods **K**.

```
$.
⬛ ajax(settings)                                                    jQuery  ▲
⬛ ajax(url [,settings])                                             jQuery
⬛ ajaxPrefilter(function(options, originalOptions, jqXHR))          jQuery
⬛ ajaxSetup(options)                                                jQuery
⬛ ajaxTransport(function(options, originalOptions, jqXHR))          jQuery
⬛ Callbacks(flags)                                                  jQuery
⬛ contains(container, contained)                                    jQuery
○ cssHooks                                                          jQuery
⬛ data(element)                                                     jQuery
⬛ data(element, key)                                                jQuery  ▼
```

J This is the list of jQuery static methods.

```
$().
⬛ add(elements)                                                     jQuery  ▲
⬛ add(html)                                                         jQuery
⬛ add(selector, [context])                                          jQuery
⬛ addClass(className)                                               jQuery
⬛ addClass(function(index, class))                                  jQuery
⬛ after(content)                                                    jQuery
⬛ after(function())                                                 jQuery
⬛ ajaxComplete(handler(event, XMLHttpRequest, ajaxOptions))         jQuery
⬛ ajaxError(handler(event, XMLHttpRequest, ajaxOptions, thrownError))  jQuery
⬛ ajaxSend(handler(event, XMLHttpRequest, ajaxOptions))             jQuery  ▼
```

K Here are the code hints for jQuery non-static methods.

Code Hints for DOM Elements

In previous versions of Dreamweaver, if you wanted to write your own JavaScript you needed to manually keep track of the named elements, **id**s, HTML tag names, and **class** names so that you could reference them using the appropriate JavaScript methods (**getElementsByTagName**, **getElementById**, **getElementsByName**, and **getElementsByClassName**). Dreamweaver CS5.5 added DOM element hinting. When you're typing in a JavaScript window, Dreamweaver shows in the code window a list of names that it collects from the DOM of the parent HTML page.

To get hints for DOM elements:

In a JavaScript document, type **document. getElementsByTagName("**. Dreamweaver pops up a list of HTML tag names Ⓛ. This is the same list that it uses for HTML code hinting.

or

In a JavaScript document, type **document. getElementById("**. Dreamweaver pops up a list of **id**s found in the parent HTML document Ⓜ.

or

```
document.getElementsByTagName('
                              <> a
                              <> abbr
                              <> acronym
                              <> address
                              <> applet
                              <> article
                              <> aside
                              <> audio
                              <> area
                              <> b
```

Ⓛ Dreamweaver lets you use code hints for DOM elements used in JavaScript, in this case, tag names.

```
document.getElementById(""
                    #) popups                    div      script06.html
                    @ searchField                input    script06.html
```

Ⓜ Dreamweaver scans the document and pops up a list with the **id**s it finds.

In a JavaScript document, type **document. getElementsByName('**. Dreamweaver pops up a list of named elements in the document **N**. If the name applies to more than one element, you'll be told that, too.

or

In a JavaScript document, type **document. getElementsByClassName('**. Dreamweaver pops up a list of the classes found in the parent HTML document **O**.

TIP Dreamweaver allows you to use either single or double quotes to get hints for DOM elements. We prefer to use double quotes, so we've used those in the steps above. But as you can see from the figures, either works.

```
document.getElementsByName(''
                      N color                                      input    script06.html
                      N direction                                 input    script06.html
                      N type                                      input    script06.html
                         "type" is used in multiple elements.
```

N If you ask for elements by name, Dreamweaver populates the hint list, and lets you know if the name has been used more than once.

```
document.getElementsByClassName(''
                         S navBar
                         S typeBtn
                         S typeBtn2
```

O Finally, if you want to manipulate elements with a particular **class** name, Dreamweaver can help you find them.

Using the Tag Inspector

If you prefer to stay in Design view but every so often just want to tweak something, the Tag inspector is one of the simplest ways to do so. Along with the Tag Editor and the Quick Tag Editor (covered earlier), it's a great way to modify existing tags, and it's an easy way to get used to the attributes that exist for each tag.

To use the Tag inspector:

1. If the Tag inspector currently isn't displaying, choose Window > Tag Inspector.

2. If you're in Design view, click an element on the page or choose a tag from the tag selector. If you're in Code view, click anywhere inside a tag. The tag and its attributes appear in the Tag inspector Ⓐ. Be sure the Attributes tab is selected.

3. There are two ways to view the attributes in the Tag inspector: by category or as a list.

   ▸ To view by category, click the Show Category view button. Categories can be open or closed. To open a closed category, click the plus (+) button (Windows) or the right-facing triangle (Mac); to close an open category, click the minus (−) button (Windows) or the downward-facing triangle (Mac). When a category is open, the list of attributes that fall into that category are displayed.

   ▸ To view as a list, click the Show List view button. This choice displays all the tag's attributes in an alphabetical list Ⓑ.

Show Category view

Show List view

Ⓐ The Tag inspector can be found in the Attributes tab of the Tag Inspector panel. Here's the Category view.

Ⓑ Or optionally, there's also the List view, which shows all of that tag's attributes in alphabetical order.

C The standard Point to File and browse icons work the same way here as they do everywhere else in Dreamweaver.

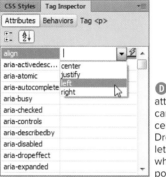

D For those attributes that can have only certain values, Dreamweaver lets you know what those possibilities are.

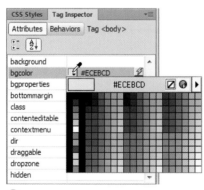

E The color picker lets you choose the color you want without having to remember odd color codes.

4. You can now modify, add, or delete attributes. There are different ways to edit different types of attributes:

▶ If you're adding or modifying an attribute whose value is a URL **C**, you'll see the Point to File icon and a browse icon to the right of the entry field. Alternatively, you can type into the entry box, which is also the case for most attributes.

▶ If your attribute has particular defined values, clicking in the value column displays a pop-up menu containing the valid values **D**.

▶ If the attribute contains a color, click- ing the small box in the value column brings up the standard color picker **E**.

5. There's no OK or Accept button on the panel; simply clicking away from the attributes or off the panel implements your changes on your page.

TIP As you might remember from Chapter 1, it's also possible to change tag attributes in the Property inspector. Because the Property inspector shows only the most commonly used attributes, you'll want to use the Tag inspector when you need to get at the others.

Using the JavaScript Extractor

Best practices for Web pages call for content to be separated from structure and behavior, so you should have separate HTML, CSS, and JavaScript documents. Separating the functions like this makes it easier to make changes in any of the documents without accidentally breaking your site. And since CSS and JavaScript documents can apply to many HTML pages on your site, changes you make in them are automatically applied to all the pages that reference those files.

Many older pages, and even pages that are created in Dreamweaver (for example, pages that use the built-in behaviors, as discussed in Chapter 12), can have JavaScript that is embedded in the HTML page. This can be within the document's **<head>** tag or in the **<body>**. The JavaScript Extractor automates moving embedded JavaScript code into an external **.js** file.

To extract embedded JavaScript:

1. Open a page containing JavaScript code.

2. Choose Commands > Externalize JavaScript.

   Dreamweaver will analyze the page, and the Externalize JavaScript dialog will appear **Ⓐ**.

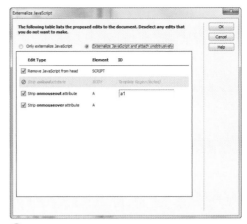

Ⓐ Choose the JavaScript you want to extract from the page.

Dreamweaver

? 1 SCRIPT block removed from the HEAD.
1 total SCRIPT block removed from the document.

2 on* attributes stripped from tags and attached unobtrusively.
2 total attributes removed from the document.

1 ID added to allow for unobtrusive attachment.
2 SCRIPT references added to the HEAD.

The following files should be uploaded
to your server along with this document:

- SpryDOMUtils.js
- index.js

OK

B When the JavaScript Extractor is done, it reports on what it accomplished.

3. In the dialog, select "Externalize JavaScript and attach unobtrusively."

   This option will move the JavaScript from the HTML page to a new external JavaScript file and add a link to the external file to the **head** section of the HTML page.

4. Select or deselect any of the proposed JavaScript edits in the dialog.

5. Click OK.

   Dreamweaver displays a dialog that gives you a rundown of what the Externalize JavaScript command did **B**. Pay special attention to the line or lines that tell you the names of the new external files, and make sure you upload those files to your server.

> **TIP** Once you externalize Dreamweaver behaviors, you can't re-edit them in the Behaviors panel, because Dreamweaver doesn't have a way to read JavaScript code from external files.

Using the Code Reference

It's often very handy to have a book close by when you're first starting to work with code (we recommend *HTML5 and CSS3 Visual QuickStart Guide, Seventh Edition,* by Elizabeth Castro and Bruce Hyslop [Peachpit Press, 2012], by the way). If you don't happen to have a book nearby, don't fret—Dreamweaver has several built-in reference books.

To open the Code Reference tab:

Right-click the element on the page that you have questions about, and select Reference Ⓐ. The Reference tab of the Results panel appears Ⓑ.

or

Follow the directions in "Using the Tag Chooser," earlier in this chapter.

or

From Dreamweaver's menu, choose Window > Reference.

Ⓐ Choosing Reference from this menu displays the Reference tab of the Results panel.

Ⓑ The Reference tab can display material about HTML, CSS, JavaScript, and more.

To insert code from the reference into your document:

1. In the Reference tab, find the code fragment you want and then click it once; the entire fragment will be selected **C**.

2. Right-click the selected text and choose Copy.

3. Paste the copied code into your document wherever you want it.

> **TIP** If you don't like the size of the text in the Reference tab, you can change it. Right-click anywhere inside the panel, and you'll have your choice of small, medium, or large text.

> **TIP** The HTML, CSS, and JavaScript reference material included in Dreamweaver is excerpted from Danny Goodman's book *Dynamic HTML, The Definitive Reference* (O'Reilly Media, 1998). It's a good book but out of date, so for learning HTML, we still recommend the Visual QuickStart Guide. Want to learn CSS or JavaScript? We're required to recommend *Styling Web Pages with CSS: Visual QuickProject Guide* (2009) and *JavaScript: Visual QuickStart Guide* (2011), both from Peachpit Press and by, well, us (so you can guess who required it).

> **TIP** Besides the reference material, the Reference tab also includes information on ColdFusion, ASP, JSP, PHP, SQL, XML, and XSLT (and probably a few other three-letter acronyms, too). There's also the *UsableNet Accessibility Reference*, a great resource for learning how to make your sites more accessible.

C Click the code sample once, and it will be selected.

Using the W3C Validator

It's important to have pages that adhere to Web standards. Although pages that you create in Dreamweaver will generally be standards compliant, changing the code by hand may introduce errors that prevent the page from being standards compliant and from rendering correctly in browsers. Or you may be reworking an old site to make use of modern Web technologies and make it standards compliant for the first time.

Dreamweaver CS5.5 introduced a W3C Validator feature that can validate, from within Dreamweaver, static or dynamic HTML documents with the W3C validation service. Any errors are displayed in the Validation tab of the Property inspector. The processes for validating static pages and dynamic pages are slightly different.

To validate static pages:

1. Open the page you want to validate.

2. Choose File > Validate > Validate Current Document (W3C).

   or

   From the Document toolbar, click the Validate button and then choose Validate Current Document (W3C) 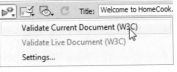.

   Dreamweaver displays a dialog letting you know it's going to send your page to the W3C validation service **B**. Naturally, you'll have to have an active Internet connection.

3. Click OK.

A To begin validating a document, choose Validate Current Document (W3C) from the Validate menu in the Document toolbar.

B Dreamweaver asks permission to send your document to the W3C validation service.

Dreamweaver sends the source code from the Code view to the validation service. When it gets a response (usually within seconds), it opens the Validation tab of the Property inspector **C**.

4. If there are any errors listed in the Validation tab, double-clicking one of them will switch to Split view and place the cursor in the Code pane where the error is, so you may fix it **D**.

To validate dynamic pages:

1. Open the page you want to validate.

2. Click the Live view button in the Document toolbar.

   As usual with dynamic sites (ones that you have created with a content management system such as WordPress, Drupal, or Joomla), Dreamweaver will go through the process of discovering and loading all the associated files.

continues on next page

Search	Reference	Validation	Browser Compatibility	Link Checker	Site Reports	FTP Log	Server Debug

File/URL	Line	Description
about.html	43	An img element must have an alt attribute, except under certain conditions. For details, consult guidance on provi...
about.html	44	An img element must have an alt attribute, except under certain conditions. For details, consult guidance on provi...
about.html	45	An img element must have an alt attribute, except under certain conditions. For details, consult guidance on provi...
about.html	46	An img element must have an alt attribute, except under certain conditions. For details, consult guidance on provi...
about.html	47	An img element must have an alt attribute, except under certain conditions. For details, consult guidance on provi...
about.html	48	An img element must have an alt attribute, except under certain conditions. For details, consult guidance on provi...
about.html	49	An img element must have an alt attribute, except under certain conditions. For details, consult guidance on provi...

Current document validation complete [11 Errors, 0 Warnings, 0 Hidden]

C If the service finds any problems, the error appears in the Validation panel in the Property inspector.

about.html ×   C:\Users\Tom\Documents

Source Code   theStyles.ssi   topNav.ssi   sidebar.ssi   footer.ssi

```
43                        <a href="http://www.google.com/profiles/dorismith
       src="images/google.png" height="16" width="16" /> Google Profile</a>
44                        <a href="http://www.linkedin.com/in/dorismith" ta
       ="images/linkedin.png" height="16" width="16" /> LinkedIn</a><br />
45                        <a href="http://friendfeed.com/dori" target="_bla
       "images/friendfeed.png" height="16" width="16" /> FriendFeed</a><br /
```

D Double-clicking the error in the Property inspector opens a code pane and highlights the problem.

3. Choose File > Validate > Validate Live Document (W3C).

or

From the Document toolbar, click the Validate button and then choose Validate Live Document (W3C).

4. Click OK.

Dreamweaver sends the source code from the Code view to the validation service. When it gets a response, it opens the Validation tab of the Property inspector **E**.

5. Since the error may have been dynamically created, double-clicking an error in the Validation tab opens the W3C Error Info window **F** (rather than taking you to the source code, as with static pages).

The error information tells you what the problem is and sometimes (not always) gives useful suggestions on how to rectify the error.

F Double-clicking an error in a dynamic page brings up a dialog that will help you zero in on the error.

TIP Validating a dynamic site is often fraught with uncertainty, because sometimes you don't know whether the error was introduced by you or by the CMS that you're using. It's nice that Dreamweaver allows you to validate live documents, but in practice you may not find it to be that useful.

TIP Have a vague recollection that you used to be able to validate your pages? You're not imagining things—up until CS5, Dreamweaver *did* have a built-in validator. It was removed in CS5, and it's now making its new and improved reappearance. The problem with the old validator was that, because it was built in, it didn't keep up with new standards such as HTML5. Now that it uses the W3C's validation service, Dreamweaver no longer has that limitation.

E With dynamic pages, Dreamweaver sends for validation the source code of the current page, which may include links to many supporting files. Any errors will still show up in the Validation panel.

Managing Your Site

As you've seen in the rest of this book, building a site means creating dozens, hundreds, or even thousands of files that work together to present a dynamic, exciting Web site. Keeping track of and managing all these files—a process called *site management*—may not be an exciting job, but it is essential.

The problem of site management gets even more complex when (as is common) you are just one member of a team responsible for building and maintaining a site. Imagine that you have several people who can all edit pages—it would be easy for one person to overwrite changes made by a coworker. That's where Dreamweaver's collaboration features come in. With Check In/Check Out, team members are notified if another person is already working on a particular file. Support for the Subversion version control system allows Dreamweaver to be integrated into even the largest sites.

In this chapter, you will learn how to manage the files and folders that make up your site; work with Dreamweaver's collaborative tools; and learn different ways to look at and work with your site.

In This Chapter

Planning for Site Expansion

When you're designing a site, you take the time to think about the site navigation so that your site visitors have an easy time finding the information they need. But what about *your* needs? When you're building and maintaining a site, it's just as important for you to plan the folder structure so that you can easily and quickly find items you need to work on. Web sites have a disturbing tendency to grow, so when you set up your site, lay out your folder structure logically, and leave room for expansion in your site structure 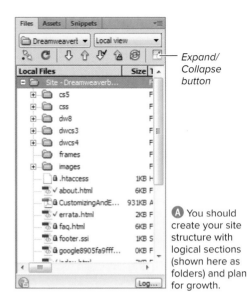.

For example, if you have different sections of a site (as represented in the site's navigation), it's a good idea to create a folder for each section (which will contain all of the pages for the section). Then consider creating an image folder inside each section folder. After all, you will probably have images for each section that are used only in that section of the site. A separate image folder in the root of your site can handle images that are used globally throughout the site.

As your site grows, you can add additional folders for new sections from the site root, or you can add folders inside the existing section folders for new subsections.

Expand/
Collapse
button

Ⓐ You should create your site structure with logical sections (shown here as folders) and plan for growth.

TIP Make sure that you name your files and folders meaningfully and understandably. While you are creating a site, you may remember what the `med_sec_hed.html` file is used for, but when you come back to the site four months later, you might not have a clue, at least without opening the file and looking at it. Instead, name the file something like `media_home.html`, and it makes it easier for you to pick up where you left off. This also helps make your site easier for other people to maintain.

TIP Don't forget that there are some characters that you can't use in file and folder names, including space, #, &, @, /, and most other punctuation. Use a hyphen or underscore as substitutes for a space.

TIP If you create image folders inside section folders, give those image folders descriptive names, too. We like to use the name of the section, followed by an underscore, then `images`, like so: `recipes_images`.

Expanding the Files Panel

The Files panel does an adequate job of showing you the files and folders in your site, but it has some drawbacks. The biggest of these is that it is cramped for space, especially for larger sites. You also can't see the local files and the remote server at the same time, making it difficult to compare items that are on your machine with those that are on the server. Dreamweaver allows you to expand the Files panel to solve these problems. You can view the local and remote sites and easily create, move, and delete files on either copy of the site. Of course, you can still use the Get, Put, Check Out, Check In, and Synchronize buttons at the top of the Files panel.

You can also select multiple files in the following categories:

- All files
- Checked Out files
- Newer Local files
- Newer Remote files
- Recently Modified files

To expand the Files panel:

1. At the top of the Files panel, click the Expand/Collapse button.

   On Windows, the Dreamweaver window will be replaced by the expanded Files panel 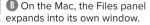.

   On the Mac, the expanded Files panel will appear in a new window **B**.

2. Create, delete, rename, or move files and folders as you like. See Chapter 2 for more details.

3. When you're done with the expanded Files panel, click the Expand/Collapse button again to toggle the window back to the normal Files panel.

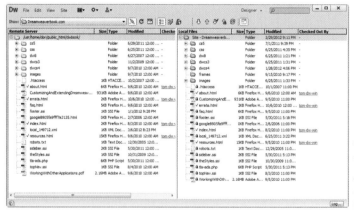

A The expanded Files panel allows you to easily see both remote (left) and local (right) files. On Windows, the panel completely replaces the Dreamweaver window.

B On the Mac, the Files panel expands into its own window.

C On Windows, the Edit menu allows you to highlight specific groups of files.

What Happened to the Site Map?

If you haven't upgraded Dreamweaver for quite some time, you may be wondering what happened to the Site Map, which was a visual tool that helped you see the links and relationships between the files on your site and which was available in all versions of Dreamweaver before CS4. The Site Map was a different view in the Files panel, and it allowed you to see the links between the different files in the site in a tree display resembling an organizational chart, descending from the site's index page. Some people preferred the Site Map because it made it easier to visualize the site structure.

In August 2007, Adobe released a list of features that it planned to remove from Dreamweaver, because research revealed they weren't being used by many people. The Site Map was on this list. Some of the features on the list were also dated and didn't conform to current best practices, such as the old Table Layout Mode (modern sites use CSS for layout). Rather than continuing to put resources into maintaining unpopular or obsolete features, Adobe chose to relegate them to the mists of history.

To select multiple files in the expanded Files panel:

1. At the top of the Files panel, click the Expand/Collapse button.

2. On Windows, from the Edit menu, choose Select All, Select Checked Out Files, Select Newer Local, Select Newer on Remote Server, or Select Recently Modified C.

   or

   On Mac, right-click in the Local Files section of the expanded Files panel, and from the Select menu choice in the context menu, choose Select All, Select Checked Out Files, Select Newer Local, Select Newer Remote, or Select Recently Modified.

   The files highlight.

TIP If you want the opposite selection of what is already selected, choose Invert Selection in step 2 above.

TIP If you select a file or folder in either the Remote Server or Local Files panes and right-click, you can easily find the corresponding file in the other pane by choosing Locate on Remote Server (if your selection is in the Local pane) or Locate in Local Site (if your selection is in the Remote pane) from the context menu.

TIP Dreamweaver usually doesn't show the hidden files it places on the remote server. For example, when you check a file out, Dreamweaver creates a small file on the server called `filename.LCK`. These `.LCK` files are how Dreamweaver knows that the file is checked out. If you want to see these hidden files, on the expanded Files panel in Windows, choose View > Show Hidden Files. On Mac, there doesn't appear to be a way to do this.

TIP It's usually a good idea to do your file management in Dreamweaver, but you can easily show a selected file in Windows Explorer or the Mac OS Finder. Select a file, right-click, and from the context menu choose Explore (Reveal in Finder).

Setting Up Check In and Check Out

In Chapter 2, you learned how to copy selected files or folders between the local and remote sites in the Files panel using the Get File and Put File buttons. Get and Put work fine when you are the only person working on a site, but you don't want to use them when you are working on a site with other members of a team. In that case, you would want to prevent one person from accidentally undoing or over-writing changes made by another member of the team when the page is transferred back to the remote site.

When you are working with other people on a Web site, you will come to rely on Dreamweaver's ability to keep track of and manage who is working on a file. Known as Check In/Check Out, this feature prevents more than one team member from work-ing on a particular file at a time. The feature also lets all members of the team know who is currently working on what file. Check In/ Check Out replaces the use of Get and Put for sites that have Check In/Check Out enabled. When you want to work on a file, you check it out, and when you are done working on the file and want to send it back to the remote server, you check it in.

Dreamweaver shows the status of files in the Files panel. Files that are checked out to you appear with a green check mark next to them, and files that are checked out by others appear with a red check mark next to them. Files that are read-only (because they are files that Dreamweaver can't edit or because the last time Dreamweaver con-nected to the remote server and checked their status they were checked out) appear with a padlock icon 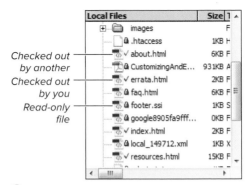.

Checked out by another
Checked out by you
Read-only file

Ⓐ These files in the Files panel show their checked-out status.

Export site definition

Duplicate site definition

Edit site

Delete site

B You use the Manage Sites dialog to set up Check In/Check Out.

To get the Check In/Check Out system to work properly, there are two cardinal rules all members of the Web team must follow:

- All members of the team must enable Check In/Check Out and Design Notes in their site definitions.

- All members of the team must *always* use Dreamweaver or Contribute (and no other tools, such as an FTP program) to transfer files to and from the remote Web server.

TIP If Check In/Check Out is enabled for your site and you use the Get File or Put File button in the Files panel rather than the Check In or Check Out button, Dreamweaver transfers read-only versions of the file to and from the remote server.

TIP When any team member checks out a file, Dreamweaver places a small text file on the remote site with the name of the checked-out file plus the extension `.LCK`. Dreamweaver uses this file to store the Check Out name and email address of the person who is using the file. When the file is checked back in, Dreamweaver automatically deletes the `.LCK` file.

To enable Check In/Check Out for your site:

1. Choose Site > Manage Sites.

   The Manage Sites dialog appears **B**.

2. In the list of sites, click to select the site for which you want to enable Check In/Check Out, and click the Edit icon at the bottom of the dialog.

   The Site Setup dialog appears, set to the Site category.

continues on next page

3. In the Category list on the left side of the dialog, click the Servers category.

The dialog changes to show the defined servers **C**.

4. Click to select the remote server in the list, and then click the Edit Existing Server button at the bottom of the server list.

The Edit Server dialog appears.

5. Click the Advanced tab **D**.

6. Select the "Enable file check-out" check box.

7. Select the "Check out files when opening" check box.

8. Enter a check-out name.

Because you may be working on a page using different programs or different systems, it's a good idea to use a name that describes the program and/or system you're working on. For example, the check-out name **tom-dw-win** indicates "Tom, using Dreamweaver, on Windows." The check-out name **tom-ct-mac** would indicate "Tom, using Contribute, on Macintosh."

9. (Optional but recommended) Enter your email address in the Email Address text box.

This allows coworkers to easily send you email if they need to communicate with you about the status of a file.

10. Click Save.

The Site Setup dialog reappears.

11. Click Save.

The Manage Sites dialog reappears.

12. Click Done.

Edit Existing Server button

C You begin enabling Check In/Check Out in the Servers pane of the Site Setup dialog...

D ...and finish the process in the Advanced tab of the Edit Server dialog.

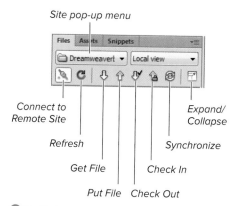

A If someone else has already checked out a file, Dreamweaver lets you know and asks what you want to do.

Site pop-up menu

Connect to Remote Site

Refresh

Get File

Put File *Check Out*

Expand/ Collapse

Synchronize

Check In

B You'll check files in and out with the toolbar in the Files panel.

C You can choose whether or not to download dependent files. If they haven't changed, don't bother.

Checking Files In and Out

When Check In/Check Out is enabled for your site and you use the Check Out button at the top of the Files panel, Dreamweaver checks to see if anyone else is currently working on the file. If someone else has the file checked out, Dreamweaver displays a dialog asking if you want to override that check out **A**. In general, it's a bad idea to do so, because it could lead to exactly the problems with multiple people working on the file that you want to avoid. On the other hand, if the person who checked out the file is you, just working on another machine, and you know the current state of the file, go ahead and override the lock on the file.

To check out a file for editing:

1. In the Files panel, from the Site pop-up menu, choose the site that contains the file you want to check out **B**.

    The site must have Check In/Check Out enabled.

2. Click the Connect to Remote Site button.

    Dreamweaver connects to the remote site.

3. Choose the file (or files) you want to check out from the Files panel.

4. Click the Check Out button in the Files panel toolbar.

    The Dependent Files dialog appears **C**.

    continues on next page

5. If you need to also edit the dependent files, such as images or external style sheets, click Yes. In most cases, however, you will click No.

   Dreamweaver transfers the selected files and puts green check marks next to the files in both the Local Files and the Remote Site views in the Files panel.

6. Make the changes you want to the checked-out files.

To check in a file to the remote server:

1. In the Files panel, select the checked-out file or files.

2. Click the Check In button in the Files panel toolbar.

   If the files you're checking in have not been saved, Dreamweaver prompts you to save them. After you save the files, Dreamweaver removes the green check marks from the files in the Files panel.

   TIP You can have Dreamweaver automatically save unsaved files before checking them in by enabling the "Save files before putting" option in the Site category in Dreamweaver's Preferences panel.

   TIP If you save and close a file without checking it in, the copy of the file on the remote site will not be updated. You should always check a file in when you are done working with it.

   TIP If you make a mistake and check out the wrong file, you can revert to the version of the file on the remote server, even if you modified and saved the checked-out version on your machine. Just right-click the checked-out file in the Files panel, and then choose Undo Check Out from the context menu. Dreamweaver removes your check-out lock from the remote server and replaces your local copy with the copy from the server, and that local copy of the file becomes read-only.

Using Design Notes

Dreamweaver's Design Notes are XML files that Dreamweaver places on the site that can be used by Web team members to annotate changes or note when a file was modified and by whom. A Design Note is associated with a file on your site, but it is a separate XML file with different fields that can be read by the Adobe programs 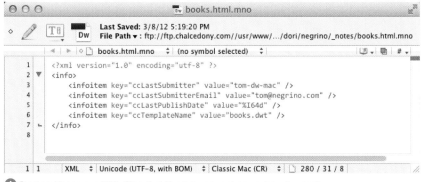. Design Note files aren't visible to your site's visitors.

You can create a Design Note yourself, and Dreamweaver and other programs in the Creative Suite can also make automated Design Note entries. For example, when you create an image in Fireworks and then export it to Dreamweaver, Fireworks creates (and places in the Dreamweaver site) a Design Note entry for the exported file, which could be in GIF or JPEG format. The entry records the name of the Fireworks source file (remember, the Fireworks file format is PNG) associated with the exported image in your site. That's how Dreamweaver, Fireworks, Photoshop, and other external image editors know how to integrate the source file with the exported site image when you go to edit it (refer to Chapter 5 for more information about editing images in Dreamweaver with external image editors).

A Design Notes are XML files that Dreamweaver knows how to read.

Dreamweaver stores Design Notes in folders called **_notes** in each of the site folders that have files with associated notes. These folders don't appear in the Files panel, but you can see them if you use an FTP program to view your site **B**. These notes folders contain one Design Note file for each site file that has a note.

To add a Design Note:

1. Open the file to which you want to add a Design Note, and then choose File > Design Notes.

   or

   In the Files panel's Local view, select the file to which you want to add a Design Note, and then right-click and choose Design Notes from the context menu.

   The Design Notes dialog appears, set to the Basic info tab **C**. This tab shows you the filename and the location of the file at the top of the dialog.

2. (Optional) From the Status pop-up menu, choose the status you want to set for the Design Note.

   The preset statuses are draft, revision1, revision2, revision3, alpha, beta, final, and needs attention.

3. (Optional) If you want to date-stamp your note, click the calendar icon in the dialog.

   The current date appears in the Notes field.

4. Type your note about the file.

5. Click OK.

   Dreamweaver saves the Design Note, and the Design Notes dialog disappears.

Name ▲	Size	Date
▶ 🗀 _baks	--	9/10/11 6:34 PM
▶ 🗀 _mm	--	5/17/10 6:33 PM
▼ 🗀 _notes	--	7/8/11 12:33 AM
antbooks.html.mno	291 B	10/25/10 5:12 PM
books.html.mno	283 B	9/10/11 1:01 PM
cttest.html.mno	279 B	5/25/10 5:54 PM
index.html.mno	235 B	6/24/11 7:18 PM
personal.html.mno	235 B	Jul 7, 2011 8:17 PM
antbooks.html	37 KB	10/25/10 5:12 PM
appearances.html	24 KB	6/10/08 3:53 PM

B Design Notes appear in the special **_notes** folders Dreamweaver creates in your site, seen here in an FTP program.

C Use the Design Notes dialog to enter your notes.

TIP Adobe Contribute also uses Design Notes to make note of when a Contribute user has updated a page. But Contribute doesn't have an interface to make specific notes; it just creates automated notes with the contributor's username and the page's modification date. Contribute Design Notes also keep track of rollbacks, which allow Contribute users to revert to previously published versions of pages.

TIP You must check out the file associated with a Design Note before you can add or modify the Design Note.

To modify a Design Note:

1. Open the file that contains a Design Note you want to modify, and then choose File > Design Notes.

   or

   In the Files panel, select the file whose Design Note you want to modify, and then right-click and choose Design Notes from the context menu.

   The Design Notes dialog appears.

2. Make changes to the Status pop-up menu, or enter a new note in the Notes field.

   If you click the calendar icon to add a new date stamp, the new note appears at the top of the dialog, and older notes appear below the newest entry, in reverse chronological order.

3. Click OK.

Setting Up Subversion

Dreamweaver features support for Subversion, which is a free, open-source *version control system* (VCS). A VCS is software that runs on the remote server and manages multiple revisions of the same bit of information. Every time a file changes, a VCS server creates a new version of the file, handles users checking files in and out of the server repository, and flags possible conflicts (when more than one user has made changes to the same file). Most VCS servers allow permitted users to get the latest versions of files, check in changed files, and revert files to an unmodified state or to a past version.

A Subversion (SVN) setup would generally be used on large Web sites or with Web sites maintained by very technically savvy users. Your site administrator will know whether or not your Web site uses an SVN version control system.

The Subversion server support in Dreamweaver allows you to move, copy, and delete files locally and then synchronize changes with your remote SVN repository.

This still does not completely replace all of the capabilities of a true Subversion client, but it's good for working with a Subversion repository without having to constantly switch from Dreamweaver to a separate Subversion client program.

To enable Subversion version control:

1. Choose Site > Manage Sites.

   The Manage Sites dialog appears **A**.

2. In the list of sites, click to select the site for which you want to enable SVN, and click the Edit icon (it looks like a pencil).

   The Site Setup dialog appears.

A Begin setting up Subversion support in the Manage Sites dialog.

B Enter the information needed to connect to the Subversion server.

Doing More with Subversion

Some of the Subversion abilities introduced with Dreamweaver CS5 further allow you to avoid resorting to a dedicated Subversion client. The Revert command allows you to quickly correct tree conflicts or roll back to a previous version of a file. From the Repository view of the Files panel in Dreamweaver, you can reduce clutter by directly performing **svn:ignore** commands to hide files you don't need to access (this is the SVN equivalent of Dreamweaver's familiar cloaking ability). To ensure future compatibility, the built-in Subversion libraries in Dreamweaver are designed to be updated by the Adobe Extension Manager.

The version of the Subversion client installed in your copy of Dreamweaver is listed in the Version Control pane of the Site Setup dialog. As newer versions of the Subversion libraries become available, they will be made available to the public as free extensions at Adobe Exchange at **www.adobe.com/cfusion/exchange**. Rather than entering that URL, you can instead click the Adobe Subversion Central link in the Version Control pane.

3. In the Category list on the left side of the dialog, click the Version Control category.

   The dialog changes to show the Version Control pane.

4. From the Access pop-up menu, choose Subversion.

   The server settings appear in the pane **B**.

5. From the Protocol pop-up menu, choose the communications protocol used by your Web site's Subversion server. Check with your site administrator if necessary.

   Your choices are HTTP, HTTPS, SVN, or SVN+SSH.

6. In the Server Address field, enter the Subversion server's URL.

7. In the Repository Path field, enter the path to the server's database. Again, you can get this from your site administrator.

8. Most of the time, the default entry in the Server Port field will be correct (it changes according to the choice in the Protocol pop-up menu). If not, your site administrator will know the correct port. Click into the field, and then enter the correct port number.

9. Enter your username and password, and then click the Test button.

   If all is well, Dreamweaver reports a successful connection to your SVN server.

10. Click OK.

    The Manage Sites dialog reappears.

11. Click Done.

> **TIP** You cannot use both a Subversion server and Dreamweaver's built-in Check In/Check Out system on the same Web site. You must choose one or the other (or neither).

Generating Site Reports

A large part of site management, especially if you are managing a team working on the site, is keeping up with all of the things that are happening to the site. For example, let's say that you want to know which pages each of your team members is working on at the moment. Dreamweaver allows you to get a report of the checked-out pages and who has checked them out. Similarly, you can get reports on many other aspects of your site, listed in **Table 18.1**. Dreamweaver splits reports into two categories: Workflow, with reports detailing who has worked on the site and when; and HTML Reports, which search through files on your site looking for HTML errors.

TABLE 18.1 Dreamweaver Reports

Workflow Category

Report name	Description
Checked Out By	Reports filename and the name of the team member who has checked it out.
Design Notes	Shows the contents of the Design Note for files that have them.
Recently Modified	Shows the last modified date for the selected files, based on search criteria you specify.

HTML Reports Category

Report name	Description
Combinable Nested Font Tags	Finds markup with font tags.
Accessibility	Checks the selected pages for adherence to accessibility guidelines.
Missing ALT Text	Flags missing alternate text attributes for images on your pages.
Redundant Nested Tags	Reports unnecessarily repeated nested tags; e.g., `<b><b>example text</b></b>`.
Removable Empty Tags	Shows any empty tags that can be safely removed.
Untitled Documents	Reveals documents in which you have forgotten to enter a title.

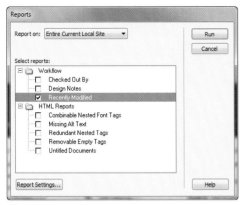

A Specify the kind of site report you want in the Reports dialog.

Some reports will let you enter parameters for the report that allow you to widen or narrow the criteria used for the report. All the reports, however, allow you to report on just the current document; the entire current local site; just selected files in the site; or files within a selected folder in the site.

To get site reports:

1. Choose Site > Reports.

The Reports dialog appears **A**.

2. From the Report on pop-up menu, choose the scope of the report.

Your choices are Current Document, Entire Current Local Site, Selected Files in Site, or Folder.

3. In the Select reports list, select the report or reports that you want to run.

If the report you have selected allows you to choose report criteria, the Report Settings button becomes active.

continues on next page

4. (Optional) For reports that allow additional settings, click Report Settings and then complete the resulting settings dialog.

Each report that allows additional settings has a different criteria dialog. **B** shows, for example, the criteria dialog for the Recently Modified report.

After you click OK in the settings dialog, you return to the Reports dialog.

5. Click Run.

Dreamweaver runs the report and shows the report output in the Site Reports tab of the Results panel below the Property inspector **C** and also in an HTML page, which it opens in your default browser.

Recently Modified			
⦿ Files Created or Modified in the Last:			OK
7 Days			Cancel
◯ Files Created or Modified Between:			Help
March ▾ 1 ▾ 2012 ▾			
And: March ▾ 8 ▾ 2012 ▾			
Modified By:			
(for Contribute Sites Only)			
This report enables you to view the pages it returns. Where do you wish to view them?			
⦿ Local Machine (for viewing static pages)			
◯ Testing Server (for viewing dynamic pages)			
http://			

B The Recently Modified dialog, brought up by the Report Settings button, allows you to specify the scope of the report. Other reports have different Report Settings dialogs.

Search	Reference	Browser Compatibility	Link Checker	Site Reports	FTP Log	Server Debug

File	Line	Description
index.html		Modified By= Tom-CT-Mac Modified Date= 1/2/2011
images\3alpacas.jpg		Modified By= Tom-CT-Mac Modified Date= 5/30/2010
about.html		Modified Date= 1/2/2011
after.html		Modified Date= 1/2/2011
before.html		Modified Date= 1/2/2011
contact.html		Modified Date= 1/2/2011
faq.html		Modified Date= 1/2/2011
services.html		Modified Date= 1/2/2011

Complete.

C The report appears in the Results panel.

Checking for Broken Links

One of the more vexing problems with Web sites is broken links—that is, links that no longer point to valid destinations within your site. Dreamweaver usually does a pretty good job of updating links when you move or rename a page, but you can still end up with broken links if you cut or copy page content from one page to another on your site. Dreamweaver allows you to check all of the links on your site to make sure they are still valid and reports any broken links it finds. You can then easily open the file that contains the broken link to fix it.

To check for and fix broken links throughout your site:

1. Choose Site > Check Links Sitewide, or press Ctrl-F8 (Cmd-F8).

   Dreamweaver checks all the pages on your site and shows you files with broken links in the Link Checker tab of the Results panel **A**.

x

y

continues on next page

Search	Reference	Browser Compatibility	Link Checker	Site Reports	FTP Log	Server Debug	

Show: Broken Links ▼ (links to files not found on local disk)

Files	Broken Links
/index.html	/Library/Untitled.lbi
/index.html	/
/index.html	/
/index.html	/food/index.html
/index.html	/wine/index.html
/index.html	reviews/saucier.html

247 Total, 124 HTML, 66 Orphaned 702 All links, 403 OK, 122 Broken, 177 External

A Files with broken links appear in the Results panel.

2. Double-click one of the results.

The file with the broken link opens, with the broken link highlighted Ⓑ.

3. Using the Property inspector, fix the broken link.

For more information about using the Property inspector to work with links, see Chapter 6.

4. Repeat steps 2 and 3 until you have eliminated all of the broken links.

TIP **Dreamweaver only checks for the validity of links to documents within your site. If you have external links on your site (links that point to other sites on the Internet), Dreamweaver does not follow those links, and so it does not ensure that those sites still exist and are reachable. If you need to validate external links, you need to follow those links manually in a Web browser.**

TIP **You can also check for broken links on just the page you are editing. Choose File > Check Page > Links, or press Shift-F8.**

Ⓑ To fix the broken link, double-click one of the report results; the file with the broken link opens with the broken link selected; in this case, the top picture is highlighted because it links to a nonexistent page.

A Choose either External Links or Orphaned Files to obtain a report on those items.

B You can change external links right in the Results panel.

Finding External Links and Orphaned Files

You can get two other types of reports from Dreamweaver. The first is a list of links from your site to other sites, called *external links*, and the other is a report of *orphaned files*, which are files that have no links pointing to them. In the first case, after Dreamweaver finds the external links, you can (if needed) easily change them. In the case of orphaned files, you should create links to the files from your other Dreamweaver pages.

To find external links and orphaned files:

1. Choose Site > Check Links Sitewide, or press Ctrl-F8 (Cmd-F8).

   Dreamweaver checks all the pages on your site and shows you files with broken links in the Link Checker tab of the Results panel.

2. From the Show pop-up menu in the Results panel, choose External Links.

   or

   From the Show pop-up menu in the Results panel, choose Orphaned Files A.

   The results appear in the Results panel.

3. (Optional) If you chose External Links in step 2, the Results panel shows a list of files and the external links that appear on them. Click one of the links to highlight it and make it editable. You can then enter a new destination for the link B.

   or

   (Optional) If you chose Orphaned Files in step 2, the Results panel shows a list of files with no links pointing to them. Double-click a filename to open that file, or open other files in the Files panel to create links to the orphaned file.

Checking Browser Compatibility

In terms of the HTML document type, Dreamweaver creates XHTML 1.0 Transitional files by default, as discussed in Chapter 3 (though you can override this in the Preferences panel if, for example, you would rather HTML5 be the default). These files are readable by and valid for all commonly used modern Web browsers. So you might consider Dreamweaver's ability to check files for HTML browser support to be somewhat vestigial. But you may find you need to work on older pages that haven't been retrofitted for current browsers. Dreamweaver allows you to check your pages for errors with targeted browsers. It does this by keeping a database of browser profiles, which details how different browsers render pages. You can check the open page for browser compatibility. Errors appear in the Results panel.

The version of this feature that has been included in Dreamweaver since CS3 is much more complete than that of previous versions because it checks the CSS—not just the HTML—for possible rendering bugs. For each bug that it finds, Dreamweaver provides an estimate of the bug's severity and a link to a discussion about the bug on Adobe CSS Advisor, a Web site that offers solutions for fixing CSS bugs.

There's a difference between browser checking and validation. Dreamweaver validates pages against W3C standards (as shown in Chapter 17) by sending the page to the W3C validation service. Browser checking compares the page against internal browser profiles. As new browsers and versions are produced, Adobe updates the appropriate browser profiles.

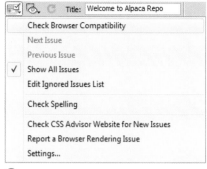

Ⓐ Use the Check Page pop-up menu to make sure your pages appear correctly in different browsers.

Target Browsers

Minimum browser versions:

☑ Chrome	7.0
☑ Firefox	1.5
☑ Internet Explorer	6.0
☑ Netscape	8.0
☑ Opera	8.0
☑ Safari	2.0

OK Cancel Help

Ⓑ Choose the target browsers for your compatibility check.

To define browsers for checking:

1. Open any file in your site.

2. From the Check Page pop-up menu at the top of the document window, choose Settings Ⓐ.

   The Target Browsers dialog appears Ⓑ.

3. To enable a particular browser, select the check box next to its name. Choose from the pop-up menu next to the name to select the minimum version of that browser you want to check against.

4. Click OK to dismiss the Target Browsers dialog.

To check for browser compatibility:

1. From the Check Page pop-up menu at the top of the document window, choose Check Browser Compatibility.

   If there are no errors found, a status line appears in the Results pane stating "No issues detected." Pop a cold one and relax.

2. If errors are found, a list appears in the Results panel 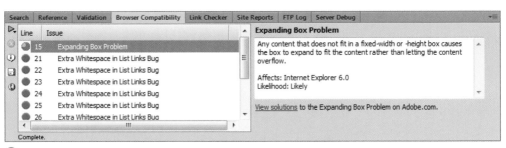.

   There are three kinds of possible errors reported in the Results panel: *errors*, *warnings*, and *informational messages*. An error indicates a problem in the code that can cause serious visual problems with the page. A warning indicates that the page won't be displayed exactly as desired in the targeted browser but that the problem isn't serious. An informational message is used for code that isn't supported in a particular browser but that has no visual effect.

3. Double-click an error in the Results panel to change the document window to Split view, highlighting the error in Code and Design views.

4. Fix the error in Code view.

TIP All browser compatibility errors that Dreamweaver finds are not necessarily errors, as such. For example, on our example site, www.alpacarepo.com, Dreamweaver dutifully reports an error against Internet Explorer 6. But that's because the page uses CSS that is more advanced than IE6 can handle, not because the CSS is incorrect. We recommend that you take the Dreamweaver report as advisory rather than prescriptive.

C Errors in your document appear in the Results panel, along with the names of the browsers affected by the errors. In this case, to show some errors, we set Dreamweaver to check errors against IE6, a browser that is so old that it doesn't understand CSS (and that hardly anybody uses anymore).

A Begin deleting a site in the Manage Sites dialog.

B When you try to delete a site, Dreamweaver asks you to confirm your action.

Deleting Sites

When you will no longer be working with a site (perhaps because the project has been taken over by another developer), you can delete its site definition. This removes the site from the Manage Sites dialog and from the Site pop-up menu in the Files panel. Of course, all the settings for the site are also deleted. You should be careful when you delete site definitions, because there's no way to undo the action.

To delete a site from Dreamweaver:

1. Choose Site > Manage Sites.

   The Manage Sites dialog appears **A**.

2. From the list of sites, click the site that you want to delete.

3. Click the Remove icon (it looks like a minus sign).

   Dreamweaver alerts you that you cannot undo this operation **B**.

4. Click Yes.

   Dreamweaver deletes the selected site.

> **TIP** Although Dreamweaver is asking if you want to delete the site, the site itself (that is, the files in the local site folder on your hard drive) won't be touched. The only things that are deleted are the site definitions: what Dreamweaver knows about your site. And of course, nothing is changed on the remote site.

Exporting and Importing Site Definitions

When you create a local site on your machine, Dreamweaver creates a local site definitions file with all the information about the site's settings, including information about the server connection, your server password, and any site-specific preferences you may have set in the Site Definition dialog. If you need to move the site from one machine to another, or if you want to add members of your Web team and have them share the same site preferences, you must export the site definition. When you do that, Dreamweaver saves the site definition information as an XML file with the **.ste** file extension.

Dreamweaver allows you to export the site definition in one of two ways. You can export it with your server username and password information (this facilitates moving the site to a different machine), or you can export the site with the site preferences but without your server login information (this is good for adding coworkers to the site).

You can, of course, also import a site definition file that you had previously exported or one you received from a colleague.

To export a site definition:

1. Choose Site > Manage Sites.

   The Manage Sites dialog appears.

2. From the list of sites, click the site you want to export.

3. Click Export.

   The Exporting Site dialog appears Ⓐ.

4. Click "Back up my settings (includes login, password, and local paths)" if you plan to move the site to another machine.

   or

   Click "Share settings with other users (does not include login, password, or local paths)" if you want to create a site definition file that does not include your server login information.

5. Click OK.

   The Export Site dialog appears.

6. Navigate to where you want to save the site definition file, make sure that the name Dreamweaver has given the file is OK (by default it gives the file the name of your site and appends the **.ste** file extension), and then click Save.

   Dreamweaver saves the site definition file onto your hard disk.

   You'll return to the Manage Sites dialog.

7. Click Done.

Exporting site 'JavaScript 8E Site'

Are you exporting this site to back up your settings or to share your settings with other users?

⦿ Back up my settings (includes login, password, and local paths).

○ Share settings with other users (does not include login, password, or local paths).

Note: Passwords are not exported in a secure or encrypted format.

OK

Cancel

Help

Ⓐ Choose whether or not you want to include your login information in the exported site definition file.

To import a site definition:

1. Choose Site > Manage Sites.

   The Manage Sites dialog appears.

2. Click Import.

   The Import Site dialog appears.

3. Navigate to and select the site definition file you want to import.

4. Click Open.

   Dreamweaver imports the site definition and adds it to the list of sites in the
   Manage Sites dialog.

5. Click Done to dismiss the Manage
   Sites dialog.

TIP You can use the ability to export the site
definition file as a way to back up your site's
settings, but this is no substitute for a regular
and comprehensive backup strategy covering all of the important documents on your
hard drive.

TIP If you happen to work on multiple computers and multiple sites, and each of the computers has a copy of Dreamweaver, you can
export your site definitions for all of your sites
and then copy them to a USB flash drive. You
could then plug in the flash drive on whichever
computer you happen to be working on, and
you will have your site settings, including your
server passwords. Of course, you would need
to resynchronize the remote site with a newly
created copy that would then become the
local site folder on the machine you are working on. See Chapter 2 for more information
about synchronizing sites.

Where to Learn More

Once you've worked through this book, you should be well on your way to creating great Web pages with Dreamweaver. But Dreamweaver is such a comprehensive program that there is plenty more to learn about it and about building Web sites in general.

In this appendix, we'll point to several of the most helpful Dreamweaver-oriented Web sites and other sites where you can learn more about building standards-compliant Web sites, and we'll even mention a few other books that will help you deepen your knowledge not just of Dreamweaver, but also of Web design and JavaScript.

As usual with products that can be found on the Internet, Web sites come, go, and change addresses with alarming regularity. The sites listed here were in existence when this book went to press and may be available when you check them out, or they may not. We are just reporting the URLs; we have no control over them. If you find a link that has become stale, we would appreciate it if you would drop a note to **dwcs6@dreamweaverbook.com** so that we can update the next edition of the book.

Find It Online!

You'll find an updated list of the sites and books in this appendix at this book's companion Web site at **www.dreamweaverbook.com**. We'll keep the Web site current with a list of Dreamweaver-oriented sites, and if eagle-eyed readers spot any errors in the book, we'll note them on the site, too.

Web Sites

Almost as soon as Dreamweaver came upon the scene, people began gathering online to discuss the program and help each other use it. There are several Dreamweaver community sites, informational sites, places where you can purchase premade Dreamweaver templates, and sites from developers who have created new Dreamweaver extensions. This list is by no means comprehensive, but it does include sites that we have found to be helpful.

Of course, Adobe has a variety of online support options as well.

Adobe Sites

Dreamweaver Support

- **helpx.adobe.com/dreamweaver.html**

  This should be your first stop when looking for answers to a Dreamweaver question (after this book, of course!) **A**. This site allows you to search not just Adobe's Dreamweaver resources but also get help from the larger Dreamweaver community. There are also tutorials, videos, articles, and documentation.

Adobe Marketplace & Exchange

- **www.adobe.com/exchange/**

  This is the place to go when you're looking for Dreamweaver add-ons and extensions. At press time, there were more than 2000 items for download **B**.

A Adobe's support site for Dreamweaver offers help on levels ranging from absolute beginner to experts who want to become, well, more expert.

B Dreamweaver Exchange should be your first stop when you are looking for a Dreamweaver extension.

Adobe's weblog aggregator brings together interesting blog posts about Dreamweaver from all over the Web.

Dreamweaver Weblogs

- `feeds.adobe.com`

  Once you go to the URL above, click the link for the Dreamweaver category. This is an aggregator site that lists posts from many people's Dreamweaver-related weblogs . It's a great way to keep up with the Dreamweaver community.

- `blogs.adobe.com/dreamweaver/`

  This blog is written by the Dreamweaver team, which makes it a great place to find out about the latest happenings directly from the people doing the work.

Dreamweaver Developer Center

- `www.adobe.com/devnet/dreamweaver/`

  Dreamweaver Developer Center has tutorials focused on the new features of Dreamweaver CS6 and articles that will help you better use Dreamweaver to build your sites. There are also some additional templates and sample layouts if the ones that came with Dreamweaver aren't enough for you.

- `cookbooks.adobe.com/dreamweaver`

  Did you come up with a slick way to accomplish something in Dreamweaver and want to tell others about it? Or maybe you're looking for someone else's slick way to accomplish something in Dreamweaver? In either case, Developer Center's Cookbook section is the place you're looking for.

Dreamweaver Forums

- `forums.adobe.com/community/dreamweaver/`

  Adobe's Dreamweaver forums are active and a good place to get help from other knowledgeable users. The Dreamweaver FAQ can also be found here.

Tutorials and Add-ons

WebAssist

- www.webassist.com

    WebAssist is one of the premier developers of Dreamweaver extensions and Web apps ready to be integrated into your sites . Its Design Extender extension helps you build customized site designs using wizards, with almost no effort. They also sell extensions that let you easily add shopping carts, database-driven back ends, advanced forms, and more to your site.

    Besides the paid products, the WebAssist site also contains many tutorials covering CSS, images, navigation, and other subjects.

D WebAssist makes a variety of great Dreamweaver extensions, including ways to make customizable site designs and add e-commerce features to your sites.

Adobe TV

- tv.adobe.com

    Tons of constantly updated video content, including podcasts, demos, and tutorials by experts and Adobe employees, are available from Adobe TV **E**, which not only covers Dreamweaver, but other Adobe products. The site shows off not just released products, but previews of Adobe products that are still in beta. For example, at press time, there were several previews of a program codenamed Muse, which is a Web animation application based on HTML5 (and is likely to be named something else by the time you read this).

Content Management Systems

Now that Dreamweaver has solid CMS support, you're likely to want to learn more about them. The three most common—WordPress, Joomla, and Drupal—are all open source, which means that you can

E Adobe TV provides a large number of video tutorials and information.

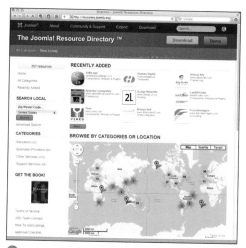

The Joomla Resource Directory is your gateway to all things Joomla.

download, install, and take a good long look at them without spending a penny.

These are our recommended Web sites to start learning about each.

WordPress

- **www.wordpress.org**

  WordPress started life as blogging software but has grown far beyond that. This is its official Web site.

- **knowit.co.nz/category/wordpress**

  KnowIT is WordPress expert Miraz Jordan's blog, and this category contains her WP-related articles and how-to's. She also has ebooks available from the site's bookstore section.

Drupal

- **www.drupal.org**

  This is the official Web site of the Drupal Project.

- **www.buildamodule.com**

  This tutorial site has hundreds of videos to help you learn Drupal—some free, but most by subscription. It covers a wide range of topics from beginner to expert.

Joomla

- **www.joomla.org**

  This is the official Web site for the Joomla CMS.

- **resources.joomla.org**

  The Joomla Resource Directory ⓕ is invaluable in pointing you to training, extension providers, support companies, and hosting resources that let you leverage your investment in Dreamweaver and your Joomla site.

Other Online Resources

You can find interesting and useful help with Dreamweaver if you look beyond just Web sites.

Dreamweaver Mailing List

`tech.groups.yahoo.com/group/adobe-dreamweaver/`

This Dreamweaver mailing list is hosted on Yahoo and is a high-volume list that's worth a look. You can also ask your questions about Dreamweaver on this list.

Wise-Women Mailing List

`www.wise-women.org`

Wise-Women is an online community with a Web site and an email discussion list . The purpose of the list is to provide women on the Web with a supportive atmosphere to deal with issues of Web development, design, and consulting. Wise-Women was founded in 1999 by one of the authors of this book (Dori) and is going strong today. You'll find lots of useful information on the mailing list about using Dreamweaver, among many other subjects. And in case you're wondering, the community is not only for women.

🅐 The Wise-Women online community offers support and help for women and men alike.

B The Creative Edge Web site offers sneak peeks of upcoming books along with ebooks and videos.

C The Lynda.com Online Training Library offers many hours of video training on Dreamweaver.

Creative Edge

www.creativeedge.com

If you're looking for ebooks on Dreamweaver or complementary technologies, Creative Edge has them **B**. Or maybe you prefer videos? Creative Edge has those, too. Or maybe you want a book that isn't available in stores yet? Creative Edge even has those. In fact, as we wrote this appendix, a Rough Cut (a work in progress) of this very book was already available for download—legally, too!

Creative Edge lets you sample books and videos before you buy them. You can even comment on Rough Cuts, giving authors feedback while they can still do something about it.

Lynda.com Online Training Library

www.lynda.com

Lynda.com offers an excellent series of video training programs that cover Dreamweaver and the rest of the Adobe product line, as well as many other software packages **C**. You can purchase these training programs as discs that you can view on your computer, or you can access the videos over the Internet through the Online Training Library, for which you'll need to purchase a subscription. Tom produced *Contribute 3 Essential Training* and *Quicken 2009 for Windows Essential Training* for Lynda.com, and Dori produced *JavaScript Essential Training* and *Ajax Essential Training*.

Other Dreamweaver Books

Though the authors would naturally like to think that the book you have in your hands is all you'll ever need to become a Dreamweaver expert, we recognize that you might just want a bit more information after you've completely devoured this book. There are approximately a million different Dreamweaver books on the market; here are two we think are the best.

Dreamweaver CS6 Bible

Joseph Lowery is well known in the Dreamweaver community, and this massive reference, published by Wiley (2012), shows why. At well over 1000 pages, we think this is perhaps the most comprehensive Dreamweaver reference book available.

Adobe Dreamweaver CS5 with PHP: Training from the Source

If you want to learn more about dynamic sites than we could cover in a QuickStart Guide, this book by David Powers (Peachpit, 2010) is your next stop. Along with its quick introduction to PHP, you'll learn how to work with databases and content management systems. It's not being updated for CS6, but it's still useful.

Web Design and JavaScript Books

Readers of previous editions of this book have asked for our suggestions for books about JavaScript and Web design. There are too many books to count about these subjects, so here are some of our favorites.

Styling Web Pages with CSS: Visual QuickProject Guide

JavaScript: Visual QuickStart Guide

Written by Tom Negrino and Dori Smith (hey, that's us!), these books are great introductions to their topics (Peachpit, 2009 and 2012). If you liked this book, you'll find more of the same solid information, delivered in an informal style.

Designing with Web Standards, Third Edition

Jeffrey Zeldman was one of the earliest and strongest voices evangelizing Web standards, and this book explains the gospel to designers in familiar terms that they understand. This book is best for readers who are already familiar with using CSS to build Web sites (New Riders, 2010).

The CSS Detective Guide

CSS is terrific and amazingly flexible, but it's not always easy to figure out the culprit when your CSS isn't acting the way you want it to. Denise R. Jacobs has written a fun, engaging book that helps you track down your CSS bugs and teaches real-world troubleshooting skills. It also has one of our favorite topics, "The Case of the Browser Who Hated Me." This book was published by New Riders (2010).

Customizing and Extending Dreamweaver

One of the best things about Dreamweaver is that it is both customizable and incredibly extensible. What's the difference? *Customizable* means that you can change the keyboard shortcuts to suit your style of working, and of course you can customize using Dreamweaver's Preferences dialog. That's fine, but *extensibility,* the ability to add new features to the program, is where the real action is.

As you've seen in the rest of our book, Dreamweaver can do an awful lot. But just because Dreamweaver is amazingly capable doesn't mean that it does absolutely everything that people want it to do. Adobe allows software developers to write add-ons, called extensions, that add new features to Dreamweaver. These new features can range from the mundane (adding improved form handling abilities) to the amazing (creating full site generators with associated page templates and navigation bars).

In this appendix, we'll show you how to customize Dreamweaver's keyboard shortcuts and how to find, acquire, and install Dreamweaver extensions.

In This Chapter

Customizing Keyboard Shortcuts

Sometimes the keyboard shortcuts that come with Dreamweaver aren't quite what you want. For example, some shortcut keys used for editing code with BBEdit (on Mac) or, for longtime users, the now-defunct HomeSite (on Windows) aren't the same as the shortcuts used for the equivalent commands in Dreamweaver. No problem; you can change Dreamweaver shortcuts to match those in your favorite code editor. In fact, Dreamweaver comes with shortcut key sets for those two code editors, which makes it a snap to change shortcut keys and increase your productivity.

Of course, you can also change any keyboard shortcut, add shortcuts to menu items that may not already have them, or delete shortcut keys you don't like. You can also print out a cheat sheet of keyboard commands to help you learn them.

To change between shortcut key sets:

1. Choose Edit > Keyboard Shortcuts (Dreamweaver > Keyboard Shortcuts).

   The Keyboard Shortcuts dialog appears **Ⓐ**.

2. Choose the keyboard shortcuts that you want from the Current set pop-up menu.

   Your choices are: Dreamweaver Standard, which includes the standard shortcut keys for the current version; Dreamweaver MX 2004, a slightly different set found in a previous version of Dreamweaver; BBEdit, which modifies the code editing keyboard shortcuts to match those used by the popular Macintosh code editor; and HomeSite, which modifies the code editing keyboard shortcuts to match the popular (yet discontinued) Windows code editor.

3. Click OK.

   Dreamweaver changes its keyboard shortcuts to match the set that you chose.

Commands list

Rename set   Export set as HTML

Duplicate set   Delete set

Add shortcut   Delete shortcut

Ⓐ Begin customizing your Dreamweaver experience in the Keyboard Shortcuts dialog.

To create a personalized set of keyboard shortcuts:

1. Choose Edit > Keyboard Shortcuts (Dreamweaver > Keyboard Shortcuts).

   The Keyboard Shortcuts dialog appears **A**.

2. From the Current set pop-up menu, choose the keyboard shortcuts set that you want to use as the basis for your personalized set.

   Dreamweaver won't let you change any of the included sets, so you must duplicate one of them, then modify the duplicate.

3. Click the Duplicate set button.

   The Duplicate Set dialog appears **B**.

4. Type the name for your duplicate set.

5. Click OK.

   Dreamweaver creates the duplicate set and makes it the active set. You can then personalize it, as shown next.

To add or change a keyboard shortcut:

1. In the Keyboard Shortcuts dialog, choose the kind of command you want to modify from the Commands pop-up menu **C**.

   This pop-up menu differs on Windows and Mac, with more choices (and more functionality) on Windows. Besides Menu commands, Code editing, Document editing, and Snippets keyboard shortcuts, Dreamweaver for Windows also allows you to set keyboard shortcuts for the Files panel options menu, the Site panel, and the Site window.

   Depending on what you chose, the Commands list changes.

B Enter the name of your new keyboard shortcuts set.

C You can customize keyboard shortcuts for more items on Windows (top) than on Mac (bottom).

D Click the + buttons to display menu choices in an indented tree form.

E Select the shortcut key that you want to change.

2. In the Commands list, navigate to the command that you want to change. Click the + icon next to the name of the menu to expand the choices for that menu. On the Mac, click the disclosure triangle next to the name of the menu.

   The menu choices are shown with any existing shortcut keys **D**.

3. Click the command that you want to change.

   The shortcuts assigned to the command appear in the Shortcuts text box **E**.

4. To add a shortcut, click the Add shortcut button (marked with a plus sign).

   A new blank line appears in the Shortcuts text box.

   or

   To change an existing shortcut, select it in the Shortcuts text box.

5. Click in the Press key text box.

6. Press the key combination you want to use for the shortcut key.

   If the key combination is already in use, Dreamweaver lets you know with a message at the bottom of the Keyboard Shortcuts dialog.

7. Click Change.

   The new shortcut appears in the Shortcuts text box.

8. Click OK to save your changes and dismiss the Keyboard Shortcuts dialog.

To export a keyboard command cheat sheet:

1. Choose Edit > Keyboard Shortcuts (Dreamweaver > Keyboard Shortcuts).

   The Keyboard Shortcuts dialog appears Ⓐ.

2. Click the Export set as HTML button.

   The Save as HTML file dialog appears.

3. In the Save as text box, give the exported file a name, then navigate to where you want to save the HTML file.

4. Click Save.

   Dreamweaver saves the list of keyboard commands to your hard disk as an HTML file. You can then open it in Dreamweaver or any Web browser Ⓕ.

Ⓕ You can print your keyboard command cheat sheet from a Web browser.

Finding and Installing Extensions

You add extensions to Dreamweaver using Adobe Extension Manager, a program that was installed when you installed Dreamweaver on your system. After you install an extension, it appears as part of Dreamweaver. Where it appears within the program depends on what kind of extension it is. For example, if you have installed an extension that allows you to easily add Google search boxes or maps, that extension would appear in the Insert menu. An extension that provides new ways to add pop-up menus may appear in the Commands menu. And extensions that add new scripting behaviors will appear in the Behaviors panel. Because Dreamweaver is almost infinitely extensible, the extensions you add can appear almost anywhere within the program.

You can find extensions in a variety of ways. Some extensions are free for downloading, and others are paid products. Many extension developers have Web sites where they host (and sometimes sell) their extensions. A Google search for "Dreamweaver extensions" will result in a large number of useful results.

But the most common way to find Dreamweaver extensions (and also extensions for other Adobe products, such as Photoshop, Fireworks, Flash, and so on) is to use the Adobe Exchange site, at **www.adobe.com/exchange/**. The Dreamweaver Exchange portion of the site has lists and short descriptions of more than 2000 extensions.

In Dreamweaver, it's easy to go to the Dreamweaver Exchange site. Just choose Help > Dreamweaver Exchange, and your default Web browser opens to the site Ⓐ. From the Exchange site, or from an extension developer's site, download the extension file to your hard disk. Then you're ready to use Adobe Extension Manager to install the extension.

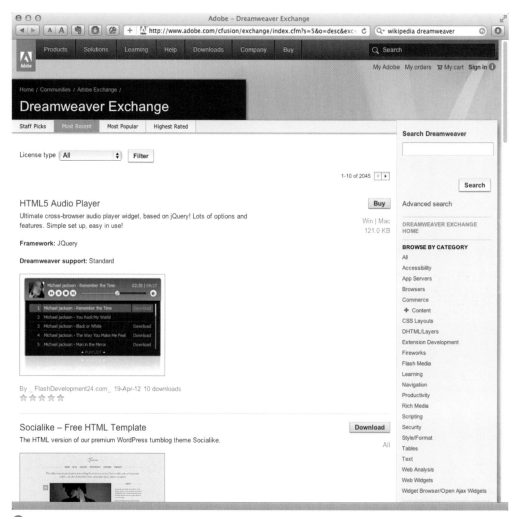

Ⓐ The Dreamweaver Exchange site lists more than 2000 extensions.

To install an extension:

1. If it's running, quit Dreamweaver by choosing File > Quit (Dreamweaver > Quit).

2. Launch Adobe Extension Manager by double-clicking its icon.

   On Windows, launch the program from the Start menu. On Mac, you'll find it in **/Applications/Adobe Extension Manager CS6/**.

   The Adobe Extension Manager window appears **B**.

continues on next page

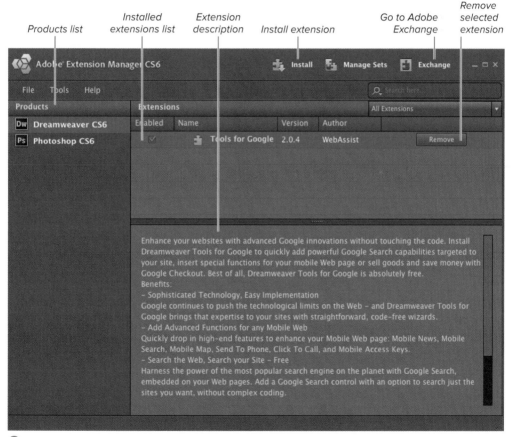

Products list | Installed extensions list | Extension description | Install extension | Go to Adobe Exchange | Remove selected extension

B Use the Adobe Extension Manager program to install or remove extensions.

3. From the Products column on the left side of the window, choose Dreamweaver CS6.

Any extensions you have installed for Dreamweaver CS6 appear in the Installed extensions list.

4. Click the Install button.

The Select Extension to Install dialog appears **C**.

5. Navigate to and select the extension file you wish to install.

6. Click Open (Select).

A license dialog appears.

7. Click Accept.

The Extension Manager installs the extension and reports success with an alert dialog.

8. Click OK to dismiss the alert dialog.

The new extension appears in the Installed extensions list.

9. Choose File > Exit (Extension Manager > Quit Extension Manager).

10. Launch Dreamweaver to use the new extension **D**.

> **TIP** If you have more than one version of Dreamweaver installed (perhaps you didn't want to remove an older copy immediately when you upgraded to Dreamweaver CS6), you can have different sets of extensions installed for each version.

> **TIP** Because each extension works differently, you need to refer to the instructions that came with the extension to discover how to access the extension from within Dreamweaver.

C Find and select the extension file that you want to install.

D Extensions can provide a complete user interface, as in this example, Tools for Google, which helps you easily create a Google search box, map, or other Google service on your site.

Index

Symbols

(pound sign) using with anchors, 177
  using with **id** selectors, 189, 194, 195–197
( ) (parentheses), selecting in Coding toolbar, 417
. (period), before class selectors, 194
// comments, applying from Coding toolbar,
  417–418
/* */ comment, applying from Coding toolbar,
  417–418
[ ] (square brackets) selecting in Coding toolbar, 417
_ (underscore), preceding targets with, 174
{ } (braces), selecting in Coding toolbar, 417
<!-- --> comments, applying from Coding
  toolbar, 417–418
</, ending tags with Code Hints, 437
' comments, applying from Coding toolbar,
  417–418
2-column liquid layout, 233–234
2-up view, 78–79

A

absolute links, 168
absolute positioning, 229, 230, 317
accessibility
  and alternate text for images, 65, 134, 135
  and new browser windows, 348
  preferences, 65, 135, 303
  recommended book on, 447
access keys, 303
Action menu, 125
active links, 83, 84, 173
Add Web Font dialog, 224
Adobe
  BrowserLab, 15, 71, 76–79, 230
  Business Catalyst, 15, 18, 20, 392, 394, 395
  Contribute, 392, 395, 457, 463
  Creative Cloud, 18, 392
  Creative Suite, 392
  Dreamweaver. *See* Dreamweaver
  Exchange, 366, 493
  Extension Manager, 493, 496
  Fireworks, 140, 143, 359–360, 461
  InContext Editing, 18, 392

  Media Encoder, 160, 162
  Photoshop. *See* Photoshop
  Web sites, 480–483
  Widget Browser, 366–371
Adobe Dreamweaver CS5 with PHP, 486
Adobe TV, 482
Advanced Settings category, 30, 52, 171, 224, 330
Ajax Essential Training, 485
alignment
  cell, 286
  with HTML, 105–107
  shortcut keys, 107
  table, 285
All mode, CSS Styles panel, 198–200
All Rules pane, 255
alternate text, 65, 134, 135, 136
anchors, 175–177
animations, 158–159
Apache, 382
AP elements, 230. *See also* absolute positioning
App Developer workspace, 20, 421
Appearance (CSS), Page Properties dialog, 80,
  81–82, 212
Appearance (HTML), Page Properties dialog,
  82–83, 212
Application bar, 6
Application frame, 8
ASP, 447
Assets panel
  accessing library items from, 404–406, 408, 410
  accessing templates from, 394, 398–400
  buttons/controls, 138
  inserting images from, 138
  updating Smart Objects in, 153
Attach External Style Sheet dialog, 255
authentication, 32, 33, 36

B

<b> tag, 102
backgrounds
  color, 82, 83, 234–236, 287
  CSS rule definitions, 190
  images, 82, 154–155
base URLs, 87

L

`<label>` tag, 302, 303
LAMP, 382–383
layout blocks, 265, 266
Layout tab, Insert panel, 17
layouts
    for coders, 420–421
    CSS-based. *See* CSS-based layouts
    and CSS box model, 228–230
    jQuery-based, 58, 338
    for mobile devices, 22, 58, 325
    starter, 204
    using Dreamweaver's included, 231–232
    using tables for, 267, 268–269
layout tables, 268
layout tools, 315–338
    fluid grid layouts, 332–337
    grids, 316–317
    jQuery, 338
    media queries, 328–331
    multiscreen preview, 325–327
    rulers/guides, 318–320
    setting page dimensions, 323–324
    zooming in on page, 321–322
`.lbi` file extension, 404
`.LCK` file extension, 457
`Library` folder, 404, 409
library items, 403–410
    creating, 403–404
    defined, 392
    deleting, 405
    detaching, 409, 410
    editing, 406–408
    file extension for, 404
    inserting, 405
    naming/renaming, 404, 408
    and Property inspector, 409–410
    re-creating missing/deleted, 410
    updating, 407
    vs. snippets, 411
    vs. templates, 403
line breaks, 104
line numbers, 422
link properties, 83
Link Relative To, 170–171
`<link>` tag, 226
links, 165–181
    adding anchors to, 175–177
    adding to graphics, 178
    checking for broken, 469–470
    creating, 62–63, 166–167
    to email addresses, 181
    formatting, 172–173
    purpose of, 165
    removing, 167
    setting color for, 83
    targeting, 174, 180
    types of, 165, 168–169

Links (CSS), Page Properties dialog, 83–84, 212
Linux systems, 219, 382
liquid layout, 233–234
List, CSS rule definitions, 191
List Properties dialog, 110, 112
lists, 108–112
    creating, 109
    nesting, 111–112
    scrolling, 309, 311
    setting properties for, 110
    types of, 108
List Values dialog, 310
Live Code view, 11, 388, 426–427
Live view
    displaying screen sizes in, 73
    enhancements, 23
    navigation, 388–389
    previewing pages in, 69
    purpose of, 11
    using CSS inspection in, 258–259
    and WebKit, 11, 74
Live View button, 347
Live View Options menu, 389, 390, 426
Load Query button, 117
Local Info category, 30
local root folder, 26
local site
    alternate name for, 26
    building pages for, 53
    creating, 28–31
    displaying contents of, 42
    moving items to/from, 46–47
    naming, 29
    saving pages for, 66–67
    switching between remote site and, 41
    synchronizing remote site and, 49–51, 402
    viewing/changing, 39
locked regions, 393, 397
Lock Guides command, 320
Lowery, Joseph, 486
Lynda.com, 485

M

Macintosh
    and Application frame, 8
    Dreamweaver menu bar on, 6
    encodings, 81
    font considerations, 219
    getting rid of tabs on, 8–9
    keyboard shortcuts, xiv
    mouse considerations, xv
    previewing pages on, 70
    and Submit/Reset buttons, 314
    testing server package for, 382
    using Dreamweaver on, xiv–xv
magnification tools, 321, 322
mailing list, Dreamweaver, 484
Make Template command, 394

MAMP, 382–383
Manage Sites dialog, 34, 38, 457, 475
Manage Workspaces dialog, 21
margins, 82, 83, 191
Mastering Regular Expressions, 131
Media Encoder (Adobe), 160, 162
media files, 133, 163–164
Media Queries dialog, 328–331
media query style sheets, 315, 329–331
menu bar, 6
Menu List, 110
menus
   context, xv, 20, 92
   jump, 296, 340, 353–355
   pop-up, 359–360
Merge Cells command, 280
`<meta>` tag, 87–88
Microsoft
   Excel. *See* Excel
   Internet Explorer. *See* Internet Explorer
   Web-safe fonts, 220
   Windows. *See* Windows systems
   Word. *See* Word
Mobile Applications workspace, 20
mobile devices, 22, 73, 220, 325, 328
Mobile layout, 336
Mobile Starters, 58, 338
mouseovers, 345
Move Guide dialog, 320
Move To External Style Sheet dialog, 252
MP3 files, 163
Multiclass Selection dialog, 209
Multiscreen button, 73
Multiscreen Preview feature, 23, 325–327
MySQL, 382

N

Named Anchor dialog, 175
naming conventions, 396
naming/renaming
   anchors, 175
   buttons, 312
   classes, 193
   editable regions, 395, 396
   favicons, 157
   files, 44, 45, 452
   folders, 29, 44, 45, 452
   forms, 298
   host directory, 36
   images, 141
   library items, 404, 408
   local site, 29
   radio groups, 307
   remote server, 35
   snippets, 412, 414
   styles, 244–245
   Web pages, 66–67
   workspaces, 21

navigation
   laying out, 237–238
   Live view, 388–389
   modifying, 239–242
   ` ` (non-breaking space), 113
nesting
   HTML elements, 195
   lists, 111–112
   tables, 270, 272
Netscape browsers, 352
New CSS Rule dialog
   creating classes in, 193, 213–214
   creating compound styles in, 195–197
   creating inline styles in, 213–214
   creating style rule for tags in, 188–189
   formatting links in, 172–173
New Document dialog
   changing document defaults in, 57
   creating new external style in, 249
   creating new page from, 3, 56–57
   and HTML5, 204
   previewing CSS style sheets in, 58
   using included CSS layouts in, 231–232
   vs. Files panel, 43
   vs. Welcome screen, 54
New Editable Region dialog, 395
new features, 4, 22–23
New File command, 44
New Folder command, 44
New from Template command, 398
New Site command, 28
non-breaking spaces, 113
numbered lists, 108, 110. *See also* lists

O

OK/Submit buttons, 314
Onion Skin view, 76, 78, 79
online magazines, 379
online newspapers, 379
online resources, 479–485
opacity values, 203
Open Browser Window dialog, 349
Open dialog, 68
Opera, 69, 210, 268
operators, 128, 130
Optimize command, 147
optional regions, 397
ordered lists, 108. *See also* lists
O'Reilly HTML Reference, 123
orphaned files, 471
Outdent Code button, 422
Over state, 347
OverWhileDown state, 347

WATCH
READ
CREATE

Unlimited online access to all Peachpit,
Adobe Press, Apple Training and New
Riders videos and books, as well as content
from other leading publishers including:
O'Reilly Media, Focal Press, Sams, Que,
Total Training, John Wiley & Sons, Course
Technology PTR, Class on Demand, VTC
and more.

No time commitment or contract
required! Sign up for one month or
a year. All for $19.99 a month

SIGN UP TODAY
peachpit.com/creativeedge

creative
edge